WAR AS THEY KNEW IT

WAR
AS THEY KNEW IT

Woody Hayes,
Bo Schembechler,
and America
in a Time of Unrest

MICHAEL ROSENBERG

NEW YORK   GRAND CENTRAL
PUBLISHING   BOSTON

Grand Central Publishing
Hachette Book Group USA
237 Park Avenue
New York, NY 10017

Visit our Web site at www.HachetteBookGroupUSA.com.

Printed in the United States of America

First Edition: September 2008

10 9 8 7 6 5 4 3 2 1

Grand Central Publishing is a division of Hachette Book Group USA, Inc.
The Grand Central Publishing name and logo is a trademark of
Hachette Book Group USA, Inc.

Library of Congress Cataloging-in-Publication Data

Rosenberg, Michael

War as they knew it: Woody Hayes, Bo Schembechler, and America in a time of unrest / Michael Rosenberg. — 1st ed.

p. cm.

Includes index.

ISBN-13: 978-0-446-58013-7

ISBN-10: 0-446-58013-9

1. Hayes, Woody, 1913–1987. 2. Schembechler, Bo. 3. Football coaches—United States—Biography. 4. Ohio State University—Football—History. 5. Ohio State Buckeyes (Football team)—History. 6. University of Michigan—Football—History. 7. Michigan Wolverines (Football team)—History. 8. Sports rivalries—United States. I. Title.

GV939.A1R68 2008

796.332092'2—dc22

2007049595

For Erin

Contents

WAR AS THEY KNEW IT

Towards all this external evil,

the man within the breast assumes a warlike attitude, and

affirms his ability to cope single-handed with the infinite

army of enemies. To this military attitude of the soul

we give the name of Heroism.

—**Ralph Waldo Emerson**, *"Heroism"*

GIFT RECEIPT

Barnes & Noble Booksellers #2280
301 NE Northgate Way #1100
Seattle, WA 98125
206-417-2967

R:2280 REG:004 TRN:5894 CSHR:John B.

ar As They Knew It: Woo
9780446580137   11
(1 @ VZ.HH)   VZ.HH G

Thanks for shopping at
Barnes & Noble

101.15   10/20/2008 07:34PM

within 14 days of purchase, or (iv) original purchase was made through Barnes & Noble.com via PayPal. Opened music/DVDs/audio may not be returned, but can be exchanged only for the same title if defective.

<u>After 14 days or without a sales receipt</u>, returns or exchanges will not be permitted.

Magazines, newspapers, and used books are not returnable. *Product not carried by Barnes & Noble or Barnes & Noble.com will not be accepted for return.*

Policy on receipt may appear in two sections.

Return Policy

<u>With a sales receipt</u>, a full refund in the original form of payment will be issued from any Barnes & Noble store for returns of new and unread books (except textbooks) and unopened music/DVDs/audio made within (i) 14 days of purchase from a Barnes & Noble retail store (except for purchases made by check less than 7 days prior to the date of return) or (ii) 14 days of delivery date for Barnes & Noble.com purchases (except for purchases made via PayPal). A store credit for the purchase price will be issued for (i) purchases made by check less than 7 days prior to the date of return, (ii) when a gift receipt is presented within 60 days of purchase, (iii) textbooks returned with a receipt within 14 days of purchase, or (iv) original purchase was made through Barnes & Noble.com via PayPal. Opened music/DVDs/audio may not be returned, but can be exchanged only for the same title if defective.

<u>After 14 days or without a sales receipt</u>, returns or exchanges will not be permitted.

1

What Kind of Game?

It was time for Woody Hayes to adjust. Halftime, late October 1967: Hayes's Ohio State Buckeyes trailed Illinois. Hayes stood at the locker room chalkboard, like any other football coach, to perform the most basic football-coach task: diagramming a play. And Hayes tried, he really did, but then he caught a glimpse of his fullback, Jim Otis, who had fumbled twice in the first half, and suddenly Hayes wanted to smack Otis.

Did it matter that Otis was one of Hayes's favorite players? Or that Otis's father roomed with Hayes for two years at Denison University? Or that Hayes had known Otis for years—and that Otis had spent his whole life preparing to play fullback for Woody at Ohio State?

Hell yes. Of course it mattered. With such close ties to Woody Hayes, Otis knew goddamn well not to fumble.

Hayes turned and rammed through the first two rows of players, then attacked with such force that Otis's Coke popped up in the air. And as he pounded away, Hayes screamed that Otis would never play for Ohio State again.

The Buckeyes had seen the flash of Hayes's temper many times. Normally, there was a way to prepare for it: make him stand on your right side. Hayes was left-handed; when he stood on your right side, he had to take a step back to throw that left-fisted punch, and you had a chance to get out of the way.

But Otis, wedged into the third row, had nowhere to go, and at that moment, so much seemed to be ending. The season was lost—Ohio State's record was about to fall to 2–3. There were rumblings that if Hayes lost the big season finale at Michigan, he would be fired. Otis, a sophomore, thought his career was finished (and in fact, he would be benched for the rest of that Illinois game and the two after that).

Had a picture been taken at that moment—an image frozen and passed around the nation, designed to provoke an instant reaction—most people would have reached quick, obvious conclusions: Hayes and Otis would never speak again; the coach would lose the respect of his players; and the Woody Hayes era at Ohio State would probably end. Every conclusion would have made sense—and every one would have been wrong.

Jim Otis never considered leaving Hayes's program; his love for the coach only grew stronger over time. As for the other players, Hayes sometimes angered them, but he never lost them. His influence on them was overwhelming.

The sheer size of a football team limits individual interactions between the head coach and each player, but Hayes was so powerful in those moments that many Buckeyes would say he was like a second father to them. He insisted that they graduate, and when they did, he coaxed many of them to go to law school. Some players considered him so morally incorruptible that long after they left Ohio State, they feared disappointing him.

Hayes told his players that their closest friends in the world would always be their Ohio State teammates. That was true, but when those friends got together, they inevitably started talking about Hayes so much that they started to sound like him. Hayes had such a profound effect on his players that years after he died, they would often speak of him in the present tense: "Woody has two rules: no drugs and no haters," they would say. Or: "He is the best teacher. When he goes to the board in a classroom, he is magnificent."

And on the topic of endings: the Buckeyes would win their final four games of 1967, saving Hayes's job. From there, they would put together one of the most dominant stretches in football history. And their excellence would trigger the greatest decade in the most storied rivalry in college football.

Nothing ended in that cramped locker room at Ohio Stadium.

This was actually one of the great *beginnings* in the history of sports.

But the Buckeyes could not possibly know that at the time. They just knew the Old Man was pissed off again. And that somebody ought to detach him from Jim Otis.

One of Woody's assistant coaches, Hugh Hindman, pulled him off.

Bo Schembechler was lost in Ann Arbor, Michigan.

It was a snowy night in late December 1968, and Schembechler and his staff had piled into two cars in Oxford, Ohio, and headed north. They had left Miami University in Ohio for the University of Michigan, if only they could find it. Except for Schembechler and his defensive coordinator, Jim Young, none of the coaches had ever been to Ann Arbor. Now they were lost.

Where to go? Schembechler couldn't ask for directions to the school's football facility, because there wasn't one; the Wolverines had a dingy locker room tucked into a corner on the second floor of Yost Fieldhouse. The locker room had few toilets and poor ventilation; the resulting smell was so foul, players wanted to run out as soon as they could. But that was risky: the stairs outside the locker room were built for small men in loafers, not football players in cleats. When the players got downstairs, they had to go outside, through a parking lot, over a set of train tracks (or over couplings if there was a train stopped on the tracks), through another parking lot, and finally into Michigan Stadium, where they could begin practice.

Schembechler could have asked for directions to the national convention of Students for a Democratic Society, which was being held in Ann Arbor that week. SDS had been founded a few years earlier by Michigan alumnus Alan Haber and *Michigan Daily* editor Tom Hayden, and it had become the most powerful student organization in the country. As the Vietnam War became more unpopular, SDS grew in size and influence, and now it was about to crumble under its own weight, leaving splinter groups that favored more violent methods.

(Haber had left Ann Arbor and SDS because there were too many factions pulling the organization in different directions.) But Schembechler, a thirty-nine-year-old footballaholic with a military buzz cut and very little interest in politics, surely didn't know about the convention.

If he got closer to campus, Schembechler could have listened for the strains of "2 + 2 = ?," one of the first anti-Vietnam rock 'n' roll songs. Written by Ann Arbor native Bob Seger, it outsold the Beatles in local stores; it would be rereleased in the autumn of 1969, as Seger's song gained resonance by the week.

But Schembechler was unlikely to listen to rock 'n' roll, or a protest song, and especially a rock 'n' roll protest song. Dissent did not sit well with the coach. (His new players would discover that quickly.)

Schembechler and his assistant coaches pulled over to a pay phone, called somebody from the athletic department, and finally found the campus. The university was on break, and because of a fuel shortage there was no heat in the campus buildings. The coaches had to meet Michigan athletic director Don Canham in the Pin Room of the Colonial Lanes bowling alley. Colonial Lanes was owned by Canham's friend Bob Ufer, who was broadcasting Michigan games on tiny WPAG in Ann Arbor.

After first making overtures to Penn State coach Joe Paterno, Canham had hired Schembechler for a salary of $21,000, only $1,000 more than the coach had made at lower-tier Miami. Schembechler's assistants planned to discuss their contracts in the Pin Room at Colonial Lanes, but that was a problem, because there were no contracts. Canham told the coaches they probably had five years to build a consistent winner. If the coaches failed, Canham said, they would all be fired—Canham included.

As Schembechler and his staff settled into Ann Arbor, Woody Hayes and Ohio State wrapped up the 1968 national championship by beating Southern California in the Rose Bowl. It was the fourth time Hayes had won at least a share of the national championship—among modern-day coaches, only Alabama's Bear Bryant had comparable credentials. Hayes celebrated by staying up until 6 a.m. editing the game film, then catching a flight to his favorite vacation spot: Vietnam.

This was Hayes's fourth trip to Vietnam. He spent most of his time showing Rose Bowl film to U.S. troops (they were eager to see Southern California star O. J. Simpson) and taking messages to relay to the troops' families when he returned home. Though much of the United States had grown disenchanted with the war, Hayes described it as his "best" trip. The national championship surely contributed to his mood. The 1968 team was considered Hayes's finest, but that distinction wasn't supposed to last very long; the 1968 Buckeyes started eighteen sophomores, so the 1969 team was expected to be even better.

Everything was looking up for Woody Hayes in January of 1969. Three weeks after he left for Vietnam, his old friend Richard Nixon would be inaugurated as president of the United States. The Ohio State Marching Band would perform at the inauguration. Nixon had opened the new year by watching Hayes's Buckeyes beat USC. (Anne Hayes, the coach's wife, had watched the Rose Bowl with a special guest: Tom Brownfield, a marine pilot who was recovering from burns suffered in Vietnam.)

Hayes and Nixon had met in 1957, when Nixon was vice president and the nation's most prominent football fan. Nixon later said that when he met Hayes for the first time, he wanted to talk about football and Hayes wanted to talk about foreign policy . . . so naturally, Nixon said, they talked about foreign policy. In conversation and on the football field, Hayes went right where he wanted to go. He now had a direct line into the White House, and calls would be made in both directions.

Ostensibly, Hayes was just another celebrity on a Bob Hope–esque tour of Vietnam. But the coach saw his trips as tours of duty. He ate in mess halls with troops. He insisted on boarding choppers to dangerous areas, against the advice of military personnel. He asked troops for their parents' phone numbers, and when he got home, he called dozens of parents to pass along messages from their children.

On this Vietnam trip, Hayes met Colonel George Patton III, whose father, the famous general, was one of Hayes's biggest heroes. The colonel was stunned at how much Hayes knew about his dad, but nobody who knew Woody Hayes would have been surprised. Two shelves of his tiny office at Ohio State were filled with Patton books. Hayes knew military history well enough to teach it—which he often did, to anybody who would listen.

Hayes rarely spoke of his own service in the Navy in World War II, though he privately (and proudly) told friends he was the only enlisted man to rise to the command of two ships. It's unclear whether he was actually the *only* man who achieved that, or how he could even confirm it. In any event, he did not dwell on the point. Hayes was far more inclined to speak of career military men—or even make them part of his program.

In 1967, when Jim Otis finally emerged from his fumble-induced benching to run for 149 yards against Iowa, he gave the game ball to Marine Corps general Lewis Walt, a friend of Hayes and one of the chief U.S. commanders in Vietnam. Walt also spoke to the Buckeyes at halftime of the 1968 Purdue game; with the score tied 0–0 and the national championship in jeopardy, Hayes turned his locker room over to a Marine general.

Why not? To Hayes, military conflict was not just a passion he pursued outside of football. It was as much a part of his coaching as blocking sleds. For years, when an Ohio State quarterback wanted to change a play at the line of scrimmage, he barked "Patton!" (if the Buckeyes were advancing on the ground) or "LeMay!" (if, like Air Force general Curtis LeMay, they preferred to annihilate their opponent through the air).

Hayes said the first safety blitz was not designed by Amos Alonzo Stagg or Pop Warner; it came from English admiral Lord Howard, who split the Spanish Armada in 1588, confusing the Spanish and securing victory. Germany lost World War II because it was caught in a double-team block from the Allies on the west and the Russians on the east. When the weather was nasty, Hayes held practice outdoors, telling his team, "If you're going to fight in the North Atlantic, you have to train in the North Atlantic." To emphasize the point, he wore a T-shirt at every practice, no matter how cold it was.

Hayes was infatuated with successful plans of attack, and though his teams were known more for stifling defenses, he was an offensive coach. He barely spent any time with the Buckeyes' defense. Hayes and his offensive assistants met in the Biggs Facility on the Ohio State campus, while the defensive coaches worked over in the school's basketball venue, St. John Arena.

Hayes gave his defensive coaches only a few directives, and chief among those was that when the opposing offense had the ball near a hash mark (i.e., close to a sideline), the Ohio State strong safety would be on the wide side of the field. That way, the offense would either run into the strong safety—one of the best athletes on the team—or be trapped, like a retreating army, against the sideline, which Hayes referred to simply as "the alps."

Bo Schembechler quickly figured out the lay of the land in Ann Arbor, which was not the same thing as understanding the landscape. George Mans tried to help. Mans was one of two coaches whom Schembechler had retained from the previous coaching staff, and he knew that in early 1969, the distance from Oxford, Ohio, to Ann Arbor was much greater than it appeared on a map.

Although Mans didn't use these words, the reality was that if the University of Michigan had not already had a football program in that winter of 1969, nobody would have dared start one.

The sport was built on rigidity, a single authoritarian leader, repression of personal desires in favor of the team, and brute force. The campus favored experimentation, individual expression, free love, and peace. The university was a buffet of causes—racial harmony, sexual freedom, nuclear nonproliferation, Marxism, gay rights—and everybody seemed to pick at least one. The stunning part was the completeness of it all; Ann Arbor seemed like one city in which the Establishment's power was limited.

In March of 1965, a group of faculty announced they would cancel classes for a day to protest U.S. involvement in Vietnam. They eventually backed down and decided on a different approach: they would hold an extra class at night at Angell Hall, one of the main academic buildings on campus. Approximately three thousand students showed up for what became known as a "teach-in," the first of its kind. It would be copied by faculties around the country, and it put Ann Arbor at the forefront of the antiwar movement. By 1969, university president Robben Fleming had publicly stated his opposition to U.S. involvement in Vietnam.

When students protested, Fleming would plead with police: *Let them protest.* He even helped. In 1968, students had taken over the school's Administration Building, demanding higher black student enrollment. Fleming, figuring that he had plenty to do outside his office that day, simply let them stay there; every once in a while he would drop by and ask, "How are you coming?" The students left with the impression that their demands would be addressed.

The power of Students for a Democratic Society was diminishing, but only because more radical groups were gaining prominence. In March 1969, two months after Schembechler arrived, a faction of SDS called the Jesse James Gang locked itself in a room with a military recruiter to prevent interviews from taking place. Fleming refused to call the police. The Gang and the recruiter remained in the room for five hours. (The students were disciplined under the campus judiciary system.)

A year earlier, Black Panther Party founder Huey Newton told an interviewer that if white people wanted to help, they could form a White Panther Party. Ann Arbor residents Lawrence "Pun" Plamondon and John Sinclair took Newton's advice and created the White Panther Party. The party pushed a program of "rock 'n' roll, dope, and fucking in the streets," and one of its stated goals was "the end of money." Sinclair and Plamondon promised a "total assault on the culture."

Adding to the sense that everything was under siege, a serial killer had been terrorizing the Ann Arbor area, strangling and sexually assaulting young women; between 1967 and 1969, seven were killed and left nude or seminude where they could be easily discovered. The killings, known as the Michigan Murders, ended with the arrest of a twenty-one-year-old Eastern Michigan University student, John Norman Collins. Even the new Briarwood Mall on the outskirts of town contributed to the feeling that the town was slipping away from the townspeople, who feared downtown businesses would lose customers to the mall.

Because the counterculture movement was not just political but cultural, it seemed even greater than it was. Long hair, tie-dyed T-shirts, and bell-bottom pants were in style, even for political agnostics. Not everybody was a hippie, but to people of the previous generation, everybody *appeared* to be a hippie. The school's central campus was filled with "longhairs." When a longhair was arrested, the local sheriff, Doug Harvey, was known to have the young man's hair cut off.

Sometimes a group of conservative, middle-aged men would drive by and watch the longhairs through the car window, as one might watch animals on a safari; these men were Michigan football coaches on their lunch break. The coaches, both amused and appalled by what they saw, would soon return to their offices. Their players could not distance themselves so easily. They split time between the athletic grounds and the rest of the university, and it often seemed like they were attending two different schools or leading dual lives.

Michigan lineman Dan Dierdorf, one of the most talented players in school history, rarely wore his letter jacket on campus. As a large man with short hair, Dierdorf could not possibly blend in, but he tried. There were good reasons to stay anonymous. In the fall of 1967, Michigan freshman Pete Newell was chatting with a classmate before an introductory philosophy class. Newell played for the freshman football team (first-year students were not yet eligible for the varsity) and the classmate asked him about his game the previous weekend. The professor heard the question and looked at Newell.

"Game?" the professor asked. "What kind of game?"

A freshman football game, Newell replied.

"You're a football player?"

"Yes."

"What are you doing in my class?"

Newell was crushed. He had come to Michigan for the education as much as the chance to play Big Ten football, and now here was this professor basically telling him that was impossible. Newell decided not to tell any other professors that he played football.

In the autumn of 1967, Michigan's big rivalry game against Ohio State had only drawn 64,144 people to 101,001-seat Michigan Stadium. Periodically, reporters would ask Bob Forman, the executive director of the Michigan Alumni Association, if there was a serious movement afoot to fire coach Bump Elliott. Forman replied truthfully: No.

After the 1968 season, Elliott resigned anyway. His final team had been surprisingly successful; unranked at the start of the season, the Wolverines had climbed all the way to No. 4 in the country entering their last game, at Ohio State. But then Ohio State clubbed them, 50–14. It was Woody Hayes's greatest triumph to that point, and even more humiliating for Michigan than the score indicated.

Late in the game, with Ohio State leading 44–14, Hayes sent star Jim Otis back onto the field to score another touchdown. The Buckeyes then tried for a two-point conversion, which the Wolverines took as Hayes's attempt to rub it in. In fact, the two-point attempt was simply miscommunication—when Hayes realized what was happening, he tried to get his team to call timeout, but it was too late. When the game ended, Ohio State fans mobbed the field, forcing some Michigan players to use chairs as shields as they waded through the crowd to the locker room. When they got there, junior tight end Jim Mandich pulled the returning players together and told them, "We will not forget this." They vowed revenge.

Two months later, they were playing for a new coach. When Schembechler's hiring was announced, players immediately split into two camps: those who had never heard of Schembechler and those who *wished* they had never heard of Schembechler.

One of Michigan's running backs, Billy Taylor, grew up in Schembechler's hometown of Barberton, Ohio, and briefly considered join-ing him at Miami (Ohio). But when Taylor saw the hard-driving coach up close, he decided he was "nuts." Dierdorf had also been recruited by Miami but wasn't interested; when Miami assistant coach Jerry Hanlon showed up at Dierdorf's high school unannounced, Dierdorf slipped out the back door and went home. On one of Schembechler's first days at Michigan, Dierdorf sat in the coach's office and thought, *This can't really be happening.* Not only was Schembechler the new head man, but Hanlon was now Dierdorf's position coach.

Schembechler knew about the fears; they seemed to please him. In individual meetings with the players who had rejected him at Miami, he snarled, "You thought you were getting away from me, didn't you?" Elliott was beloved by his players. He rarely raised his voice and treated them like adults, not replaceable parts. The Wolverines had heard him use profanity just once—before a game at Duke in 1968, when he was annoyed that the visitors' locker room was so far from the field, he snapped and said, "Let's go kick the shit out of them!"

Schembechler suspected the players were soft. His conditioning drills seemed designed to return them to simpler times, when Nean-derthals roamed the earth.

One drill was called the "Slap and Stomp." Two players would face each other in a wrestling ring and keep their feet moving as they slapped and pushed each other. The purpose of the drill was a mys-tery. During spring practice, Schembechler held two full practices a day, every day. He made the Wolverines hop up the fieldhouse steps—sometimes on one leg, sometimes with another player on their back.

At times, the players felt like caged animals—especially when Schembechler put them in cages. He had his reasons: the coach wanted his offensive linemen's first move to be out, instead of up, so he told them to assume their stance in a cage, where they had no choice but to jump forward. Nothing was left to chance. Schem-bechler wanted his linemen three feet apart—he measured with a yardstick, and if they were off by more than an inch or two, he would smack them in the calf with the yardstick. Sometimes he smacked them so hard that the yardstick broke.

Some players left the program. Many thought about leaving. And some who stayed did so simply to spite Schembechler. (That was fine with the coach—he didn't care what motivated them, as long as something did.) In Schembechler's first month on the job, a player named John Prusiecki walked into his office. Prusiecki hadn't played much the year before.

"I'm quitting," Prusiecki told Schembechler.

"You can't quit!" Schembechler barked. "Who do you think you are to quit?"

"This isn't the Army. I can quit if I want to quit."

Schembechler looked at Prusiecki.

"Okay," the coach finally said. "What's your name?"

Prusiecki cleared out his locker and started walking out of Yost Fieldhouse. He saw the sign that Schembechler had hung there, almost taunting those who thought about leaving the program: THOSE WHO STAY WILL BE CHAMPIONS. Prusiecki grabbed a magic marker and wrote underneath, "And those who leave will be doctors, lawyers, engineers, architects, bishops, generals, statesmen and captains of industry." And then he left.

Prusiecki was not alone. The only reason the players did not stage a full mutiny was that Schembechler was working even harder than they were. When players passed the athletic campus late at night, his car was usually in the parking lot.

Don Canham, the athletic director, liked that Schembechler was a "details man." Every assistant coach had specific responsibilities. (Larry Smith, for example, was in charge of finding the players who avoided Schembechler by hiding behind the steel support posts at Yost Fieldhouse.) Under Schembechler, meetings began five minutes early: players who showed up at 1:57 p.m. for a 2 p.m. meeting were considered late. Even his personal life was a model of efficiency: between the 1967 and 1968 football seasons, he had met his wife, Millie, married her, and adopted her three children. Now he was preparing for the birth of his first child.

As Prusiecki discovered, Schembechler was not going to let some nameless player change how he operated. With every near-rebellion, the coach grew more intense. At one practice, Schembechler got so mad at assistant coach Dick Hunter that he chased Hunter down the practice field—a fifty-yard sprint, one coach chasing after another, while the players watched in amazement, wondering what Schembechler would do if he caught his assistant. Tackle him? Beat him up? Luckily, they never found out—Hunter outran his boss. Another time, safety Barry Pierson and Mandich got in such a wild fight, it even stunned Schembechler. He kicked Pierson out, then turned to his tight end.

"And Mandich!" Schembechler screamed. "You precipitated the fracas!"

Players tried not to laugh.

Precipitated the fracas?

Who says that in anger?

As they were discovering, Schembechler's greatest gift was with the language. He spoke every sentence like nobody had ever uttered those words before—hitting the phonetic high point of every word, making it his own. This skill pre-dated his desire to coach. When he was a student at Miami from 1947 to 1951, he aspired to be a sportscaster; as he walked to class with friends, he would announce a baseball game being played in his head.

Schembechler surely would have been an excellent sportscaster, but it was probably best that he never pursued that dream. Most sportscasters of the day had a signature phrase, and Schembechler's was "son of a bitch." Once you heard him say "son of a bitch" (and it didn't take long), you wondered why anybody else would even try. When warning players to stay away from alcohol (at this point, the coach was comically oblivious to the drug culture), this is how he phrased it: "Don't dissipate your body." They didn't necessarily take the advice, but they remembered the words.

Ann Arbor had not always been a leftist stronghold. From 1931 to 1957, the city's mayors were all Republican. In 1952 and 1956, Republican Dwight D. Eisenhower beat Democrat Adlai Stevenson by a ratio of more than two to one in Ann Arbor. In a 1960 campus straw poll, Richard Nixon beat John F. Kennedy for president (though ultimately Kennedy barely carried the city).

But the city's political profile had changed at a startling pace; in less than a decade, the campus had become a counterculture mecca, and the effect was jarring. In 1960, Ford Motor Company president Robert McNamara had lived in the Geddes neighborhood in Ann Arbor. He would take peaceful evening walks through the university's Diag, the unofficial center of campus. McNamara had left Ford to be the U.S. secretary of defense. In that position, he oversaw the escalation of the war in Vietnam. By the end of the decade he would not have been welcome in Ann Arbor at all.

The actual number of true believers in "the movement" was hard to quantify, but it seemed like the radicals were swallowing up new chunks of society at every turn.

It was the kind of development that deeply upset Woody Hayes. He preferred the 1950s, when "the air was clean and sex was dirty." He did not understand how so many people could openly question military leaders, the president, or other authority figures.

He told his players many times, "We're tearing down all our heroes in America."

It pained him to say it. Hayes had many heroes. Most had a military background, but one of his favorites was Ralph Waldo Emerson, the nineteenth-century author, poet, and philosopher. Hayes owned a copy of almost everything Emerson had ever published, and he quoted him as a religious zealot might quote the Bible. His favorite essay was "Compensation," which began:

"Ever since I was a boy, I have wished to write a discourse on Compensation: for it seemed to me when very young, that on this subject life was ahead of theology, and the people knew more than the preachers taught."

Hayes himself was not a particularly religious man. He said his religion could be summed up in the words of his mother, Effie: "God made you and put you on earth, and the rest is up to you." In that sense, he was devout. Woody Hayes saw every waking moment as a chance to shape the world.

Hayes spent more time in hospitals than some doctors; he would drop in, ask the nurses, "Who hasn't had visitors today?" and make his rounds. He did not advertise his hospital visits—if a reporter had written about them, he would have been furious—but because of his fame word filtered out, and Ohio State fans often asked him to visit sick friends or family members. He almost always complied. Hayes told his players they had been blessed with the chance to play the world's greatest sport for Ohio State University, but the proper response was not to pay back Woody or Ohio State.

"You can never pay back," he said, "but you can pay forward."

Hayes repeated it so often, people assumed he had coined the saying. He was quick to correct them. This too had come from Emerson's "Compensation":

"In the order of nature we cannot render benefits to those from who we receive them, or only seldom. But the benefit we receive must be rendered again, line for line, deed for deed, cent for cent, to somebody. Beware of too much good staying in your hand. It will fast corrupt and worm worms. Pay it away quickly in some sort."

Hayes rarely enjoyed any downtime, even with his own family. He often slept on a cot in his office instead of at home with his wife, Anne. (They had a son, Steve, who was a student at Ohio State's law school.) Hayes had very few hobbies and was not inclined to relax with friends. He much preferred an intense discussion of world affairs.

Every conversation had a purpose. Whenever possible, Hayes dined at the Ohio State Faculty Club, where he would engage other members of the faculty in a conversation about the Battle of the Coral Sea or ancient Greece or something of similar gravity. The Faculty Club appealed to him because it was open only to faculty members and their guests, and Hayes, in addition to being a football coach, was a tenured professor in the department of physical education. He was especially proud of that, because his father, Wayne Hayes, had been the schools superintendent in his hometown of Newcomerstown, Ohio.

It was fair to wonder why a man with such disparate interests and such a deep desire to affect society would devote his life to coaching a game. To Hayes, that was a flawed question. Football was not just a game to him; he believed that within the Ohio State football program one could find the ethos that had made America great. Football players sacrificed for the betterment of the team. They did not question their coach. They stayed clear of drugs (or so he believed). Hayes often said his players were the finest students on the Ohio State campus, because the combination of athletics and academics forced them to work harder than other students.

Football created heroes for a country that badly needed them. Following the basic tenet of his mother's "religion"—God created him and the rest was up to him—Woody Hayes's Sunday mornings were spent not at church but behind a film projector.

Hayes rarely sought publicity of any kind, but he liked the public nature of the football program. Unlike most coaches, he never hid in his office. His phone number was listed and his address (1711 Cardiff Road) was common knowledge in Columbus. He was proud to have his team's discipline and tenacity on display every Saturday in the fall. The people in the stands could learn from it. Like most esteemed lecturers, he did not appreciate when people questioned his teachings; in postgame press conferences, he often gave terse, coarse answers to the most innocuous questions.

Hayes did not even like when his assistant coaches suggested a change. He believed his program had an inherent rightness—or even righteousness—and that others should feel the same way. In 1956, he had given small loans to poor players out of his own pocket, and was so sure this was within the spirit of amateurism that he told *Sports Illustrated* about the loans without prompting. The Big Ten placed him on probation for his transgression, but the coach did not believe he had done anything wrong.

"To believe your own thought," Emerson wrote, "to believe that what is true for you in your private heart is true for all men, that is genius."

With the exception of his military service, Hayes lived his entire life in the state of Ohio. He grew up in little Newcomerstown, on the east side of the state; attended Denison University, thirty-two miles outside Columbus; and only coached in the state. Hayes was proud of that. He felt that Ohio represented all that was great and pure about America, and Columbus was central Ohio in every way: geographically, culturally, temperamentally. It was a city of steeples and front porches, and it was dominated by three pillars of the Establishment: the state government; more than three dozen insurance companies with headquarters there; and Ohio State football.

The Buckeyes were more than just a local team. They were the prism through which Columbus viewed itself. The passion was so great that it had consumed the three men who coached before Hayes; Paul Bixler, Carroll Widdoes, and Wes Fesler had all resigned at least partly because of the intense pressure, earning Ohio State its tag as the "graveyard of coaches."

Hayes had survived for eighteen years in Columbus. By 1969, coming off one national championship with another one surely on the way, he had raised his profile. He was not just the head coach at Ohio State. To many, he *was* Ohio State.

Hayes understood instinctively that the key to longevity in Columbus was beating Michigan. In 1934, Ohio State coach Francis Schmidt had spoken for his whole school when he said the Michigan players "put their pants on one leg at a time, the same as we do!" Since Schmidt's declaration, any Buckeye who beat Michigan received a miniature pair of gold pants.

While other coaches fled from that pressure, Hayes elevated the rivalry's importance. He made it clear that the Ohio State–Michigan rivalry was not just between schools but between states. He said the rivalry started in 1836 when President Andrew Jackson forced Michigan to cede Toledo to Ohio in order to gain statehood. (One hundred and thirty-three years later, Toledo was still split territory: Michigan fans were as prominent in the city as Ohio State fans.)

Hayes was famous among fans and reporters for never saying "Michigan"—he always called it That School Up North. This was not just a show for the public. Hayes's players and assistant coaches never heard him say the word "Michigan." It was always—always—That School Up North.

Some figured this was just a motivational ploy. Others believed that Hayes had a certain disdain for Michigan, which thought of itself as a "public Ivy," academically superior to other Big Ten schools. (By 1969, Ann Arbor's radical bent surely didn't endear the town to him.)

Whatever Hayes's true feelings, his public comments clearly made him more popular in Columbus. The city felt like an overgrown college town. Its chief industry, insurance, took hold in the first half of the twentieth century, when businessman Murray Lincoln determined that the risks in rural areas were lower than in urban ones, and insurance rates should reflect that. Woody Hayes, a champion of the American small town, would have agreed instinctively. Lincoln's company, Farm Bureau Mutual, grew so much that in 1955 it changed its name to Nationwide.

Like Murray Lincoln, Hayes had a philosophy that meshed with his vision of Middle America. More than any other great coach in football history, he thrived on simplicity.

In 1961, Ohio State had no more than a dozen offensive plays—that's all the Buckeyes ran for the entire season. That meant that in a given game, every play would be called a few times, and his favorite plays (basic off-tackle runs) were called so often, everybody in the stadium could recognize them. The team had Paul Warfield, who would go on to make the Pro Football Hall of Fame as a wide receiver—but Hayes put him at running back and defensive back, and Warfield barely caught any passes.

When he wanted to pass that season, Hayes would often remove his normal running quarterback for a superior passer, telegraphing his play preference to the other team. Ohio State used a single snap count the whole year—when the quarterback shouted "Go!" the center would snap the ball. Naturally, opposing defenders figured this out rather quickly. "They're snapping it on 'Go!'" they told each other excitedly, as though they had just cracked some top-secret code.

The Buckeyes would just laugh. They had reason to. That year, with a dozen offensive plays, gross misuse of one of the best re-

ceivers in football history, and the most obvious snap count imaginable, they won the national championship.

And they won it largely because of coaching. Hayes demanded
that his players repeat a technique one thousand times, until every
muscle and joint moved in precisely the right way. Then he would
make them do it again. He wanted to take the entropy out of the
game; he loathed fumbles, penalties, and any other mental errors,
and his teams seldom made mistakes. If every man executed his
individual assignment better than the opponent, then Hayes's
eleven would outplay the other coach's eleven on that play—and if
that happened repeatedly, his troops would march down the field
efficiently.

Patton said wars were fought with weapons but won by men.
Woody Hayes let others invent new weapons. He made sure he had
the best men.

His players quickly discovered that it was not enough to perform
the same technique again and again; Hayes wanted maximum effort
on each attempt. To that end, he used extreme motivational techniques. If a player made a mistake in practice, Hayes often hit himself
in the head—not just the occasional slap to the forehead, but all-out
punches to the face.

At other times, he would take off his glasses and step on them (he
went through a dozen pairs a year) or take off his watch and break
it. Players suspected that some of it was an act—there were whis-
pers that Ohio State trainers cut Hayes's hats before practice, to make
them easier to tear later—but they knew it wasn't *all* an act, and part
of Hayes's genius was the mystery. Players could never quite tell when
he was acting and when he had lost his mind. It was not the sort of
question one asked.

One of the stars on that 1961 national championship team, offensive lineman Daryl Sanders, had two dreams about Hayes when he
was in college. Actually, Sanders had the same dream twice. (That's
how thorough Woody Hayes was—his players even repeated their
dreams.) In the dream, Woody was in full tirade mode at halftime when
men in white lab coats walked into the locker room and carried him

away. Then Sanders's position coach stood up and said, "It's okay, men. *Let's go!*"

The position coach was named Bo Schembechler.

Like many people, Bo Schembechler heard the legend of Woody Hayes before he saw it—and like many people, Schembechler didn't believe his ears. In the spring of 1949, he was an offensive lineman and left-handed pitcher at Miami University, which meant he skipped spring football practice to play baseball. His buddies told him about this crazy new coach, who grabbed players and screamed like they'd never heard before.

Schembechler figured nobody could be that tough. He was wrong.

Once he returned to the football field, Schembechler quickly joined in the team pastime: hating Woody Hayes. It was easy, and they were good at it, but by the next year, Hayes was . . . well, maybe not beloved, but appreciated. The Miami players realized that his methods produced winning results, and that Hayes gave as much as he asked.

Schembechler became especially fond of the coach—without ever saying it, Schembechler and Hayes saw their own stubbornness and fire in each other. At the end of that season, the Ohio State job came open. During a game of handball, Hayes asked Schembechler if he had any idea who should get the job. Schembechler told Hayes he deserved it. Then they resumed playing handball, a game that suited their dispositions: man against man, alone in a room with no equipment.

Before Hayes left for Ohio State, he told Schembechler to take summer classes and that Hayes would make sure the tuition was covered. (Schembechler was on an athletic scholarship, but it did not automatically cover the cost of summer classes.) As Schembechler was nearing graduation, he received a bill for the classes. He could not afford to pay it. He called Miami athletic director John Brickels and told him of Hayes's promise, but Brickels said he knew nothing about it.

Schembechler then called Hayes at Ohio State. Hayes promised to take care of it—and did. Schembechler never found out how Hayes paid the bill; it was quite possible that he paid it himself. Woody Hayes never worried about money, except when somebody else didn't have enough. When he got to Ohio State, he regularly turned down pay raises. (He said he was doing his part to fight inflation.)

The handball games resumed a few years later, when Hayes hired Schembechler as an assistant at Ohio State. Their lockers were next to each other. Hayes would call Schembechler at 6 a.m. on Sundays and tell him that if he didn't come down to the handball court in the next twenty minutes, he was obviously not man enough to face him.

Officially, Hayes decried profanity, but in competitive situations he could not help himself. He and Schembechler would paint the air blue. Schembechler, the younger man and better natural athlete, always won. One day Schembechler was annoyed at having to play and he let Hayes win. Woody then told all of his assistants he had beaten Bo at handball. It was as if all the other games didn't count because Woody Hayes didn't count them.

That bullheadedness could be infuriating, but it was part of what made Hayes so successful. In Schembechler's first year on Hayes's staff, he tried to suggest a different blocking scheme for one of Hayes's running plays. Hayes insisted he was wrong, Schembechler persisted, and they went back and forth until Hayes finally said, "Oh yeah? How many games did you win last year?" Schembechler had been an assistant under Ara Parseghian at Northwestern. The Wildcats had gone 0–9.

Schembechler shut up.

Despite the arguments (or maybe because of them), Hayes loved having Schembechler on his staff. Schembechler lived for football, and he had no inclination to establish a personal life outside of his work—he was even married, briefly, to Hayes's secretary.

Hayes and Schembechler were so alike that Ohio State beat reporters took to calling Bo "Little Woody." Schembechler told them he didn't understand the moniker and he resented it. But privately he would chuckle. He knew it was accurate. So did Hayes. In another handball game, after the 1963 season, Schembechler told Woody that he wanted to leave Ohio State to take the Miami head coaching job.

"You can't take it," Hayes said. "You're going to be the next coach at Ohio State."

Hayes then explained that he only planned to coach for three to five more years. Schembechler was skeptical. He left for Miami. If Schembechler had stayed he would have hung on forever: Hayes would coach sixteen more years at Ohio State.

At least Schembechler would have had job security. Hayes proudly told people he had never fired an assistant coach. If a coach wasn't getting the job done, Hayes would somehow make up for it.

Oh, Hayes had often *told* coaches they were fired; it was his way of ending the conversation and letting the assistant coach know who was in charge. Most assistants had to be fired a few times before they caught on. When Hayes told assistant coach George Chaump he was fired during Chaump's first meeting at Ohio State, Chaump walked out of the meeting embarrassed, only to hear Woody call after him: "George, goddammit, get back here! I never fired anybody—I'm not going to break my record on you."

Schembechler thought that if he showed similar loyalty—and got similar on-field results—then his players would deal with his brutal methods. Other Michigan coaches weren't so sure. They advised him to ease up. But Schembechler would not soften. He told his coaches they had been hired to beat one team: Ohio State. If they needed extreme measures to do it, that was fine with him.

They were practicing karate. They would get up before the sun rose over southeast Michigan and repeat all sorts of kicks and punches. It was an odd skill set, and it is unclear why they needed it, but they were determined to topple the biggest and most powerful foe they had ever faced: the U.S. government.

There were maybe thirty of them in a park in Detroit, radicals with revolution in mind. Of the thirty, around a dozen had attended the University of Michigan. Others had lived in Ann Arbor. Most had been part of Students for a Democratic Society. They were sure that the peaceful demonstrations of the antiwar movement did not go far enough. The United States was bombing its enemy, so why couldn't they?

One of them, a young man named Bill Ayers, had tried to walk on to the Michigan football team a few years back. Ayers was a 145-pound offensive lineman; the Michigan program had been down, but not *that* far down, and Ayers never joined the team. Now he was on a different kind of team: fighting the Vietnam War . . . fighting the status quo . . . fighting, fighting . . . and now he was in Detroit, punching the early-morning air.

More than a year had passed since President Lyndon Johnson spoke of "peace in Vietnam" in a nationally televised address. The night of Johnson's speech, Ayers and school president Robben Fleming shouted at each other through bullhorns on the steps of Fleming's house. Despite Fleming's antiwar, tolerate-the-protests stance, he was still considered part of the Establishment to many radicals, and Ayers would let him know it with his favorite greeting: "Fuck you, you motherfucker!" Fleming was not the type to curse back.

"Congratulations," Fleming told Ayers on the night of LBJ's address. "You've won. The war will end soon."

That was March 31, 1968. Now it was the summer of 1969 and the war had not ended. Ayers and his comrades were going to do something about it. They formed their own guerrilla army. Inspired by a lyric from Bob Dylan's "Subterranean Homesick Blues" ("You don't need a weatherman to know which way the wind blows"), they called themselves the Weathermen.

In mid-June 1969, Michigan safety Thom Darden was relaxing in front of the Michigan Union. The area was known as a good spot to check out girls. That reputation was about to be enhanced. He thought he was watching a drama club practice when the actors, both male and female, stripped off their clothes and ran naked down South University Avenue.

A riot was under way. Well, the police called it a riot; others said they were merely trying to "liberate" South University Avenue. (Fleming, the university president, said most of the rioters were not students, and as always, he begged police not to overreact.) It lasted two days. There were forty-seven arrests and twenty-two injuries, but what Darden would remember most was people having sex in the street as pedestrians watched and celebrated.

On the second day of the uprising, police tear-gassed a number of people in front of East Quad, including Pun Plamondon of the White Panthers, who became disoriented and ran into a stop sign, splitting his forehead. The next day, Plamondon joined Michigan student leaders in denouncing the massive police presence on the rooftops along South University. They then led the crowd toward a plaza by the Michigan Union, where they drank beer and smoked pot next to the newly acquired sculpture there: a fifteen-by-fifteen-foot cube, balanced on one of its corners, which could whirl around with just a little push.

Bo Schembechler surely never saw the riot/liberation. He spent his days over on the athletic campus, working the dawn-to-midnight shift. On his only real break from work that year, he took his family to the Leelanau Peninsula on the western side of Michigan for what was supposed to be a two-week vacation. After five days, Schembechler left to attend a football clinic in Milwaukee. He picked up his family on his way home.

Another time, restaurateur Win Schuler held a picnic for the Michigan and Michigan State staffs. The highlight was supposed to be a donkey race between Schembechler and Michigan State coach Duffy Daugherty, but alas, nobody informed the donkeys. They refused to move. The race was declared a draw (which must have annoyed Schembechler, who hated ties).

Though it failed, the Win Schuler picnic was an appropriate promotion for Michigan in 1969: new athletic director Don Canham loved unconventional marketing and Schembechler loved hamburgers. The coach's sole concern was football; he had given up handball and regularly blew past his recommended daily allowance of junk food, which he ate while he worked.

Canham had been the Michigan track coach before becoming athletic director, but unlike most athletic directors, he was a highly successful businessman. His company, Don Canham Enterprises, sold video, athletic, and educational materials. When Canham became athletic director in 1968, the company was valued at $5 million, renamed School-Tech, and put into a trust. Canham immediately sat down with outgoing athletic director Fritz Crisler to look at the budget. The department was projecting a $200,000 loss.

"Fritz," Canham said, "whaddya say we put the athletic department in a trust and work at School-Tech?"

Canham stuck around, but School-Tech was never far from his thoughts—he knew he could always go back to his company if he got fired, so he was free to run the athletic department as he chose. He was full of ideas. Canham remembered the 37,000 empty seats for the 1967 Michigan–Ohio State game, and he was determined not to let it happen again. In July 1969, with 25,000 tickets still unsold, he advertised the game in Ohio newspapers. It was a highly unusual move. Football games were seen as community events, not commercial ventures. But Canham wanted a sellout, and when Ohio State fans gobbled up the remaining tickets, he got it.

Some Michigan boosters thought Canham had gone too far. In truth, he was just getting started. A few years earlier, on a track team road trip to UCLA, he had walked into a campus bookstore full of UCLA pennants and sweatshirts. This was unusual. Canham asked UCLA athletic director J. D. Morgan how the athletic department got into the sweatshirt business, and to Canham's surprise, Morgan said UCLA wasn't really in the sweatshirt business. The bookstores had complete rights to the items.

Canham filed that away. When he became athletic director at Michigan, he immediately designed several logos on his kitchen table at home—a block "M" with a wolverine in the middle, a block "M" with the word "Michigan" written through it—and slapped them on all sorts of items: T-shirts, ashtrays, playing cards. Other schools weren't even selling sweatshirts, and here was Canham, hawking everything.

Canham was a born salesman. As a student at Michigan in the early 1940s, he bought used sweatsocks for eight cents a pair, then resold them for a quarter. A man who has sold used socks for a 200 percent profit tends to feel he can sell anything. In Canham's first year as athletic director, he expanded the athletic department mailing list from 100,000 to 400,000, and paid for the increased mailing partly through merchandise sales.

This could be big, Don Canham thought. Really big.

How revolutionary was Canham's vision? In 1969, Woody Hayes's old tackle Daryl Sanders interviewed for a job as president of something called NFL Properties. In that role, he would be in charge of all merchandising for the pro football league. But Sanders didn't like what he heard at the interview. He got the impression the company was happy just to break even.

Canham thought the ceiling was higher. But not even he understood just how high. Before he left work each day, he walked through the hallways to make sure everybody had turned the lights off. The electric bill wasn't going to pay itself.

"I do not wish to treat friendships daintily," Emerson wrote, "but with roughest courage. When they are real, they are not glass threads or frostwork, but the solidest thing we know."

When Bo Schembechler got the Michigan job, Woody Hayes did not send him a note or a card. Hayes did not even call his protégé to wish him well. This is what Schembechler expected, and maybe even what he preferred. Their kinship was based on being so much alike, and one way they were alike is that they did not express their deepest feelings. Besides, Hayes had never fraternized with a coach from That School Up North before. He was not going to start now.

Their relationship—which started as coach-player, then became coach-assistant—was about to enter a new phase: competitors in the nation's most storied football rivalry. To a generation of football fans, their names would be intertwined. NCAA rules in 1969 allowed schools to appear on national television only three times in a two-year span, so for many fans the only chance to see Woody Hayes or Bo Schembechler was when Ohio State played Michigan.

In all the years of their rivalry, Hayes and Schembechler would rarely speak to each other. There would be a few exceptions: on the field before their annual season-ending game; at Big Ten meetings in the summer; and on a few occasions when circumstances were so grave that even these two men had to confront their feelings. In this time of self-enforced separation, a decade would pass, each man's public image would change drastically, and their country would become a much different place. And yet their competition would be so intense—and the value they placed on it so great—that in the ten years in which they rarely communicated, Woody Hayes and Bo Schembechler would become closer than ever.

2

The Fall of '69

As predicted, the 1969 Ohio State Buckeyes were Woody Hayes's best team; Hayes said so himself near the end of his life. By most accounts, he had two of the best teams in the country: his starters and his backups. And it was hard to tell which was which.

The competition was especially fierce at fullback, the primary weapon for any Woody Hayes team. Senior Jim Otis was an All-American candidate, but many Ohio State players and coaches believed junior John Brockington was even better. There was no doubt that Hayes favored Otis, but the groundswell for Brockington was so strong that Hayes asked his offensive assistants to vote for either Brockington or Otis. Brockington won in a landslide.

"Well," Hayes said in response, "you're all wrong."

Hayes was so sure that he ignored both his assistant coaches' advice and the potential racial implications: Otis was white and Brockington was black. Hayes's lone black assistant, running backs coach Rudy Hubbard, wondered if Brockington's race was hampering his candidacy. He eventually concluded that this was not about race. Hayes, in fact, had been aggressive in recruiting black players and rooming black and white players together. It was about loyalty, stubbornness, and understandable admiration for Otis.

Once Hayes made his decision, it was final. General George Patton said all his tactical ideas came to him full-born. The same was true of Woody Hayes.

Yet for all his love of military strategy, Hayes often perplexed his team with his own battle plans. He clung to his antiquated, predictable "robust" offense—a T formation with three running backs and everybody else bunched together. While other coaches were starting to spread the field—creating mismatches and outfoxing the opposition—Hayes preferred to overpower.

His favorite plays were "26" (an off-tackle run to the right) and "27" (the same play to the left.) They were good, necessary plays, but Hayes called them so often that they lost any element of surprise. When Hayes asked each of his assistants to write a critique of the team in 1968, assistant coach George Chaump wrote that the Buckeyes were "way too dependent" on 26 and 27. Hayes scrawled his response in bold red ink across the top of the critique: "BULLSHIT!" Chaump eventually convinced Hayes to install the more advanced I formation, though Hayes still used the "robust" in short-yardage situations. The change helped Ohio State win the 1968 national championship.

Despite the grumbling of players and coaches, there were advantages to Hayes's authoritarian style. For one, it gave everybody something to hate. Hayes despised satisfaction; he said he never saw a man make a tackle with a smile on his face. It also meant that every detail was covered by somebody. Every year, Hayes put an assistant coach in charge of the weather—the coach would give him a weather report every morning, like a schoolchild reciting the Pledge of Allegiance, and Hayes would then determine if he needed to make any changes to account for inclement weather. Another coach was in charge of choosing which movie the team would watch the night before road games.

And finally, Hayes's authoritarianism meant that everybody stayed on message. Ohio State Buckeyes were not taught three different ways to block a defensive end or two different techniques to catch a ball over the middle. They were taught one way—Hayes's way—and they practiced it until they got it right. One reason Hayes admired Patton was that the general had a lower casualty rate than other military leaders. Hayes aspired for the football equivalent.

Ohio State's opening game in 1969, against Texas Christian University, was expected to be a stiff test. TCU had scored 35 points against highly regarded Purdue the week before and was considered a real threat to beat the Buckeyes. It would be hard to argue that Hayes's personnel choices hurt his team. On Ohio State's first play from scrimmage in 1969, quarterback Rex Kern threw a 36-yard pass to Bruce Jankowski, down to the TCU seven-yard line. The play was nullified by a penalty. The Buckeyes moved back 15 yards . . . and so Kern promptly threw a 58-yard-pass to Jankowski. Touchdown.

Ohio State went on to beat TCU 62–0. It should have been 64–0; the Buckeyes missed two extra-point attempts, which would be their only real weakness throughout the season. But even that weakness underscored their overall supremacy: if ever there was a team that didn't need any extra points, it was this one.

"They are the finest college team ever assembled," TCU coach Fred A. Taylor said afterward, and that opinion soon became accepted as fact. Even Hayes, always wary of complacency, had to admit that this year he had the goods.

"I'm not one to hide our light under a half-bushel," Hayes said. "If you talk your players down, they may start to believe you. This is the best material we ever had at Ohio State."

In the next week's *Sports Illustrated*, Dan Jenkins, the nation's premier college football reporter, wrote, "In that towering gray edifice known as Ohio Stadium, the Buckeyes of Woody Hayes again look like No. 1—and No. 2 and 3."

It was not just a funny line; it captured the depth and dominance of this team. Backup quarterback Ron Maciejowski, like John Brockington, would have starred on most teams. At one practice before the 1969 season, Maciejowski completed every pass he threw, at least a dozen straight, until he finally threw one off a receiver's fingertips in the end zone . . . and for that, he got kicked out of practice. It had nothing to do with that incomplete pass. Maciejowski had played too well on the day when a traveling group of newspaper reporters known as the Big Ten "skywriters" was watching Ohio State practice.

Hayes did not want the reporters to think too highly of Maciejowski, because the coach had no intention of starting him in 1969. That spot was reserved for Rex Kern.

As Hayes proudly noted, Kern was from Lancaster, Ohio, the

same hometown as William Tecumseh Sherman. (Hayes was so fond of Sherman that the coach sometimes referred to him as "Billy Sherman," as though Sherman were a sophomore linebacker instead of a Civil War general who had been dead for seventy-eight years.) Sharing a hometown with a famous general was not enough to earn the starting quarterback job at Ohio State—not even Woody Hayes loved the military *that* much—but it was fitting, because if the term "field general" had not already been used to describe quarterbacks, it would have been coined for Rex Kern.

Kern was a natural leader and an exceptional athlete (he had come to Ohio State to play basketball.) His only weakness was that he had a bad back—and combined with his fearlessness, that meant he was always an injury risk. He was precisely the kind of leader that Woody Hayes wanted on the field in the closing minutes of a tight game . . . and yet, these Buckeyes were so good that they never played tight games. They followed the TCU win with a 41–14 blowout at Washington and a 54–21 win over 19th-ranked Michigan State.

It seemed that the toughest task for Ohio State would be picking the Friday night movies. And in a way, it was. The assistant coach in charge of movies, Earle Bruce, knew nothing about them. (As Bruce explained to Hayes, "I never go to a movie—I work for you.") Hayes had a few rules: no profanity, no gore, and especially no sex. The players told Bruce they had another rule: no more Disney movies.

On the eve of Ohio State's fourth game, at Minnesota, Bruce scanned the movie listings and came upon a film called *Easy Rider*. The players said it was about motorcycles. Bruce figured it was about a motorcycle race. It was actually about two hippie drifters, played by Peter Fonda and Dennis Hopper, who were snorting cocaine ninety seconds into the film.

The moral of the movie?

"You know, this used to be a hell of a good country," Jack Nicholson's character tells Hopper's, before adding, "They're gonna talk to you and talk to you and talk to you about individual freedom, but they see a free individual, it's gonna scare 'em." It could not have helped that Nicholson said this while wearing a blue sweater with a yellow block "M" on it.

Hayes immediately fired Bruce from movie-picking duty; he later said that the movie "depressed" the Buckeyes and accounted for their poor performance at Minnesota. It is just as likely that the Buckeyes were distracted by the coach himself. On Ohio State's last trip to Minnesota, in 1966, the Old Man had supposedly gotten so angry that he slammed his fist through a door, and now the Buckeyes wanted to see the evidence. They were thrilled to find that the hole was still in the door, and although they didn't play particularly well, it hardly mattered: No. 1 Ohio State cruised to a 34–7 victory.

"Michigan Football Offers New Excitement in '69."

So read the newspaper advertisement. Below that were the words, "Parents—Why Not Share the Action?" And below that, almost as an afterthought: "What About Michigan's Football Ability?"

Michigan athletic director Don Canham wasn't going to let something as silly as the quality of his team keep him from selling football tickets. "Until we start planting shrubs there," he said, "we're going to have to fill seats." Most athletic directors figured that if the team won, the people would come, but Canham wanted to draw fans regardless of how the Wolverines fared. He emphasized the game-day experience.

Canham encouraged tailgating when the concept was in its infancy. Michigan Stadium's capacity of 101,001 was the largest in the nation, and though anybody could see the upside—Michigan could sell more tickets than anybody else—Canham understood the downside: even with a crowd of 60,000, the stadium was barely more than half full. Canham sold two-dollar tickets to high school students. He organized "high school band day," when high school band members were allowed in for free (and got a chance to perform on the field). Canham wanted a product that *seemed* to be in demand. If he couldn't engineer a sellout, he at least wanted the *appearance* of one.

Canham's predecessor, Fritz Crisler, was like a lot of athletic directors: he thought that if a game was too appealing on television, nobody would come to the stadium. Crisler had allowed cameras in the press box only. The result was a standard, uninteresting view from the top of the stadium.

Canham thought television could sell the game (and the Michigan brand) to a mass audience. He let a friend at ABC know that Michigan had a new policy: whatever the network wanted, Canham would try to provide. ABC Sports president Roone Arledge called him back immediately. ABC now felt welcome in Michigan Stadium. With the new emphasis on the game-day experience, Canham hoped non–football fans felt welcome, too. He even advertised the new artificial playing surface, Tartan Turf—he hoped the field would attract people no matter how the Wolverines played on it.

The installation of the Tartan Turf epitomized the Canham approach to business. He installed what most believed to be a superior surface, saved $10,000 in annual maintenance costs, and donated the old sod to the new St. Francis of Assisi Church down the road. That way, Canham saved the grass and didn't have to pay anybody to get rid of it; church volunteers came and took it away.

Don Canham's marketing approach was progressive, but it was also pragmatic. What about Michigan's football ability? Canham couldn't answer with confidence.

The Bo Schembechler era began at home against Vanderbilt, and he was at odds with the referee before the opening kickoff. The referee, Jerry Markbreit, had officiated one of Schembechler's games at Miami the year before, and Schembechler was so upset with some of the calls that he told Markbreit, "I'll make you a promise: you'll never work another game for me!" Of course, referees didn't work for coaches, but that didn't matter to Schembechler. Like Woody Hayes, he was so accustomed to players and coaches following his orders that he often figured everybody did.

Schembechler also believed in the same style of football as Hayes. He ran the "belly" offense, basically the same as Hayes's beloved "robust." It was not terribly appealing to the casual fan. Schembechler rarely called passing plays on first down and seemed to be happy if his team didn't pass at all.

The day before the opener, University of Michigan president Robben Fleming told five thousand students at a teach-in that the war in Vietnam was "a colossal mistake." (He added, "We have also the rather naïve notion that our political institutions have served this country so admirably that they must be applied to every other country in the world.") The next day, Michigan beat Vanderbilt, 42–14; afterward, 12,000 spectators marched from the stadium to the school's central campus to protest the Vietnam War, and it was unclear whether the game or the protest had drawn the crowd.

Or maybe it was very clear: "Politics and Tartan Turf were, at 1:30 yesterday, the major attractions in the Michigan Stadium for the 70,183 not-so-screaming fans that came to drink away a Saturday afternoon," read the lead paragraph of the game story in the school newspaper, the *Michigan Daily*.

Three days after the Vanderbilt game, Michigan fullback Garvie Craw became a father. The day after that, Millie Schembechler gave birth to a son, Glenn Edward Schembechler III, nicknamed Shemy, just like Bo's father. Craw and his coach visited the hospital together. The doctors first wheeled out Stacey Craw, and Bo and Garvie cooed appropriately. Then they wheeled out Shemy.

"I don't know if it's any indication of what's to come," Bo said, "but that child has the largest gonads I've ever seen."

The coach was apparently unaware that newborn boys have swollen scrotums—he, like Craw, was learning on the fly, and he wasn't afraid to admit it. It was one reason the Michigan players put up with their new coach.

The next week, the Wolverines beat Washington. They were suddenly No. 13 in the country. Then, in a flash, they weren't: Missouri drilled them, 40–17, thanks in part to a blocked punt, precisely the kind of play that infuriated Schembechler. At the next practice, the coach told the Wolverines that anybody who blocked a punt would get a free milkshake. The football field was surely the only spot on campus where a milkshake was considered a wild indulgence, but in any event, Schembechler had no intention of handing out any.

"We will never get a punt blocked ever again in the history of Michigan football!" Schembechler shouted, with such conviction that his players believed it, right up until the next play, when a punt was blocked.

Downfield, offensive lineman Jim Brandstatter looked up for the ball. He saw none. Then he heard the phrase that they all knew so well by now: "*Yoooooouuuuu son of a BITCH!*"

"Oh, shit," Brandstatter thought. "Someone's in trouble."

Brandstatter was sure it wasn't him. He had blocked his man. He had no doubt. He replayed the punt in his head, from snap to "son of a bitch," right up until Schembechler's left elbow nailed him at the top of his chest—Schembechler had left his feet to make the hit. The coach grabbed Brandstatter's facemask and screamed, "You dumb son of a bitch! You'll never play another fucking down for Michigan! Get out of here! I never want to see you again!"

Brandstatter was used to being called names. He was in the Reserve Officer Training Corps, and when he wore his ROTC uniform to class, his fellow Michigan students would scream "pig!" and "asshole!" and spit on him. Four days before the opener, sixty demonstrators had seized the ROTC building; soon after, a faculty panel recommended that the school sever all financial ties to ROTC and stop giving credit for ROTC classes.

Brandstatter's father was a retired brigadier general, and he always figured he would serve in the military. He had no use for hippies, their culture, or the music they called poetry. He had tried smoking pot but didn't like it. For all these reasons—plus the fact that he played offensive line, the position Schembechler had played and loved above all others—Brandstatter should have been Schembechler's ideal player. Yet the coach had taken to calling him "Wide Butt," and Brandstatter had written letters to his parents complaining about the new coach. Now Brandstatter started walking up the stadium tunnel to go home, possibly for good. His position coach, Jerry Hanlon, stopped him.

"Don't go, don't go," Hanlon said. "It wasn't your fault." Senior

Dick Caldarazzo had missed the block. Schembechler was wrong. But the message was clear: mistakes would not be tolerated.

The following week, Michigan bounced back to beat ninth-ranked Purdue. That set up their *other* big rivalry game, against Michigan State. Before his team took the field, Schembechler started to thank his players for sticking with him, even when they didn't want to.

"You guys have accepted me as your coach," he said. He appeared to have tears in his eyes. His players immediately went out and gave him another reason to cry: they lost, 23–12. Michigan was now 4–2, and some of the seniors decided they'd had enough. They went into Schembechler's office and told the coach that team morale was low. He was crushing their spirits. He had to ease up.

Schembechler thought for a moment.

"I'll tell you what I'm gonna do," he said. "I'm gonna make it *harder*. To hell with you."

The next game was at Minnesota. Schembechler told his players that if they were hurt and didn't practice, they wouldn't make the trip. He left a few starters home. His players responded just as he hoped: they whipped Minnesota, 35–9, and the key was the Wolverines' conditioning—they got better as the game wore on. They came home and beat Wisconsin, 35–7, in their homecoming game.

The Wolverines were starting to roll. But getting attention was another matter. There were more than 40,000 empty seats in Michigan Stadium for the homecoming game. For many students, the only reason to go to the stadium was the antiwar "moratorium rally" in mid-October: the rally drew 20,000 people and class attendance was reportedly 60 percent below normal that day. (Schembechler was very concerned about the burning of draft cards at the rally; he feared it would damage the new Tartan Turf.) Other students crashed a regents meeting (in a dispute over the university-run bookstore), held sit-ins and teach-ins, or built bomb craters on campus. And some weren't satisfied with mere craters: since 1968, Ann Arbor had seen the bombing of a local CIA office, of an engineering laboratory that was conducting classified government research, and of an ROTC staff car.

The Weathermen, having wrested control of Students for a Democratic Society, took their hopes for a revolution to Chicago. In early October, they bombed the famed Haymarket Statue there and set off several days of riots. Cars were overturned, windows were shattered, dozens were injured, dozens more were arrested . . . and it was all predictable. The night before the Haymarket bombing, the *Chicago Tribune* went to press with this warning, buried in a news story on page 30: "Hit-and-run guerrilla tactics, confrontations with police, and disruption of the Federal building and high schools are among the plans being made by radicals. . . . The plans were discussed by William Ayres, [*sic*] educational secretary of the SDS and other national leaders at a recent meeting."

It was, as the White Panthers had promised, a total assault on the culture. The Panthers were doing their part, too. Like many radicals, they felt that marijuana laws were being used to stifle their political activity; since police could not easily arrest hippies for their views, they went after them for recreational drug use. John Sinclair, the blues musician who cofounded the White Panthers, decided to fight fire with smoke. He openly flouted the marijuana laws, almost begging to be arrested, and the cops happily complied.

Sinclair figured when he got arrested, people would see the absurdity of treating marijuana possession like a serious crime against society, and the law would change. It is perhaps worth noting that Sinclair was taking a lot of LSD when he came to that conclusion. In 1969, he was sentenced to nine and a half to ten years in prison for possession of two marijuana cigarettes. The case made national headlines—the idea that a man could spend a decade in jail for holding a pair of joints got plenty of attention—but it also intensified the government's focus on the White Panthers.

Sinclair's Panthers cofounder, Pun Plamondon, got used to a black police car following him around. When he wanted to lose his tail, he would walk into a pinball arcade on South University Avenue, open a seemingly useless door, walk downstairs until he was under the sidewalk, then walk through an underground tunnel and end up a block away, inside Ulrich's bookstore.

Was Plamondon avoiding the cops so he could do harm? The

government thought so. On October 8—as the Weathermen clashed with police in Chicago—Plamondon, Sinclair, and fellow White Panther Jack Forrest were indicted for bombing the CIA office in Ann Arbor. (Sinclair and Forrest were accused of conspiring; Plamondon was accused of actually setting off the bomb.) Sinclair was already in jail for his pot charge. Forrest was arrested. Plamondon was in the Panthers' house at 1520 Hill Street, just off campus, when news of his indictment came over the radio.

Plamondon didn't know what would happen when he was arrested and he didn't want to wait to find out. His fellow Panthers removed the backseat of a late-model Buick belonging to Elsie Sinclair, John's mom . . . Plamondon climbed in where the seat used to be, so it would appear nobody was in the backseat . . . and then Plamondon got the hell out of Ann Arbor. He went to a hippie commune in the mountains of Northern California, and then to San Francisco, Seattle, and New York . . . and Toronto . . . and Germany, Italy, and Algeria. By the spring of 1970, he would be on the FBI's Ten Most Wanted List.

Pun Plamondon had been an outcast all his life, from the moment he was born in a state mental hospital, to an alcoholic father and a mother who had syphilis. (He was conceived while they were institutionalized.) His friends hoped he would stay out of the United States for as long as necessary. But Pun Plamondon would return. And then he would get his own stunning payback.

The banner headline was splashed across the front page: "Big Ten Can Change Its Outdated Rose Bowl Rule!" The editors of the *Football News* somehow withheld the word "Woo-hoo!" from their November 1 issue, but they did not hide their agenda. The story began, "The Football News campaign to get the Big Ten to repeal the nonrepeat Rose Bowl rule and send the likely champion Ohio State to Pasadena Jan. 1 is gaining momentum."

Every year since 1947, the Big Ten had sent its champion to the Rose Bowl. But teams were not allowed to go two years in a row, and the conference forbade teams from going to any bowl other than the

Rose. So repeat champions had to stay home. Since Ohio State had earned the Rose Bowl bid in 1968, the Buckeyes were ineligible for any bowl for the 1969 season. But other conferences had looser rules—the Pac-8, which also sent its champion to the Rose Bowl, gladly sent repeat teams. And this year the Buckeyes were so good that it seemed outrageous for the Big Ten to send anybody else.

"I don't believe they should go to the Rose Bowl," said Illinois coach Jim Valek, after Ohio State drilled his team 41–0. "I don't think any team should go to the Rose Bowl two years in a row. But I'd like to see them give Tennessee or one of those other teams a thrill. I'd like to see them against Missouri or Texas." Then Valek cracked, "I don't want to be piggish. I want somebody else to have a thrill like I had today."

Ohio State followed its victory over Illinois with a 35–6 win over Northwestern and a 62–7 win over Wisconsin. The gap between Ohio State and Wisconsin was so large that the losing coach, John Coatta, didn't even seem upset.

"Not much you can do about it," Coatta said afterward while munching on an apple. "I was about to go over and see if they had a big 'S' on their chests."

Five Buckeyes would earn All-American honors: defensive backs Jack Tatum and Ted Provost, noseguard Jim Stillwagon, fullback Jim Otis, and quarterback Rex Kern. The Rose Bowl debate continued through the fall. It was not just a debate about the 1969 Buckeyes; it cut to the heart of college football's purpose. The "no-repeat rule" was instituted because administrators saw the Rose Bowl as a reward for a long, successful season, to be shared by as many conference schools as possible. If the rule was changed, the conference would be saying that the desire for the best possible intersectional games was more important than the experience of a bowl trip. Even Ohio State athletic director Dick Larkins said he liked the no-repeat rule.

Ultimately, the Big Ten decided to leave the rule in place. Woody Hayes would spend the holidays in Columbus instead of Pasadena, and though he would have loved to showcase his team in the Rose

Bowl, he was always happy to be in Columbus. He was a dominant figure in the Ohio capital. His favorite restaurant, the Jai Lai, had a billboard advertisement with pictures of Hayes and the Eiffel Tower. The caption: "In All the World, There's Only One."

Hayes had recovered from his mid-1960s swoon, when his recruiting hit a rare dry spell, mostly because of a flaw in his philosophy. In the early 1960s, Michigan State had built a Big Ten powerhouse largely by recruiting players from outside the state—in particular, black players. Hayes, who took so much pride in working at his state's public university, was late to that trend. Michigan State won national championships in 1965 and 1966, while Ohio State went six seasons without a Big Ten title in the mid-1960s, a streak that nearly got Hayes fired. But once he adapted, he quickly returned the Buckeyes to the top of the conference. In Ohio or elsewhere—and in cities, suburbs, and rural areas—no coach in the country recruited better than Woody Hayes.

Hayes rarely spoke to recruits about football, except to say that if a player was good enough to be recruited by Ohio State, he was obviously outstanding. Mostly, he promised the player's parents that their son would leave Ohio State with an undergraduate degree. This was not just empty talk. In 1965 Hayes had hired James Jones as academic adviser to the football team, an almost unprecedented move. Hayes, who was never big on pretentious titles, referred to Jones as his "brain coach" and held him to the same high standards as every other assistant. Each position coach was also responsible for knowing the class schedule and academic progress of every player he coached. Every Ohio State freshman football player received a copy of a grammar textbook called *Word Power Made Easy* for mandatory English lessons. The lessons were taught by an Ohio State professor named Woody Hayes.

On road trips, the Buckeyes left on Friday mornings for a Saturday afternoon game, even if the game was only a short flight away, so that Hayes could take his players on an educational outing when they landed. Sometimes they attended a lecture. Often he took his players to a place of historical significance. In 1964, the day before they played Iowa, the undefeated Buckeyes visited the Herbert Hoover Presidential Library and Museum in West Branch, Iowa. Hoover had died ten days earlier, and the guards were still on duty at the burial site. At Hayes's request, a young man who worked at the museum started giving a lecture on Hoover to the Ohio State players, only to hear a voice in the crowd say, "No, I don't think so." And again: "No, I don't think so."

The voice belonged to Woody Hayes. He felt the lecture was inaccurate. Finally the coach stood up, relieved the young man of his duties, and gave his players an hour-long talk on Herbert Hoover.

Ah, if only it were always so simple. If only Woody Hayes could stand up whenever he objected to a speaker and take over the lecture. Instead, too many people were taking the stage *away* from football coaches.

In November 1969, fourteen black football players at Indiana University told coach John Pont they were unhappy with the racial atmosphere in the football program—they said it was "mentally depressing and morally discouraging to blacks." Pont was stunned. He believed radicals were using his players to advance their agenda. Nine Hoosiers quit, devastating the program—not just by their absence, but because of the implications.

Two years earlier, Indiana had been a Rose Bowl team, and with Ohio State ineligible in 1969, the Hoosiers had a chance to go back to Pasadena. Pont sensed that his program was about to disintegrate. He was right. Keeping the team together would be difficult and recruiting would be impossible—other coaches would use the incident against Pont. The Hoosiers lost their final three games of 1969, and twenty of twenty-two over the next three seasons. And for the life of him, Pont couldn't think of anything he had done wrong.

The same thing had happened at other schools—notably Wyoming, Washington, and Princeton. Still, when it happened to Pont, it must have hit home with a couple other Big Ten coaches. Pont had played football at Miami for Woody Hayes. He had lived across the hall there from his buddy Bo Schembechler.

*   *   *

The genius was in the simplicity. Folk musician Pete Seeger didn't realize that, not initially. When he first heard the song, he thought it was barely a song at all. But nothing else was catching on that day, so Seeger decided to give it a shot . . . and the next thing he knew, fellow musicians Peter, Paul, and Mary joined in, and soon tens of thousands, *hundreds* of thousands, were singing along, swaying their bodies:

"All we are saying . . . is give peace a chance."

That was literally almost all they were saying—they repeated the line, written by John Lennon a few months earlier, over and over again: *All we are saying . . . is give peace a chance.* How many people were singing in Washington, D.C., that November day in 1969? At least a quarter million. The federal government put the number at 325,000. By any estimate, it was the biggest antiwar rally in U.S. history. The rally concluded in front of the White House, which seemed like a surefire way to get the attention of the president of the United States. But Richard Nixon never came out to acknowledge the crowd. He stayed inside and watched Ohio State beat Purdue.

President Nixon must have known it was a big game. To the Buckeyes, it seemed like the *biggest* game. Purdue, in that era, was the measuring stick for Ohio State's return to prominence. In 1967, the Boilermakers had whipped the Buckeyes, 41–6, the most lopsided defeat of Hayes's career. In 1968, Ohio State got revenge and stamped itself as a national contender with a 13–0 win over the No. 1–ranked Boilermakers. Now, in 1969, Purdue came in as the No. 10 team in the country, averaging 37 points per game. The weather was so cold and windy that Woody Hayes actually wore a jacket, but only a blizzard could have kept this game close. Hayes's best team drilled Purdue, 42–14.

Afterward, with thousands of protesters standing behind a fifty-seven-bus barricade outside the White House, President Nixon called Hayes to congratulate him. Ohio State had clinched a share of the Big Ten title. The Buckeyes only needed one more win, against Michigan, to capture a second straight national title, and there was little doubt they would get it.

"I knew they were good from looking at films, but they're too good for anybody, I guess," Purdue coach Jack Mollenkopf said. "Unless it would be the Minnesota Vikings."

Was this the best college football team ever?

"I don't think I've ever seen one with everything they've got," Mollenkopf said. "They've got it all."

The only thing they didn't have, of course, was a chance to go to Pasadena. In that week's *Sports Illustrated*, Dan Jenkins suggested an alternative: the Woody Bowl, featuring Ohio State's offense against Ohio State's defense.

"It would be some crash, boy," Jenkins wrote, "but it might be the only way this dazed collegiate world of 1969 would ever find out what the best team in the country is."

Meanwhile, over in Iowa City, Bo Schembechler's Wolverines ripped Iowa, 51–6. The week before, they had beaten Illinois 57–0. Now, as they walked off the field after besting Iowa, the Michigan players immediately started chanting: "Beat the Bucks! Beat the Bucks!" They actually thought they could do it.

The next day, Schembechler gathered his Wolverines for their weekly Sunday meeting and asked defensive lineman Pete Newell to stand up.

"He's our defensive player of the week," Schembechler said of Newell, a sophomore philosophy major with a liberal bent. "And this means an awful lot, because Pete was out there in Iowa City with the rest of the team, and not in Washington with the damn hippies where he really wanted to be."

Newell laughed. It was as close as Schembechler came to discussing politics with his players. Even in coaches' meetings, when the conversation turned to politics, Schembechler was uncharacteristically quiet. He was focused on football—and specifically, on whomever Michigan played next.

As much as Bo Schembechler burned to beat Woody Hayes and Ohio State, he rarely mentioned it to his players. The Wolverines didn't realize that he had installed the same defensive scheme as Ohio State largely so the Wolverines could practice against it. Or that their two best running plays—off-tackle right and off-tackle left—came straight from Hayes, right down to the names of the plays: "26" and "27." Or that every day in practice, without telling his players his true motivation, Schembechler made them do something to prepare for Ohio State.

Now Schembechler had nothing to hide. When Michigan players arrived at practice the week of their game against Ohio State, they found the scout team in scarlet jerseys—Ohio State's color—with a big gray 50 on it. It was a not-so-subtle reminder of the Buckeyes' 50–14 triumph over Michigan the year before.

On Tuesday of that week, a snowstorm hit Ann Arbor. Michigan players weren't sure if they were going to practice inside or outside. They turned to Schembechler. The coach knew exactly what to say:

"If you're going to fight in the North Atlantic, you have to train in the North Atlantic!" he shouted, then grabbed a shovel and cleared the field with his players.

But as they said at the Jai Lai, "In all the world, there's only one." Woody Hayes's Buckeyes were not worried. They were a 17-point favorite over Michigan. They had been so good all season—winning every game by at least 27 points, outscoring their opponents by an average of 46–9—that their talent seemed to supersede all of Hayes's deepest beliefs.

Hayes was a staunch advocate of the running game, but the 1969 Buckeyes passed so well that he opened up the playbook. His program was designed to wear down opponents by the fourth quarter, but in 1969, his starters never even *played* in the fourth quarter. Hayes always built his season around beating That School Up North, but in 1969, many of his players felt Purdue was the biggest game of the year. And after beating the Boilermakers, Hayes told reporters, "Our defense was the best I've ever seen it." This was standard for him in 1969—he had already admitted, after only one game, that his roster featured "the best material we ever had"—but it violated a fundamental tenet of the Hayes philosophy: never, ever feel too good about yourself.

In the wake of the Purdue triumph, Ohio State captain Dave

Whitfield sensed that the Buckeyes were too cocky. Some of the younger players were acting like the undefeated season was assured. Whitfield and fellow captain Alan Jack met with the coaches and then the players to try to recapture the Buckeyes' focus. Whitfield sensed that he wasn't getting through. They had the best defense in school history—the Old Man had said so himself. Hadn't Whitfield read the newspaper?

"I hate to be defended in a newspaper," Emerson wrote. "As long as all that is said is said against me, I feel a certain assurance of success. But as soon as honeyed words of praise are spoken for me, I feel as one that lies unprotected before his enemies."

There was an unusual buzz on the Michigan campus that week. For many Wolverines, it was the first time they felt that the student body was behind them. That was partly because Michigan had been playing very well, but the opponent—powerful, monolithic Ohio State—was a factor, too. The Buckeyes were college football's Establishment team.

Michigan offensive lineman Dick Caldarazzo walked down the Michigan Stadium tunnel an hour and a half before the game, just to get a sense of the atmosphere. When he reached the other end of the tunnel, he could not believe what he saw. Ninety minutes before kickoff on a cool late November day, there were already at least 20,000 fans in their seats, maybe 30,000 . . . and almost every one of them was wearing Ohio State scarlet and gray. Don Canham had gone to Ohio to get his sellout, and he couldn't ask Ohio State fans to give their tickets back now.

The opening kickoff was moved from 1:30 p.m. to 1:15 to accommodate ABC. President Nixon cut off a budget meeting at one o'clock so he could watch some of the game in his office before heading to a dental appointment. By the end of the day, Nixon would have a TV hooked up in his dentist's office. Once this game started, it would be impossible to turn away.

* * *

Woody Hayes tried a little gamesmanship in pregame warm-ups. He had his team stretch on Michigan's side of the field. Woody was clearly testing Bo, but it was a tactical mistake: Schembechler simply asked Hayes to move to the proper side of the field, Hayes had no choice but to comply, and the Wolverines felt like their coach had stood up to the legend.

Hayes had other worries. Kern had injured his back, so Hayes told his backup, Maciejowski, that he would probably play 95 percent of the game. But when kickoff came, Hayes stuck with Kern, his leader and star.

Kern immediately drove the Buckeyes straight down the field. They scored on a one-yard run by Otis. Then, as was their custom in 1969, the Buckeyes missed the extra point. It was almost funny: in the last game of the year, the best team in America still couldn't execute the easiest play in the game. But then Michigan responded with a touchdown and kicked the extra point. Ohio State trailed for the first time all season.

The Buckeyes came right back and scored another touchdown, and this time they made the extra point . . . but Michigan jumped offside, and now Hayes had a choice: decline the penalty and hang on to his 13–7 lead, or accept the penalty, move the ball half the distance to the goal line, then try a two-point conversion. He went for two. His team failed to get it. Ohio State's lead shrunk to 12–7.

Michigan responded again with a long drive. Schembechler's experience under Hayes was proving invaluable: other teams knew what Ohio State did, but Schembechler knew how the Old Man *thought*. Schembechler knew that if he ran away from All-American safety Jack Tatum, as most teams did, then he was just playing into Hayes's hands; Hayes would line Tatum up on the strong side of the field and let the other teams run the other way, into the alps. Schembechler also knew that when Tatum blitzed, like Lord Howard splitting the Spanish Armada, that would leave Michigan tight end Jim Mandich open downfield.

The Wolverines mixed off-tackle runs with passes over the middle, keeping Ohio State off balance. Finally, fullback Garvie Craw pounded the ball in for a touchdown. Michigan led 14–12.

The Wolverines had believed all week that they could play with Ohio State. Now they knew for sure. And the Buckeyes, who thought (like everybody else) that they were invincible, started to realize they were not. They were forced to punt on their next possession. Michigan needed one big play to break the game open and put serious pressure on the Buckeyes for the first time all season. They got it.

Michigan's Barry Pierson fielded the punt at his own 38-yard line and took off. By the time Ohio State tackled him, Pierson had run all the way down to the Ohio State three. The Wolverines banged in another touchdown to take a 21–12 lead.

Woody Hayes talked to his offensive players before sending them back in the game. But as he did, a television cameraman zeroed in on him. Hayes gave the cameraman a shove and resumed coaching.

Michigan added a field goal to push its lead to 24–12 at halftime. The Buckeyes had to play catch-up, and although they clearly had the firepower to do it, they also had a quarterback with an injured back and no history of playing from behind. On Ohio State's first possession of the second half, Pierson intercepted a Kern pass. On the next possession, Pierson intercepted Kern again. Hayes eventually turned to Maciejowski, but that changed nothing: he too was intercepted by Pierson.

For the day, Michigan would intercept six Ohio State passes. Hayes didn't like throwing six passes in one game to his *own* team, let alone to the opponent. The halftime score stood up: Michigan won, 24–12.

ABC announcer Bill Flemming immediately called it the "upset of the century." The Michigan players tried to carry Schembechler off the field in celebration. They managed to carry him, but not off the field—it was mobbed with Michigan fans, and nobody could move.

The Buckeyes had outgained Michigan 374–373, but they had ruined their chances with those six interceptions. Ohio State had thrown 28 passes and completed only 10. In the pandemonium afterward, Hayes seemed to realize that he had lost by playing somebody else's game. He put his arm around Otis's shoulder and said, "Jim, if you would have run the ball fifteen more times today, we would have won the game."

Schembechler refused to gloat. The closest he came was in discussing the Rose Bowl: "Those people wanted a Big Ten champion. We'll give them one." He added that Woody had congratulated him on the field.

What did Bo say in response?

"Nothing," Schembechler said. "He's my coach."

The Buckeyes had rolled over everybody that season, and now they were literally stuck: mobbed by Michigan fans outside the stadium. It took their bus a solid hour to get out of the parking lot.

That night, Schembechler had a party at his house. He wasn't much of a partier—he'd have a couple of beers and a cigar, and that was it. He rarely attended other people's parties. But on this night, the greatest of his career, he was happy to celebrate.

Over on campus, the Michigan players partied more willingly—and voraciously. When the team gathered for a meeting the next morning, many of the Wolverines were still drunk. But even in that altered state, they had a new appreciation for the sign Schembechler had hung in Yost Fieldhouse during those brutal winter workouts: THOSE WHO STAY WILL BE CHAMPIONS. And while Schembechler tried to downplay the importance of beating his mentor, the storyline was too good, and too obvious, to avoid. It was summed up on the bumper stickers that appeared in Ann Arbor that winter: "Goody, Goody! Bo Beat Woody!"

The news spread all the way to Vietnam, to the third brigade of the 82nd Airborne Division of the U.S. Army, to a young soldier from Oxford, Michigan, named Mike Lantry.

That Schembechler guy beat Woody Hayes.

Lantry was on the front lines of a war with ill-defined front lines, trying to follow the Wolverines as a mental escape. It was not easy. Scoring updates were scarce—Lantry usually got them by word of mouth, or from *Stars and Stripes*, the military newspaper, several days after a game was played.

Lantry was thrilled to hear Michigan had won. He had no idea that someday, he would be a pivotal figure in the Michigan–Ohio State rivalry. He had barely even thought of playing college football. Every day in the fall of 1969, Mike Lantry had only one goal: survive.

Michigan arrived in Southern California for the Rose Bowl in mid-December. Bo Schembechler acted like it was August. The coach instituted a training program straight out of preseason conditioning: two practices each day for the two weeks they were in California.

But the Wolverines didn't need more conditioning; they needed to heal. Predictably, they paid a price. Fullback Garvie Craw, one of the team's stars, suffered a hematoma in his thigh—he couldn't even jog until the day before the game. Glenn Doughty, another valued running back, injured his knee. The rigorous workouts even wiped out the Michigan coaches: before one of Michigan's last practices before the Rose Bowl, several assistants were lying down with their heads on blocking dummies.

Schembechler walked over to a mirror, shirtless, and admired himself. "There's only one tough son of a bitch that never goes down around here," he said. "*I'm* the tough one. I never go down!"

Despite the grueling practices, the Wolverines still believed they would beat USC; after the victory over Ohio State, they naturally figured they could beat anybody. So they were a confident bunch as they gathered for a team meeting on New Year's Day. By this point, they knew the rules: be there five minutes early. Most were so excited about playing in the Rose Bowl that they were in their seats fifteen minutes early. Ten minutes later, the coaches still hadn't shown up. Finally, defensive coordinator Jim Young walked in.

"Bo won't be with us today," he said.

The players were stunned. Schembechler never even missed a practice drill. There was only one plausible explanation for their coach missing the Rose Bowl:

He was dead.

For all Young knew, they were right. The night before, Schembechler had felt a sharp pain in his chest as he walked up a hill to a team dinner. A few hours later, he cut off his traditional night-before-a-game meeting with his coaches in his room; Schembechler, who never tired of football, was suddenly too tired to talk football the night before the Rose Bowl.

The body Schembechler saw in the mirror at Pasadena Junior College was not the same one he saw in his dorm room mirror at Miami, back when he was a lefty pitcher working on his pickoff move. All those on-the-run cheeseburgers and marathon film sessions had come with a price. Schembechler, who had weighed 195 pounds when he took the Michigan job, now weighed 220. He had dissipated his body. And on the eve of the Rose Bowl, he'd had a heart attack. He was forty years old.

Young didn't tell the players about the heart attack, mostly because he didn't really know what had happened, or how Bo was doing. He just told them he would be the head coach for the game.

On the surface, that should not have made much difference. Young was an outstanding coach with a similar philosophy to Schembechler's. (How similar? When Young was a high school coach in Lima, Ohio, a woman who taught at his school asked him every Monday why he never threw on first down.)

But the Wolverines were now an emotional wreck. Cecil Pryor, one of the most fun-loving players on the team (he had snuck out of his room after curfew the night before and didn't come back for several hours), was crying. Scanning the field before the game, some spectators mistook Michigan assistant coach Jerry Hanlon for Schembechler, but when Hanlon left for his usual spot in the press box, they realized Schembechler was gone.

Slowly the news of the heart attack filtered down to the players. Maybe if the Wolverines had known that Schembechler was going to be okay—or if they had a couple days to digest the news—then it would have been different. But they had no time to recover. Dan Dierdorf, the star lineman, later said it was the first time a Rose Bowl team ever *walked* out of the tunnel.

For so much of 1969, Michigan players dreamed of life without Bo

Schembechler. Now Bo was gone, and they were devastated. Young and his coaches tried to keep the team energized against fourth-ranked Southern California. The game was tied 3–3 as the Michigan Marching Band formed a peace symbol on the field at halftime.

Schembechler was never far from anybody's mind. In the third quarter, somebody handed Young a telegram—a *telegram*, handed to the acting head coach, in the middle of the Rose Bowl. This had to be a message from Schembechler to the team, or perhaps an update on Bo's condition from the hospital. Young opened it. It read:

> Don't forget to pass on first down.
>   *Sally Berry*
>   *Lima, Ohio*

USC took a 10–3 lead on a 33-yard touchdown pass in the third quarter. Michigan failed to score again. Schembechler spent eighteen days in the hospital, where he received a stunning amount of mail from fans and fellow coaches. One letter stood out.

Dear Bo:

If you were going to have a sick spell, why didn't you have it at our game, for your team didn't look the same without you. On television it appeared that they stuck in there real well, but they lacked the coordination that they had against us. Anne is always accusing me of practicing medicine without a license, but even at that hazard I'm going to offer a little free advice. A few years back I headed up the Central Ohio Heart Fund Drive two years. During that time I talked with scores of good heart doctors and with hundreds of "happy cardiacs" who were the best and most enthusiastic fund raisers we had. In their cases their complete recovery was truly amazing. At one luncheon a man thirty-two years old told me he had suffered an attack a year and one-half before while playing tennis. That morning his doctor had told him that he could start playing tennis again. I'm not suggesting that you go back to handball for you never were very good at it. . . .

All I'm trying to say is: If you won't get stubborn and heroic you can be in better health than ever.

I'll see you next November 21st.

Your old coach and long-time friend,
Woody

November 21, of course, was the day of the 1970 Ohio State–Michigan game. As soon as his team arrived in Columbus after the stunning 1969 loss to Michigan, Hayes had gone straight to his office to begin preparing for the rematch.

Never again would a Woody Hayes team be accused of taking Michigan lightly. Hayes had the 1969 score woven into a rug, along with a blank score for the 1970 matchup; he then laid the rug at the door of the Buckeyes' locker room, where they would have to walk over it every day. He planned to visit Vietnam again in the offseason, but other than that, he would focus on That School Up North.

And now that Schembechler had established the Michigan program with the stunning upset, his obsession with Ohio State was no longer a secret. For the next nine years, Hayes and Schembechler would spend part of almost every day planning for The Game. But before they could face each other again, so much would happen on their campuses—so little of it planned.

The Old Man.

Hayes (second from left) watches film with his assistant Bo Schembechler (seated at his left) in 1959. *Courtesy Grandview Heights Public Library*

Woody in the Ohio State locker room, 1970.
Courtesy Grandview Heights Public Library

Hayes and President Nixon. *Courtesy Grandview Heights Public Library*

From left: Bo Schembechler, Don Canham, and Bump Elliott, at Bo's introductory press conference. *Courtesy Bentley Historical Library*

Schembechler (left) and Don Canham, December 1969.
Courtesy Akron Beacon-Journal

Outside Ohio Stadium, spring 1970. *Courtesy Ohio State University Archives*

The Black Action Movement on the Michigan campus.
Courtesy Bentley Historical Library

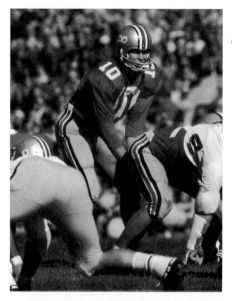

(left) Rex Kern. *Courtesy Chance Brockway*

(below) Dan Dierdorf.
Courtesy Michigan Athletic Department

Glenn Doughty.
Courtesy Michigan Athletic Department

Reggie McKenzie.
Courtesy Michigan Athletic Department

John Sinclair. *Courtesy Detroit Free Press*

Sinclair, after his
release from prison.
Courtesy Detroit Free Press

LAWRENCE ROBERT PLAMONDON

Pun Plamondon's
FBI photos.

Nixon visits Ohio State, October 1970. *Courtesy Ohio State University Archives*

Hayes clowning on one of his Navy ships. *Courtesy Ohio State University Archives*

Woody and Anne Hayes, with their son, Steve. *Courtesy Ohio State University Archives*

Hayes, flanked by Brian Baschnagel (left) and Archie Griffin.
Courtesy Grandview Heights Public Library

Hayes (seated at right) with Archie Griffin and Champ Henson (Hayes picked out the sports coats himself). *Courtesy Grandview Heights Public Library*

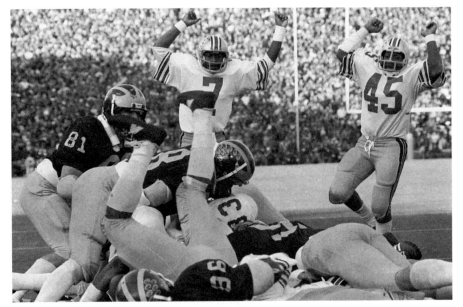

Cornelius Greene (7) and Archie Griffin celebrate a Pete Johnson touchdown in Ann Arbor. *Courtesy Chance Brockway*

Cornelius Greene doing a postgame interview. *Courtesy Chance Brockway*

Archie hits the hole against Michigan.

Courtesy Chance Brockway

Dennis Franklin.

Courtesy Michigan Athletic Department

Mike Lantry in college (left), and in the Army. *Courtesy Mike Lantry*

President Gerald Ford and
Bo Schembechler, September 1976.
Courtesy Gerald R. Ford Presidential Library

Hayes and Gerald
Ford on the eve of
the 1976 election.
*Courtesy Grandview Heights
Public Library*

Bo and Woody before the '76 game in Columbus. *Courtesy Chance Brockway*

Rick Leach.
Courtesy Michigan Athletic Department

Calvin O'Neal.
Courtesy Michigan Athletic Department

Rod Gerald.
Courtesy Chance Brockway

Art Schlichter.
Courtesy Chance Brockway

"To Woody Hayes, for whose loyal friendship I shall always be grateful."

Courtesy Ohio State University Archives

Woody getting his honorary degree from Ohio State.
Courtesy Grandview Heights Public Library

Hayes, after his retirement, across the table from Schembechler.
Courtesy Bentley Historical Library

3

Using the Enemy's Tactics

The United States of America did not fight wars on its own soil. This, the Weathermen thought, was part of the problem: the United States was always on the attack, never on the defensive. They decided to bring the war home.

Their thought process involved one small step in logic, one giant leap for their kind: the U.S. government was bombing people in Vietnam; the Weathermen deemed this bombing "immoral" and wanted to combat it; therefore, the Weathermen would bomb U.S. government targets. The Haymarket Statue bombing in Chicago and subsequent "Days of Rage," as they came to be called, were just the beginning. The Weathermen went underground, split into four- or five-person "cells," and prepared to strike.

In the first week of March 1970, the New York cell gathered in a town house in Greenwich Village—just a few young activists and a hundred pounds of dynamite—and plotted to bomb Columbia University. One of the Weathermen there, twenty-eight-year-old Diana Oughton, had been running a preschool in Ann Arbor less than two years earlier with her boyfriend, Bill Ayers—trying to change the world through education. Now her tactics had changed.

Did the Weathermen plan to use the hundred pounds of dynamite to kill people? Or would they "merely" bomb buildings, as they had done with the Haymarket Statue, inflicting symbolic and financial damage? The world never found out. The Weathermen were inexperienced at warfare; the bombs were assembled incorrectly and exploded in the town house, taking the lives of Weathermen Terry Robbins and Ted Gold, as well as Oughton, whose remains were identified only by a print on the severed piece of a finger.

After the tragedy, the Weathermen went on the lam. They fanned across the country, assuming false identities and contacting each other with calls from one pay phone to another at designated times. They would keep bombing government targets—often with a warning, to avoid killing any people. To avoid getting caught, they decided to stay away from the radical hotbeds where they would likely be recognized—places like Berkeley, California; Madison, Wisconsin; and, of course, Ann Arbor.

Nearly two years had passed since students took over the University of Michigan's Administration Building, demanding higher black student enrollment, leading school president Robben Fleming to drop in and merrily ask, "How are you coming?" In early 1970, the students gave Fleming an answer: not fast enough.

A group of black students formed an organization called the Black Action Movement and pressed Fleming for increased black enrollment, which was just 3 percent. Fleming offered a series of plans and promises, none of which satisfied the BAM leaders.

If Fleming was slow to respond, that might have been because he was a busy man. That winter, eighty faculty members formed a group called the Radical College and threatened a strike if Students for a Democratic Society was expelled from campus. Whenever corporate recruiters arrived on the Ann Arbor campus, they ran the risk of getting locked in a building; it happened at least four times that winter. Recruiters from DuPont, Dow Chemical, and General Electric were all harassed. Another, from Chase Manhattan Bank, canceled an appearance rather than face the inevitable protests.

Fleming said he would give the names of students who disrupted the university to the government, in compliance with federal and state laws. He was harshly criticized on campus for saying he would comply with the law. Fleming apologized and said he would write a letter to authorities explaining why he was not complying with the law. One day, without cause or explanation, a single bullet was discovered on the grounds of his home.

In February, a group of leftists known as the "Chicago Seven" were convicted on riot charges for their conduct at the 1968 Democratic National Convention, leading to an instant three-mile protest march through Ann Arbor by two thousand people, some of whom broke windows and threw rocks at patrol cars. Ann Arbor police chief Walter Krasny called the protesters "a bunch of criminals." One of the marchers was Pete Newell, starting defensive lineman for the Wolverines; he made it all the way to city hall before looking down and realizing he was wearing his letter jacket. Fearful of his photograph appearing in a newspaper, and the newspaper ending up in the hands of Bo Schembechler, he turned around and went home.

In truth, the Chicago Seven protest march was not the greatest potential threat to Schembechler's program. Black Action Movement leaders could have destroyed it simply by making their way over to the athletic campus—and as February turned to March, BAM rapidly swept through Ann Arbor, trying to shake the administration into action. More than a hundred black students—at least 10 percent of the entire black student population, including graduate students—stormed the Undergraduate Library, putting some books on random shelves and throwing some others in the trash. The next day, at least four "stink bombs" exploded in campus buildings; they were attributed to BAM leaders, who denied setting them off.

The BAM leaders kept pushing—disrupting classes, and demanding that nine hundred new blacks be admitted by the fall of 1971. On a campus with fewer than six hundred black undergrads, some felt the demand was extreme—one of the school's publicly elected regents warned Fleming not to give in to "coercion" by black students. But coercion was coming.

On March 9, 150 students marched to the admissions office. The widespread appeal of BAM was written on their faces, most of which were white. The regents finally agreed to meet with BAM leaders, to try to reach a settlement, but now the students felt empowered—they did not want to settle for anything. On March 19, they called for a student strike.

Even on a campus with so many activists, the odds were stacked against the strike organizers. Earlier in his career, Fleming had been an expert labor relations negotiator, while the BAM leaders were students in uncharted territory. They had a loose organization—anybody who wanted to join was welcome. (Later they would wonder about one "student" who showed up around the time of the strike, got actively involved, then vanished when it was over. Was he an FBI or CIA plant? Nobody knew.) But BAM leaders felt like most of the school would support them. They were correct.

Almost immediately, class attendance dropped to 50 percent. Soon it hit 40 percent. A week into the strike, attendance in the main undergraduate school, the College of Literature, Science and the Arts, was estimated at 25 percent. Despite their inexperience, the BAM leaders had several advantages over Fleming. Striking, though it sent a powerful message, was a passive act; one simply had to skip class, which many students were all too happy to do. With the state's strong union roots, a lot of students were not going to cross any picket line on principle. There was also the fear of being thought of as a racist simply by attending class—some BAM sympathizers dressed as Ku Klux Klan members, walked into classes, and mockingly thanked the students for "refusing to support niggers and long-haired communists."

But there was also plenty of genuine undeniable support. Letters supporting the strike flowed into the *Michigan Daily*, the student newspaper, signed by a hundred people or more—including many faculty. A group of faculty members paid $1,200 for an *Ann Arbor News* advertisement condemning strike violence, but they were in the minority, and their ad energized the strikers. And with each side aware of the publicity machine, it was fair to wonder if BAM would enlist the only blacks on campus who were sure to generate media coverage: football players.

The Michigan players probably figured their coach was the last man in the world who would understand what it was like to start a student strike. But that wasn't true. As a student at Miami, Schembechler had tried to organize a strike himself. He was a dishwasher in Hamilton Hall, a women's dormitory. One day he got so fed up with cleaning so many dirty dishes that he sharply told his friends they were all going on strike. Alas, his powers of persuasion were not quite honed yet; his friends thought he was insane. He went back to work.

So Bo Schembechler had some experience with student strikes. But it was hard to see how it could help him here.

Schembechler believed that his program was a model of outstanding race relations. But then, so did his old college suitemate John Pont, and black protests were destroying Pont's program at Indiana. Schembechler had tried to defuse any possible problems with humor; in 1969 he told his players that he would be fair to players of all races, except the "goddamn Italians"—at which point he looked over at lineman Dick Caldarazzo, and the room cracked up. That same year, one of his black players, Jim Betts, convinced Bo to relax his no-facial-hair policy for the blacks because it was part of their "heritage." Schembechler complied, to the amusement of the rest of his players, both black and white, who believed Betts was full of shit. Betts was one of the only players with the audacity to challenge Schembechler like that, and maybe the only one with the charisma to pull it off.

Now the blacks had a chance to really take it to Schembechler—with one word from the players, BAM leaders would have added him to their list of targets. Bump Elliott, Schembechler's predecessor, had recruited the first sizable group of black players in school history—seven recruits in the class of 1972. The cause resonated with the players, who joined BAM. But the players made it clear that their roles would be among the masses, not the leaders. They were acting as students, not football players.

Schembechler never expressed a strong opinion on the strike. He simply told his players that he expected them to fulfill their scholarship obligations. He certainly never thought of getting involved—he was there to coach football, not mediate social issues. His primary concern was that the strike did not affect his team, which was in the middle of spring practice.

In that sense, Schembechler was lucky that it took black students almost two full years, instead of one, to strike. The delay might have saved his career.

The year before, black defensive lineman Cecil Pryor had put too much slap in the "Slap and Stomp" drill. Pryor decked his opponent. Schembechler stepped in the ring, grabbed Pryor, and told him if he wanted to fight, he might as well start with the coach. He immediately suspended Pryor. Pryor then called a meeting of the black players to discuss their options. If a BAM strike had broken out at that moment, Schembechler's Michigan tenure might have ended before he ever coached a game. At that time, most of his players resented his tactics and would not have defended him.

But by March of 1970, Schembechler had led the Wolverines to the Rose Bowl. Pryor had grown to love the coach; after the Rose Bowl, he somehow slipped past hospital security to see Schembechler in his room when only family members were allowed to visit. Schembechler had also hired a black assistant coach, Tirrel Burton, after having none on his staff in his first year. (Schembechler never mentioned race to Burton, but Burton assumed he was hired partly to help recruit black players.) By 1970, the black players still felt that Schembechler could be a brutal son of a bitch, but they knew he was not a racist son of a bitch.

"He treats us all the same," Betts told BAM organizers. "Like dogs."

The strike was settled April 1, with the administration capitulating to almost every major BAM demand. Fleming promised that black enrollment would increase to 10 percent by the fall of 1973. He also promised to increase student aid to blacks and to recruit more black faculty members. The vice president of the United States, Spiro Agnew, immediately ripped into the school's "surrender," calling it "a callous retreat from reality."

Though Schembechler's 1970 team avoided race-inspired implosion, graduate assistant coach Garvie Craw would notice another, more subtle division of the roster. Craw had been a fullback on the

1969 team. That had been a fun-loving, alcohol-drinking group. In 1970, Craw noticed that a significant number of players had started to smoke marijuana—and on weekends, the drinkers and pot-smokers went separate ways.

Schembechler wasn't worried about that, or his heart attack, or even the BAM strike. He wanted another Big Ten championship. Any notion (or hope) that he would go soft after the heart attack quickly faded as he returned to his old grumbling self. There were rumors that he would hold "three-a-days": one practice in the morning, one in the early afternoon, one in the early evening.

As part of his new commitment to fitness, Schembechler started jogging; his doctors asked him to ease into the workouts, but pretty soon he was running against a stopwatch, three miles in twenty-seven minutes, trying to set new post–heart attack personal bests. It was not enough for him to exercise—he needed to compete. His doctor made him get rid of the watch. Schembechler found the distance running so invigorating, he decided his players should do it, too. The Wolverines ran constantly that offseason. In the wake of the Big Ten championship, Schembechler now had more credibility with his players and was less likely to face resistance. But he still pushed too hard sometimes.

After the team's spring game, Schembechler told reporters, "Billy Taylor hasn't shown us anything since the Ohio State game." Taylor, the starting tailback, was furious—he had been suffering from tonsillitis and thought the coach was singling him out. He briefly left the program. He missed his high school coach, Tom "Red" Phillips, who was more supportive and less critical than Schembechler. In fact, Taylor strongly considered reuniting with Phillips, who had taken an assistant coaching job at a college near Taylor's boyhood home. He even visited Phillips at his new school to discuss the possibility. The school was Kent State.

Many people at Ohio State would forget, even a month later, what started it all. It was a list of black demands. Afro-Am, a black student organization at Ohio State, wanted increased black enrollment; a black cultural center on campus; a spot in the School of Journalism building for their publication, *Our Choking Times*; and assorted other requests for better representation and access to university resources. They decided to organize a campuswide strike. There were serious doubts about pulling this off—even those in the movement joked about the "fair-weather radicals" who could not be counted on to join a protest.

Other causes were adopted—like female students asking for daycare for their children—which made sense. The more causes, the more people would rally behind them, and Afro-Am leaders needed all the help they could get. In recent months, student activism had bubbled up in a few places on the Ohio State campus, like water that was not quite hot enough to boil. There had been a strike at the College of Social Work and another at the School of Journalism. The local chapter of Vietnam Veterans Against the War was well organized.

Still, a campuswide strike? In the hundred-year history of the university, it had never happened. The Afro-Am leaders set April 29 as the strike date. They would march on the Oval at the center of campus and hope that a few hundred people would show up.

The crowd on the Oval was estimated at two thousand. Black students (and their white supporters) peacefully picketed campus buildings, starting at 11 a.m. A group of 350 protesters marched through the university to rally support for the strike. It was a significant number, certainly, but on a campus of 50,000, it was hardly a groundswell. For years, the Ohio State campus had been called "the Big Farm"; the nickname came from its agricultural education, one of the first disciplines offered by the school, but it came to represent all the rural kids who formed the heart of the university.

Many students were among the first in their family to attend college, and they weren't going to blow their chance with a protest. They were not natural activists. They weren't going to get involved unless they had a reason.

The Ohio State administration gave them one.

The strike leaders had complained that the administration was detached and unwilling to listen to their complaints. Two and a half hours after the picketing began, school president Novice Fawcett left for a trip to Syracuse, New York. The administration called in twelve hundred National Guardsmen to stifle the protest, but the Guardsmen only caused it to escalate. When students blocked the corner of Neil and 11th avenues, university vice president James A. Robinson called the Ohio Highway Patrol and asked them to take care of it. Soon students were throwing rocks at the patrolmen and the crowd swelled to three thousand.

Some students predictably saw the strike as an excuse to skip class and party. Fraternity brothers with no interest in politics blasted stereos on their front lawns along 15th Avenue. But when patrolmen sprayed tear gas up and down the streets, the partyers decided the protests had some merit. Forty-nine people were arrested. Fifty were injured, including six by gunshot. The police blamed the gunshots on snipers atop buildings. Protesters blamed the police. The strike was one day old.

The next day, it just got worse—more than four hundred arrests (many for violations of curfew, which had been set at 8 p.m) and at least 131 injuries were reported in the Ohio State *Lantern*, the student newspaper. Several times, the National Guard and highway patrolmen tried to move the protesters into a small section of the Oval, and when the crowd was deemed unruly, tear gas was fired.

That night, President Nixon announced on national television that American troops had attacked a Communist base complex in Cambodia.

"This is not an invasion of Cambodia," the commander in chief assured the nation, but it sure seemed that way. It spurred protests across the country and inflamed the rioting at Ohio State. The Afro-Am strike had morphed into an antiwar protest.

With rioters on one side and young, inexperienced National Guardsmen on the other, it was natural to worry about what could happen, and on May 4, the answer came outside Cleveland, 140 miles to the northeast. At a rally on the campus of Kent State University, National Guardsmen fired sixty-seven shots into a crowd of protesters, killing four students.

Two days later, Ohio State officials announced that their school would be closed until further notice. After what happened at Kent State, the administration had no choice. Three hundred protesters roared their approval at the news; one ran to Ohio Stadium and rang the victory bell. But victory was not really theirs—disruption charges had been filed against several strike organizers, and several took refuge in a farm in northern Ohio, where the cops wouldn't find them.

On May 19, the school reopened—but the protests continued. That day, a familiar figure was spotted forty feet behind the speakers' podium. There, in a burgundy sport coat and narrow black-and-red-striped tie, was Woody Hayes.

Hayes told *Lantern* reporter Jay Smith that he was "here as an interested observer—as a citizen." He gave terse non-answers to a few more questions, stayed for a half hour, and left.

Smith printed the interview in its entirety in the next day's *Lantern*. (Q. *"Were you here to see if any of your players became involved in the strike?" Silence again. "Well, Mr. Hayes, at least have the decency to say no comment." A. "No comment."*) The seemingly innocuous interview sure got somebody mad; Ohio State financial aid director Rodney Harrison told Smith that several people asked him to take away Smith's Evans Scholarship as punishment.

Even Hayes's brief comments weren't totally accurate. He was not there merely as an interested observer. Woody Hayes was *never* just an interested observer. Technically, his job was to coach Ohio State's football team, but in his mind, he was the head coach for the school, not just the team. He could not stand to see his university torn apart. Two days after his first appearance on the Oval, Hayes decided to address the crowd.

By this point, the protest had become mostly about the war in Southeast Asia, and there was no doubt about where Hayes stood. The protesters wanted the Ohio State administration to publicly state opposition to the war. Hayes believed in the "domino theory": that a Communist regime in one country would lead to a spread of communism in the region, and so he supported the war.

The protestors also wanted the school to stop awarding credit for ROTC classes. Hayes's position on ROTC was clear, too: one of his players at Miami, Carmen Cozza, once complained to the registrar that he had been mistakenly enrolled in ROTC classes, only to discover that it was no mistake. Hayes had signed him up. (By the late 1960s, Cozza was the head football coach at Yale, ordering his players to keep their hair short, and fighting off attempts to put black armbands on his team's jerseys to honor the war dead.)

What would Hayes say now, with the school engulfed by chaos? Ringed by some of his players, he asked for peace—not peace in Vietnam and Cambodia, but on campus. He wanted a democratic solution. Go through the system, he said, not around it.

But it was the *way* he asked for it that struck some observers. He told the students they could "win together" and added, "Sometimes you can't get a touchdown—you go for a field goal."

Football talk? Hundreds injured, hundreds more arrested, four dead at Kent State and the Ohio State campus shut down for two weeks, and the Old Man was talking about *football*?

Students derisively chanted, "First and ten—do it again!" as though the mighty Buckeyes were moving in for a touchdown. Football talk! To the true believers on the Oval, the comments were callous at worst and simplistic at best, but to those who knew Hayes—who had heard him compare Ohio State's offense to Sherman's march through the South and say Lord Howard invented the safety blitz—they were no surprise. Hayes was at ease talking to governors, senators, or the president of the United States, but he once got so rattled in the presence of Vince Lombardi that when he tried to introduce his top three quarterbacks, he mangled two of their names. If it seemed like Hayes was minimizing the campus turmoil by comparing it to football . . . well, it could not possibly have seemed that way to him. He revered the game too much.

In the wake of the riots, Ohio State would establish a minority affairs office, a Department of Black Studies, and a Black Cultural

Center. The protestors accomplished their initial goal: to earn a place in the school's power structure. But the school's administration never bought into the notion that the protests had been started in good faith. At least one organizer was banned from Ohio State for a year for his role. Administrators also pointed out that many of the protesters were not students at all—they were radicals from other places who arrived on campus after the riots began.

In an attempt to clear racial tension, Ohio State professor Art Adams, one of Hayes's friends, invited the most important campus leaders (naturally, that included Woody) to a dinner to discuss how each would deal with race relations. And when one black activist recited a list of white sins—and started telling everybody what had to change—the Old Man cut him off: "I was putting black kids through college before you were born!"

On July 23, 1970, a Michigan state trooper stopped a Volkswagen van in northern Michigan. Passengers had been tossing beer cans out the window. The cop checked the passengers' identification and ordered them to pick up their trash, then sent them on their way.

One of the passengers had identified himself as George Edward Taft III of Chicago.

After letting the van go, the cop discovered that George Edward Taft III was actually Lawrence "Pun" Plamondon, who had returned to Michigan and remained a fugitive on the FBI's Most Wanted List.

The trooper chased down the Volkswagen. When the cop stopped the van again, Plamondon sat with a .38 caliber Derringer handgun in his hands, wondering, *Should I shoot the pigs?* This is why his friends wanted him to stay out of the country: if the police found him, what would keep them from shooting him on sight? He was a hippie with no real family, an accused felon who had skipped town when he was indicted. Who would defend him?

Plamondon gripped the Derringer and thought about firing before the cops did. He turned himself in instead. (He later attributed the tossing of beer cans to "a lack of revolutionary discipline.")

Pun Plamondon was off to jail—finally—to find out what kind of evidence the government said it had.

Many of the biggest upsets in sports only seem like big upsets at the time. They follow a certain formula: The favorite has been winning for so long, nobody considers the possibility of a loss. Meanwhile, the underdog is far better than it is perceived to be. In 1964, nobody could imagine Cassius Clay beating Sonny Liston. Years later, when Clay had become Muhammad Ali and one of the greatest champions ever, his victory over Liston in Miami made perfect sense.

The same could be said of the 1969 Ohio State–Michigan game. Ohio State was the best team in the country, but Michigan was among the best, and with the game in Ann Arbor and Rex Kern injured, the Wolverines should have been given a better chance than they were. The game was immediately stamped as the "upset of the century," but that was only true if you looked at what happened beforehand instead of what happened afterward. In 1970, the Wolverines showed just how good they really were.

They still felt unappreciated—ranked eighth in the country to start the 1970 season and picked for second in the Big Ten, behind Ohio State, by most sportswriters. Hadn't they beaten Ohio State by 12 points? Didn't people remember? Now the Wolverines were comfortable in Schembechler's system. They had faith in Schembechler and his staff—they knew that if they followed orders, the results would literally be something straight out of a textbook: the *Official University of Michigan Football Notebooks*, called *Offensive Football* and *Defensive Football*, which were published after the 1969 season through athletic director Don Canham's company.

Canham's company touted the books as the only official notebooks ever published by a major football program, but they were hardly revolutionary. Woody Hayes had self-published *Hot Line to Victory*, a similar football textbook, the year before. The book was intended for the general public—Hayes wanted to share strategy and tactics with anybody who would listen. The Michigan books were designed for high school coaches. They detailed most of Michigan's plays and explained techniques for every position. They sold for five dollars each—and Canham, ever the salesman, used the notebooks to advertise another item: 16-millimeter instructional films of Michigan's best plays. The films were $24.95 each, $89.95 for a package of four.

But the notebooks and films, as comprehensive as they were, could not turn any staff into the Michigan staff. Schembechler and his assistants were exceptional teachers, particularly of line play, the essence of their team. The notebooks also did not come with infusions of Schembechler's charisma, an essential component in the Wolverines' success.

One day before the season started, Schembechler called offensive tackle Dan Dierdorf into his office.

"You're the best player on this football team, regardless of position," Schembechler said.

Dierdorf was pleased—Schembechler had never complimented him before—and he thanked the coach.

"No," Schembechler said, "you're not going to thank me in a minute. Here is the reality of being the best player on this team: I am going to treat you worse than everyone else. Everyone on this team is going to look at how I treat you, so if they sense favoritism, I've lost them. I don't care if you're an all-American or not. Whatever you do isn't going to be good enough for me."

Dierdorf was not happy. But Schembechler was right, in every way: Dierdorf was not just the best player on the team—he was the best offensive lineman in the country. Behind him, the Wolverines would rush for 276 yards per game in their first nine games (compared to just 90 for their opponents). Among those nine games, the only really close one was at home against Texas A&M; Michigan scored with three minutes remaining to win, 14–10. Two weeks later, the Wolverines avenged their 1969 loss to Michigan State. And when November arrived, they were peaking, just like the year before—they beat Illinois and Iowa by a combined score of 97–0. Heading into the season-ender at Ohio State, they were 9–0, ranked No. 4 in the country, and had won fourteen consecutive regular-season games.

Schembechler kept his word to Dierdorf: the coach was harder on his star than on anybody else. Before the season, Schembechler made the mammoth lineman get down to 245 pounds, which nearly required the removal of a couple of limbs. Then he asked Dierdorf to get down to 240; the lineman was so mad that he immediately went to Burger King and ate six Whoppers. But Dierdorf also became the embodiment of the Michigan program: big, powerful, refusing to step aside for anybody. Schembechler did not tolerate egomaniacs on his team, but the collective ego of the Wolverines was huge; in coming years, the rest of the conference would view it as arrogance.

Before one game in 1970, as Dierdorf stretched on the field, Schembechler hovered over him and told him to watch the opposing players warm up.

"Look at 'em down there!" the coach shouted. "*Look* at 'em! You know what?"

"What, Coach?"

"They're *afraid* of us! Right now they're warming up and they're *scared*! And do you know *why* they're scared?"

"Why, Coach?"

"Because we're *MICHIGAN*!"

And then he walked off.

In mid-October 1970, President Nixon made an appearance at the Statehouse in Columbus. Woody Hayes appeared on the podium with him. Afterward, the president decided to divert his motorcade to the campus Oval before going back to the airport, surprising even his Secret Service men. When the president arrived, he got out of his car and was swarmed by students. Some Ohio State students climbed trees just to get a look at him. Nixon listed his Vietnam record and told the students, "I'm proud of [the soldiers] and I'm proud of you."

A few students chanted antiwar slogans, but the majority booed them into silence.

The Oval was the same spot where protesters had shut down the campus just a few months earlier. The riots faded as quickly as they had erupted. Some campus activists felt that if there was a pressing social question that dominated the Ohio State campus that fall, it was this: were the 1970 Buckeyes the best team in school history?

Ohio State was ranked No. 1 in the country heading into the season. The thirteen sophomores who started for the 1968 season and dominated most of the 1969 season were now seniors. Senior quarterback Rex Kern was a favorite to win the Heisman Trophy, which would add to his aura of perfection. (Fathers all over Ohio would have loved for their daughter to marry Kern, but he married the princess of the Rose Bowl court from his sophomore year instead.)

The undefeated 1968 team was considered the best in school history. The 1969 team was even better, but it lost to Michigan. Logically the 1970 team, with most of the same players, should have been the best.

But it wasn't. Woody Hayes would not allow it.

Hayes reverted to his old T formation offense—he took the best array of offensive talent in the country and stuffed it into a meat grinder. The Buckeyes ran one running play after another, each more boring and predictable than the last.

What was Woody thinking? The answer could be found in a movie released in 1970. It instantly became one of Woody's favorites, and for the rest of his career, every assistant coach who wanted to avoid another *Easy Rider*–type disaster could choose this film for the Friday night before a game. Every Buckeye would see it at least a few times in his career. The movie was *Patton*, starring George C. Scott as General George Patton.

George Patton had written a memoir called *War As I Knew It*. But for those who hadn't read it and hadn't studied him, the movie provided insight into the famous general. The Buckeyes knew that Patton was one of Woody's biggest heroes, right up there with Emerson. Watching the film, Ohio State players and coaches got the feeling that Patton was not just the Old Man's hero. Eerily, it seemed like Patton *was* the Old Man: commanding any room he entered, always saying exactly what he wanted to say, never caring what anybody else thought of him.

"Goddammit, I don't want these men to love me," Patton says in the movie. "I want them to fight for me!"

When was Woody really mad and when was he faking it—ripping apart a pre-torn hat for effect? The Buckeyes never knew.

"It isn't important for them to know," Patton says, when told that his troops couldn't tell when he was acting and when he was not. "It's only important for me to know."

The film focuses on the most famous, most eventful era of Patton's career, World War II, and the morality of the war is scarcely discussed. It is about war itself, the strategy and courage of it—and a general who is inescapably drawn to it.

"I love it," Patton says. "God help me, I love it so. I love it more than my life."

Patton's passion for combat is shown through his intense desire to defeat an enemy he admired: German field marshal Erwin Rommel. To defeat Rommel's army, Patton must first climb into the bunker inside Rommel's head—and Rommel is shown to be every bit as obsessed with Patton as Patton is with him.

After hearing an underling recite Patton's résumé, Rommel responds, "You're not telling me anything about the *man*."

Patton, looking through binoculars across a battlefield, shouts, "Rommel . . . you magnificent bastard, *I read your book!*"

Hayes's only complaint about the film was that Scott's Patton believes in reincarnation. Hayes didn't think the real Patton felt that way. (He apparently thought Patton lived by the words of Woody Hayes's mother: "God made you and put you on earth, and the rest is up to you.") But otherwise, Hayes loved every minute.

Hayes would have loved *Patton* if it had been released any other year, but in 1970, he had even more in common with Scott's Patton than normal. He too was trying to defeat an enemy he admired. In June of 1970, he inscribed a copy of *Hot Line to Victory* to "a truly great coach and friend, Bo Schembechler," and sent it north. He then resumed his yearlong pursuit of Schembechler. The 1970 Ohio State

Buckeyes did not even fake a "one game at a time" mentality. They only had one goal that season: beat Michigan.

The Buckeyes had dominated everybody else in 1969, but Hayes wasn't worried about replicating that performance—he wanted to avenge the 24–12 loss in Ann Arbor. His message to Jim Otis after that game—*Jim, if you would have run the ball fifteen more times today, we would have won*—set the tone. In Woody parlance, the 1969 Buckeyes had too much LeMay and not enough Patton. In 1970, he would go back to his roots. In doing so, he would frustrate many of his stars, including his biggest.

The players had long joked that Kern was Hayes's second son, and in 1968 and 1969, all of Columbus seemed ready to claim him as well. But one reason Kern was so good was his freewheeling style. In the first half of his first game as a starter, he had waved off the punting team (and pissed off Woody) on fourth down and 10 near midfield, then scrambled for the first down. Now "King Rex" was handcuffed. He had his worst season. Fans at Ohio Stadium started to call for backup Ron Maciejowski to replace him, and Hayes occasionally complied. Hayes had mostly spared Kern from his temper, but now the coach was riding the quarterback for the first time. Maciejowski played more and more. Kern developed ulcers; Maalox was visible on his lips at practice.

The joy of routinely building a four-touchdown lead in the first quarter was gone. The Buckeyes just wanted to make it to the Michigan game with an unbeaten record—and they almost didn't do that.

Ohio State's final game before the Michigan showdown, at Purdue, took place on a rainy, snowy November day. Hayes, wary of weather-induced mistakes, became even more conservative. He told his players they would try to grab an early lead, then let their defense hold on. In the first quarter, Ohio State pounded its way to a 71-yard touchdown drive. It was precisely as Hayes planned. He told his troops they had their lead—now the defense would take care of the rest. Just as he said it, Purdue returned the ensuing kickoff 96 yards for a touchdown.

The teams slogged through the rest of the game, and in the fourth quarter, with the score tied at seven, Maciejowski replaced Kern again. Ohio State's undefeated season was in serious jeopardy. Punter Mike Sensibaugh fumbled a snap and Purdue got great field position. (Sensibaugh's only consolation was that he also played safety, so he got to stay on the field and face Purdue's offense instead of going to the sideline and facing Woody.) Ohio State finally won on a late field goal. The key play was a 52-yard pass from Maciejowski to Bruce Jankowski; Maciejowski had ignored Hayes's play call and told Jankowski to run a post pattern.

When Hayes asked Maciejowski why he had changed plays, the quarterback snapped, "Well, Coach, you sent in a play that hadn't worked all day." Hayes quickly changed the topic.

President Nixon called afterward to offer his congratulations and say he was sorry he would not be able to attend the Michigan game the next week. The narrow margin dropped Ohio State to No. 5 in the polls—they had already dropped from No. 1 to No. 2 to No. 3—but that didn't matter much to the Buckeyes. The only game they really wanted to play was upon them.

For the first time in history, Michigan and Ohio State were both undefeated heading into their season-ending clash. Coupled with the stunning 1969 result, the game became one of the most hyped ever. But there was something else, too: a mystery about these teams that added to the aura. Because the NCAA only allowed teams to appear on television a total of three times every two seasons, most people watching this game would have never seen either team play that season, let alone both. They were discovered through newspaper stories and scores: Ohio State 56, Texas A&M 13 . . . Ohio State 34, Duke 10 . . . Ohio State 29, Michigan State 0.

On Sunday mornings, one of Don Canham's staffers would splice a 55-second highlight package out of the Michigan game film, drive forty miles into Detroit, get a dozen duplicates made, and send the copies to television stations around the state. The highlights would usually air on Tuesdays, three days after the game. The Michigan

Alumni Association would take the game film and bring it to alumni gatherings in Detroit, Chicago, Grand Rapids, Flint, Saginaw, and Lansing. The film then would be shown, unedited, to the alumni, with whoever brought it giving a narration.

Interest was higher at Ohio State, but it was tough to cash in: a closed-circuit telecast of the 1969 Ohio State–Minnesota game was cut short when the red color tube in the projector went out, leaving a broadcast that was all greens and blues.

The 1970 version of the game would give everybody in the country a chance to see Ohio State and Michigan. This time, Michigan was the team that couldn't go to the Rose Bowl, having gone the year before. When he was asked about Michigan after the Purdue game, Hayes was coy.

"We haven't formulated our plans yet," he said, though he had been formulating them for a year.

The hype was so intense that Hayes put his players in a local hotel two nights before the game, instead of the customary one, to give them a chance to rest.

They were rested, all right—and revved up. The Buckeyes forced a fumble on the opening kickoff, recovered it, and immediately took a 3–0 lead. Michigan responded with a field goal. Because both defenses were so stout—and both offenses were so conservative—special teams play became even more important than normal, and Michigan appeared to take advantage. Paul Staroba unleashed a 73-yard punt, the equivalent of a long pass downfield—but the Wolverines were whistled for a personal foul on the play.

Schembechler was irate. He was told it was a facemask penalty while the punt was in the air, and who ever heard of a facemask penalty while a punt was in the air? Impossible! He was right: there was no facemask penalty. But Michigan offensive lineman Reggie McKenzie had jumped on a Buckeye's throat on the play, and not by accident, either—McKenzie was so fired up, he wanted to break somebody's neck. Considering that charges could have been filed, a 15-yard penalty wasn't so terrible, but it gave Ohio State an extra 35 yards in field position, and the Buckeyes scored a touchdown to take a 10–3 lead into halftime.

Michigan was in the same position Ohio State had been in the year before: trailing at halftime on the road. Hayes's return to his "robust" offense was paying off. Ohio State's defense was shutting down the vaunted Michigan running game—now Bo would have to pass while Woody could keep pounding away. For a while, the Wolverines pulled it off—they drove down the field and threw a touchdown pass that would have tied the game, except that Ohio State blocked the extra point. The Buckeyes led 10–9, and a one-point lead never seemed so big.

Michigan's offense simply could not move the ball in the second half. Ohio State added a field goal to make it 13–9. Then the Buckeyes got the kind of play that Michigan got the year before: Stan White intercepted a Don Moorhead pass and ran down to the Michigan nine-yard line. The crowd sensed victory. Leo Hayden ran in for the touchdown, and Ohio State led 20–9. The score would hold up: Ohio State 20, Michigan 9, and it really wasn't that close; Ohio State outgained Michigan 329–155 in the game, including 242–37 on the ground.

When time ran out, the crowd rushed the field. As Hayes tried to escape to the safety of his locker room, he was surprised to see a man stop right in front of him, and even more surprised to see that it was Schembechler. The Michigan coach wanted to make sure he shook the Old Man's hand. When the Buckeyes finally made it to the locker room, President Nixon had called in to congratulate them, but Hayes said, "The president will just have to wait this time."

Hayes had something to say to his team. He held up an *Official University of Michigan Football Notebook*.

Then Woody Hayes shouted, "I read your book, you son of a bitch!"

Though Schembechler was gracious on the field, he was not so polite to reporters afterward. He waited as long as he could to talk to the press, then answered questions in a voice that was barely above a whisper. When a writer asked him to speak up, he snapped back, "Can't you hear anything?" By the time he was finished and the locker room was open, the Wolverines were all gone. They would grant no interviews that day.

Thankfully for reporters, Hayes held court with the press for almost an hour. He had a well-earned reputation for being ornery with the media, but after big wins, he was a writer's dream. And there were plenty of writers at Ohio Stadium that day: more than six hundred people crammed into the press box, leading Hayes to call it "the most publicized and televised single game in college football history."

Hayes even let reporters into the locker room. He told them President Nixon "was greatly impressed with our ballclub. I've got to feel this was our greatest victory. This makes up for what happened last year. This justifies in the minds of our seniors that they are the greatest group of players we ever had here."

The celebration was one of the most raucous in school history—surpassing, perhaps, the party after the 1968 Michigan game. Among the merriment, there were several instances of looting and violence—it reminded some of the riots in the spring. Ohio State's win swallowed up the front page of the next day's *Columbus Dispatch*, which featured a rare front-page editorial that announced, "Although the pollsters may not agree, we declare the Buckeyes are No. 1." Another front-page story, headlined "FOOTBALL WIDOWS KEEP ON THE MOVE," noted, "While menfolk huddled around the television sets devouring the action, women did the shopping, had their hair set, and got the car washed and filled up."

And of course, there was ample coverage of the game itself, including the play that sprung Leo Hayden for a game-high 118 rushing yards.

"It's a funny thing," Hayes said. "The Japs got their plan for attacking Pearl Harbor from our own Fleet Problem No. 14 of 1934. The Germans got the tank from the British. Guess where we got that play? It's in my book [*Hot Line to Victory*] and I got it originally from the fellow at Oklahoma [Chuck Fairbanks]. But Michigan refined it.

I saw it in their highlight films from last year—we bought a copy for $80—and so we borrowed it back. I'm totally grateful.

"I truly relish turning an opponent's play against him."

This was not the first or last time Woody Hayes would call a victory his "greatest." He made similar comments after other wins. But the 1970 win was especially important. With a loss, Hayes would have been 0–2 against Schembechler, with most of his starters graduating and the 1971 game in Ann Arbor. The win also put the Buckeyes in great position for their second national title in four seasons.

Ohio State rose to No. 2 in the polls with the victory, behind defending national champion Texas. The National Football Foundation actually named Ohio State and Texas co–national champions before the bowl games, which was not an unusual gesture. In 1969, after Michigan's stunning victory over Ohio State, the Texas-Arkansas game in December suddenly had national title implications. President Nixon presented the winning Texas team with a plaque honoring the Longhorns as national champions—even though Texas still had to play Notre Dame in the Cotton Bowl three weeks later. Many people still regarded the bowls as festivals instead of championship games.

Now Texas was headed for a Cotton Bowl rematch with Notre Dame. Ohio State would face the lightly regarded Stanford University Indians in the Rose Bowl. Woody Hayes's senior class had won a remarkable twenty-seven of twenty-eight games in three years of eligibility, and had just avenged that lone defeat in impressive fashion.

Hayes wanted to make sure they didn't get soft after the big win over Michigan, so in one of the first practices for the Rose Bowl, while the Buckeyes were still in Columbus, he ordered his quarterbacks to practice their blocking. It was classic Hayes—he always expected his quarterbacks to be *football players*, damn it, not just passers, and he wasn't going to get soft just because his team was undefeated.

Nonetheless, it was a bizarre request on several levels. Hayes's quarterback, Kern, was prone to injury and only had one game left—asking him to hit a blocking machine a few weeks before the Rose Bowl was awfully risky. Sure enough, Kern injured his right shoulder—his throwing shoulder—during the drills. Asking quarterbacks to block also established a tone of heavy work for the Rose Bowl preparations. The Buckeyes, who had been frustrated by Hayes all season, were wary of a repeat of their first Rose Bowl trip after the 1968 season, when Hayes had them tape up on the plane so they could begin practice when they landed, then put them through brutal training camp–like practices.

But mostly, asking the quarterbacks to practice blocking was astounding because they wouldn't really need to block in the Rose Bowl.

And why wouldn't they need to block?

Because Woody Hayes, after winning twenty-seven of his last twenty-eight games with the I formation, decided to institute a wishbone offense.

Hayes surely liked the wishbone because it was a running scheme. The Old Man could get tight in big spots. On the verge of another unbeaten season, he wanted to do something, but he didn't want to do too much, and somehow he came up with the wishbone. He never fully explained it to his team, but that was the beauty of being the head coach: he didn't have to.

The wishbone was a risky offense, heavily reliant on timing and coordination, which meant that players needed a lot of practice time to master it. Since almost all of Ohio State's starters were seniors, they would basically spend one month learning the offense, use it against Stanford, and never play together again.

To ease any concerns about taping up on the plane again, Hayes promised his players a day off when they arrived in Southern California—they would pose for some official pictures, do a light walk-through, and enjoy the rest of the day. But on the flight to Los Angeles, Hayes ordered his players to get taped. He said it was raining in Southern California and he was just being extra cautious.

But when they got to the practice field, it wasn't raining. Hayes put them through a rigorous practice that ended with a series of "gassers"—sprints that left the Buckeyes exhausted and furious. That night, the seniors had a big blowout meeting with their coach in a meeting room at Huntington Sheraton. Captain Jim Stillwagon presented a list of grievances to Hayes, who was in no mood to hear them. From then on, many Buckeyes simply wanted the season to end. They became more disenchanted with every practice.

Meanwhile, Stanford was fired up for its shot at mighty Ohio State. Indians head coach John Ralston was reading *Hot Line to Victory* in his hotel room every night.

Stanford, which had lost to Purdue, Air Force, and California, jumped to a 10–0 lead in the game. Ohio State came back to tie it at 10. At halftime, the always creative Stanford Band assembled in the formation of an outhouse and played "Yellow River." It was an appropriate salute to Ohio State's second-half performance. Stanford's Heisman-winning quarterback, Jim Plunkett, threw for 265 yards; Kern, with the injured shoulder, completed only four passes for 40 yards.

Ohio State could have won the national championship—Notre Dame beat No. 1 Texas in the Cotton Bowl, opening the door. Instead, Ohio State's season ended with a 27–17 loss. But as many Buckeyes would later say, at least it ended.

4

Napoleon; or, The Man of the World

In early 1971, several Ohio State seniors played a series of basketball games for charity—and for themselves. They had a brief window of time to capitalize on their fame—when they were no longer subject to NCAA rules (because their college careers were over) yet were still in shape, living in the same city, and famous enough to draw a crowd when they played another sport. They traveled around Ohio playing low-stress hoops at high schools, which would charge fans for a chance to see Woody Hayes's Buckeyes up close. They got fifty bucks a man; all other revenue went to the host school.

And since Michigan's football program copied pretty much everything Ohio State did, the Wolverines soon had their own little traveling team. It was probably inevitable, then, that somebody would try to get Ohio State and Michigan to play each other. And so they did, on a Friday night in May 1971, at Napoleon High School in Napoleon, Ohio.

With the Ohio State–Michigan rivalry at an all-time high, the players negotiated a 50 percent pay raise: $75 per player. Before the game, as the Buckeyes and Wolverines sat in a locker room, a school administrator walked in and said that the school had not raised as much money as they had hoped, and would the players mind taking $50 each instead? The players said they would discuss it.

It did not require much discussing. As soon as the door was shut, the Wolverines and Buckeyes agreed: they had come for 75 bucks, and that's what they would take. If there was ever going to be any tension between the Ohio State and Michigan players (and there was never any indication of that), it ended right there.

The game itself was thrilling—or as thrilling as a pickup basketball game among ex–football players can be: with time running down, Michigan's Pete Newell banked in a shot to tie the game, and then Ohio State won in overtime. This was fitting. For the next several years, Ohio State and Michigan would play breathtakingly close football games.

But the players would remember the experience more than the basketball game. They had a rare chance to learn about their biggest rival—and naturally, the conversation centered on the two head coaches.

Two meetings into the Bo Schembechler–Woody Hayes rivalry, the coaches were painted as two of the same: Woody and Little Woody, plotting against each other all year long. But the players didn't know much about the opposing coach beyond caricature. The Buckeyes knew that Schembechler was a Woody disciple, but since they couldn't imagine anybody on the planet being just like the Old Man, they weren't sure what that meant.

The Wolverines suspected that Hayes was crazy, but whenever they said so, one of the Michigan coaches would sharply insist that Hayes knew exactly what he was doing. Schembechler wasn't the only Woody pupil on the Michigan staff; assistant coach Gary Moeller had been a Buckeyes captain, and defensive coordinator Jim Young had played two years at Ohio State before transferring to Bowling Green. The Michigan players had grown fond of Schembechler, and since their coaches spoke so highly of Hayes, they naturally assumed that the Buckeyes liked Hayes as much as the Wolverines liked Schembechler. They did not.

It quickly became clear in that locker room in Napoleon, Ohio, that while the Michigan players felt a kinship with Schembechler, the Buckeyes never got as close to Hayes. When the Buckeyes said Hayes was like a second father, they were talking about his influence on their lives, not his relationship with them.

The Ohio State players were in awe of their coach—and it is difficult to get close to somebody when your dominant feeling is awe. This was partly a function of age: Hayes had won his first national title seventeen years earlier and acted like a professor. Schembechler was a young coach who had lived, just a few years earlier, like a student. At Miami in the late 1960s, he had virtually no furniture in his apartment. His fridge was usually empty except for maybe some beer or Coke and a piece of fruit. When he moved to Ann Arbor, his wife, Millie, and fatherhood gave him a more balanced life, but he was still a football junkie at heart. Sometimes he didn't even remember to pick up his paycheck—Don Canham's secretary had to call Millie at home and tell her to come get it.

Both coaches instilled fear in their players, but with Schembechler it was largely a fear of what he would say, while with Hayes it was more a fear of what he would do. "I'd kick you in the ass," Schembechler would tell his linemen, "but I'm afraid I'd lose my foot." Schembechler would scream at any son of a bitch who missed a block, but Hayes's temper was physical, and not just in practice; in an incident that had become part of Woody lore, Hayes had slammed a chair into the ground in the 1959 game against That School Up North.

In the late 1960s, Ohio State fullback Jim Otis worried that Hayes would walk up to him on the practice field and kick him in the testicles. Otis had known and admired Hayes since he was a little boy, and in all that time he had never seen Hayes kick anybody in the balls. Yet Otis couldn't shake the image. And if Woody had known about Otis's fear, he probably would have been pleased—the threat of getting kicked in the testicles could only make a fullback run harder.

The Michigan players loved being around Bo largely because Bo loved being around them. The camaraderie of a locker room was a major reason Schembechler got into coaching. When he was an Ohio State assistant, he was closer to many players than Hayes was. They took orders from Hayes but they turned to Schembechler for support.

Bo Schembechler was one of the guys. Woody Hayes was *never* one of the guys. He never wanted to be, especially around his players and coaches—he was there to lead. Hayes was often funny, but he was never *light*. He seemed to prefer when life was difficult—not only would he sleep in the office a couple nights per week in the fall, but he did so on a little couch in a spartan office that could have belonged to a graduate assistant.

He kept hundreds of books in the office, almost all of which were about international politics or military history. Besides the books, the office had only the most basic and necessary items: a desk, a chair, a vertical locker, and that couch. It was the office of a coach who had yet to prove himself, which was precisely how Hayes wanted it. When the athletic department decided to lay carpet in the coaches' offices in the early 1970s, Hayes objected. Ohio State officials couldn't lay carpet in the rest of the building and leave its most famous tenant with bare floors, so they waited until Hayes went home one night. They installed the carpet before he returned the next morning.

Football fans across the country pictured Hayes and Schembechler obsessing about each other, watching film of each other's teams throughout the year. The picture was accurate. But it was also incomplete.

Nobody ever had to talk Bo Schembechler or Woody Hayes into watching film. They loved it. And the sheer volume of film-watching did not fully explain its significance. Film-watching is a skill. Some coaches can pick up more information in an hour than lesser coaches get in a day.

Schembechler was an exceptional film-watcher. He had an uncanny ability to see what every player did on every play. He rarely took notes. He just watched. He would mumble to himself, as if agreeing with his own conclusions—"um-hum, um-hum, um-hum"—then hop up to tell his assistants what he had just learned. He and a few of his assistants enjoyed smoking cigars, and sometimes they would light up as they studied film—with the windows closed and the smoke clouds filling the air, it was the ultimate men's club.

Once in a while assistant coach Gary Moeller would smoke a pipe, and Schembechler would get on his case: "You're getting *placid.*" But occasionally Schembechler would smoke a pipe. And Moeller would tell him he was getting placid, too.

Bo had extraordinary screaming matches with some of his assistant coaches, especially offensive line coach Jerry Hanlon. But everybody knew that Schembechler and Hanlon were buddies, that Schembechler affectionately referred to Hanlon as "Rocco," and that when they coached at Miami, they had practically lived together, with Schembechler picking Hanlon up in the morning, going to breakfast with him, working alongside him all day, and then dropping him off at night.

And for all his toughness, Schembechler had an air of fun about him. He was always humming something—Frank Sinatra's "Strangers in the Night" was a favorite, but it could have been anything. When his wife, Millie (or any other woman he knew well), walked in a room, he would burst into song: *Here she comes . . . Miss America . . .* When he exercised, he would take off his shirt, turn to somebody else in the gym, and ask, "What do you think of the world's most perfectly developed man?" As always, the inflection on every syllable was perfect.

Woody Hayes never wanted fun to get in the way of work. He kept his film room extremely cold year-round. He wanted his coaches *alert*—the assistants would put on their coats just to watch film. Woody also had somebody tape the curtains shut so that absolutely no light filtered in. The coaches could not even see each other clearly. And if a reel of film had the audacity to show a Buckeye mistake, even in practice, the coaches would sometimes hear (not see) a projector hitting a wall. But the assistants knew that as hard as Hayes pushed them, he pushed himself harder: sometimes, in the early-morning hours, he fell asleep at the projector, only to wake up at the *snap-snap-snap* of the finished reel.

Most fans would have thought it was the other way around—that the Ohio State players knew Hayes better than the Wolverines knew Schembechler. After all, the public knew far more about Hayes. When a reporter asked about, say, Ohio State's fullback, Hayes might respond with a monologue about academics or D-Day or staying away from drugs. He would quote Emerson at length. He was the one who voiced his views on a campus strike—and the one who walked up to random longhairs to urge them to support their school. Hayes was easily found: a huge billboard announced that his favorite restaurant was the Jai Lai, and he often ate lunch at the Big Bear supermarket, about as public a lunch spot as one could find in Columbus.

Schembechler rarely voiced a public opinion on anything other than the off-tackle play. It wasn't just that he disliked talking to reporters. He didn't understand why reporters were so interested in talking to *him*. His own players didn't know where he stood on the Black Action Movement or Vietnam protests.

Schembechler often talked to his players about the importance of schoolwork, but some of them felt he had a narrow definition of academic achievement: they were supposed to graduate. He did not necessarily want them to take the most challenging classes. When he arrived in Ann Arbor, Schembechler was taken aback to see Pete Newell majoring in philosophy and another player, Frank Titas, majoring in English. He was worried their class load would interfere with football.

Schembechler's free time was spent at home with Millie and the kids. Every Christmas, Millie would make hot fudge and Bo would deliver it around town—to people like Don Canham and Michigan Marching Band director William Revelli. His last stop would be former Michigan player and coach Bennie Oosterbaan; when Schembechler got there, the two coaches would sit down and talk football.

After every Michigan game, there was a gathering at the Schembechler house. Kids would play football in the yard. Millie, having already served lunch at the pregame tailgate, would be preparing another round of food. And Bo would park at his house at 870 Arlington Boulevard on the east side of Ann Arbor, walk through the breezeway, go through the kitchen, stop at the living room to say hello to everybody, and announce that he was going to the basement to watch the game film. His friends would join him.

When Woody Hayes watched film at home, he set the projector up in his living room; Anne and any guests would be confined to the kitchen. Film-watching was serious business, and besides, Hayes wasn't big on recreation. It was inconceivable, for example, that he might take a few hours to go play golf with his friends. When he walked near the Ohio State golf course, his assistant coaches would duck behind trees rather than be seen playing golf. They learned that when they were on vacation, they needed to get out of town—if they stayed in Columbus, Hayes was liable to call them into the office to watch film all day, even if it was the middle of May.

Even if a coach refused to answer the phone, Hayes could track him down. His ability to know everything about everybody was scary. Thanks to his "brain coach," he always knew which players were slacking off, and he would not only confront the offending player— he would grab the textbook and lecture the kid. And, since he spent much of his free time roaming the academic campus, players were always in danger of running into their coach.

The news did not travel in both directions, though: everybody in Columbus knew who lived in the white house at 1711 Cardiff Road, but only a few were invited to socialize there.

Woody famously kept a listed home phone number for his whole life, but since he was barely ever home, Anne was usually the one to deal with the angry fans. She would not hang up on the callers. That would only encourage them. Instead, she would either convert them into Woody fans or soften them up with a good-natured barb; no matter who called, Anne was assuredly the wittiest person on the line. When a caller said he was mad at her husband, Anne is said to have replied, "If you find him, tell him I'm mad at him, too."

Anne was den mother to the Buckeyes; she cooked meals and knew their girlfriends and wives. She was also an exceptional public speaker (even better, some thought, than her husband), and when Woody had to miss a speaking engagement, she often filled in. Anne—more socially aware and more balanced in her views—told Hayes's friend Harold Schechter that she never understood why her husband got involved in politics.

Hayes spent much of his free time at hospitals, trying to cheer up strangers. Or he would be at the Faculty Club discussing politics and history with other faculty members. Professors expecting an angry, foul-mouthed coach were surprised—Hayes did not bring his on-field demeanor with him, and never cursed around a woman. He was often joined at the Faculty Club by his close friend Paul Hornung, the sports editor and Ohio State beat writer for the *Columbus Dispatch*. (Hornung was not related to the famous Green Bay Packer of the same name.) Hayes sparred with most sportswriters, but Hornung was more like a younger brother than a journalist—he spent much of his time praising Hayes, in person and in print. He rarely wrote a critical word about Hayes.

On the rare occasions when somebody didn't recognize him, Hayes would talk at length without mentioning football. If he was asked what he did for a living, he would say, "I'm a football coach up at the university."

Hayes's only indulgence was food, especially sweets. He devoured desserts like a little kid, which made sense: when Woody was a child in Newcomerstown, his mother baked pies and sold them out of a basket so his father, Wayne, could remain in college. Woody never forgot the taste or the lesson: education came above everything else. Like his father, Woody read newspapers and magazines ravenously. During football season, when his time was limited, he would mark up the stories he wanted to read and hand the newspaper to a secretary, who would cut them out and place them in a binder for him to read when he had a chance.

Before the 1970 season, Hayes read that Americans could reduce their reliance on foreign oil by driving less. Naturally, he decided to tackle the problem; naturally, he decided to reevaluate his own habits first; and just as naturally, Woody Hayes could not just reduce his driving a *little*. He decided to walk to work every day.

The trek was nearly three miles. The distance did not discourage Hayes, even in cold weather, but the walk took up a lot of his time. One problem was that he kept stopping to talk to passersby; many knew him, many just wanted to chat, and the few who didn't want to talk—the hippies and rebels—were confronted by the Old Man, who wanted to know why they were so disenchanted with America or Ohio State.

When Woody finally arrived at his office, he would begin his fifteen-hour-plus workday. On nights when the coaches worked particularly late, assistant coach Rudy Hubbard would give him a lift home, ostensibly to save time. But then Hayes would suggest they stop for a pecan roll, or maybe a piece of pie, and then he would want to sit down with the snack and a cup of coffee and chat for a while, and that's when it would hit Hubbard: *He doesn't want to go home.* Woody clearly loved Anne, and nobody could imagine him cheating on her. But relaxing at home did not come easily to him. He needed to be out, sticking his fingers into the world.

Woody's vacations usually consisted of a few days alone at his cabin in the hills of Noble County, Ohio, where he grew up. He would hike for hours—a restorative experience, certainly, but hardly a relaxing one. His cabin was barely large enough to hold him and the reading material he would bring with him—books and those binders filled with news stories—but even so, it was more than he needed.

On many nights, Hayes didn't even sleep inside the cabin. He would lay out a bed of straw on the back of his Ranchero pickup truck and sleep under the stars.

"The stars awaken a certain reverence," Emerson wrote, "because though always present, they are inaccessible."

Woody Hayes did not visit Vietnam after the 1970 season, but the Big Ten was well represented. Michigan running backs Glenn Doughty and Billy Taylor went on a State Department–sponsored trip to Southeast Asia between semesters of their junior year. On the players' first night in Vietnam, Doughty heard sirens outside their Saigon hotel; he peered out his window to check out the commotion. He later found out that a bomb had been found—if it had not been disabled, both the players and their hotel might not have survived the night.

The trip only got more frightening from there. Doughty and Taylor spent three weeks in Vietnam, much of it in military hospitals, where the carnage of war was right in front of them. Doughty talked to one soldier on his way into surgery for his leg, only to see him again later with the leg amputated. One soldier wanted to talk football with Taylor, but Taylor couldn't get his mind off the soldier's head (which had been hit by shrapnel and was severely swollen because of an infection) or abdomen, which was split by a long gash. Taylor became nauseous.

He and Doughty should have felt better when they arrived in the central Vietnamese town of Pleiku, a major U.S. military base, and ran into several soldiers who had attended Pershing High School in Detroit with Doughty. But the Pershing guys only told them what others had suggested: they didn't understand why they were there, and they didn't see how the United States could win. By the time Doughty and Taylor returned to Ann Arbor, they were convinced the war was a mistake.

As Glenn Doughty and Billy Taylor watched the war unfold in Vietnam, former U.S. Army specialist E-4 Mike Lantry was getting ready for his first classes at the University of Michigan.

Lantry walked into his new dorm, West Quad, and went up to the third floor. As he walked down the hallway toward his room, he heard loud music. The more he walked, the louder the music got. Lantry realized that the music was coming from *his* room.

He arrived and knocked on the door. The music stopped.

Lantry walked in and saw two young men with a guitar, a set of drums, and an amplifier. One of the men wore leather pants and had hair that draped all the way down to the middle of his back. His face was bright red, like he'd been in the sun all day, even though it was the middle of winter.

"I'm your new roommate," Lantry said.

He put his bags down.

"I'll be right back."

Lantry went straight to the university's housing office and requested a transfer to another room. He was just out of the Army, he explained to the housing office, and this was his one chance at a college education, and there was no way he would make it through the semester living with those guys, whoever they were. He moved to another room.

Lantry had decided to try out for the track team, but in his first month on campus, some of the football players convinced him to try their sport, too. Lantry decided he would be a placekicker. He joined the football team for winter conditioning drills.

Bo Schembechler was on a recruiting trip at the time, and when Schembechler returned to Ann Arbor, he walked into Crisler Arena to watch his Wolverines run around the concourse. (Don Canham was using his new revenue streams to build a new football practice facility, but the building wasn't finished yet.) Schembechler scanned the crowd of a hundred or so players and realized there was one he had never seen before. He pulled Lantry out of the pack and sat him down.

"Don't you think if you want to go out for the University of Michigan football team, you ought to talk to the head coach first?" Schembechler asked.

Lantry and Schembechler agreed to meet the next day. And when they did, Schembechler gave his blessing: Mike Lantry would be a walk-on placekicker for the Wolverines.

Don Canham was selling Michigan to people all over the country, but with the turmoil on campus, he was reluctant to sell the school in his own home. His daughter Clare had witnessed the Black Action Movement protests firsthand when she was a junior at St. Thomas High School in Ann Arbor. Don and his wife, Marilyn, who had attended Michigan in the late 1930s, questioned whether the 1971 version of the University of Michigan was right for their daughter. They suggested to Clare that she attend a small, private school instead— Middlebury, maybe, or St. Mary's College in South Bend, Indiana.

Eventually, the Canhams agreed that Clare could attend Michigan but would live at home for her freshman year. Don would drive Clare to class in the morning, and somebody would pick her up at the Michigan League in the late afternoon and bring her home.

In August 1971, as Clare prepared for her first classes at Michigan, Don got a glimpse of what his job might be like if he could promote sports with no strings, politics, or university attached.

Canham brought the NFL's Detroit Lions and Baltimore Colts into Michigan Stadium for an exhibition game. A year earlier, these same two teams had drawn only 16,000 fans to their exhibition game. Canham thought he could do better. He guaranteed Lions general manager Russ Thomas that he could get 35,000 fans, a bold prediction that Canham wasn't sure he could fulfill.

As part of the deal, Canham insisted on splitting all revenue with the Lions; the standard contract was 15 percent for the host school, but Canham wasn't big on standard contracts. In addition, he agreed to pay the Colts $75,000.

Canham's gamble paid off: the game drew 92,000 spectators. Canham had luck on his side: between the signing of the contract and the game, the Colts won the Super Bowl. But a lot of it was Canham, who sold the uniqueness of the event to anybody who would listen. ("The first NFL game in historic Michigan Stadium!")

Still, Canham wasn't satisfied with the huge crowd or the $300,000 profit for his athletic department. He knew that most of the fans at the game had probably never been to Michigan Stadium before, and he figured that if they enjoyed the day, they might want to come back. Since taking over as athletic director, Canham had sold the game-day experience, regardless of how Michigan fared. The next logical step, then, was selling the experience regardless of who was playing. He placed Michigan season-ticket applications on many of the seats.

Before the game, Colts owner Carroll Rosenbloom walked out of the stadium tunnel, took one look at the crowd, and became furious. Rosenbloom turned to the first man he saw and told him that there was no way the Colts would play in front of a full house for a measly $75,000.

He had to hunt down this Don Canham guy.

"I think he's up there," replied the man, pointing to the press box.

Rosenbloom stormed off. The Colts owner was outfoxed twice that day: first by agreeing to such a low fee, and then by the guy who sent him to the press box: Don Canham himself.

*   *   *

In the fall of 1971, an Ann Arbor activist asked Michigan captain Frank Gusich if his team was against the war. Gusich's reaction: "Of course we're not *for* the war." Good, the activist replied. They wanted to stage an antiwar protest at halftime of the homecoming game. Would the players help out?

Gusich took a petition into the locker room and came out with the signatures of two-thirds of the team—including, of course, star running backs Glenn Doughty and Billy Taylor. Schembechler was not happy. He sternly told Gusich that the petition could distract the team in the middle of the season. They were entitled to their opinions, but nothing should interfere with football.

Thanks in part to the players' support, Michigan's official 1971 homecoming parade theme was "Bring All the Troops Home Now; Let's Have a Real Homecoming." As the Michigan Marching Band played "Taps," fifty war veterans lined up on the sideline and released one hundred helium-filled black balloons in remembrance of the war-related deaths in Southeast Asia.

At halftime of the homecoming game, the PA announcer intoned, "In the words of the student body, there cannot be a real homecoming unless a date is set now for the withdrawal from Southeast Asia of all American forces, equipment, and war aid."

The crowd of 75,000 went silent.

There was only one Vietnam veteran on the Michigan football team, and he wasn't in the stadium for the homecoming game. Mike Lantry was in the Detroit suburb of Grosse Pointe, getting married. (Lantry was just a freshman, and freshmen were ineligible for the varsity.)

Lantry had not signed the petition. He was still processing his feelings about the war. He saw the protesters on campus and understood that he should keep quiet about his war experience. He rarely socialized with anybody outside the football program. He just wanted to prove—mostly to himself—that he could stay afloat academically at the University of Michigan. In a sense, he had the same goal in Ann Arbor as at his post outside Saigon: survive.

Despite Schembechler's fears, Michigan somehow survived the

halftime distraction and squeaked out a 61–7 homecoming win over Indiana. Nothing, it seemed, could possibly derail the 1971 Wolverines. In the first four games of that season, Michigan outscored its opponents 161–6. In another four-game stretch, the Wolverines trounced their opponents 194–27.

In a blowout of Iowa, the Wolverines scored 63 points and only gave up 97 yards—and for that, they earned an unusual but fitting tribute from Hawkeyes coach Frank Lauterbur, who began his postgame press conference with an announcement: "We got the fucking shit kicked out of us today."

The amazing thing about all this was that the Wolverines were basically a one-dimensional team; their quarterback, Tom Slade, was a mediocre passer, and for the year, they would run the ball almost seven times for every pass they threw. They just ran so well that they didn't have to pass. Michigan was on track for another mammoth showdown at the end of November. Ohio State, however, was not.

Ohio State had lost the best class in school history and was supposedly rebuilding—even on the coaching staff. Defensive coordinator Lou McCullough, considered by many to be Hayes's likely successor, had left to become Iowa State's athletic director, for the same reason Schembechler had left Ohio State for Miami in 1964: he wondered if Woody would ever retire. George Hill replaced him.

At Hayes's urging, Ohio State had installed artificial turf for the 1971 season. The turf was easy to maintain and was supposed to cut down on injuries. Even the best grass surfaces were naturally uneven, but turf was nice and flat, which should have reduced ankle and foot injuries. It also should have helped Hayes eliminate fumbles and slippage and any other damn thing that could keep his eleven from overpowering the other guy's eleven. (And That School Up North had installed it two years earlier—what took Ohio State so long?)

Unfortunately, the grip on the turf was too strong. It clung to the Buckeyes' shoes, and after a few days of preseason training, a bunch of players had sore muscles and could barely walk. The solution,

Hayes decided, was to water down the field before every practice. But that created its own problem: the ball got slippery, which made it harder to throw, and the Old Man went ballistic whenever a quarterback misfired a pass.

Hayes did not want to hear about a wet ball. That was just another excuse, and Ohio State football was not built on excuses. A wet ball? That was like complaining about the goddamn *weather*, and Woody wouldn't stand for that, either—if he saw a player with his hands in his pants or under his jersey, trying to stay warm, he'd pull the guy's hands out and give him a little smack.

Alas, the turf contributed to another excuse: just about anybody who stepped on it in the fall of 1971 got injured. By the week of the Michigan game, eight starters were missing and several reserves had been injured. The Buckeyes hung in as long as they could—when they got by Minnesota in late October, they were 6–1, still in the Big Ten race.

But the next week they scored only 10 points in a home loss to Michigan State. And the week after that, they scored 10 again in a home loss to Northwestern. All-American center Tom DeLeone tore up his knee in the Northwestern game—he was the tenth Buckeye to have a knee operation that fall—and the game against That School Up North appeared a formality. Ohio State was given no chance to win in Ann Arbor.

The same day that Ohio State lost to Northwestern, Michigan clinched the Big Ten title with a 20–17 win at Purdue. It was the first Michigan game of 1971 decided by single digits, and Schembechler, eager to prop up his team before the Ohio State game, was unusually bold afterward.

"We are the best," Schembechler said. "Why shouldn't we be No. 1?"

With Michigan already in the Rose Bowl and Ohio State limping to the end of the season, the big rivalry game would not even be televised live. Why bother? What could possibly happen that would make compelling television around the nation?

Locally, though, interest was still high. The game had long been sold out, and even with the forecast of lousy weather and a blowout, there was no doubt that Michigan Stadium would be full for the first time all season. It was as much about the theater as the possibility of a close contest. As Don Canham said the night before the game, "A lot of people bought tickets just to see what Woody will do."

Michigan Stadium was widely called the nation's biggest football stadium, but that referred to capacity, not structure size. The stadium itself was surprisingly small—just an oval bowl sunk into the ground, with a press box and two digital scoreboards (installed by Don Canham) attached. It was tucked away in a predominantly residential area away from the central campus. Instead of looming over the rest of the university, Michigan Stadium seemed to be hiding from it.

The stadium's appeal was that when it was filled, more than 100,000 people felt close to the action. Now 104,116 people, the biggest crowd in NCAA history, were packed in for what everybody figured would be a Michigan blowout.

The Wolverines led the Big Ten in rushing, rushing defense, scoring, scoring defense, total offense, and total defense. They had scored more points and allowed fewer yards than any team in the country. Nebraska, Oklahoma, and Alabama also had exceptional teams that year—top-ranked Nebraska would beat No. 2 Oklahoma five days later in one of the greatest games in college football history—but with two more wins, Michigan would at least be in the conversation for No. 1.

Ohio State realized what it was up against. Hayes even slipped while making his early-week comments to the press—he said, "We know what kind of battle we're against up there in Michigan," the only time anybody could remember him saying the word "Michigan" in public. (Although, as Paul Hornung of the *Dispatch* pointed out, he was referring only to the state, not the school.) On the morning of the game, Ohio State defensive end Tom Marendt was stricken with appendicitis. Marendt was the ninth Buckeyes starter lost to injury. That's why the record crowd was stunned to see Michigan walk off the field at halftime with just a 3–0 lead.

It had been a snowy, rainy, sleety day, and the North Atlantic conditions probably helped the underdog Buckeyes. The injuries had ruined Ohio State's season, but for one game against That School Up North, Hayes had his men ready. At Ohio State's traditional last practice drill before the game, a public ceremony known as the Senior Tackle, Woody noticed that the blocking machine was facing south.

"We're going to tackle toward the north," he said, and the crowd cheered.

Now it was clear that Hayes's wounded team would not fold. Unfortunately, they couldn't really move, either—Ohio State would gain only 138 yards for the whole game. If the Buckeyes were going to win, they would need a turnover or special teams play to do it . . . and late in the third quarter, they got it. Tom Campana returned a punt 65 yards for a touchdown. Ohio State led, 7–3.

Pretty soon, there were barely seven minutes on the clock, now-or-never time for Schembechler's crew. Starting quarterback Tom Slade had injured his hip and been replaced by Larry Cipa. The Wolverines needed to go 72 yards for a touchdown. Otherwise, Ohio State would pull off an upset that would be just as stunning as Michigan's 1969 shocker. (And more impressive, really, considering the Buckeyes' injuries, and the fact that, unlike the '69 Wolverines, they were playing on the road.)

Other than a couple of passes (one of which was complete), Schembechler stuck with his ground game. The Wolverines doggedly moved down the field to set up the play of the game—or at least what appeared at the time to be the play of the game.

Michigan had a first down on the Ohio State 21-yard line. The Buckeyes went to their "Omaha" defense (as in Omaha Beach), forming a wall of defenders on the line of scrimmage.

If Hayes were facing that kind of defense, he would have cited Sun Tzu, the ancient Chinese general: "The worst policy of all is to besiege walled cities." Bo Schembechler was the best student Woody Hayes ever had. Schembechler's quarterback, Cipa, saw the Omaha defense and called for a sweep around the walled city.

The Wolverines blocked the play perfectly. Billy Taylor, who began the year with a visit to Vietnam, ended it with a 21-yard touchdown run.

Now the Buckeyes had two minutes to drive down the field and at least kick a field goal, which would create a 10–10 tie. Considering each team's outlook that morning, a tie would be viewed as an Ohio State triumph.

With so little time on the clock, Hayes was forced to call pass plays so his team could move downfield quickly. He had no choice. Quarterback Don Lamka dropped back and saw receiver Dick Wakefield open on the left side of the field. Lamka threw a decent pass to Wakefield—high, but catchable—and Wakefield went up to catch it.

But Michigan defensive back Thom Darden leapt over Wakefield and snatched the ball from behind for the interception.

When Wakefield got up, he saw a penalty flag on the field, and he was thrilled: *They called pass interference . . . we can win this game!* Darden would admit, years later, that he hit Wakefield before the ball arrived—and that if he had merely knocked the ball away, instead of intercepting it, the officials probably would have called pass interference. But they didn't. The penalty flag Wakefield saw was for unsportsmanlike conduct on the head coach at Ohio State.

Woody Hayes had sprinted onto the field, to within inches of referee Jerry Markbreit, and demanded that Markbreit reverse the call. Markbreit would eventually become the most famous referee in the NFL, but now he was just a young official getting chewed out by Woody Hayes. Markbreit threw the penalty flag.

Hayes was just getting warmed up. As Markbreit walked off the 15 yards for the penalty, Hayes was right in his face, screaming—after a few minutes, the Ohio State assistant coaches literally dragged him off the field. The stadium was rocking. Nobody had ever seen anything like this before.

On the other sideline, Bo Schembechler thought Hayes was acting—he was trying to distract everybody from the fact that his team was 6–4 that year. In the stands, Hayes's old tackle Daryl Sanders felt the same way.

To most of the fans, though, it was pure, unfiltered anger. And it only got wilder: on Michigan's second play after the interception, as Cipa took a knee to down the ball and run out the clock, Ohio State linebacker Randy Gradishar burst through the line and decked the quarterback. He was immediately ejected. Markbreit started to walk him to the Ohio State sideline, but . . . hold on . . . what was this?

The Old Man was tearing up the first-down markers! He threw one out onto the field. Then he threw the other one out there, too. Then he ripped a piece of plastic off one of the markers. It looked like he was actually trying to rip the chains apart, but the chains weren't like his pre-torn hats—they didn't rip apart easily. Markbreit had one of the other officials walk Gradishar to the sideline. He had heard enough from Woody for one afternoon.

The crowd was going nuts. In the press box, new Big Ten commissioner Wayne Duke was wondering what he had gotten himself into—this was his first game in his new job.

Through it all, Markbreit noticed something else: the Ohio State players remained silent.

When the clock finally, mercifully ran out, the sky was suddenly clear—the snow and sleet and rain had given way to a rainbow. Michigan fans rushed the field and tore down the goalposts. In the pandemonium, Schembechler and Hayes never shook hands. ("It was a little confusing out there," Bo explained.)

The press waited forty-five minutes for Hayes to emerge from the locker room.

Finally, a team spokesman announced, "He's talking to no one today." No one, indeed: Ohio State athletic director Ed Weaver and his deputy, Hugh Hindman (one of Hayes's old assistants), said that Hayes had not spoken to *anybody* after the game. Hayes left through a side door and was jeered by Michigan fans as he boarded the team bus.

Even Woody's pal Paul Hornung wrote that it was Hayes's "most explosive outburst in 21 years at Ohio State" (though Hornung barely mentioned it in the first twelve paragraphs of his game story in the *Dispatch*). And when the video was shown around the country . . . well, who could resist the image?

Jim Murray of the *Los Angeles Times*, whose syndicated column appeared in hundreds of newspapers, wrote that if Hayes were so sanctimonious about officiating, he should forfeit any game in which Ohio State benefited from a blown call. Pete Waldmeir of the *Detroit News* called the display "shameful . . . Woody was a raving lunatic." Roy Damer of the *Chicago Tribune* wrote that it was a "clown act . . . he belittled himself."

Even in Ohio, Woody took heat: Tom Loomis of the *Toledo Blade* wondered if it was "time for him to quit," and Hal Lebovitz of the *Cleveland Plain Dealer* wrote that "it was ludicrous, then revolting. . . . It's one thing to be a fierce competitor, which he is. It's quite another to be a horse's rear end."

Lebovitz's column was headlined "Apologize, Woody," but nobody who knew Hayes expected an apology. His position on apologies had been clear for some time: if you were right, you needn't apologize, and if you were wrong, an apology sounded too much like an excuse. In this case, he believed he was right. He called the interception the worst blown call in the history of college football.

"When you see officials decide the ballgame, I'm bitter," Hayes said on his television show that night. "I went out there to let them know I was bitter."

He said he expected "to get called on the carpet. I hope I do." He said he just wanted to know "whether the calls were correct or not." The idea that he was right about the pass interference call but wrong to react the way he did . . . that never occurred to Woody. He had built a career on reactions—hitting himself in the face when a player fumbled in practice, screaming in the face of a lineman who jumped offside. He seemed to think any action was the appropriate reaction as long as he was right.

"The only right is what is after my constitution," Emerson wrote, "the only wrong is what is against it."

For all his popularity, Hayes had always faced a small but vocal group of critics at Ohio State. They did not like the image he presented of the university, and their leader was Jack Fullen, the now-retired head of the Ohio State Alumni Association. In a scathing letter to the *Lantern*, the school newspaper, Fullen wrote:

> The latest Ann Arbor asininity outdid his chair-throwing hysterics up there a few years back . . . this time the Angry One is not mad at one football official, the *Miami Herald* quotes him as saying, "I hate them all." It figures. They're the only persons connected with any phase of his life whom he can't bully or browbeat. . . . And who spoiled the brat? The university which could have averted its shame at Ann Arbor by cracking down on the Hayes histrionics long ago.

Hayes had long ridiculed Fullen and his like. They were either liberal academic types who had never fought for a damn thing in their lives or they were using football to prop up their own careers—or both. Hayes appeared before the Ohio State athletic council and was reprimanded by Duke, the Big Ten commissioner, but he was not suspended or even publicly rebuked by his boss. Weaver, the Ohio State athletic director, offered to repay That School Up North for any damage Hayes had done, but Don Canham dismissed the offer.

"I'll buy all the down markers Hayes wants to break," he told reporters, "because Ohio State without Hayes would mean 30,000 less people in the stands."

In a private letter to Weaver, though, Canham wrote, "My big concern was that he very nearly started a riot with his antics." A few days later, during a speech in Cleveland, Hayes suggested a remedy for blown calls: "We can have electronic machines on the sidelines to make things right. . . . If a fellow on the sidelines in a football game wants a replay, it should cost him a timeout . . . they look at the 'instant replay' . . . and if he's wrong let it cost him five yards."

He didn't understand that outside of Ohio, the only video replay anybody wanted to see was of his tantrum. In the 103-year history of college football, a lot of calls had been blown. Many coaches had won national championships. But an eruption like *that*? Who could ever forget it? To much of the country, Woody Hayes was now the coach who stalked a referee and tore up a sideline marker, sure as Bear Bryant was the guy in the houndstooth hat.

To Hayes, tearing up that sideline marker was as natural as speaking on the Oval during the 1970 student strike. As he told the crowd in Cleveland, "All I was trying to do was defend truth and justice."

John Lennon thought this would be the start of something big. The former Beatle had decided to hold a national concert tour urging young people to vote. (The voting age had just been lowered from twenty-one to eighteen, which would presumably help Democrats defeat President Nixon.) Lennon's plan never quite took off. He only appeared at one concert. It was December 10, 1971, at the University of Michigan's basketball venue, Crisler Arena, for something called the John Sinclair Freedom Rally.

The good news was that Sinclair and fellow White Panthers Pun Plamondon and Jack Forrest had been cleared (at least temporarily) of bombing the CIA building in Ann Arbor. The case hadn't even made it to a jury. Detroit judge Damon Keith had ruled that the government had obtained its evidence through illegal wiretaps. The Nixon administration vigorously appealed the ruling; Nixon said the government had "less than fifty" wiretaps in the whole country, and they were necessary for national security.

As the case made its way through the courts, the Panthers should have been free, but they were not. Sinclair was still in jail for his possession of two joints, and Plamondon was in jail for possessing illegal draft cards.

Now Lennon was taking up Sinclair's cause, along with Stevie Wonder, Bob Seger, and Black Panthers founder Bobby Seale. Lennon had a new song that would have suited the audience: "Happy Xmas (War Is Over)." But he wrote another new one just for this concert. It was called "John Sinclair."

As Lennon sang, an undercover FBI agent in the Crisler Arena crowd wrote down every word. The agent then filed a report to FBI director J. Edgar Hoover. Hoover had made radicals a top priority—at the time of the John Sinclair Freedom Rally, eight political activists were on the FBI's Ten Most Wanted List. The Nixon administration began deportation proceedings for Lennon. The official reason was that Lennon had pleaded guilty to cannabis possession, a misdemeanor, in Britain three years earlier. Lennon believed he was singled out because of his activism; as he sang in the song he wrote for John Sinclair, "Was he jailed for what he done? Or for representin' everyone?"

Two days after the concert, John Sinclair was freed on appeal. His legal problems were not over, but at least he was out of prison. He hugged his four-year-old daughter, Sunny, for the first time in two and a half years.

A TV interviewer asked Sinclair if the whole experience would make him reconsider his stance on marijuana.

Sinclair shouted, "Let's go smoke some joints!"

Michigan had won twenty of its last twenty-one games, including all eleven in 1971. Yet Bo Schembechler's team was still only ranked fourth in the country.

"We have played our schedule and won every game, and yet we've never been considered as the national champion," Schembechler said, before adding, "which maybe we're not."

The Wolverines had only one weakness: they couldn't pass. They had gotten away with it because nobody in the Big Ten really passed. It was a rushing league. But that brought up another problem: the Wolverines had not faced a great passing team all year. Of course, these were considered minor concerns. Michigan entered the Rose bowl as a 10-point favorite over Stanford, which had lost to lowly Duke and San Jose State.

There was no reason to worry. But Don Canham was worried anyway. Before the game, he stood in the press box and muttered to nobody in particular, "Is anyone as nervous as I am? I don't know what it is . . . but I just can't sit down." For the second straight game, Canham's words would be prescient.

The Wolverines dropped into deep coverage to guard against the

Stanford passing game, but Indians quarterback Don Bunce made Michigan pay with one short pass after another. Michigan ran successfully, as always—290 yards for the day—but the Wolverines couldn't find the end zone. Still, it seemed like they would survive; midway through the fourth quarter, they led 10–3. Then Stanford tried a fake punt—a trick play that shouldn't have tricked anybody, since Michigan had prepared for it all week. Inexplicably, the fake punt went for 31 yards.

Stanford soon tied the score. And after a Michigan safety, Bunce led his team downfield. With twelve seconds left, Stanford's Rod Garcia kicked a 31-yard field goal for the Indians' second straight Rose Bowl upset.

For the Michigan program, this was not just an end to a season. It was the last game for most of the players Schembechler had inherited from predecessor Bump Elliott; as of 1972, the Michigan team would be comprised mostly of Schembechler recruits. The rest of the Big Ten hoped that Schembechler's success was largely due to Elliott's players—and that Ohio State's 1971 stumble signaled a decline in Hayes's program. The hope would not last.

5

Only the Good Ones

Dennis Franklin and Steve Luke had been playing sports together since they could walk. They were born eleven days apart in the same hospital in northeast Ohio, their mothers were friends and they were best friends by grade school. When Franklin was a high school quarterback in football-mad Massillon, Ohio, Luke both snapped the ball to him (as a junior center) and caught passes from him (as a senior tight end). Both Franklin and Luke were excellent athletes, highly coveted by Big Ten schools.

Word quickly spread among college recruiters that Dennis Franklin and Steve Luke were a package—pick up one and you'd get the other, too. They took all of their recruiting trips together. So when Luke told Woody Hayes he was coming to Ohio State, Hayes called Franklin and asked him for a decision—the implication being that if Franklin didn't commit today, there might not be a scholarship available tomorrow.

That kind of tactic usually worked for Hayes with Ohio kids. But Franklin was turned off. Bo Schembechler had told Franklin that he could take as long as he liked and Michigan's scholarship offer would stand. Franklin took Schembechler at his word. He dragged the process into spring of his senior year. Michigan assistant coach Jerry Hanlon would visit Franklin in Massillon between the Wolverines' spring practice sessions. Hanlon had no choice. In the early 1970s, the recruiting season was year-round. Boosters did much of the legwork for schools, especially close to home; an alum could take a recruit to dinner weekly without arousing the interest of the NCAA. But coaches spent weeks at a time on the road, driving from one high school to the next.

Eventually, the NCAA would respond with strict recruiting guidelines, including a National Signing Day in midwinter and restrictions on coach-player contact. In the meantime, the process was endless and exhausting—and the price for giving in to exhaustion could be severe.

In the spring of 1969, Hanlon was supposed to recruit prospects at Cathedral Latin and John Hay high schools in Cleveland, which were adjacent to each other. Hanlon went to Cathedral Latin first. When he walked out, it was raining, and he decided not to walk across the parking lot to see the player at John Hay. *Heck*, Hanlon thought, *John Hay never has any big-time players. How good could this kid be?*

Hanlon would regret the decision. The prospect's name was John Hicks. By 1972, he was considered one of the finest offensive linemen in the country—for Ohio State.

Then again, Arizona State coach Frank Kush would argue that Hanlon simply saved himself some time by staying away from Hicks. Whenever Kush saw an Ohio player he liked, he started his research with one question: does Woody want him? If the answer was yes, Kush didn't even bother recruiting the kid. There was no point. Kush had a rising program in a beautiful climate and extensive contacts in the Midwest. But he knew he couldn't beat Woody Hayes in Ohio. He didn't even try.

Bo Schembechler did not have that option. He *had* to try to recruit in Ohio. The state of Ohio had a deeper talent pool than the state of Michigan, and since Michigan State would inevitably win some in-state recruiting battles against Michigan, it was essential that the Wolverines reach into Ohio for top players. Schembechler realized this as soon as he arrived in Ann Arbor in 1969, and since he already had many contacts in the state from his Miami and Ohio State days, he decided to challenge Ohio State on Hayes's home turf.

Schembechler somehow made inroads in Ohio, which was a testament to his own recruiting ability. He was extremely organized—just as he planned every Michigan practice down to the minute, he made sure that the Wolverines' recruiting machine was as efficient as it could be. His exceptional ability to see skills on film helped him figure out which prospects to recruit.

And once he was in a player's home, Schembechler wowed families with the same verbal skills that had won over his players. He had the poise and charisma to get him out of any jam. Once, when he was recruiting a Catholic player to Miami, he mentioned that there were priests at most Miami practices. The player's mother asked for the priests' names. Schembechler didn't know the answer. He calmly turned to assistant coach Jim Young.

"Jim," he said, "tell her the names of the priests."

Schembechler knew Young didn't know the priests' names, either. But better for the assistant to blank than the head coach.

Schembechler's charisma, coupled with Hayes's push for a decision, helped Dennis Franklin make his college choice. Instead of playing with his childhood buddy Steve Luke at Ohio State, Franklin decided to play against him, for Michigan.

Besides being a towering figure in his home state, Woody Hayes had the nation's best booster organization laying the groundwork. Originally known as the Frontliners, and now known simply as the Athletic Committee, the boosters blanketed the state. There were committeemen assigned to every high school in Ohio, checking out prospects, taking recruits to dinner, and alerting Hayes whenever Bo Schembechler or another major-college coach came to town.

And Hayes was one of the great recruiters in history. When he visited any part of Ohio, word would quickly spread that the great coach was coming. Since Hayes was such a legend, the mother of each recruit would naturally make sure she had a home-cooked meal ready for him—and not just any home-cooked meal, but the mother's specialty. Hayes would eat the meal and lick his fingers and make her think it was the greatest thing he'd ever eaten. The mothers never realized that Hayes often visited four or five homes in one night. By the time he was on his fifth house (and fifth dinner) of the evening, he was surely full. But he never let on.

With all that in his favor, Hayes could pick and choose among the best athletes in the Midwest, if not the country. But he looked for something more than just athletic ability.

In the spring of 1972, Hayes sat in a western Pennsylvania high school gym while recruit Brian Baschnagel finished volleyball practice. Baschnagel kept glancing up at the bleachers to see if Hayes was evaluating his athletic ability. But Hayes never looked up from the book he was reading: *Animal Farm*, by George Orwell. That night, Hayes and Baschnagel spent more than two hours at dinner. They talked about history and Baschnagel's desire to go to business school or law school after college.

Nothing galled Hayes more than a player who betrayed the state of Ohio for That School Up North. Now, in the spring of 1972, one of those players would be Michigan's starting quarterback.

Dennis Franklin had beaten out incumbent Tom Slade, who had merely come within two points of a perfect season in 1971. Schembechler did not hesitate to give Franklin the job. He was clearly the superior athlete.

Before the 1972 season, when a reporter asked Franklin why so many Ohio kids played for Michigan, he cracked, "Only the good ones." At least that's how he was quoted. Franklin swore he said "*a lot* of the good ones." But the "only the good ones" quote quickly made its way to the Ohio State locker room, where the Buckeyes asked Steve Luke what was wrong with his friend. They asked Luke if Franklin was talking about *him*.

Luke thought Franklin's comment was intended in good fun. He also knew it wouldn't be taken that way.

Whether Franklin said them or not, those four words—"only the good ones"—summed up everything Ohioans had hated about the University of Michigan for decades. Those people at That School Up North thought they were so damn superior to the farm kids down in Columbus—smarter, richer, more sophisticated. In Ohio, the last game of the regular season was not just about Big Ten supremacy. It was a chance to stick it to the arrogant folks up north.

Although Woody Hayes seethed when a player left Ohio for That School Up North, he rarely fired back by plucking a kid from the state of Michigan. It had taken him a few years to recruit *anywhere* outside of Ohio, and recruiting in Michigan did not make much sense. For one, Hayes would have to beat two in-state Big Ten schools to land a player. For another, he had been deliberately inflammatory about That State Up North.

But in February 1972, Ohio State assistant coach Ed Ferkany convinced Hayes to look at a pair of recruits in Michigan. Hayes was wary, and he was even more wary when he and Ferkany visited the players on the night of their all-conference football banquet: here he was, going against Sun Tzu's advice and besieging a walled city. To Hayes's astonishment, he was treated like royalty by the high school coaches.

"A prophet is without honor in his own country," Hayes cracked. His disdain for the state of Michigan seemed to be thawing, at least for a night.

A heavy snow fell as Ferkany drove Hayes back to Columbus. Ferkany's vision was limited, not just by the snow but because the light was on inside his car so Hayes could read one of his books about war. Hayes also insisted that the radio be turned off. He almost never allowed the radio on in the car, no matter who was driving. As they drove on I-75 through downtown Detroit, Ferkany noticed that he was very low on gas. He said they had to stop.

"Bullshit," Hayes replied. "Keep going."

Ferkany didn't know why Hayes was so insistent, but he didn't ask. He had been on the job for just three weeks and his association with Hayes had been a series of surprises. When Hayes first called him to say he wanted to interview him to be Ohio State's offensive line coach, Ferkany thought it was a practical joke—one of his coaching friends pretending to be the great Woody Hayes. When he finally realized that this was, indeed, the real Woody Hayes, he agreed to fly in for an interview, which is when the next surprise came: like most visitors, Ferkany was shocked that Hayes worked in such cramped quarters. He had figured Hayes would have a palatial office, if only to impress recruits. But the Old Man never cared what players thought of his office. He wanted them listening to *him*.

"If the king is in the palace," Emerson wrote, "nobody looks at the walls."

Then came the interview. Ferkany arrived in Hayes's office on a Saturday morning in early February, a time when even the ultra-dedicated Hayes had a light workload. Ferkany had to be back at the airport by 6 p.m. so he could fly back to his job at the Naval Academy, where he had recruits waiting.

Hayes began the interview with a long discussion of the Navy. He then took Ferkany to lunch at the Big Bear supermarket on Lane Avenue, which he proudly noted was "Ohio's original supermarket, built in 1934." He went through the lunch buffet and picked out meals for both himself and Ferkany, without asking Ferkany what he wanted.

By this time it was 1:30 and the men had not mentioned football.

They then went to pick up Hayes's dry cleaning (Hayes spent a half hour chatting up customers while Ferkany waited outside in the coach's Ranchero pickup) and headed to Hayes's house to watch a Michigan-Purdue basketball game, which would have a major effect on Ohio State's Big Ten championship hopes. A few minutes into the game, Hayes fell asleep on his couch. Ferkany now had three hours left in his eight-hour interview, his prospective employer was taking a nap, and they *still* hadn't talked any football.

Anne Hayes walked in and saw her husband asleep on the couch while this stranger watched a basketball game in her living room.

"Well, you're here for the interview," she said to Ferkany. Anne then kicked her husband and snapped, "Woody, damn it! Jesus!"

Hayes woke up and quickly rushed Ferkany to the office, where they could finally start talking football. Ferkany was well prepared. He launched into a spirited analysis of sprint-draw plays and the I formation, but Hayes cut him off: "Aw, screw it. That's not what I want to run, anyway." Ferkany briefly discussed his recruiting philosophy and why he could make the transition from running backs coach at Navy to offensive line coach at Ohio State. He then flew home and told his wife the day had been a waste of time. Obviously, Hayes had no interest in him.

A week later, Hayes offered Ferkany the job. When Ferkany took it, Hayes handed him a book and ordered him to read it.

Ferkany expected a playbook. What he got was *Memoirs: Ten Years and Twenty Days*, by German navy commander Karl Dönitz.

Hayes knew all he needed to know about Ferkany's football knowledge before the interview. Ohio State assistant coaches George Hill and Dick Walker had recommended him, which was good enough for the Old Man. The whole point of the interview was to make sure that the two could get along.

Hayes's only reservation was that Ferkany grew up in Michigan, and as Ferkany drove through the snow in Detroit, with the light on and the gas tank nearing empty, he found out just how seriously Woody Hayes took this rivalry. Ferkany drove past metro Detroit's "downriver" towns and watched the gas gauge dip again.

"Coach, we gotta stop," Ferkany said.

"Keep that fucking car going!" Hayes barked. *"We're not stopping in this goddamn state and paying taxes in the state of Michigan!"*

Ferkany and Hayes somehow made it to the Ohio border and got off at the first exit, Alexis Road. They filled up the tank and headed back to Columbus.

In mid-March 1972, the Michigan Supreme Court overturned John Sinclair's pot conviction on the grounds that the state's marijuana law was unconstitutional. Sinclair still had to deal with his CIA-bombing charge (the wiretapping appeal was winding its way through the courts), but this decision was a major victory for him.

The ruling put Michigan in a state of flux—the new marijuana law would not go into effect until April 1, leaving the state without any pot laws. Federal laws and local ordinances were still in effect, but legal experts said law enforcement officers would have an extremely difficult time pursing marijuana convictions before the new law kicked in.

Ann Arbor police chief Walter Krasny could only muster this weak warning to pot-smokers: "Proceed with caution."

Sinclair and many other Ann Arborites proceeded, but not with caution. They openly smoked pot all over town. And when the new law took effect on April 1, 1972, they protested by holding the "First Annual Ann Arbor Hash Festival" on the university's Diag. Five hundred people braved freezing temperatures and snow showers to smoke weed. They weren't all radicals or even college-aged people—some women with babies and older folks smoked, too. One participant gave out free "vegetable hash," and told people it was kosher for Passover.

The smokers were not worried about getting caught. They had no reason to worry. As police lieutenant Eugene Staudenmeir stood on the smoke-filled Diag, he told the *Michigan Daily*, "I don't see anything."

The festival became known as Hash Bash. It would be an annual event on the Ann Arbor calendar for the next few decades.

Eleven weeks later, John Sinclair sat in the U.S. Supreme Court and waited to hear about the rest of his life. Pun Plamondon's wiretapping case had made its way to the highest court in the land. (At the moment, Plamondon was in jail on another charge.) The government had never said what was on the tapes (and since Sinclair was not the one who was wiretapped, he couldn't be sure, either). But President Nixon's administration had vigorously defended its practices at every step of the judicial process; the administration obviously believed the stakes were high, not just for this case but for the precedent that it would set.

The stakes were high for Sinclair and Plamondon, too. If the Supreme Court ruled in favor of the government, the pair would face a trial for bombing the CIA offices in Ann Arbor—and given their well-earned reputation as politically active hippies, they weren't sure they could get a fair trial. A long jail term was possible, maybe even probable.

By a vote of eight to none, the Supreme Court sided with Plamondon. The wiretaps were illegal.

The youngest member of the court, Justice William Rehnquist, abstained because of a conflict of interest; Rehnquist had served as Nixon's assistant attorney general, during which time he helped frame Nixon's policy on wiretapping American civilians. Rehnquist had warned of "the danger posed by the new barbarians," and said that "if force or the threat of force is required in order to enforce the law, we must not shirk from its employment."

In his majority opinion, Justice Lewis F. Powell Jr. wrote:

"The issue before us . . . involves the delicate question of the President's power, acting through the Attorney General, to authorize electronic surveillance in internal security matters without prior judicial approval. This case brings the issue here for the first time. . . . The price of lawful public dissent must not be a dread of subjection to an unchecked surveillance power. Nor must the fear of unauthorized official eavesdropping deter vigorous citizen dissent and discussion of Government action in private conversation. For private dissent, no less than open public discourse, is essential to our free society.

The decision would have long-lasting implications for the U.S. government and was major news around the country. Naturally, the *Ann Arbor News* put the story on page 1 of the afternoon paper. But a daily newspaper is only a first rough draft of history; in retrospect, the biggest headline of the day could be found on page 5:

"GOP Denies Break-In Role."

Two days earlier, five men had been arrested for breaking into the Democratic National Committee headquarters in the Watergate complex in Washington, D.C. One of them, James McCord, was a former CIA agent who was security coordinator for the Committee to Re-Elect the President.

Years later, Plamondon's attorney William Kunstler would find the timing curious: the wiretapping decision was reached Friday, June 15. The next day, the burglars broke into DNC headquarters for the second time. Two days later, the wiretapping decision was announced.

Maybe Kunstler was overly suspicious. Maybe he was prone to conspiracy theories about the president and his minions.

But Kunstler believed that Rehnquist, fresh off his time in the Nixon administration, had leaked the decision to his old bosses, who ordered the removal of wiretaps that had been installed in the Watergate building just weeks earlier, which led to the Saturday night burglary, which led to the arrests, which led to headlines like "GOP Denies Break-In Role," which led to . . .

Woody Hayes often told his players, "The Young Turks have to step up." The original Young Turks were a group of army officers who tried to reform the Ottoman Empire in 1908. Hayes wanted his players to know that even though they were young, they could make a difference in society and for their team.

In 1972, the phrase had special meaning. Freshmen were eligible to play varsity football for the first time. Hayes didn't like the rule change. He did not understand why freshmen were allowed to play a football game before they actually entered a college classroom. But he wasn't stupid. He said in the spring that some freshmen would make an immediate impact on some major-college teams, and he wasn't going to make all his freshmen sit on the bench just to prove a point.

Pretty soon, Hayes had a reason to embrace the new rule; as he would say after Ohio State's second game of the season, "Archie Griffin made me change my mind."

Griffin was a freshman running back from Eastmoor High School in Columbus. Hayes had always been reluctant to recruit Columbus kids—he thought there would be too much pressure from fans to give the local boys playing time. Hayes did not recruit Griffin until he found out Northwestern was interested, and when he found out *Michigan* was interested, the coach went after him hard.

The young tailback had also considered Navy, and he was stunned when the assistant who had recruited him for Navy, Ed Ferkany, showed up in Griffin's driveway on behalf of Ohio State. Ohio State running backs coach Rudy Hubbard, who had recruited Griffin along with Ferkany, begged Hayes to put Griffin in the lineup. Hayes relented in the first game.

And on his first carry, Griffin fumbled.

The freshman thought he would be glued to the bench for the rest of the year, maybe longer. But the next week Hayes gave Griffin the ball again. Two hundred and thirty-nine yards later, Griffin had rushed for more yards than any player in school history.

"You could sell more seats with a guy like that," Hayes said. "What makes a kid that good, I don't know . . . I know you'll have to write about him. Then we'll have to bring him back down [to earth]." It sure seemed that way two days later, when Griffin did not practice because of minor injuries.

Brian Baschnagel, his fellow freshman running back, thought Griffin was milking his success. Baschnagel was staring at four years on the bench behind this prima donna, and naturally he thought about transferring. But as he showered after practice that day, Griffin came up to him, fully clothed.

"Brian," Griffin said, "I've been meaning to talk to you. You're from Pittsburgh, Pennsylvania. I'm from Columbus, Ohio. If it had been the other way around, they would have asked you to go in the game on Saturday and you would have done what I did."

Baschnagel was stunned. He knew that wasn't true. But the fact that Griffin went out of his way to say it told Baschnagel all he needed to know about Archie Griffin.

Archie Griffin was joined in the backfield by another Columbus-area guy who nearly went to Michigan: Harold "Champ" Henson, a fullback who grew up on a farm thirty-five miles from Ohio Stadium. Hayes was late to recruit Henson, too, but once he homed in, he got him.

Thanks largely to Griffin and Henson, Ohio State only lost one game before the clash with That School Up North: at Michigan State in mid-November. Longtime Michigan State coach Duffy Daugherty had announced his retirement the week before, and the combination of fired-up Spartans and five Ohio State turnovers was too much for the Buckeyes to overcome. Hayes blamed himself. His team was supposed to avoid mistakes and get better in the second half, and on this day it did neither. Afterward, he spoke to reporters for a total of fourteen seconds before retreating to the training room.

But that Michigan State loss was an aberration. Though the Buckeyes were young, they formed a nucleus to rival the 1968–69–70 teams, which went 27–2 and won a national championship.

Those teams had been scared of the Old Man. The new group was different. These new guys were already starting to challenge the coach.

Hayes had kicked offensive lineman Chuck Bonica off the team, ostensibly for repeated lateness. The Buckeyes thought the coach was being unfair and said they wouldn't practice unless Bonica was reinstated. Hayes relented. Another time, a few black players threatened to skip practice because they thought Woody was favoring white guys. Griffin and another black freshman, quarterback Cornelius Greene, were petrified. Griffin and Greene could either join the black players (and implicitly accuse the coach of racism) or openly disagree with them (and risk being called Uncle Toms). When the other black players met with Hayes to air their grievances, Griffin and Greene sat in the back of the room. The meeting could not end soon enough for them.

There was another difference between the new stars and the old ones: Archie Griffin's class would be the first to spend all four years in college without the cloud of the Vietnam War hanging over them. In late October 1972, Secretary of State Henry Kissinger announced that "peace is at hand" in Vietnam. Peace wasn't really at hand; the North Vietnamese government hadn't agreed to a deal. But the war was clearly in its final days. In January of 1973, Nixon would order a halt to the bombing of North Vietnam, and by March the last U.S. combat soldiers would leave the country. The February 1972 draft lottery had been the last of the war.

Ohio State offensive lineman Jim Kregel had seen the horrors of war affect his brother Mike, an infantryman in Vietnam. Jim Kregel was opposed to the war but felt like he was cheating by playing football instead of fighting alongside his brother. And the incredible attention that the Buckeyes received in Columbus, where the war seemed of peripheral concern, made Kregel question the town's priorities. Rather than stay silent, he had participated in sit-ins on campus. Kregel knew the Old Man would not approve, and he worried the coach would find out. But he went anyway.

For radicals in Ann Arbor and around the nation, the end of the war was a dream come true. It had been their greatest objective; for most, it was the reason they became politically active in the first place. But the radicals' greatest triumph also triggered the decline of their power. Without the war to motivate them, young Americans would be less inclined to join a total assault on the culture. Nothing else would galvanize the generation like Vietnam had.

When people asked Bo Schembechler if he had served in the Army, he replied, "Well, no—not *really.*" He had served from 1951 to 1953, during the Korean War. But he was never sent overseas, and he would never pretend he had the same experience as a soldier who fought on the front lines. For him, serving in the Army was not a life-changing event. It was just something he did.

On the rare occasions when Schembechler talked about his time in the service, he would recount a few stories—always impeccably told, with a tinge of humor. He would talk about one captain, who was "the biggest phony that ever lived." When this captain had to send a soldier to Korea, he would act like he had done everything in his power to send the guy to war-free Europe instead. Nobody believed him. And one time at a party—with the captain and all his officers in the front row—the soldiers goaded Schembechler into giving his impression of the phony son of a bitch. Schembechler was drunk—they all were—so he took the bait.

"Jones," Schembechler said dramatically, pretending he was weeping, "I didn't want to do it. I wanted to send you to Germany, but I couldn't do it." His buddies howled with laughter. The captain just sat there.

In another story, Schembechler played on a football team at an Army base and another captain asked him to be defensive coordinator. Schembechler decided to have some fun: he installed a 6–1 defense, designed to keep all blockers away from the middle linebacker. He then made himself the middle linebacker. The team won the championship.

The stories were intended to entertain, but they said something about Schembechler: he hated phony leaders and he could organize a winning football team in almost any circumstance. Now, in 1972, he had his handpicked recruits playing for him instead of the players he inherited from Bump Elliott. Schembechler had been Woody Hayes's ideal player at Miami: an offensive tackle who loved practice and almost never made any mistakes. He wanted to build his program around similar players—and Schembechler, like Hayes, had learned that talent alone was not enough.

Of all the players on Schembechler's first three Michigan teams, the most talented might have been a running back named Preston Henry. Henry never taped up before practice—he would arrive a few minutes before the start of practice, quickly put on his pads, and head to the field. Henry also never iced anything down and did very little stretching. Yet he never got hurt. In the spring of 1970, with most of Michigan's running backs injured, he volunteered to play halfback for both teams in the spring game. He did it, too. But Henry was a knucklehead—always getting into some sort of trouble, never gaining Schembechler's trust. When he finally earned a starting halfback job, he missed the bus to the team plane.

Schembechler wanted players he could lead—and nobody in college football commanded a team's attention better than Schembechler. His players joked about his military-like discipline, but Schembechler didn't learn to lead in the military. He was a leader when he got there. When he enlisted in the Army, he had avoided Officer Candidate School. He didn't want to be an officer. He wanted to be an enlisted man, fulfill his duty, and get out. Yet Schembechler was a natural leader—they kept giving him duties anyway. He served in the Army for twenty-one and a half months and walked out as a sergeant first class, six ranks above private.

Schembechler's Wolverines always looked disciplined, even when they walked into a hotel for a team meal. And if the meal wasn't ready on time, Schembechler would throw a fit—not necessarily because he was mad, but just to let the hotel know that he expected timeliness. The team would rarely have another problem the rest of the weekend.

That translated to the field—Schembechler had gone 28–5 in his first three years, but if anything, his program actually improved in 1972. Michigan's quarterback, Dennis Franklin, was proving to be every bit as good as Schembechler and Hanlon had hoped. For the first time under Schembechler, the Wolverines relied heavily on the option play, where the quarterback can choose to pitch the ball to a tailback or keep it himself. It was perfect for the athletic and decisive Franklin.

With Franklin at quarterback and all–Big Ten players at fullback (Ed Shuttlesworth) and on the offensive line (Paul Seymour and Tom Coyle), Schembechler's troops did not aim to please; they aimed to annihilate, and they did so without any hint of compassion. In their second game, the Wolverines traveled to Los Angeles to face sixth-ranked UCLA, which had upset top-ranked Nebraska. Michigan didn't just beat UCLA by 17 points. The Wolverines totally shut down Bruins quarterback Mark Harmon, whose father, Tom, had won the Heisman Trophy for Michigan in 1940. Three weeks later, Michigan State coach Duffy Daugherty said his team played its "best game of the season" against Michigan. Daugherty would have liked it even better if his Spartans had actually scored. Michigan won, 10–0.

The Wolverines bludgeoned opponents with brutal efficiency, one running play after another, all the way to the end zone. Subtle tweaks to blocking assignments were crucial to their success, but to the average fan, it looked like Schembechler was calling the same play over and over again. Wayne DeNeff of the *Ann Arbor News* vigorously defended the Wolverines.

"To say it was dull football would be to ignore all those excruciating blocks down there along the line of scrimmage," he wrote after Michigan beat Michigan State.

But others weren't so thrilled by those excruciating blocks. In late October, after Michigan beat Minnesota 42–0, *Detroit Free Press* columnist Joe Falls wrote a column headlined "Winning at U-M: It's a Big Bore." Falls questioned whether run-dominated blowouts could really hold people's attention.

"Schembechler is doing what he was brought in to do—put Michigan back on the football map," Falls wrote. "But he's putting a lot of people to sleep in the process . . . it just isn't very exciting to see his team move relentlessly from one end of the field to the other."

Bo faced criticism on another front, too. One autumn day in the early 1970s, Michigan president Robben Fleming called Schembechler and said he wanted to have lunch. Schembechler wasn't fond of lunch meetings in the middle of the season, but he couldn't exactly say no to his school president, especially since Fleming so rarely requested anything from the athletic department. Schembechler met Fleming in the Michigan Union. There was a room set aside with only a table for two. They ate and chatted for a while with no apparent purpose. Schembechler wanted to get down to business, whatever it was. He leaned toward Fleming.

"Hey, Mr. President," the coach said. "Why are we havin' this lunch?"

Fleming replied, "You know, Bo, I wonder . . . do you really have to get on the officials the way you do?"

Schembechler was stunned—of everything he did, *that* was what Fleming wanted to discuss?

"Let me just say one thing to you, President Fleming," he said. "When I'm on one side of the field and Woody Hayes is on the other side of the field, if I just stand there and not say a word, he is going to have the officials in the palm of his hand. I'm not gonna let him do that."

Fleming was not alone in his concern. Bennie Oosterbaan, one of the best players and coaches Michigan ever had, told Schembechler he was doing a wonderful job in every way, but why did he have to throw such fits on the sideline? Schembechler never made as much of his tantrums as everybody else. In his mind, he was acting, just as Woody Hayes was acting when he stomped on a cheap watch or ripped up a pre-ripped hat. But others thought his act was unbecoming for a university that fancied itself a public Ivy, and in the Big Ten, Schembechler's carping at referees and almost uninterrupted dominance gained him a reputation as a bit of a bully.

The reputation spread to the rest of the athletic department. In 1967, the year before Don Canham became athletic director, Michigan had only drawn 64,000 people for the Ohio State game—and many of those were Ohio State fans. In 1972, Michigan drew at least 81,000 people for five of its six home games. The Wolverines led the nation in attendance—snapping a fifteen-year streak for Ohio State.

Canham's success had put heat on other athletic directors, who were simply overmatched by comparison. (He would be quoted as calling his fellow Big Ten athletic directors "a bunch of donkeys"; he denied saying it.) He parlayed his burgeoning reputation into increasing power in the Big Ten, and he wasn't afraid to wield it. He had already killed Northwestern's plan to rent Dyche Stadium to the Chicago Bears. Canham felt it was okay to stage one exhibition game in a college stadium, but if an NFL team played all its games there, the school would have trouble drawing people for its own games.

For the moment, however, the critics could only grumble. Michigan won its first nine games with ease. The Wolverines got a scare in the tenth game, against Purdue. They were tied 6–6 in the fourth quarter. But with 1:04 remaining in the game, sophomore placekicker Mike Lantry kicked a 30-yard field goal to give Michigan a 9–6 victory.

Lantry was still conflicted about his time in the Army. It seemed like a huge waste. He had risked his life for a war that President Nixon concluded was unwinnable. But Lantry also felt that without the skills and discipline he learned in Vietnam, he never would have stayed afloat at the University of Michigan.

Now Lantry wasn't just staying afloat. He was an important part of a national title contender. For the third straight year, Michigan was undefeated entering the season-ending game against Ohio State. The Wolverines had allowed only 4.3 points per game, the lowest mark in the country. The annual showdown would have special significance, because for the first time in the Woody-Bo era, both Ohio State and Michigan could go to the Rose Bowl with a win. The Big Ten had repealed its no-repeat rule—and just as significantly, the Big Ten had *kept* its ban on bowls other than the Rose.

One of these teams would go to the most famous bowl game in the country. The other would stay home.

The two teams were so evenly matched and the defenses were so strong that a low-scoring tie seemed like a real possibility. There, too, Michigan had the edge. Ohio State's loss to Michigan State meant that in the event of a tie, Michigan would win the Big Ten title. (A tie would hurt Michigan's national title chance, but maybe not that much—the Wolverines, ranked third in the country, would still get a shot at undisputed No. 1 Southern California in the Rose Bowl.)

If he had a chance, would Bo play for a tie rather than risk losing?

"We don't like ties," he said. "But you have to consider situations. The first thing we're going for down there is the outright championship. Can't we win that with a tie? Yes.

"Does that answer your question?"

Former Ohio State captain Dave Whitfield had just come back from military service—in Germany, not Vietnam, because the war was winding down. Now he was back at the site of his greatest days: the Ohio State locker room. Woody Hayes had asked him to give the Buckeyes a pregame talk. Hayes had reason to be nervous. His team, though extremely talented, was young and a four-point underdog to That School Up North. If the Buckeyes lost, Hayes would be an unthinkable 1–3 against Schembechler heading into the next year's game in Ann Arbor.

Earlier that week, Hayes looked out from his practice field—*way* out, across a four-lane highway and up to a window on the tenth floor of the Fawcett Center for Tomorrow, and he saw . . . a spy? Could it be? Hayes took no chances. He called the campus police. The cops arrived on the scene to find a Michigan fan filming Ohio State practice with a telephoto lens.

Whitfield was searching for the right words to describe the intensity of this rivalry. He kept thinking of his last game, when he thought the Buckeyes were too cocky and they lost, 24–12, in Ann Arbor. At the end of his speech, he said, "This is not a game . . . This is *war.*" Young Archie Griffin thought he understood the rivalry—he had grown up in Columbus. But as Whitfield spoke, Griffin looked around the room and saw that his teammates had tears in their eyes. Then he looked at Whitfield and saw that he, too, had tears in his eyes.

As the eighth-ranked Buckeyes walked out of the locker room, some guy who appeared to be drunk, stoned, or both broke through security and started ranting and raving. The cops quickly knocked the guy to the ground and arrested him. And because the Old Man was known to go to extreme lengths to motivate, defensive tackle Pete Cusick would later wonder whether Hayes had set the whole thing up himself to incite his young team.

Third-ranked Michigan struck first with a 35-yard field goal by Mike Lantry. Ohio State came back with a classic Woody Hayes touchdown: fullback Champ Henson ran three times, starting at the Michigan four-yard line, until he finally scored. Ohio State led, 7–3.

Michigan's polished offense came right back, though—the Wolverines moved from their own 20 deep into Ohio State territory. Pretty soon, the Wolverines were on the Ohio State one-yard line.

First and goal from the one. Schembechler called on tailback Chuck Heater. Heater lost a yard. Second and goal from the two. Schembechler gave it to Heater again. Heater gained the yard back. Third and goal from the one. This time, fullback Bob Thornbladh got the carry. He was tackled for no gain.

Fourth and goal from the one. There were eleven seconds left in the first half. Schembechler called timeout, presumably to decide whether to kick the chip-shot field goal to cut the margin to 7–6 or go for the touchdown.

Schembechler wanted that touchdown.

Ohio Stadium, arguably the most famous structure in Ohio, looked like a modern-day Roman Colosseum. Known as "the Horseshoe" because it was open on one end, it was designed to be imposing: it was the first college stadium to feature a second deck, and visiting players felt as though all of Ohio was descending upon them. Ohio State had lost the attendance title to Michigan, but the Horseshoe was by far the more intimidating stadium. And now, with the Buckeyes needing one more stop for a stunning goal-line stand, the crowd roared like the players had never heard it roar before.

Quarterback Dennis Franklin took the snap and . . . hold on, did he even take the snap? Franklin had fumbled it. He covered the ball but could not advance it. Ohio State had stopped the Wolverines.

It seemed to be a game of inches. Ohio State had punched it in from inside the five-yard line and Michigan had come up just short. But the next score came on a longer play: a 30-yard run by Archie Griffin. Ohio State led 14–3.

Michigan came back with another drive, and this time, the Wolverines scored from the one-yard line. They got the two-point conversion, too. Ohio State led 14–11.

The Wolverines had moved the ball better than Ohio State. They just needed another chance to score. And pretty soon, they had it: with 8:53 left in the game, they had the ball on the Buckeye five-yard line.

First and goal from the five: Wolverines tailback Harry Banks, a Cleveland native, pounded out two yards. Second and goal from the three: Banks ran again for two more. Third and goal from the one. Banks got the call again and was tackled by Ohio State lineman Pete Cusick right around the goal line. Banks and the Michigan coaches were convinced it was a touchdown, just as the Buckeyes were convinced that Michigan had committed pass interference a year earlier. But for the second year in a row, the officials sided with the home team. They said Cusick had stopped Banks short of the goal line.

Fourth and goal from the one.

Earlier in the week, Schembechler had strongly hinted that he would go for a tie and clinch the conference championship. Now he had his chance. He just had to call Mike Lantry in from the sideline to kick an 18-yard field goal. If Lantry converted, the game would be tied 14–14—and since Michigan would win the conference with a tie, the Wolverines would effectively be in the lead. Ohio State would still have several minutes to score, but Schembechler had the best defense in the country and a running game that could salt away a lead as well as anybody. He had to feel like a field goal would clinch the Big Ten championship.

But Bo Schembechler had been preparing for this moment for much of his adult life. He had learned the concepts of a power running game from the Old Man; he had recruited big, tough offensive linemen and speedy backfield players to beat Ohio State; he had done something in practice every day of the year to prepare for a tight game against the Buckeyes; and he sure as hell hadn't done all that so he could abandon his running game so close to the end zone.

Unlike most kickers, Lantry was not just some scrawny kid with a strong leg—he would earn three letters as a shot putter for the Michigan track team. He had even been a left-handed pitcher in high school, just like Schembechler. But Lantry was still a kicker. Schembechler didn't come all this way—from the practice field at Miami all the way down to the one-yard line in the south end at Ohio Stadium—to show the Old Man that his kicker could force a tie.

A pass play surely would have caught the Buckeyes off guard, but of course, Schembechler didn't come all this way to pass the ball, either.

And he didn't even come all this way to deceive the Old Man by running the option.

Bo Schembechler and Woody Hayes believed football was built

on the power running game, on brute force and technique, on *want*. Schembechler called on Dennis Franklin to run a quarterback sneak, just as he had in the first half. This time Franklin took the snap cleanly, then pushed into the line. The first Buckeye to get to Franklin was linebacker Randy Gradishar, who had grown up in a town outside of Youngstown, Ohio. The name of the town was Champion. Gradishar stopped Franklin short of the goal line. Ohio State had stopped Michigan again. The stadium erupted. It was as though the entire state of Ohio was screaming: *Only the good ones, huh?*

The Wolverines got one last chance, in the final two minutes, and they drove to the Ohio State 41. On third down, Franklin threw a pass out of bounds, stopping the clock with 13 seconds left. The fans at the Horseshoe thought the game was over; they poured onto the field to tear down the south goalposts. Not surprisingly, Woody Hayes ran out there to stop them—he pulled a calf muscle doing it. Order was restored a few minutes later, though the goalpost was not, and Michigan tried to pass on fourth down. Franklin threw incomplete.

The game was effectively over. Fans rushed the field again. But it wasn't *technically* over—there were six seconds left—so the fans had to be cleared again. For the Wolverines, this was excruciating. How many times would they have to watch Ohio State fans rush the field?

The Buckeyes ran one play to end it. Now it was official: Ohio State 14, Michigan 11.

Afterward, Hayes explained why he ran onto the field to stop the pandemonium.

"Each year it gets a little worse," he said. "A couple of years ago I was trying to help out when we had some trouble on campus and one of those people said to me, 'How about the way your football crowd behaves?' And you know, he had a point."

But neither the unruly crowd nor his pulled calf muscle could dampen Hayes's mood. Those goal-line stands were reminiscent of the Battle of Britain, when the British, backed up against their own end zone, held off the Germans. Hayes was so happy, he even apologized to reporters for making them wait for him.

"A game like this brings kids together," Hayes said. "They all pull together. If society as a whole could learn from this . . . then no one could put us down."

Schembechler was beside himself. Michigan had outgained Ohio State 344–192, earned 21 first downs to Ohio State's 10, *and* won the turnover battle. Under those circumstances, it was almost impossible to lose. But the Wolverines had run seven plays from the Ohio State one-yard line and scored just once.

"I just wish there was some way we could have gotten in the end zone," Schembechler said. "I'm sick that we didn't . . . we never dominated a team so much and lost the game." Schembechler said flatly that this was the best Michigan team of his four-year reign. He knew it didn't matter. The Buckeyes were heading to Pasadena.

Ohio State was a 14-point underdog to Southern California in the Rose Bowl, which was mostly a testament to USC's dominance. The Trojans had five All-Americans and had won their eleven games by an average of four touchdowns. USC coach John McKay, who had already won two national championships, said it was the best team he had ever had. Even Hayes agreed with the oddsmakers: "We deserve to be underdogs," he said.

The apparent mismatch would have no bearing on the television audience; the Rose Bowl was an American institution. Between 60 and 70 million people were expected to watch the game on NBC.

As his team warmed up a few minutes before the game, Hayes huddled with his assistant coaches on the sideline. Several photographers were shooting photographs of the coaches, including a fifty-five-year-old from the *Los Angeles Times* named Art Rogers. Hayes was always wary of the press, but he was especially wary at the Rose Bowl, where he had long believed the West Coast media was out to get him. Rogers wanted an artistic photo of Woody—shot from the ground, through an assistant coach's legs. Hayes saw Rogers near his huddle— *in* his huddle, as far as he was concerned—and shoved Rogers's camera into his face.

The shove injured Rogers's right eye; he would have double

vision for several weeks. He stayed in the stadium to shoot photos of the first half, then left. As far as the Buckeyes were concerned, Rogers saw the best part of the game. The halftime score was 7–7, and considering all the hype for USC, this was a major surprise. But the Trojans' McKay was not worried. He knew he had the better team, and in the second half the Trojans proved it. They were unstoppable. By the time the game finally ended, USC had secured a 42–17 victory and the national championship. Hayes later said Southern California had the best team he had ever seen.

As the writers waited for Hayes to address them after the game, the Columbus reporters made a plea to the West Coast guys: Please, fellas, wait until the end of the press conference to ask about the photographer. They worried that as soon as somebody brought up Art Rogers, the Old Man would storm off—and they would be left, once again, without any quotes about the game. The Columbus reporters squeezed in five questions about football. Then the *Los Angeles Times*'s Mal Florence asked Hayes about assaulting Rogers.

Hayes swore, kicked over the microphone stand, and shouted, "If that's all you have to ask me, then forget it! These are big stories for you, aren't they?"

They sure were. Hayes stormed off, but as far as the public was concerned, the Art Rogers incident went into his unofficial personnel file. Hayes was now the guy who tore up the sideline markers and pushed a cameraman at the Rose Bowl.

For some who knew Hayes well, though, there was another, more telling episode on this Rose Bowl trip.

Six days before the game, Hayes and McKay were asked to speak at a Rose Bowl luncheon. Naturally, McKay spoke about his team. When Hayes's turn came, he gave a long, heartfelt eulogy for President Harry S. Truman, who had died that day. He spoke for a half hour without mentioning football. McKay finally walked out. The speech seemed like a filibuster by a paranoid coach to avoid talking about the game. It was not.

On the car ride out of the banquet, Hayes's friend Paul Hornung teased him about the speech. Hayes, the well-known Republican, had glowingly praised a Democrat!

But Woody wasn't amused. When he arrived at practice, he gathered the Buckeyes together and told them about what had happened. He said he couldn't believe that nobody had mentioned that President Truman had died.

And then, for one of the rare times in his career, he started telling his players about his own military experience.

In the summer of 1945, Hayes was captain of the USS *Rinehart*, a two-hundred-sailor U.S. Navy ship. The *Rinehart* was expected to have a major role in the upcoming invasion of Japan—it would help secure the coastline as fighter planes attacked. The *Rinehart* was ill-suited for the job. It had originally been built for convoy duty in the Atlantic Ocean, escorting tankers from one location to another. It did not have particularly large weapons on it: three-inch guns, mostly. Its top speed was around twenty knots, which was fine for convoy duty but not fast enough for combat so close to enemy shores. The *Rinehart* had been refitted for the impending invasion of Japan, but it was still a slow, deliberate vessel.

In truth, the men aboard the *Rinehart*, particularly Captain Wayne Woodrow Hayes, seriously doubted they would survive the mission.

On August 6, 1945, at President Truman's orders, U.S. forces dropped an atomic bomb on Hiroshima, Japan. Three days later, a second atomic bomb was dropped, on Nagasaki. Shortly thereafter, Japan surrendered. As a direct result, the plans for the USS *Rinehart* were scrapped.

Woody Hayes believed that by using such overwhelming force, doing what was necessary and ignoring the inevitable criticism, President Harry Truman had saved his life.

6

Books

And now this Watergate thing comes up," Woody Hayes was saying, "and all of a sudden we've got a president who's got to go and negotiate with all the other world powers from *weakness*. Now this is one thing you never learn to do. This is a *disaster* for America."

It was early afternoon on May 8, 1973, and Hayes was furious. Everybody was attacking his president. The press simply would not let the Watergate incident go, and now millions of people seemed to think President Nixon had done something wrong. Seven men had been convicted in the wake of the Watergate break-in. There were rumblings about a cover-up. Nixon aides H. R. Haldeman and John Ehrlichman had just resigned over the scandal. The Senate Watergate Committee was about to conduct nationally televised hearings.

Hayes had called the White House earlier that day, just to express his confidence in the president. Nixon was in a meeting when Hayes called, but Hayes left a message complimenting him on his visits to the Soviet Union, his establishment of relations with the People's Republic of China, the achievement of peace in Vietnam, and the release of prisoners of war. Nixon had just started his second term a few months earlier—the Ohio State Marching Band again performed at the inauguration—and Woody Hayes had high hopes for the next four years. During his phone call to the White House, Hayes called Nixon "the greatest president in history."

Hayes told anybody who would listen, "Richard Nixon can count on his old friend Woody Hayes." The president deserved that. After Woody came home from that blowout loss in the '73 Rose Bowl, one of the first letters he received was from the president of the United States. President Nixon just wanted to show his support:

Dear Woody:

I have always liked your statement—"show me a good loser and I'll show you a loser." . . . your team has a great deal to be proud of . . . I predict that Ohio State, under your leadership, will be back in the Rose Bowl before too long.

That was loyalty. *That* was what the country needed. Of course, Nixon never mentioned Woody's incident with that West Coast photographer. That was just another one of those deals that was overblown by the press.

"I know just how Nixon feels," Hayes said. The president was just trying to do his job. Why wasn't he allowed to do it? Why didn't people let their leaders lead?

Nixon was only one victim. The Ohio State University was another one. Already in 1973, a court ruled that Ohio State had violated the rights of student Joel Ann Todd Flesch during its crackdown on the 1970 student riots, and the American Association of University Professors had censured the OSU administration for denying due process to a former untenured professor, who had been dismissed in 1968 for burning his draft cards. In August, a U.S. district court would rule that Ohio State's law against campus disruptions was unconstitutional. The university wasn't even allowed to run itself! The culture of mistrust was only getting worse: at the 1973 Ohio State spring commencement, FBI director William Ruckelshaus warned that Watergate was eroding public confidence in government.

"So you see why it makes me bitter when I see this Watergate inflated all out of proportion by you fellas," Hayes continued on this May afternoon. "We're tearing down all our heroes in America. There's just no respect anymore for anything, goddamnit. . . . They've gotten to and destroyed just about every sports figure and general we've ever had."

The rant was typical for Hayes. What was unusual, on this spring afternoon in 1973, was his audience. Hayes was in the hallway outside his office in the Biggs Facility, talking to a twenty-eight-year-old reporter from *Harper's* magazine named Robert Vare. Vare had shown up unannounced, hoping for an interview. As soon as Hayes found out Vare was from *Harper's*, he went off. *Harper's?* Just another one of those eastern liberal rags.

When the Old Man really got going, he was a conversational pinball. He bounced from current politics to ancient Greece to the Ohio State offense before anybody else could get a word in. Vare did not share a single one of Hayes's opinions, but he was fascinated. He had only met one other person whom he found this interesting: Muhammad Ali. Vare tried to spar with Woody a little bit—to be assertive without being threatening. When Vare mentioned that he had been a humanities major, with a specialization in ancient Greek history, Hayes talked about Pericles, Herodotus, and Thucydides.

Vare quickly saw that Hayes wanted to be seen as more than a football coach, and Hayes confirmed the suspicion that afternoon when he said that he was writing a book. It was called *You Win with People!* It would be self-published, just like *Football at Ohio State* in 1957, and *Hot Line to Victory* in 1969. But Hayes needed a professional to look at it, and despite what Hayes thought of Vare's employer, Vare *was* a professional. Hayes asked him to read a chapter.

Vare went back to his hotel and edited chapter 1 thoroughly. Hayes's first two books had basically been football textbooks. But now he wanted to say something more.

You Win with People! was not so consumed with the X's and O's of football, although Hayes recapped his greatest games and shared stories about his coaching career. He wanted to share his philosophy of football, and of life in America, which were pretty much the same philosophy. He believed a man's character and work ethic mattered more than his talent, and it was the heart of his recruiting strategy: he thought that if he brought in the best people—not necessarily the fastest or the strongest—he would win.

When Vare came back to Hayes's office the next day, Hayes thanked him for the help, and suddenly the Old Man had an editor and Vare had more time with the coach than he ever expected. After arriving in Columbus without an appointment, Vare would enjoy almost unfettered access for a month. He would spend his days around Hayes— observing everything, then darting off to the restroom to write up his notes. He realized that even in May, the slowest time of the year for college football coaches, Hayes was in no rush to go home: he would work in the morning and afternoon, take Vare over to the Faculty Club for dinner at around 6 p.m, then head back to the office.

After a while, Hayes seemed to forget that Vare was there as a reporter. When people in the program saw Vare, they didn't flinch: he was the guy helping Woody with his book. By the time Vare went home to New York, he realized he had much more than a feature story. He had a book of his own. He would spend much of the 1973 season around the Buckeyes; his book was scheduled to come out the following year.

Woody Hayes asked his friend Paul Hornung of the *Columbus Dispatch* to write the first chapter of *You Win with People!* ("We have worked closely together for 22 years," Hayes wrote.) Then Hayes took over. He began with the belief that had shaped his coaching career.

"I have a deep and abiding respect for football," he wrote in his first sentence, "for it has paralleled the great achievements of this nation." He went on to write, "Without winners, there can be no civilization, and without heroes, there can be no winning. I can see a conscious or subconscious effort in our country to tear down heroes, and yet I ask what success, what achievement could there have been without heroes?"

Hayes did not understand how citizens could fail to support their own military in a war, their own students in a football game, or their own president at such a crucial time in history. His views were no secret to his staff. By the early 1970s, he was holding 7 a.m. meetings with his offensive coaches to discuss current events—he brought his newspaper, which he had already read, and quizzed the coaches on world affairs. The "right" answer wasn't necessarily the factually correct answer; Hayes expected his coaches to share his opinions too, especially about Watergate and Vietnam. He was, after all, the expert on military strategy. He was the one who had visited the troops in Vietnam four times and raved about the experience. He had befriended Generals Lewis Walt, William Westmoreland, and Creighton Abrams, all of whom had major roles in directing the U.S. Army in Vietnam.

But the famous battles of the past, which Hayes studied at length, mostly featured traditional combat: two sides trying to occupy the same piece of land. In Vietnam, the United States tried to help the South Vietnamese stave off the spread of communism, despite doubts about the commitment, stability, and integrity of the South Vietnamese government. The combat was often nontraditional and unpredictable: guerrilla attacks and ambushes in the jungle.

Woody Hayes either did not understand, or would not accept, that Vietnam was a different kind of war.

After teaching political science to his assistant coaches for a half hour each morning, Hayes would be ready to move on to football. Sometimes he would tell his assistants to diagram something on the blackboard and then he would head to the restroom. When Hayes walked out, the assistant coaches would often sneak out for a little while, which pissed the Old Man off. He thought they were hiding from him.

During that break, assistant coach Ed Ferkany would go off to smoke with the equipment guys. Hayes wrote in *You Win with People!* that none of his assistant coaches smoked. He likely believed that because he wanted to believe it.

In *You Win with People!* Hayes also gave five reasons why his coaches did not get divorced.

1. "The coach is not always underfoot at home, for his are long hours at work."
2. The coach and his mate are "well-adjusted."
3. "The wives have some opportunity of recognition in their husband's profession."

4. "The wife realizes that she has a husband who is happy in his work, and consequently, she is willing to make sacrifices.

5. "Economically, the coach's salary is large enough for him and his family to live comfortably and with dignity. However, it is small enough that certain economic priorities must be set. This sharing and sacrificing within helps to create a good family— or a good football team!"

The Ohio State assistant coaches would roll their eyes. They wanted more money and they would have loved some more time at home. But as long as the Buckeyes were winning as much as any team in the country, the assistants were reluctant to leave.

By keeping salaries low and his demands high, Hayes ensured that only the most dedicated coaches would want to work for him. He was not looking for *happy* assistant coaches. He wanted coaches who outworked their opponents, who stood for something. If football was the best of America, and Ohio State represented the best of football, then the Ohio State coaches had to be some of the finest men in the country. *You win with people!*

How seriously did Hayes take this mantra? In the spring of 1973, a recent Yale graduate named Jeff Kaplan interviewed for graduate assistant coaching positions at both Ohio State and Michigan. Kaplan's coach at Yale, Carm Cozza, had played alongside Schembechler under Hayes at Miami. Cozza set up the interviews.

Kaplan went to Ann Arbor first. Schembechler was friendly and helpful, but at the end of the hourlong interview, he told Kaplan that he only had two graduate-assistant positions and he was going to fill them with guys who had played for him at Michigan. Kaplan understood.

Then Kaplan went down to Columbus, where Hayes also had two graduate-assistant positions open. They chatted extensively, mostly about Yale and Cozza. At the end, Hayes told Kaplan he had already talked to ten people for the job, and every one of them was more qualified than Kaplan.

"But if you apply to law school at Ohio State and get admitted," Hayes said, "I'll hire you."

Kaplan didn't really want to go to law school, but he was dying to coach at a place like Ohio State. He enrolled in the school's College of Law and accepted a job as graduate assistant and academic adviser/brain coach for the football program. On its surface, Hayes's prerequisite for Kaplan was odd. The coach was basically saying that since Kaplan was underqualified, he had to spend a solid forty hours per week working at something other than the football program in order to get hired. But Hayes believed strongly in the value of law school. He had urged dozens of former players to get law degrees and occasionally said he wished he had gotten one himself.

Why law school? Hayes never encouraged anybody to go to business school. He held medical school in high regard, but he never pushed anybody into that, either. Law school was different. Laws meant order. They kept the United States anchored where it needed to be. The hippies and liberals were all too happy to break the law—they didn't understand that the law was the very foundation of the United States of America. It was bad enough that so many longhairs were flouting laws; even worse, some of them were *creating* laws. In *You Win with People!* Hayes wrote incredulously, "The town council at one Big Ten University has passed a law that pot smoking is punishable with merely a $5.00 fine and quite often the $5.00 is not collected." The town, of course, was Ann Arbor.

"How do you tell them about pot when you never smoked it?" Bo Schembechler asked. "I'm not naïve. Any coach who believes drugs are not a problem is putting his head in the sand. I think almost every youngster in college has tried some sort of drug, just out of curiosity if nothing else."

Schembechler was talking to Joe Falls, a popular sports columnist for the *Detroit Free Press*. Schembechler made it clear to Falls (and his players) that he disapproved of marijuana use. He just wasn't sure how to address the issue, and the last thing he wanted to do was preach to reporters.

So why was Schembechler talking to Falls at all? He had no choice. He had agreed to write a book with him.

Falls had come up with the idea for *Bo Schembechler: Man in Motion* in the fall of 1972. He wanted to write about Schembechler's recovery from a heart attack and his rise as the hottest young coach in the country. Falls knew that Schembechler probably wouldn't cooperate, so one afternoon in the Michigan Stadium press box, he enlisted the help of the one man who could convince Bo: Don Canham.

Canham loved the idea. As with so many Canham-endorsed projects, the book had multiple benefits. Obviously, it would provide free publicity for the program. It would also give Schembechler a little extra money without raising his salary. Although he was a millionaire, Canham was still a child of the Depression, and he was notoriously cheap. He closely monitored every aspect of his department's budget and was stingy with salaries. Getting extra cash for his coach without paying it himself—well, that was Don Canham's kind of business plan.

Schembechler couldn't understand why anybody would want to read a book he had written, but Canham talked him into it. Canham was still fighting Michigan State for attention in the Detroit media market—WJR, the biggest, most powerful radio station in the state, carried Michigan State games instead of Michigan's. Now Detroit's most popular sports columnist was working *with* the Michigan football coach.

While Schembechler tried to keep reporters at a distance, for fear they would disrupt his team, Canham wanted to bring reporters closer, out of a hope that they would boost his department. It helped that Canham genuinely enjoyed the company of reporters and had been friendly with many Michigan media types since his days as the school's track coach. When *Detroit News* columnist Pete Waldmeir was going through a divorce in the early 1970s, he stayed on Canham's boat at the Grosse Pointe Yacht Club for three weeks.

The athletic director's old company, School-Tech, published the book. Falls tried to get the same kind of access from Schembechler that Robert Vare got from Woody Hayes. But Schembechler had built a reputation for shutting out the media. He kept a file on individual writers—if a guy wrote something Schembechler didn't like, Schembechler would stop talking to him. For a while, he had even shut out all of *Sports Illustrated*, which was merely the most important and influential sports publication in the country. The night before home games, Michigan held press "smokers," or cocktail parties; Schembechler attended the smokers his first season, then stopped going.

Falls asked Schembechler why he didn't do more to help reporters.

"I can give you something every day," Schembechler replied. "All I have to do is act like Woody Hayes. You'll have something to write. But that's not my way."

Schembechler gave Falls a window into his program, but it was a very small window.

"I don't know how much a football coach can do to help the young people," Schembechler told Falls, "but I have one policy here and it is that although I help the players as much as I can, the most important people in my program are assistant coaches."

Eventually Schembechler decided he'd had enough. He told Falls he was finished working on the book. Falls scrambled to interview other Michigan employees; he even reprinted several of his own *Free Press* columns in the book. While Woody Hayes wrote and published his book himself, Schembechler never really wavered from his initial aversion.

Why would anybody want to read a book by Bo Schembechler? Years later, he would say even *he* never read *Bo Schembechler: Man in Motion*.

"No man can write anything," Emerson wrote, "who does not think that what he writes is for the time the history of the world."

All Bo Schembechler wanted to do was coach, and with a team like this, who could blame him? The 1973 Michigan Wolverines won their first ten games by an average of 26.2 points, and the margin wasn't inflated by a couple of lopsided results, either. They won every game by at least two touchdowns and never trailed in the fourth quarter.

The Wolverines were so good that they sucked the suspense out of every game. Against Indiana, for example, Michigan took a 42–0 lead, then went into the locker room for halftime. In the interest of sportsmanship, Schembechler rested his starters for the entire second half, but he wasn't happy about it. "I'm not sure our guys got a lot out of it," he said. "That really hurts the momentum of any football team."

Quarterback Dennis Franklin, in his second year as starter, had turned into one of the most lethal weapons in school history. The Michigan offensive line was as skilled as any in the country, and the defense simply overwhelmed opponents.

Football experts knew there was a method to the domination. In 1973, Dan Dierdorf was a dominant offensive lineman for the NFL's St. Louis Cardinals—often blocking for former Buckeye Jim Otis. The Cardinals had an exceptional coaching staff: Don Coryell had just taken over as head coach, future Hall of Famer Joe Gibbs coached the running backs, and Jim Hanifan, who would gain a reputation as one of the greatest offensive line coaches in history, was Dierdorf's position coach. Early in training camp that year, Hanifan marveled at Dierdorf's blocking technique and pulled him aside.

"Where did you learn how to block like that?" Hanifan asked.

Dierdorf said his offensive line coach at Michigan, Jerry Hanlon, had taught him. At the end of that season, Jim Hanifan would make a trip to Ann Arbor to meet with Hanlon.

Jim Hanifan visited a very different campus than the one Dierdorf had left. Just three years earlier, Dierdorf had refused to wear his letter jacket on campus because he didn't want other students to know he played football. By 1973, it was cool to be a football player again. Even placekicker Mike Lantry—a Vietnam veteran who was wary of how his fellow students would treat him—proudly wore his letter jacket to class.

The hippie movement was receding, but the hippie culture was becoming more prevalent. When Schembechler arrived in Ann Arbor, long hair, bell-bottoms, and pot-smoking were all seen, to varying degrees, as political statements. Now they were just part of being a student at Michigan.

Schembechler still kept a military-style regimen for his team—players wore blazers and ties to and from the games, and punctuality was mandatory—but he had to make some concessions. Although he hated when players grew their hair long, he never did anything about it. And he couldn't control what his players did off the field, so they did what other students did: pretty much anything they wanted.

One time, a few players stole a drink vending machine out of a dorm and put it in their room. They had no reason. They were just tired of walking down the hallway to get a drink. The Wolverines would plug the drains in their team's shower room with towels, fill the room with four inches of water, and start playing some kind of "water rugby"—somebody's hat would be the "ball" and the radiators were the "goals."

If they wanted to drink some beers, they went down to Fraser's Pub on Packard Road, east of campus. If they wanted some food with their beer, they went to the Village Bell downtown. If they wanted to dance and get high, they went to a place called The Scene on Main Street. The Scene had a lighted dance floor and played loud music, everything to amplify the senses—not that the senses needed amplifying. A lot of customers were stoned when they showed up. Pot, hashish, Quaaludes, and harder drugs were readily available to any student who wanted them. Most Michigan players experimented with pot, some more frequently than others.

Schembechler was aware of the drug use and worried about it. But he kept coming back to the same question: "How do you tell them about pot when you never smoked it?"

"The players know I've never taken any drugs," Schembechler told Falls. "They know I really don't know what I'm talking about because I never tried them myself. Damnit, that bothers me."

At least the partying did not hamper Michigan's performance. By the second half of almost every game, all lifelong Michigan football fans could relax.

Well, almost all.

From her seat in Michigan Stadium, where she had been attending games since she was a child, Linda Lantry was always nervous for her husband, Mike. She couldn't help it. Linda knew that placekicking required a precise combination of snapping, holding, blocking, and kicking, but it didn't look that way from the stands. Mike just seemed so *alone* out there.

Linda also had a tough time following the trajectory of the ball. Mike kicked it so damn high—sometimes the ball went over the top of the upright. Linda, sitting with the other players' families behind the Michigan bench, could not always tell if a kick was good or wide. She had to watch the officials.

In most games Mike Lantry's field goals were (literally) a footnote. Michigan was going to win no matter what Lantry did. For the rest of the Big Ten, the worst part of playing the Wolverines was not the beatings. No, the worst part was that Michigan appeared to be only the second-best team in the conference.

It looked like President Nixon was right: Ohio State would "be back in the Rose Bowl before too long." The Buckeyes played nine games before facing Michigan, and they won each one by at least 24 points. The scores looked like a series of misprints: 56–7 . . . 37–3 . . . 27–3. In one five-game stretch, Ohio State whipped Wisconsin, Indiana, Northwestern, Illinois, and Michigan State by a combined score of 186–7. Woody Hayes's team seemed impervious to injury. When star fullback Champ Henson blew out his knee, Bruce Elia stepped in and led the Big Ten in scoring.

Sometimes the Buckeyes' opponent would think it had done pretty well, all things considered. Hey, Indiana lost by only 30 points. Not bad, under the circumstances. But what the Hoosiers didn't realize is that the Buckeyes had barely prepared for them. The Old Man would spend the first three days of the week gearing his offense up for That School Up North. He wouldn't even tell his guys what kind of defenses Indiana ran until Thursday.

The Buckeyes carried that confidence to game day. Offensive tackle John Hicks, maybe the most dominating player in the whole country, would look across the line of scrimmage before getting into his stance and tell some poor defensive lineman, "We're coming your way." Then Hicks would plow through the guy and Archie Griffin would pick up six yards.

This was Hayes's best team since that 1969 Team of the Century—the one that blew the national title in Ann Arbor with those goddamn interceptions. Like the 1969 squad, these Buckeyes excelled at Hayes's goal-line package, the six plays known as Patton One through Patton Six. But the 1973 Buckeyes were a much different group. The 1969 team had been embodied by Rex Kern, the tough, straight-arrow quarterback from central Ohio. The 1973 team was embodied by the new quarterback, Cornelius Greene, an electrifying runner from inner-city Washington, D.C.

Greene's friends in D.C. had told him Ohio State would never play a black quarterback. Certainly nobody expected him to get the job in 1973. Greg Hare had expertly quarterbacked the Buckeyes to the 1972 Big Ten title and was now a senior co-captain. Yet Hayes held a rigorous competition between Hare and Greene. The two split duties in fall practice until Hare suffered an injury, at which time Greene took the reins and never let go.

Hayes never told Greene he had won the job. Greene found out from a newspaper. Reporters repeatedly referred to him as "Ohio State's first black quarterback" and no doubt meant it as a positive development, but Greene wanted to shed the label. The writers soon moved on, but others did not: Greene received plenty of hate mail that fall. He tore it all up, but he noticed that his roommate Archie Griffin barely received hate mail at all. The message was clear: running backs were expected to be black, but quarterback was a white man's job.

Greene's blackness went beyond his skin color. Griffin, born and raised in conservative Columbus, typified his city, but Greene was a product of black culture. He had starred at Dunbar High School in Washington; Dunbar had been an elite public school in the 1950s, but by the time Greene arrived, it was a run-down city school. The football field was more dirt than grass. Greene was low-key, polite, and street smart. He once told *Washington Post* photographer Dick Darcey that anytime Darcey came to Dunbar, Greene would have his boys make sure nobody stole his hubcaps.

But on the field, Greene was unlike anybody Ohio State had ever recruited. In high school, he painted his shoes red so his uncle (who didn't really understand football) could find him easily. Greene had unbelievable ball skills. He would fake a handoff and keep the ball on his hip, and by the time the defense figured out what had happened, he was long gone. And that was a sight, too: Greene and his Dunbar teammates attached tassels to their game pants (around the knee) so the tassels would shake when they ran.

He was "the flamboyant flim-flam man," wrote *Washington Post* sportswriter Leonard Shapiro, and soon everybody was calling him Flam. Greene even wrote the nickname on a piece of tape and stuck it on the front of his helmet:

FLAMBOYANT.

Flam celebrated his first touchdown at Ohio State by dancing in the end zone. Woody Hayes's Buckeyes *never* danced in the end zone. But what could Hayes do? If he insisted that Flam act like Rex Kern, would the players say the Old Man was out of touch? Or worse: would they say he didn't understand black players?

Before Flam's second game, against Texas Christian University, Hayes enlarged the TCU team picture and held it up in front of his team. "Does anybody know why we're going to win this game?" he asked. A couple of Buckeyes said Ohio State had better coaches. Two or three more said Ohio State simply had a better team.

Hayes looked at the TCU team picture and gave his answer.

"They don't have enough black players," he said.

To make his point, he would tell his guys that Duke Ellington needed both the black and white keys to play the piano.

In *You Win with People!* Hayes wrote, "Almost every smoker becomes an automatic pusher either to get someone else to try it and often later to sell it." In fact, it was tough to know just who was smoking pot. Once, when the team was staying at Stradley Hall for preseason practices, an assistant coach thought he smelled marijuana on the freshman floor, so he asked straight-arrow lineman Kurt Schumacher if any of the freshmen were smoking marijuana.

"Coach, you gotta be kidding me," Schumacher said. "You can't think anybody is doing that." Schumacher told one of his teammates what the coach had said, and the teammate nervously asked, "What did you tell him?" Schumacher realized how naïve he had been.

For two decades, Woody Hayes had seen his program as a model for the rest of society, a counter to the counterculture. But now the counterculture was simply the campus culture, and it was not remotely political. Ohio State had never been a haven for radicals, but now there was hardly even a hint of activism. The new rage was streaking: students would run naked across the Oval or into Mirror Lake, just for the hell of it.

University president Harold Enarson told a gathering of donors that "student interests have shifted from the writings of Che Guevara to that best seller, *The Exorcist*, from the waving of placards to the tossing of Frisbees, from frantic rallies to private pursuits (boy of girl and girl of boy), from fascination with hard drugs to rediscovery of the drug of their parents—alcohol. No more is heard of Vietnam, ecology, Earth Week, or the plight of the Third World."

On those occasions when students *did* push for a change, the university was inclined to comply without a fight. In 1973, the Ohio State Marching Band admitted women for the first time. So did the Ohio Staters, a leading student organization. The school started to permit beer in student rooms and apartments.

Woody Hayes knew that if the university changed, he would have to try to change too. He got rid of his ban on facial hair. Sideburns grew long and afros sprouted. Hayes also let his players live off campus for the first time.

It seemed like the Old Man was adapting to the times. But was he really? Hayes didn't like either of his new policies. He wanted his players to be clean-cut, and he really wanted them in the dorms, where they didn't have to worry about paying bills, could easily get balanced meals at the cafeteria, and could mix with the rest of the student body. He railed against the new campus culture. "These days everybody wants to do their own thing," he would tell his players. "*Fuck* doing your own thing."

On the scoreboard, these 1973 Buckeyes might have looked like the 1968 and 1969 teams. Hayes knew better. One time, in a story the players would later recall with pride, Hayes sat down with equipment manager John Bozick, a longtime confidant, and told him that his players were crazy. He couldn't control them.

Then the Old Man perked up and said:

"But goddamn can they play football."

One night Woody Hayes was visiting some Buckeyes in their dorm as they watched the Dallas Cowboys play on *Monday Night Football.* One of the announcers mentioned Cowboys receiver Drew Pearson, and Hayes went into a lecture about that Drew Pearson bastard . . . well, not *that* Drew Pearson bastard. The mention of Pearson reminded Hayes of the famous newspaper columnist of the same name.

The journalist Drew Pearson had opposed the Vietnam War and been critical of the military. In one of his most famous scoops, in 1943, Pearson reported that U.S. Army general George S. Patton Jr. had accused two soldiers of cowardice and slapped them. The report made international news, and Patton, Woody Hayes's hero, was relieved of his command of the Seventh Army.

On November 17, President Nixon held an hourlong question-and-answer session with four hundred Associated Press managing editors in Orlando, Florida. The session was televised. Most of the questions were about Watergate, but Nixon was also accused of illegally profiting from public service. In response to one question about what he would do when he left office, Nixon quipped that it depended on when he left. Ultimately, the session would be remembered for Nixon's five-word defense of his character: "I am not a crook."

While the president was under siege, his old friend Woody Hayes was riding high. Hayes's team whipped Iowa 55–13 that day to keep the No. 1 ranking in the country for the eighth consecutive week. The Buckeyes were undefeated heading to their season-ending game against That School Up North. The hype had been building for weeks.

After each Michigan or Ohio State win, the losing coach was asked to compare the two powerhouses, like a boxer who had been knocked out by both the champion and the leading contender.

"It is almost as if they were both stamped out of the same machine," Indiana coach Lee Corso said after losing to Michigan.

And whom would Corso pick in the season-ending showdown? He hesitated.

"I predict that it will be decided in the fourth quarter on the kicking game," he said.

In the first sixty-eight editions of their rivalry, Michigan and Ohio State had never met when both were undefeated. Now it would happen for the second time in four years. Every aspect of the game seemed to make it bigger. Ohio State was ranked No. 1 and Michigan was ranked No. 4. Schembechler and Hayes had each won two games against each other, so the winner would get bragging rights. The teams had outscored their opponents by a combined score of 146–0 in the first quarter.

Ohio State was third in the nation in scoring and first in scoring defense. Would such a dominant team actually lose? It seemed impossible. But Michigan had not lost in Ann Arbor in four years.

The last time the teams were undefeated entering the game, in 1970, Michigan was ineligible for the Rose Bowl because it had gone the year before. The Big Ten had since repealed its no-repeat rule—but unlike other major conferences, it still barred its teams from any other bowl. And this time the Big Ten winner would be the clear favorite in the Rose Bowl against either Southern California or UCLA.

To both the Wolverines and Buckeyes, the conclusion was obvious: the loser of their game would stay home and watch the winner capture the national championship.

The day before the game, best-selling author James Michener visited Don Canham. Michener was working on a book about the evolving world of American sports, and naturally, he wanted to talk to the most successful athletic director in the country.

While some Big Ten schools were experiencing a decline in ticket sales, Canham's team was leading the nation in attendance—and he kept building his customer base. Canham had been running an advertisement in national magazines that read "How To Mix Business With Pleasure . . . Try Michigan Football." College games were considered community events, but Canham thought he could convince businessmen to entertain clients at Michigan football games. With every success, he gained more influence on college sports. That fall, he helped quash attempts to form a "super-conference" of all the top football programs in the country.

Canham marketed everything but Michigan's success, because he knew he couldn't control that. Yet he knew that Schembechler's wins had played a huge part in the building of Michigan's burgeoning athletic empire. The two men had a reciprocal relationship: Schembechler won, so Canham provided him with better facilities and a bigger recruiting budget, which helped Schembechler win more. When Schembechler wanted a state-of-the-art weight machine that the Cleveland Browns were using, Canham didn't blink at the $13,000 price tag.

But on Saturday afternoons in the fall, Canham was back where he started: he still couldn't influence the outcome on the field.

"I'm so excited about this damned game," he told Michener. "I don't think I'll be able to stay and watch it."

Canham was serious. He often left Michigan Stadium before half-time. He would get to the press box several hours before the game, schmooze with reporters and administrators, make sure everything was in order, check with the vendors to see what was selling—and then, while everybody else watched the game, he would walk out, hop in his car, and drive ninety minutes to his vacation home on Harsens Island on Lake St. Clair, northeast of Detroit.

He had a room at the Harsens Island retreat where he would paint with oils. Canham would often create street or nature scenes—bright, colorful paintings, which were even more impressive because Canham was color-blind. He never asked anybody if he had the blues and greens right, just as he dismissed his wife or kids when they told him his clothes didn't quite match. Don Canham never worried about his vision.

He *did* worry about football games. There was no immediate financial incentive to winning—Big Ten schools split the Rose Bowl revenue evenly—but Canham was always looking two steps ahead of everybody else. The winner of this Michigan–Ohio State game would get free publicity for two weeks at the Rose Bowl, including three hours on national television on game day, with much of the country watching. The loser wouldn't go to *any* bowl game.

"Is television that important?" Michener asked.

"It's everything," Canham said. "Ohio State went out last year. Woody Hayes was all over the screen, pre-game, middle of the game, post-game. Very quiet. Very gentlemanly. Saying all the right things. I could visualize families in every small town telling their boys, 'That's the kind of coach you ought to have, son.' . . . If we don't win tomorrow and get Bo Schembechler on national TV, we're in trouble.

"We've got to win. We've simply got to win."

The Ohio State Buckeyes were determined to disrupt all of Michigan's plans—even the ceremonial. Before every game at Michigan Stadium, the Wolverines ran out from the stadium tunnel and under a huge banner with "GO BLUE" written on it. But the Buckeyes, as the visiting team, ran onto the field first, and led by offensive tackle John Hicks, they went straight for the banner. They yanked it down and jumped around in celebration, as though they had captured the enemy's flag. It was the kind of stunt the 1969 team never would have tried, out of fear of the Old Man. For the shaggy-haired, off-campus-living 1973 Buckeyes, it was instinctive. Nobody even knew why it happened. They just wanted to do it, so they did.

Not to be outdone, the Wolverines sprinted out of the tunnel and veered right, so they could jump up and down in front of the Buckeyes, as if to announce that they were not intimidated one bit. The Michigan players then ran under the "GO BLUE" banner, and finally, after a season of buildup, the most hyped game in Michigan–Ohio State history could begin.

From the beginning, it was clear that the defenses would dominate. Ohio State ran on three straight downs and punted. The Wolverines were even less successful—they got the ball and fumbled on second down. Then the Buckeyes ran three more times and punted again. Nobody could score. At the end of the first quarter, Michigan had five first downs and Ohio State, which had averaged an astounding 372 rushing yards against the rest of its schedule, did not have any. That, however, was about to change.

On the first play of the second quarter, Archie Griffin ran for 38 yards. The Buckeyes' ground machine was starting to crank up. Griffin ran again. Then Bruce Elia ran. Then Griffin again. Then Elia. Then Griffin. The Buckeyes made it all the way to the Michigan 21-yard line without throwing a single pass, which was just how Woody Hayes wanted it. Cornelius Greene had injured his thumb the week before, and though the swelling had gone down by the end of the week, the Old Man did not want to take any chances. He did not want to pass, period.

But now it was third and long, an obvious passing situation. Greene dropped back to pass for the first time all day. Nobody was open. Flam scrambled down to the Michigan 14, short of the first down, and Ohio State had to settle for a field goal.

Later in the quarter, the Buckeyes got the ball on their own 45-yard line, and Griffin and that dominating line took over. Six yards, eight yards, seven, fourteen. Finally, fullback Pete Johnson punched it into the end zone.

As the Ohio State Marching Band took the field to play "Jesus Christ Superstar" at halftime, the Buckeyes led 10–0.

In the Michigan locker room, Bo Schembechler told his players not to worry. They were going to play well in the second half, and they were going to win. It was one of those coaching moves that made Schembechler such an effective leader. He knew that yelling at his players would only convince them the 10–0 deficit was insurmountable. They needed confidence, and he supplied it.

Meanwhile, over in the Ohio State locker room, the Buckeye coaches were thrilled. They had prepared for this moment all year long. They had worked on the game plan since the spring: Griffin would run off-tackle, usually to the right side, behind John Hicks. Then, once that play had been established and a Michigan safety started creeping up toward the line of scrimmage, Greene would fake the handoff to Griffin, then roll out and pass.

With the Wolverines stacking the line, an Ohio State receiver would be open downfield almost every time—and since the Buckeyes had practiced this all year, they were sure they could hold their blocks long enough for Greene to release the ball. They even had a play where Griffin would fake a run, then throw a halfback pass.

The Ohio State assistant coaches were confident, even giddy. After a year of preparation, they just had to complete one big pass to defeat That School Up North. Just throw downfield and—

"Bullshit," Woody Hayes said.

What?

Hayes said the Buckeyes would not pass. They would run the ball between the tackles and avoid turnovers. They had a 10–0 lead and a dominating defense and didn't need to risk any passes, especially by a first-year quarterback with an injured thumb.

The coaches were stunned. Run it inside? What? What happened to the game plan? Didn't the Old Man understand that Schembechler's defense would adjust? The Buckeyes *had* to throw—not a lot, but at least a few times, to keep Michigan's defense honest.

Hadn't they worked all spring and summer on this?

"We are reformers in spring and summer," Emerson wrote. "In autumn and winter we stand by the old."

The assistants were furious. Ralph Staub, the offensive coordinator, and George Chaump, the quarterbacks coach, tried desperately to convince Hayes to stick to the game plan, but as with so many arguments with Hayes, this one was over as soon as he uttered that one word: *bullshit*. Griffin had carried 17 times for 101 yards in the first half. The Buckeyes would ride him the rest of the way.

Michigan opened the second half by driving all the way down to the Ohio State 32. But then Franklin tried to hit receiver Larry Johnson in the end zone; the pass was intercepted, and you could almost hear the Old Man scolding his protégé: *Do you see what happens when you pass?*

Hayes was not going to risk it. Staub, the offensive coordinator, tried calling plays, but Hayes overruled him and sent in his own. The Buckeyes' next drive sounded like a military chant: Archie left, Archie left, Archie right, Archie right, Archie left. On that last play, a third-and-five, Ohio State didn't even fake an interest in passing. The Buckeyes lined up with a single receiver. Michigan stacked nine defenders on the line of scrimmage. Griffin gained only one yard and walked off with a slight limp.

Schembechler mostly kept the ball on the ground, too, but he mixed in a few passes, and he at least had some variety to his running plays. Sometimes Franklin would hand to fullback Ed Shuttlesworth, who would burst through the line; sometimes Franklin would pitch to Gil Chapman; and sometimes he would run the option. With that approach, Michigan rumbled deep into Ohio State territory, where Mike Lantry had a chance at a 30-yard field goal.

The snap was poor. But holder Larry Gustafson somehow caught the ball and got it down before Lantry's foot arrived. The field goal was good. Less than a minute into the fourth quarter, the score was Ohio State 10, Michigan 3.

Would Hayes let Greene pass now? No chance. The Buckeyes ran the ball three straight times and punted.

The Wolverines had the ball on their own 49. They had plenty of time for a long, ground-oriented drive, and it started off that way, with a five-yard run by Shuttlesworth. But then Schembechler mixed it up. Franklin faked a handoff and threw 27 yards to Paul Seal. Michigan quickly moved inside the Ohio State 20-yard line. Then Shuttlesworth powered his way for five yards, then for two more. Then two more again.

It was fourth and inches. Schembechler had a chance to make up for the 1972 goal-line stands, to pound the ball down Ohio State's throats, to show the Old Man who had the toughest team in the Big Ten.

Everybody in Michigan Stadium expected a quarterback sneak or a fullback dive. Franklin took the snap, turned, and reached out toward his big fullback, Shuttlesworth. The Buckeyes collapsed on Shuttlesworth. But he didn't have the ball. Franklin had kept it. Franklin spun right and sprinted straight for a touchdown—he got through the line so cleanly, he high-stepped into the end zone, his arms in the air in exultation, a year's worth of frustration lifted off his shoulders. *Only the good ones!*

Mike Lantry kicked the extra point. With less than ten minutes remaining, the score was tied 10–10, forcing everybody to ask the question:

What if nobody wins?

If the game ended in a tie—and the teams therefore tied for the Big Ten championship—the conference's athletic directors would vote on who went to the Rose Bowl. But Michigan was considered a lock to win that vote—Ohio State had gone the year before, and even though the Big Ten had repealed its no-repeat rule, the spirit remained. Besides, Michigan needed only a 5–5 split to earn the bid. Ohio State would need six votes because the Buckeyes had gone to the Rose Bowl the year before.

Now the Buckeyes had to pass . . . didn't they? *Bullshit.* Hayes stuck with his game plan: Archie, Archie, Archie, Archie—four carries for 29 yards. On the last carry, Griffin's twenty-ninth of the game, he got up slowly. Elmer Lippert replaced him. Even then, Hayes did not waver—Lippert carried on the next two downs. Then Griffin reentered the game on third down and five. Griffin gained three yards. The Buckeyes still had not thrown a pass. They punted.

For the second straight year, Schembechler had a chance to go for a tie and near-certain Rose Bowl bid. And for the second straight year, he went for the win. Michigan was backed up on its own 11-yard line, but Schembechler didn't care. He called for two passes on the first four plays. Pretty soon the Wolverines were on their own 44-yard line.

Schembechler called for another pass.

As Franklin dropped back, most of the 105,000 sets of eyes in Michigan Stadium were watching him and his receivers. But Schembechler was still an offensive lineman at heart; he rarely took his eyes away from the line for long.

And so he surely noticed that Michigan center Dennis Franks tried to block Ohio State's noseguard instead of executing his assignment, which was to block a defensive tackle . . . which forced Michigan's left guard, Mike Hoban, to turn and try to block the noseguard . . . which forced Michigan's left tackle, Curtis Tucker, to try to pick up Hoban's assignment, instead of blocking Ohio State defensive end Van DeCree. All this switching was almost impossible to do on the fly, and now it was an old offensive line coach's worst nightmare. It was a jailbreak.

Franklin nimbly avoided the first Buckeye to get to him. He stepped to his right and managed to throw a pass to fullback Ed Shuttlesworth just as DeCree drilled him.

By the time Shuttlesworth caught the pass, Franklin's season was over. DeCree had broken the quarterback's collarbone.

The Wolverines did not have time to worry about their quarterback. There were barely two minutes left to play. Larry Cipa replaced Franklin. Schembechler called for two consecutive running plays, which brought moderate gains. That set up fourth down on the Ohio State 41, and a chance for junior placekicker Mike Lantry to kick arguably the most memorable field goal in college football history: 58 yards, likely to decide the game between two legendary rivals, both undefeated, with the national championship on the line.

Nobody in the history of either school had ever converted on such a long field goal attempt. Yet Schembechler knew that Lantry had the leg to do it. Earlier in the year, Lantry had connected from 50 and 51 yards against Stanford.

The ball was lined up even with the left upright. Soccer-style place-kicking, where the kicker attacks the ball from an angle, was becoming more popular, but Lantry was a straight-ahead kicker: he stood directly behind the ball and waited for the snap. One could have drawn an imaginary line from Lantry to the holder's hands to the center to the left upright.

Under this kind of pressure, would Lantry be able to kick it so far?

The answer came as soon as Lantry kicked the ball: absolutely. There was no doubt it was high enough and long enough. Incredibly, on a 58-yard field goal attempt, he had several yards to spare.

But was it straight enough?

On a cool, breezy November day like this, it was hard to know which way the wind blew. Sometimes it swirled.

The ball started straight down that imaginary line, from Lantry over the center and toward that left upright . . . then it curled slightly to the center of the field, clearly inside the upright . . . if the football would just stay between the uprights, Mike Lantry would finally be greeted as a hero, three years after returning from the most unpopular war in U.S. history . . .

Finally, at the last moment, a gust of wind blew the ball back the other way.

Wide left.

The score remained tied, 10–10.

Now Ohio State had to pass for the first time all day. The Old Man had no choice. Hayes sent Greg Hare, his best passing quarterback, in to replace Greene, even though Hare had not played all day. Hare threw his first pass into coverage. Michigan's Tom Drake intercepted it. With 52 seconds left, Michigan had the ball on the Ohio State 33.

That is when Schembechler made a tactical mistake. After Gil Chapman ran for five yards on first down, Schembechler had Cipa throw out of bounds to stop the clock. Then Schembechler sent Lantry out to try a 44-yard field goal. But it was only third down, and there were 28 seconds left—Schembechler could have called at least one extra running play instead of having Cipa throw out of bounds, both to give Lantry a shorter field goal try and to kill the rest of the time on the clock.

Lantry was determined not to miss wide left again. Maybe he overcompensated. This one went wide to the right. The score was still tied, 10–10.

Hare chucked a desperation pass that had the makings of a miracle. It flew 46 yards in the air, bounced off at least three players (including two Buckeyes), and finally came to rest on the back of Ohio State's Brian Baschnagel, without hitting the ground. It was a live ball for anybody to grab. Finally it rolled to the turf, incomplete.

Hare threw one more pass. It too fell incomplete.

The most hyped game in Michigan–Ohio State history had ended in a stalemate, and nobody knew what to make of it. A few children ran onto the field. Other than that, the crowd sat in relative silence.

This much was certain: Michigan was going to the Rose Bowl, and Ohio State was going home. Everybody could see that. Michigan would benefit from the spirit of the no-repeat rule and the fact that the Wolverines had outgained Ohio State.

The Buckeyes needed the support of six Big Ten athletic directors. Five of those—Michigan's Canham, Michigan State's Bert Smith, Wisconsin's Elroy "Crazy Legs" Hirsch, Iowa's Bump Elliott, and Indiana's Bill Orwig—had either played or coached at Michigan.

Ohio State safety Steve Luke was too mad to ask how Franklin, his childhood friend, was feeling. As Ohio State senior guard Jim Kregel walked off the field, he found his brother Mike, a Vietnam vet, in the stands. Jim always felt guilty that he got to play football before an adoring city while Mike was off fighting a war that didn't make any sense to him. So Jim handed Mike a keepsake: the jersey and helmet from the final game of his college career.

On his way out of Michigan Stadium, Hayes took a swat at a photographer. He missed.

When reporters asked Hayes why his team had not passed more, he told them, "Our passing is not good. It hasn't been good all year." Then why call those passes at the end? "We knew we had to win this one to go," Hayes said.

Hayes asked reporters how Dennis Franklin was doing, and when he was told that Franklin had broken his collarbone, he replied, "Oh, for God's sake. That is a shame, a dirty shame. That will keep him out of the Rose Bowl."

Concern for Franklin was so widespread that when Big Ten commissioner Wayne Duke arrived at Detroit Metro Airport to fly home after the game, he called back to the Michigan Stadium press box to see how the quarterback was doing.

Schembechler felt so good about his team's performance that he told reporters he would vote his team No. 1 in the country in the coaches' poll—after all, the Buckeyes had been No. 1, and Michigan had outplayed them.

That night, Schembechler hosted a party at his house, and although it had been planned before the game, it quickly took on the feel of a victory party. Schembechler was thrilled and relaxed. His team was going to its third Rose Bowl in five years. The next morning, the *Ann Arbor News* splashed a big headline across the top of page A1: "It Smells Like Roses!"

On Sunday morning, Hayes visited Riverside and University hospitals in Columbus. Hospital visits were part of his routine, but this time he wasn't just making his rounds. Ohio State trainer Alan Hart was undergoing cancer treatment at Riverside. When Hayes got off the elevator, a nurse told him Hart had just died, at age thirty-seven. The news at University was not as grim but still wasn't good: punter Tom Skladany had broken his foot against Michigan.

Meanwhile, up in Ann Arbor, Bo Schembechler was still flying high. Michigan sports information director Will Perry picked up Schembechler in his station wagon to drive to Detroit, where Schembechler was scheduled to tape his weekly television show. The athletic directors' vote was due to be released any minute, but Schembechler didn't even turn the radio on. He was too busy planning for the Rose Bowl. This time it would be different, he promised Perry. He would not treat the Rose Bowl practices like a second training camp. He would make sure his players were fresh and healthy when they played Southern California. They would go out there and win the game.

When Schembechler and Perry arrived at the WWJ television studio in downtown Detroit, they were surprised to find a group of reporters and cameramen waiting. Bill Halls of the *Detroit News* was the first to reach Schembechler.

"Have you heard the vote?" Halls asked.

"No," Schembechler said with a smile. "How'd it go?"

"Ohio State," Halls said.

If Bo Schembechler had any experience to draw upon, it came from Woody Hayes. In 1961, when Schembechler was an Ohio State assistant coach, he and Hayes were in Cleveland for an alumni banquet when they found out that the Ohio State administration had voted to decline a Rose Bowl bid. The administration feared that Buckeyes football was becoming too big and was detracting from the school's academic mission. Ohio State students were furious and began to protest. Hayes was furious, too. But he didn't want any protest.

"I don't agree with those 28 'no' votes," Hayes said then, as Schembechler watched, "but I respect the integrity of the men who cast them, if not their intelligence. I would not want football to drive a line of cleavage in our university. Football is not worth that." The protests soon died down. If the fiery head coach was willing to accept the decision, how could anybody else object?

Yes, Bo Schembechler could have copied the Old Man if he wanted. But he was in no mood for peacemaking. His team, easily one of the top five in the country, was now shut out of the bowl season entirely. Schembechler had promised his players that if they did what he asked, they would win the Big Ten and go to the Rose Bowl. They had lived up to their end. Now the Big Ten was taking away their reward.

Ohio State had won the vote 6–4. Athletic directors from Michigan, Iowa, Minnesota, and Indiana voted for Michigan. Wisconsin's Elroy Hirsch and Michigan State's Bert Smith had both voted against Michigan, their alma mater, and ADs from Purdue, Illinois, Northwestern, and of course Ohio State had voted for the Buckeyes.

Almost immediately, there was speculation that some athletic directors had voted out of resentment for Canham. Northwestern was still bitter that Canham had killed its stadium lease for the Chicago Bears. Schembechler referred to "petty jealousies." But mostly it seemed like the athletic directors had simply voted for the team with a healthy quarterback. Illinois athletic director Cecil Coleman said he would have voted for Michigan if not for Franklin's injury. Michigan State's Smith acknowledged he hadn't watched the Michigan–Ohio State game and said "it's only natural" that Franklin's injury would have an effect on the vote.

Schembechler smelled a conspiracy. Hadn't Wayne Duke, the Big Ten commissioner, called to check on Franklin? Schembechler was convinced that Duke had influenced the vote.

Duke and the athletic directors all denied it. Even Don Canham believed them. But Schembechler would not let it go. Every day brought a new outburst. He said that if quarterback was so important, then why was the Big Ten sending Ohio State, a team that "admittedly has no passing attack"?

On Monday—two days after the game—Schembechler ended a speech to the Ann Arbor Quarterback Club with this: "A great wrong has been done to these kids. I wouldn't trust the older generation either. All they do is scurry around worrying about themselves. The players don't factor into it at all." He was in tears.

The nation was becoming engrossed by the Watergate scandal. That week, President Nixon's secretary, Rose Mary Woods, said that Nixon had known for weeks that there was an eighteen-and-a-half-minute gap on Nixon's White House tapes. But many in the Midwest could not stop talking about the Rose Bowl vote.

Letters of support poured into Schembechler's office at the rate of three hundred per day. The Michigan state House of Representatives passed a resolution honoring the Wolverines. State legislators were furious at Michigan State's Smith, a Michigan grad who had voted for Ohio State. Schembechler said Michigan State should have supported its "sister institution"—a strange charge, since Michigan had rarely treated Michigan State like an equal. (Two decades earlier, Michigan had even tried to block Michigan State's entry into the Big Ten.) Even a columnist from the Ohio State student newspaper, the *Lantern*, criticized the system.

On Tuesday, a forty-three-year-old Michigan doctoral student named Gerald Faye filed a lawsuit seeking to overturn the vote. Canham called the suit "ridiculous." Canham was as mad as anybody, but he knew the vote was legal and unchangeable, and he wasn't about to tear down the conference. A master at public relations, he knew that complaining would only make Michigan look worse. The problem was that Canham couldn't shut up his football coach.

On Wednesday night, Schembechler spoke at the football banquet at Ann Arbor's Huron High School, where his stepson Chip had just earned a letter, and he used the forum to take more shots at the Big Ten brass.

"I'll be a thorn in their side," he warned. "I have a football team that is almost totally disillusioned with college football."

Hold on.

What did he just say? Totally disillusioned with college football? Hadn't Schembechler read the first sentence in Woody Hayes's new book?

I have a deep and abiding respect for football, for it has paralleled the great achievements of this nation. Twelve years earlier, when Ohio State's regents had voted to decline the Rose Bowl bid, Hayes had accepted it. Why couldn't Bo do the same?

Hayes angrily told an Ohio State alumni group in Cincinnati that the controversy was "typical of today, where every decision is questioned. The problem today is we don't accept decisions. I've always accepted decisions and the one twelve years ago was pretty hard to take." When he calmed down, Hayes said, "I lost my cool out here for the first time. If I don't watch out, I'll end up like Bo Schembechler." It was an apparent reference to Schembechler's heart attack.

The Big Ten slapped Schembechler with a one-year disciplinary probation for his complaints. Hayes had bigger problems, though. The Old Man had a revolt on his hands.

If the Ohio State assistant coaches had their way, Michigan would have gone to the Rose Bowl. The coaches didn't want to go out to Pasadena and let Woody destroy their chances again. They got together and voted not to go. The players were just as fed up. Even Archie Griffin, the loyal star, privately said that Hayes should have called some passes.

Hayes worked on the coaches first. They told him that he had to let Staub call the plays in the Rose Bowl—and that meant the Buckeyes would pass. Hayes reluctantly agreed. He then gathered the players. Some of them had been freshmen in 1970, when Hayes made them tape up on the plane, and most of them had gone to Pasadena the year before, when Hayes had tried to suck the fun out of the experience. But Hayes was smart: he wasn't going to let them file secret ballots. He asked his players, "Now, who *doesn't* want to go?"

Well, nobody was going to stand up in front of the whole team and tell Woody to forget about the Rose Bowl. Besides, Hayes made a few promises. He would loosen his curfew restriction. He would let the married players sleep in the same bed as their wives. He would keep the team in a hotel the night before the game, instead of moving to a monastery like he usually did.

The Buckeyes were wary, but Hayes lived up to every promise. For the first time in memory, the Ohio State players actually had fun on their Rose Bowl trip. The Old Man loosened up, too. He went on *The Tonight Show*. He sat on Santa Claus's lap at a Christmas party. He even got along with Art Rogers; the *Los Angeles Times* photographer was working the Rose Bowl again and had no problems with Hayes. (Rogers had no problems seeing, either—his double vision had cleared.)

For Ohio State's first play of the 1974 Rose Bowl, Staub called for a pass. Cornelius Greene promptly threw an interception.

Flam went to the sideline and tried to hide from Hayes. But Woody found him and said, "We're still going to pass today." To Greene's shock, the Buckeyes did just that—they threw twelve passes, completed six, and Ohio State drilled USC, 42–21.

Notre Dame had beaten Alabama in the Sugar Bowl to claim the national championship, but Ohio State's Rose Bowl victory confirmed the Buckeyes' feeling that *they* were the best team in the country. After all, Notre Dame had beaten USC by only nine points earlier in the year.

At Hayes's postgame press conference, USC president John Hubbard, an expert on British history, invited Hayes to give a lecture on World War I at USC.

"I would rather talk about World War II," Hayes said. "That was not a stalemate."

As Hayes stepped off the podium, he thanked the press.

"You've treated me just great," he said. "And not just today, but ever since I've been out here. I think I've treated you better, too. It's a two-way street, you know.

"I love you all."

Dennis Franklin watched Ohio State's triumph from his living room in Massillon, Ohio. Even though his friend Steve Luke was playing for Ohio State, Franklin was rooting for Southern California. He could not stand the thought of the Buckeyes winning the Rose Bowl—*his* Rose Bowl.

Despite the worries of Michigan's doctors and Big Ten athletic directors, Franklin's collarbone had healed by late December. When a news photographer came over to his house on New Year's Day, the quarterback said he was healthy enough to play.

To prove it, Dennis Franklin walked into his backyard and threw a snowball.

7

Television

Jeff Kaplan had been working sixty to eighty hours per week for Woody Hayes while attending Ohio State's College of Law, just as Hayes had wanted. Now Kaplan was exhausted, and he had proven his worth to the Ohio State football staff. So after the 1973 season, Kaplan told Hayes that he planned to quit law school and concentrate on coaching.

"If you want to quit law school, that's up to you," Hayes said. "But if you do, then walk out that door, shut it behind you, and I never want to see your face again."

Kaplan stayed in law school. Hayes held that kind of sway over young, ambitious assistant coaches. They would do virtually anything just to be associated with him. Older assistants were a tougher sell. After the 1973 season, Hayes lost valued running backs coach Rudy Hubbard and offensive line coach Ed Ferkany, both for the same reason: money.

Hubbard had recruited Archie Griffin and several other future stars, but he was making only $18,000 per year and desperately wanted a raise. He knew he had to leave after a meeting in Hayes's office. Defensive coordinator George Hill, the second most powerful man in the program, told Hayes that Hubbard had done such a good job that the program should pay him back somehow. Hayes told Hill he was right. They ought to do something for Hubbard. Hayes then reached up, grabbed a canteen that was hanging on the wall, and handed it to Hubbard. That was Hubbard's raise. Hubbard soon left to become the head coach at Florida A&M.

Ferkany had a similar moment of clarity: after the 1974 Rose

Bowl, when Hayes gave him a whopping $300 raise. Ferkany loved coaching at Ohio State, but he had five children, and was only making $16,500 per year. He left to sell steel for Worthington Industries in Columbus. (Former Buckeyes quarterback Ron Maciejowski, who was working at Worthington at the time, was making around $40,000.)

The Ohio State football program was a moneymaking machine, and Hayes could have offered Ferkany and Hubbard big raises to stay. He refused to do so, and it had nothing to do with their performance. Hayes never wanted anybody working on his staff simply for the money. As if to prove the point, he consistently turned down pay raises himself: in 1973, his salary was only $29,400.

After getting trained at Worthington, Ferkany drove to Canton, Ohio, on June 5, 1974 for his first real day on the job. He had a lot on his mind that day. His wife, Jeanne, was in the hospital with a disc problem, and his oldest daughter was babysitting for their other four children. And of course, Ferkany had never really wanted to leave his coaching job.

But there were perks to the new life. Ferkany didn't have to listen to the Old Man's half-hour lecture on politics at 7 a.m. every day. And without Hayes sitting shotgun, Ferkany was free to turn his car radio on. Ferkany was listening to the radio on his drive home that day when he heard the news: Woody Hayes had had a heart attack.

Hayes later said he could see the heart attack coming. He had basically worked two years straight; he had spent the offseason between the 1972 and 1973 seasons writing *You Win with People!* in addition to his other duties. But he didn't really try to stop it, either. He did not start exercising or ease off his workload. He had a book to write and a team to coach.

Jim Otis, Hayes's old fullback, was home in Celina, Ohio, when he heard the news. Otis drove straight to Columbus, went to Hayes's hospital room, listened to the doctor's plea ("You've got fifteen seconds—don't let Woody talk"), and went in.

"Coach, don't say anything," Otis said. "You're not allowed to talk. I just want to tell you how much I love you, and how much these kids need you. So you gotta do what they tell you to do in here."

Hayes looked up. It was a cool, poorly lit room. The coach was hooked up to an IV and several monitors.

"When does training camp start?" Hayes asked.

"Five or six weeks," Otis said.

"Well, goddammit, are you in shape?"

Hayes had turned sixty-one that Valentine's Day, and after the heart attack there was immediate speculation by fans and reporters that he would retire. Hayes never flinched. He decided within a few days that he would return to coach the Buckeyes, and everybody who knew him understood that he would not cut down on his hours.

Hayes made one concession: he went on a strict diet and lost twenty-five pounds before the start of the season. But for Hayes, staying healthy meant he had to do more than just lose weight, because he had another medical concern: like his father, Wayne, he was a diabetic.

Hayes did not tell many people about his diabetes. Most of his players would never know. Some of his assistant coaches wouldn't know, either, and the ones who did would never bring it up with the Old Man. Woody Hayes could not stomach sympathy; he did not want his diabetes to be construed as a weakness. And he sure didn't want anybody telling him to lay off the pecan pie.

Hayes's personality was not suited to diets. He never did *anything* in moderation. He also subscribed to the theory that your body doesn't get charged for the sugar, fat, and calories in a dessert if you eat it off somebody else's plate.

"Give this young man a piece of apple pie," Hayes would tell waiters on road trips, as he pointed to a student manager sitting next to him. "And he'd like to have a piece of cheese on it."

Sometimes, Hayes would help three or four other people with their pieces of pie or cake, then announce proudly that he had not eaten dessert.

After Hayes's heart attack, get-well letters poured in from around the country. Those who knew him well—from his former assistant coaches to Ohio State president Harold Enarson—all struck a common theme: *Woody, please listen to your doctors.* They worried he would try to do too much too soon. If anything, Hayes likely would work *harder* after his heart attack, just so nobody could say he had slowed down.

Naturally, many Ohioans wondered if the Ohio State program would be the same. The answer came quietly that very day, when Ed Ferkany arrived home. Ferkany was relieved to see that, with his wife in the hospital, his oldest daughter had his other four kids under control. But before he could settle in to his house, he heard a knock at the door.

It was Anne Hayes. She was carrying a pot of stew. Anne said she knew it was Ed's first day on the road and that Jeanne had her disc injury, so she had left Woody at the hospital to go home and make dinner for the Ferkany family.

Anne told Ferkany not to worry about Woody.

"He'll be fine," she said.

On August 8, 1974, Richard Milhous Nixon resigned as president of the United States. He was replaced by former congressman Gerald Ford, the most valuable player of the 1934 Michigan football team.

Though Ford was four decades removed from his playing days, his passion for the Wolverines had not waned. As president, he would ask his staff to provide frequent reports on Michigan's athletic teams. Naturally, he would strike up a friendship with the head coach of the football team.

Bo Schembechler was instinctively conservative, a fan of Ford's, and highly respectful of the office of president. But his relationship with President Ford would be very different from Woody Hayes's with President Nixon. Hayes and Nixon bonded mostly because of their shared political views: Hayes supported Nixon. Schembechler and Ford became close because of Ford's love of Michigan—in a sense, Ford was supporting Schembechler.

On his twenty-third day in office, Ford flew to the heart of Middle America to speak to the summer graduating class at Ohio State. Ford joked that Columbus was "sometimes known as the land of the free and the home of Woody Hayes" and said, "Woody Hayes is so popular here in Ohio, it's unbelievable. We just had our picture taken together and when that picture appears in today's *Dispatch*, I'm pretty sure what the caption will say: 'Woody Hayes and Friend.'"

That evening, the *Dispatch* did just that.

Hayes admired Ford, despite Ford's unseemly association with That School Up North, and he absolutely wanted Ford to be president—starting in 1977, at the end of President Nixon's second term. Hayes was devastated that Nixon had to leave office early. He was disappointed in his friend—not for the Watergate break-in or the other "dirty tricks" of the Committee to Re-Elect the President, or even for covering all that up. No, Hayes was disappointed that Nixon had quit.

Quitting went against everything Woody Hayes believed. Never mind that Nixon resigned only because impeachment was inevitable. He had let the bastards get to him. Hayes blamed the media for forcing history's greatest president into such a shameful act. One thing was clear: Hayes was not going to let the media—or anybody else—force him out. Many people in and around the Ohio State program thought he would never leave his job; to them, he was a coach for life.

But to those who knew Hayes well, there was a sense that the coach might retire under one circumstance: if he won one more national championship, which he openly coveted. That way, nobody could say he had quit. Nobody could say that he left as a failure.

Was the Old Man risking his health by continuing to coach? Yes. But on that front, Hayes would quote Napoleon Bonaparte.

"I'd rather die a winner than live a loser," Hayes would say, "because when you're a loser, you die a little each day."

It would be wrong to say Gerald Ford was popular in Ann Arbor simply because he was a Michigan alum. But he was certainly not as *unpopular* as a Republican president would have been five years earlier. The University of Michigan had changed dramatically since Bo Schembechler had arrived. With the end of the Vietnam draft and the resignation of President Nixon, the two major causes of campus protests had disappeared. Five years is a long time in the life of a university; in that time, a school experiences an almost total turnover in its student population. So not only had the protests died down, but many of the current students had no memory of them.

In the fall of 1974, the *Michigan Daily*, the student newspaper, printed an article on Students for a Democratic Society and the school's activist past. "Besides being 'the research center of the Midwest,'" the story began, "Ann Arbor was once, believe it or not, a center of campus radicalism." The story went on: "Finding old SDS members still in Ann Arbor isn't as easy as one might think. Many have left, and some prefer not to remember their SDS connections."

Actually, finding old radicals in Ann Arbor was not quite as hard as the *Daily* made it seem. John Sinclair and Pun Plamondon still lived there. The White Panthers were no more; they had become the Rainbow People's Party, in part to be more inclusive. Sinclair was producing a weekly radio program in Ann Arbor, Toke Time, and had organized the Ann Arbor Blues and Jazz Festival, with Plamondon's help. (Plamondon, once accused of bombing a CIA building, was in charge of squelching any disruptions at the festival.)

The 1974 Blues and Jazz Festival would be a financial disaster. The next year, Sinclair and his wife, Leni, would move to Detroit. Sinclair saw that the culture in Ann Arbor was transforming from hippie to yuppie, and the Sinclairs did not want their kids surrounded by wealthier children.

Bo Schembechler, on the other hand, wasn't going anywhere. Six years after his arrival in Ann Arbor, it was hard to imagine the town without him. His record was an unfathomable 48-6-1. And because Schembechler had never seen his program as a model for anything larger, he did not need the clear distinction between football and the longhairs. He just needed to know that his grip on his program was as firm as ever.

The 1974 Wolverines, like the 1969 group, were mesmerized by their coach's charisma. Schembechler's gift with the language was as effective as ever. Michigan booster Tom Monaghan was so impressed that he asked Schembechler to give motivational speeches to the employees of his pizza company. Monaghan had opened a store called DomiNick's in nearby Ypsilanti with his brother in 1960; he had since changed the name to Domino's and built it into a franchise operation with dozens of stores.

In the Schembechler dialect, a player who slacked off was a "ham-and-egger"; nobody seemed to know exactly where the phrase came from, but everybody knew what it meant. If a player broke up with his high school girlfriend, Schembechler would say, "Women are like streetcars—there will be another one coming by in ten minutes. Now get your head out of your ass and go play."

When reporters asked him about the 1973 Rose Bowl vote, Schembechler cracked, "We're the only football team in America trying to rebound from an undefeated season."

They rebounded just fine. Before Michigan's fifth game of the season, against Michigan State, the press made a big issue out of the Spartans' vote to send Ohio State to the Rose Bowl the year before. Schembechler quashed any talk of revenge—he wanted his team's focus to be solely on the game—and the Wolverines beat Michigan State 21–7. It was their fifth straight win over their in-state rivals. The next week, the Wolverines squeaked past Wisconsin, and then they went on a typical Schembechler late-season run, beating Minnesota, Indiana, Illinois, and Purdue by a combined score of 135–13.

For the fifth straight year, Michigan was undefeated and untied heading into the season finale against Ohio State.

The 1974 Wolverines, like all Schembechler teams, were built on a disciplined running attack and a devastating defense. Schembechler was reluctant to promote individual players, and that reluctance, combined with the steamroller quality of Michigan's victories, made the players seem like football-mad automatons.

In the fourth game of the year, at Stanford, senior linebacker Steve Strinko tore cartilage and damaged a ligament in his right knee. Strinko was given a choice: drain it, tape it up, and hobble through the rest of the year, or have an operation and miss the rest of the season. Strinko chose to play. At the end of the season, he would be named Michigan's most valuable player.

Strinko had everything that Bo Schembechler wanted in a player. He was tough, he was athletic, and he loved inflicting physical punishment on opposing ballcarriers. He had grown up in Middletown, Ohio, halfway between Dayton and Cincinnati, where he was an honors student with a 3.8 grade point average. He had a solid family (his younger brother, Greg, also played for Michigan), and Woody Hayes had recruited him hard, too.

Once he arrived at Michigan, Strinko immediately embraced all the university had to offer, except for the academics. A month before his senior season, he was academically ineligible. He needed to pass one more summer-term class or he wouldn't be allowed to play. Schembechler punished Strinko by making him run ten hundred-yard dashes after every practice. Schembechler would run against Strinko and give himself a ten-yard start. If the coach beat Strinko once, Strinko would have to run ten more.

It really didn't matter how long Schembechler kept Strinko at practice, though. Whenever Strinko left, he was going to get high. Strinko had dabbled in marijuana, mescaline, cocaine, acid, and, of course, alcohol. (He liked acid because he wouldn't just pass out—he could really enjoy the trip.) By his senior year, he was smoking pot every day.

Bo Schembechler's entire recruiting philosophy was built on getting hardworking, hungry players instead of wild kids who would party all night. The problem was that Steve Strinko was both: he approached the game with an aggressiveness that bordered on recklessness, but that is also how he approached his life. Strinko did not do anything halfway.

For fun, he and his buddies rode the elevators in South Quad, a Central Campus dorm—not *in* them, but *on top* of them. Sometimes they coaxed a couple of girls into joining them, and as the elevator rose toward the top floor, the guys told the girls they had to lie really flat or they would be crushed between the elevator and the top of the elevator shaft. (That wasn't true. But seeing the girls panic added to the fun.)

Strinko's position coach, Gary Moeller, would get on his case for enjoying the weekends too much, but there were doubts about whether Moeller knew the extent of his drug use. It was hard to separate Strinko from the crowd of casual users. One day, Strinko sat down with a copy of the Michigan roster and went through the names, trying to figure out who had smoked pot at least occasionally. He figured the number was at least 80 percent, and at least half the team smoked pot every week.

Some of his teammates would later say Strinko's estimate was high. But for the 1974 Wolverines, parties were frequent and long-lasting. One off-campus house, where several Wolverines lived, became an unofficial Party Central for much of the team. Everybody who showed up—players, friends, girlfriends, whoever—would get introduced to "Fred." Fred was a five-and-a-half-foot-tall bong.

In the summer of 1974, Woody Hayes handed one of his new graduate assistant coaches, Dutch Baughman, a book: *What I Know About Football*, by Woody Hayes.

"You'll be referring to this book for a long, long time," Hayes said.

Baughman, already thrilled to be working for the great Woody Hayes, could not wait to read it. As soon as he walked out of Hayes's little office, he leaned against a wall and opened *What I Know About Football*. The pages were blank. Baughman couldn't believe it: of all the copies of this book, he got the one with the printing error. He turned to go back into Hayes's office to get a fresh copy.

Hayes was standing in the doorway.

"You'll be amazed what you will learn from a book that has no words in it," Hayes said.

Late that summer, Hayes would be amazed by a book that *did* have words in it. *Buckeye: A Study of Woody Hayes and the Ohio State Football Machine*, by *Harper's* staff writer Robert Vare, was an immediate bestseller. Excerpts ran in *Sports Illustrated* and *Esquire*, and Hayes's dissatisfaction with modern society spilled across almost every page.

Vare quoted him as saying, "The dorms are so fucking filthy now, there's so much sex and drugs, we can't even let recruits stay there the way we used to. The permissiveness is total."

And: "I can tell in a minute when a kid's been smoking [pot] just as soon as he walks out on that field. I don't even have to ask him."

And this, about professors: "These fellas they have today leave the student in the classroom. No, sir, they don't give a fuck about their kids."

And: "They've gotten so goddamned liberal up there at Oberlin they don't even give a shit about sports anymore. I hear they're even letting w-o-m-e-n in their sports programs now. That's your Women's Liberation, boy—bunch of goddamned lesbians . . . you can bet your ass that if you have women around—and I've talked to psychiatrists about this—you ain't gonna be worth a damn. No sir! Man has to dominate. There's just no other way. Jeezus Christ, I'd like to get that goddamned Oberlin on our schedule! We'd show them what *de*-humanization is about."

And on and on.

Mostly, *Buckeye* portrayed Hayes as an autocrat, oblivious to the embers of discontent in his program. Mike Royko, one of the most widely read newspaper columnists in the country, wrote an entire column accusing Vare of copying Royko's own best-seller, *Boss*, about power-hoarding Chicago mayor Richard J. Daley. The merits of those charges were dubious, but the portrayal of Hayes as an authoritarian leader of a machine was certainly reminiscent of Daley.

Hayes was furious. His own quotes didn't bother him—he meant every word—but the comments from his players and coaches sent him over the edge. Vare detailed the near-mutiny after the 10–10 tie and quoted anonymous players questioning him. On his weekly television program, *The Woody Hayes Show*, Hayes accused Vare of being a plant from That School Up North. But Hayes's complaints only boosted sales—*Buckeye* would sell around 25,000 copies in hardcover and 100,000 in paperback—so Hayes did something that did not come easily to him. He shut up.

* * *

One of Bo Schembechler's favorite mantras was *"The team, the team, the team!"* He hated promoting individual players; he thought the stars would get complacent and everybody else would get jealous. He wanted a team full of worker bees. If they won, they would all share the credit; if they lost, they would all take responsibility. Woody Hayes was different. He was eager to tell the world about his favorite players. It was as though he was saying "You win with people—people like *this.*"

Hayes often shielded his players from reporters; many Buckeyes arrived in the National Football League, after All-American careers, without any idea how to deal with the press. Hayes preferred to tout his players himself, and by 1974 he was promoting one player above all others, more as a person than a player. If people thought Woody Hayes's way didn't work anymore, well, Hayes had proof that it did. The proof's name was Archie Griffin.

Here was a black kid with an afro and long sideburns who stayed out of trouble, obeyed his coach, and always deferred to his teammates. Archie's father, Jim, worked three jobs while his mother, Margaret, raised their eight children. Hayes would even recruit two of Archie's younger brothers, Ray and Duncan, to play for the Buckeyes.

Hayes told anybody who would listen that Archie Griffin was the greatest football player he had ever seen and the finest young man he had ever met. Teammates would vouch for Archie's character. They genuinely loved him, even the ones who rolled their eyes at the Old Man's constant promotion of his star, and the whole country could see his talent. Griffin had run for 1,577 yards in 1973. Now, running behind yet another dominant offensive line, he was gaining momentum as a Heisman Trophy candidate, even though the Heisman traditionally went to a senior and Griffin was only a junior.

Ohio State's games became more predictable than ever: Griffin would rush for at least 100 yards and the Buckeyes would win. In Ohio, the team and its coach had never been so popular. *The Woody Hayes Show* (cohosted by Paul Hornung of the *Dispatch*) was the most popular late-night television show in Ohio. Children loved this crazy grandpa, asking questions of players, then gleefully cutting them off to give his own answer. Sometimes Hayes would simply make a statement and end it with, "Now isn't that right?"

During one airing, Hayes asked defensive back Neal Colzie a question, and Colzie responded, "I ain't hip." In other words: *I don't know.* Hayes looked at Colzie and corrected him: "I ain't hip, *sir.*" Colzie responded, "I ain't hip, *sir.*"

At moments like that, it seemed like nothing could stop Woody Hayes. Ohio State president Harold Enarson knew better.

In an interview on the porch of his Rose Bowl hotel the year before, Enarson told the *Dispatch's* Hornung that "rising costs, I think, put a pall over all major college football." Enarson had spent much of his tenure fighting state budget cuts. Those cuts led to rising tuition costs, which meant rising scholarship costs. Football had always swallowed a big chunk of athletic budgets. But now those budgets were stretched thinner, partly because of the increase in the value of a scholarship, and partly because of the Federal Education Amendments of 1972—more specifically, a portion of those amendments known simply as Title IX.

Title IX was supposed to ensure that women had the same opportunities in education as men. The question was in the application of the law. The Department of Health, Education and Welfare had declared that Title IX covered all athletic costs—not just scholarships, but travel and equipment. Enarson told Hornung that columnists did not understand the economic ramifications—they spouted "the pure sweet doctrine of equality" without thinking of how to pay for it.

A faction of the Ohio State faculty had long questioned the emphasis on football. Now a government agency was doing the same. Enarson was not naturally a football fan; he attended the games mostly as a function of his job. Hayes took pride in being the prism through which people saw the university, but Enarson said there was "a bitter irony" to the success of the football team. The Buckeyes increased the university's profile but overshadowed its teaching accomplishments.

But, Hornung asked, didn't the football team help the university's academic mission, too? Didn't the school raise more money, from both public and private sources, when the Buckeyes were winning?

"I won't say that's wrong, but I've seen precious little evidence of it," Enarson said. "I think there's a curious converse of this, though. A steadily losing team in a major state university invites the most bitter controversy and convulsions and does bring down the wrath of the legislature and the powerful people."

"In other words," Hornung asked, "if you are going to have a team, it had better be a good one?"

"Yes," Enarson said.

It was in this climate—with budgets tightening, faculty questioning the importance of football, and the Ohio State University president speculating about repercussions if the Buckeyes started losing—that Woody Hayes and his Buckeyes ventured north, to East Lansing, Michigan, as the No. 1 team in America.

Woody Hayes had been nervous before his team left Columbus. He didn't even spend time preparing for Michigan that week, even though the annual showdown was just two weeks away. Hayes was totally focused on Michigan State. He felt the Spartans' talent was better than their record. (He also felt that that talent had been procured illegally, via NCAA rules violations.)

Now here he was, on a cold day in his least favorite state. His team needed to gain six yards to stay undefeated. How did the Buckeyes let it get to this point? They had led 13–3 with 9:03 left in the game, with one of the best defenses in the country on their side. Then . . . well, strange stuff started happening. Tim Fox, one of the best defensive backs in the country (almost *every* Ohio State starter was one of the best in the country), had tried to play with a separated shoulder and strained ligaments in his knee. Michigan State receiver Mike Jones beat Fox for a 44-yard touchdown pass. Fox knew what was coming and he still couldn't stop it.

Then, with less than four minutes left, Ohio State punter Tom Skladany—not just any punter, naturally, but one of the nation's best—booted a 55-yarder, pinning Michigan State all the way back on its own 12-yard line. All the Buckeyes had to do was stay disciplined, avoid careless errors, and avoid the big play. So what happened? On the next play, Michigan State's Levi Jackson ran 88 yards for a touchdown.

Ohio State suddenly trailed 16–13. The clock showed 3:17. The national championship was on the line. In the huddle, quarterback Cornelius Greene told his teammates they would score. Archie Griffin broke off a 31-yard run. Greene scrambled. Greene passed.

Now here they were, down at the Michigan State six-yard line. Less than a minute remained.

Hayes did what he always wanted to do in tight spots: he went to his fullback. Champ Henson took a handoff and ran almost all of those six yards. The officials ruled he did not make it to the end zone. Still, Ohio State had a second down inside the one-yard line.

Henson got the call again. Again he was stopped.

Henson was sure he had scored. But anyway, there were still 29 seconds left.

Plenty of time for one last play. The Buckeyes were out of timeouts.

The clock was winding down—*:29, :28, :27* . . . Four Spartans were lying on top of Buckeyes, trying to keep them from getting back up. It was a blatant delay-of-game strategy, but could they really kill all 29 seconds? The clock kept going—*:16, :15, :14* . . . Eventually, the Ohio State players got to their feet. Flam hopped around the backfield, trying to get his team in an offensive formation. Now—*:04, :03, :02* . . . Greene called a play (Patton One) and lined up under center for the snap.

The ball went through Greene's legs.

And that should have ended the game.

But running back Brian Baschnagel picked the ball up and ran into the end zone.

Touchdown? The line judge sure thought so—he put his hands in the air. The other officials were not sure. Had they gotten the play off in time? Were there any penalties? The Buckeyes left the field believing they had won, 19–16. Many Spartan fans rushed the field, believing their team had won, 16–13. A few Michigan State students grabbed Hayes's famous cap with the "O" on it; others hollered at him; and when one touched Hayes's shoulder, the Old Man turned around and smacked the kid with the back of his closed fist.

The punch was caught on television and broadcast to 80 percent of the country.

It had been one hell of an afternoon.

And *still*, nobody knew who had won.

The game officials scurried to the nearby Kellogg Center, where they were headquartered. Big Ten commissioner Wayne Duke, who attended the game, spoke to the officials twice to find out whether Baschnagel's touchdown counted. Half the Spartan Stadium crowd left without knowing if Michigan State had pulled off one of the biggest upsets in Big Ten history. In the Ohio State locker room, Hayes refused to let his players get dressed or shower until they had confirmation of their victory.

When reporters entered the Michigan State locker room, Spartans coach Denny Stolz shouted, "I am the winning coach!" Yet nobody knew for sure. Stolz said, "They snapped the ball and they didn't get it across the goal line, so we won." But they clearly *had* gotten it across the goal line. That was the one thing that was not in question.

Forty-five minutes had passed since the game's final play. Finally, Duke made an announcement:

Michigan State had won.

The Buckeyes' last play did not count, Duke said, because time had expired. Even if time *hadn't* expired, the officials said Ohio State would have been penalized anyway, because the Buckeyes did not come to the required one-second set before snapping the ball.

Hayes was furious. He grabbed Duke, pinned him up against a wall of lockers, and screamed, *"What are you going to do about it?"* Did he even care that the man in his hands was not a player, but the commissioner of the Big Ten Conference? Hayes was in a blind rage. The game officials were trying to tear down Ohio State football, and he wasn't going to sit there and take it.

Hayes ordered his Buckeyes to follow him—they were going to go over to the Michigan State locker room and beat the shit out of the Spartans! More than a few Buckeyes were ready to do it. The assistants talked them out of it. If Hayes couldn't fight Michigan State, he wanted to get the hell out of there. He ordered the Buckeyes to get on the bus in full uniforms.

In his brief meeting with the press, Hayes told one reporter, "I'm going to put my fist down your goddamn throat." When he boarded the bus, he demanded that the driver take them to the airport; the driver tried to explain that that was impossible, because there was a crowd of Michigan State fans blocking the Ohio State bus, and the driver did not want to run them over.

Hayes was incredulous. What kind of excuse was that?

"Let me drive!" Hayes said.

The driver refused to give up the wheel.

On the plane back to Columbus, Hayes sat in the window seat on the right side. The old advice about not letting him stand on your left was hard to communicate to an airplane window, and the window paid a price for its ignorance. Hayes continually grabbed his head with his left hand and banged it against the window. With each bang, he repeated:

"We lost. *Fuck*."

(Bang.)

"We lost. *Fuck*."

(Bang.)

On *The Woody Hayes Show* that night, Hayes erupted again. He accused the Spartans of "dirty football" and called the result "grossly unfair" to the Buckeyes. He asked Greene and guard Scott Dannelley about the Spartans holding down the Buckeyes to prevent a final play.

"I can't tell you how bitter I am," he said on his show. "The older you get and the more you win, the more bitter you get with a loss."

The video of his television rant quickly circulated around the country.

"Certainly losing the game is not worth the embarrassment that Hayes has brought himself, Ohio State, and the sport," Paul Attner wrote on the front page of the *Washington Post* sports section. "He gets on his weekly television program with a few of his players and goads them into explaining how those awful players from Michigan State held his boys down at the goal line so Ohio State could not run one more play."

Hayes didn't care about the criticism. Wayne Duke reprimanded him for his public comments, and warned that a seven-day suspension would follow his next outburst, but Hayes didn't care much about that, either. (Hell, Bo had been put on probation for a *year* after he complained about the Rose Bowl vote the year before.) As far as Hayes was concerned, the bastards *did* hold his boys down at the goal line, just as Thom Darden interfered with Dick Wakefield in the 1971 game against Michigan. Now he had been screwed out of a possible national championship—and maybe even a chance to go out on top, so nobody could say he was a quitter or a failure, like they said about Nixon.

A few days later, Hayes told an Associated Press reporter, "I wanted that undefeated season more than anything I ever wanted in my life. I'd give anything—my house, my car, my bank account, anything but my wife and family—to get it."

To people reading that, it seemed like the Old Man had lost his mind. Maybe he had, at least temporarily, but he meant what he said. Hayes's house had a refrigerator that had been outdated for at least a decade, maybe two—it had a coil attached to a motor in the basement. He had flatly refused to take a free courtesy car on several occasions, preferring to stick with his Ranchero pickup instead of taking anything from anybody. And he never had a clue how much money was in his bank account.

Hayes often told people that his father, Wayne, once sent him to a department store to pay a small debt. A week later, Wayne died—without owing anything to anybody.

Wayne Hayes's children shared his view of money. Woody's brother Ike, a small-animal veterinarian, refused to charge policemen, firemen, physicians, or clergy for his services. When Ike's family objected, he said those people worked too hard and he didn't feel right charging them.

Ike had died suddenly in 1955, but Woody was carrying on his father's legacy. His refusal to take cash went beyond his Ohio State salary. Woody had been paid $200 per television show in the late 1960s and had never complained. The show's producer, Gene D'Angelo, knew Hayes would resist any attempts to increase his pay, so D'Angelo simply bumped Hayes up to $1,000 per show without asking. In the early 1970s, D'Angelo told Hayes he wanted to syndicate the show. The windfall, D'Angelo said, could be $150,000 per year for Hayes alone.

Hayes told D'Angelo he wasn't interested. He proudly declared he was a tenured professor at Ohio State, and he wanted to be paid like a tenured professor at Ohio State. He did not want a dime more.

D'Angelo was not surprised by Hayes's answer. Sometimes, Hayes wouldn't even cash those $1,000 checks, which meant he was actually *losing* money on the show, since he would have to pay taxes on the income.

"The heroic soul does not sell its justice and its nobleness," Emerson wrote. "It does not ask to dine nicely and to sleep warm. The essence of its greatness is that virtue is enough. Poverty is its ornament."

The week after the controversial ending in East Lansing, Ohio State traveled to Iowa City to play Iowa. The night before the Iowa game, the team watched *The Gambler*, starring James Caan as a literature professor with a gambling addiction. The professor gambles his way into serious debt to the mob, which is not the kind of thing Woody Hayes normally liked to show his players the night before a big game. But anyway, the gambling didn't get to the Old Man. Neither did the mob violence.

No, what got to him was the *teaching*—the scene where the professor discusses an essay by William Carlos Williams, who concluded, after much thought, that George Washington was not the hero he seemed to be.

"Why is Washington disappointing?" the professor asks his class.

"Because he's afraid," says a student.

"Afraid of what?"

"Losing," says another student.

"Losing!" the professor exclaims. "Washington is terrified of failure. And if failure is the absolute evil, what must be eliminated at any cost? The element of . . ."

"Risk?" asks a third student.

"Risk! There are certain questions Washington just won't ask. Certain borders he'd rather die than cross. D. H. Lawrence says Americans fear new experience more than they fear anything. They are the world's greatest dodges because they dodge their own very selves."

"Bullshit!" yelled Woody Hayes from the back of the theater.

Hayes could not believe it. Did that professor just call George Washington a *coward*? Bullshit! When the Buckeyes got back to their hotel for their traditional Friday night meeting—these meetings were never that long or compelling, but Hayes wanted his players' final thoughts before going to bed to be about football—they were in for a surprise. Up on the blackboard, Hayes wrote all the highlights of the story of Valley Forge. He told his players about Washington's great victory there. Without George Washington, Hayes said, there would be no America, and he wasn't going to let this son-of-a-bitch professor call George Washington a coward.

There was no *Easy Rider*–esque letdown for the Buckeyes the next day—Ohio State beat Iowa, 35–10. The same afternoon, Michigan whipped Purdue, 51–0, in Ann Arbor, and that set up yet another showdown: 10–0 Michigan against 9–1 Ohio State for the Big Ten title. Who could say? Maybe the winner would get the national title, too—Michigan was ranked third in the country and Ohio State had fallen only to No. 4 after its loss to Michigan State.

"There may be some doubt about the No. 1 college football team in the United States this season," began a story in the *New York Times* the week of the game. "But there is no doubt about which school has sold its athletic program to students, fans, faculty, alumni and corporate executives more skillfully than any other institution."

That, of course, was Michigan. Don Canham's athletic empire was thriving in almost every way. His football program was unbeaten once again. Canham's call-it-like-I-see-it attitude had earned him a few detractors. He acknowledged that the vote to send Ohio State to the Rose Bowl might have been a vote against him. ("You know, I couldn't win a popularity contest and maybe that was a factor," he told a reporter in the fall of 1974.) But he was still seen as the smartest man in college athletics. He would be named 1974's Man of the Year by the *Football News*.

Yet Canham felt the empire was under siege. Six years after taking over a department running a large deficit, he had turned Michigan into the biggest cash cow in college sports, and what happened? The government was messing with his business.

"There is no distinction made between revenue-producing sports and other sports," he wrote in a *New York Times* op-ed piece that December. "At certain institutions basketball revenue exceeds $500,000 per year. To generate that income, the team must probably compete in basketball classics in Los Angeles or New York City or some other points far from campus. To field this hypothetical team would cost in the neighborhood of $200,000. The total net to the athletic program would be $300,000. Does this mean that we must fund a women's basketball team with $200,000?"

Canham called Title IX "a good law," but he was baffled by the Department of Health, Education and Welfare's interpretation. Among other things, HEW had said that a university's student body should vote on which sports the school participated in each year. Given the year-to-year changes in facilities and scholarships that would be required, Canham thought the proposal was "just ridiculous," and he said so.

Canham said this had nothing to do with gender equity and everything to do with common fiscal sense. Although he had attended

Michigan on a track scholarship and spent two decades as the school's track coach, he didn't really understand why schools gave out full scholarships for track, or golf, or any other nonrevenue sport. He was a child of the Depression. This was a man who would sift through the lost-and-found box at Crisler Arena for a "new" pair of reading glasses. Now he was supposed to spend tens of thousands of dollars on women's sports just because some government bureaucrat said so?

Some women on campus thought Canham and Bo Schembechler were not just against Title IX. The women thought they were against women's athletics, period. Canham and Schembechler gave the women reason to believe that: they fought to keep female athletes from receiving letter jackets (though the women eventually won that battle).

Canham would not give up on the Title IX battle. But in the meantime, the most important day of his professional year was looming.

Canham went down to Columbus with Bo Schembechler, Dennis Franklin, Steve Strinko, Mike Lantry, and the rest of the Wolverines. Franklin had aggravated an ankle sprain against Purdue. Strinko had ongoing knee problems. They did not care. They had been pointing to this week for a year, ever since that Sunday when Schembechler showed up for his TV show and found out that Ohio State had won the Rose Bowl vote.

Ten Michigan starters were from Ohio, and they were tired of hearing about Ohio State's dominance. Defensive end Larry Banks even told reporters that Archie Griffin, who had rushed for at least 100 yards in twenty-one straight games, would only rush for 100 against Michigan "over my dead body."

Whatever happened, Michigan would end the season with the best record of any team in the country from 1972 to 1974. The only question was whether they would ever play in a bowl game. The traditional season-ender against Ohio State generated hype that would have seemed insane just five years earlier but was now routine. Ohio University and Marshall moved their kickoff time up to 11 a.m. so everybody would be home in time to watch Michigan–Ohio State. It was the kind of tension that normally made Don Canham leave before halftime—but because the game was in Columbus, Canham could not do that. This time, he would stay to the end.

So would everybody else.

Nineteen seventy-four had been a transitional year for ABC's college football broadcasts. ABC was no longer content to simply show the game. The network wanted to televise the *event*. Chris Schenkel, the staid voice of college football for thirteen years, was ushered out to make way for charismatic forty-five-year-old Georgia native Keith Jackson, whose passion for the college game was evident in every sentence. Schenkel's color analyst, Bud Wilkinson, was on his way out, too; in 1974, ABC used a rotation of retired head coaches and current coaches whose teams were off that week.

The changes went beyond the broadcast booth. ABC Sports president Roone Arledge wanted to show what made college football different from the National Football League: the relationships between teams and college towns, the games as growing centerpieces of campus social life, the bands, the mascots, and the seniors who had one last chance to be heroes. With that goal in mind, ABC had conducted a nationwide search for two "college-age" reporters to roam the sidelines during games. The network had employed sideline reporters before, but the duties were usually limited to injury updates and occasional football analysis. Now ABC wanted reporters to bring the games to life.

Arledge and his assistant, Dick Ebersol, settled on Don Tollefson and Jim Lampley as their college-age reporters. Lampley almost missed out because, at twenty-five, he was considered too old for the gig, and because he had broadcasting experience—the network had sought a true novice. Arledge decided at the last minute to hedge his bets with somebody who at least wouldn't embarrass the network, and so he chose Lampley.

From the start of the season, Lampley was determined to land an interview with Woody Hayes. Ohio State told him no. And no. And also: no. Hayes was opposed on principle—he didn't trust reporters he didn't know, especially TV people, and he sure didn't trust some shaggy-haired twenty-five-year-old from out of town. Lampley would not give up. Finally, the week before the Buckeyes played Michigan, he got a call from an Ohio State administrator: show up in Columbus at our chosen time and Coach Hayes will talk to you. For five minutes. Not six minutes. Not ten. Five.

Lampley had also tried to secure an interview with Bo Schembechler. Schembechler complied without a fight (Don Canham had obviously told him about the importance of television) and said nothing interesting. When Lampley asked about the 1973 vote, Schembechler spoke evenly of the seniors on the 1973 team. Dennis Franklin, sitting next to Schembechler, said, "I always felt like if you work for something you should be rewarded." Lampley tried to coax good television out of Schembechler, but it was almost impossible. The coach didn't care how he looked or sounded on TV. The interview was just something he had to do between practice and film study.

When Lampley sat down for his allotted three hundred seconds with Woody Hayes, he knew the first question would be crucial. So he asked about the topic that was most likely to endear him to Woody Hayes: military history.

Hayes talked to Lampley for more than a half hour.

As Lampley introduced the interview, he said Hayes had "been called dictatorial, dogmatic, a tyrant." Hayes told Lampley he would "rather be regarded as a benevolent despot." He reiterated his views that football players were better people than other students ("they live a more disciplined life") and that "there are a lot of people in the news media today who don't care about telling the truth. They simply want to make a story out of it. There is a sport in this country much bigger than football, or basketball, or baseball. It's that sport of tearing down . . . this is the worst thing that's happened to our society."

As for his critics, Hayes proudly told Lampley he was on a one-year contract.

"Anytime they don't like the results I get, or the way I run it," he said, "they can fire me."

Lampley asked Hayes why he continued in such a stressful job after his heart attack.

"I did not have a serious heart attack," Hayes said. "If I can get through this season without one, and then get back into better shape again, I can avoid a heart attack for a long time. But if I don't, it happens, and so what?"

After that interview, the actual game figured to be a letdown for Jim Lampley. It was not. Lampley would spend three seasons as an ABC sideline reporter and cover almost every major rivalry in the sport: Auburn-Alabama, Nebraska-Oklahoma, Texas–Texas A&M, Notre Dame–Southern California. As a college student at North Carolina, he had watched his school face archrival Duke in basketball. Yet none of those games made him feel such palpable tension as he felt when Michigan played Ohio State.

Especially in Columbus.

And especially in 1974.

As the national television audience watched Lampley's prerecorded interviews with Woody Hayes and Bo Schembechler, Hayes and Schembechler met at midfield for the traditional coaches' chat before the game. This was always a strange talk. The two men still considered themselves good friends, but they had been plotting against each other all year. Their only conversations were at the Big Ten meetings in Chicago in the summer and right now, on the field before their season-ending game. They talked for a while, and as Hayes went back to his team, he walked past Michigan's kicker and said, "Good luck, Mike."

And such was Hayes's aura that Mike Lantry thought, *Wow. He knows who I am.*

Meanwhile, on the east side of the famed Horseshoe, Mike's wife, Linda, settled into her seat alongside her husband's friend Mike Oliver. Mike Lantry and Mike Oliver had played on the same Little League team (the Cardinals in Oxford, Michigan) when they were eight years old. They had been buddies ever since. Like Lantry, Oliver had been shipped off to Vietnam, and like Lantry, he was still sorting through his feelings about the experience. He had become accustomed to a chilly reception when people found out he had been a soldier. (He got a similar reception when he entered Ohio, too—he was ticketed for speeding in his blue Volkswagen Beetle with its Michigan license plate, even though cars with Ohio plates were cruising past him.)

On the sidelines, Jim Lampley had his last chance to set up the game for the national television audience.

Lampley had discovered that the original mission of the "college-age reporter" had only lasted a month or two; the constraints of televising a football game made it too difficult for him to do long features on fraternities or mascots or anything that was not directly related to the game. Jackson, the play-by-play man, wanted to be the one speaking as a play developed. Lampley generally had twenty-four seconds to speak before saying, "Back to you, Keith."

At parties, Lampley turned this into a shtick—he would do "royal family succession in twenty-four seconds," or "the history of the world in twenty-four seconds." During games, he found that the best use of his twenty-four seconds was to compromise: he would inject some drama or emotion, but he would not stray too far from the field. He would provide storylines. Jackson and his color commentator (on this day it would be Penn State coach Joe Paterno) would say what was happening. Lampley was there to say why it mattered—and to make the viewers feel like they knew the men beneath those helmets.

Now, as Michigan and Ohio State went through final preparations for the Big Ten game of the year, Lampley talked about a few of the most prominent names on the marquee. The last player he mentioned (and the last player the camera focused on) was Mike Lantry.

"Keep in mind," Lampley said, "that a year ago, if Lantry had hit only one of two late-game field goal attempts, it would have been the Wolverines, and not the Buckeyes, who would have headed out to Pasadena on January first."

Lampley then sent it back to Jackson for Mike Lantry's opening kickoff.

*   *   *

For all the Wolverines' complaints about the 1973 vote, even they had to admit they were badly outplayed at the start of that game. They were determined not to fall behind again. Michigan forced Ohio State to punt on the opening drive, then took over near midfield. They ran the ball twice. Then they decided to get aggressive.

Dennis Franklin faked a handoff, then dropped back to pass. He saw Gil Chapman open in the middle of the field and threw a strike. Chapman plucked the ball out of the air and just kept going. Forty-two yards later, Michigan had its first lead over Ohio State in two years. Mike Lantry kicked the extra point to make it 7–0.

The Wolverines got the next scoring chance, too, after Steve Strinko recovered a Cornelius Greene fumble. This time, Schembechler sent Mike Lantry out to try a 37-yard field goal from the right harsh mark.

The ball split the uprights. Now, in a reversal of the 1973 game, it was Michigan leading 10–0 on the road.

Ohio State responded with a drive into Michigan territory. They stalled on the Wolverine 30-yard line as time wound down in the first quarter. Woody Hayes would have to send kicker Tom Klaban in for a 47-yard field goal try. The wind was gusting at up to twenty miles per hour in the Buckeyes' faces, and Schembechler probably should have called timeout to force Klaban to kick before the teams switched sides at the end of the quarter. Instead, Schembechler saved his timeouts, the quarter ended, and Klaban got to kick with the wind at his back.

The snap was bad, but holder Brian Baschnagel somehow placed the ball on the tee properly. Klaban nailed it. Michigan's lead was down to 10–3.

On Michigan's next drive, Franklin was intercepted by Ohio State's Bruce Elia, which just confirmed the strength and depth of the Buckeyes: Elia, who had led the Big Ten in scoring as a fullback the year before, had switched back to linebacker and led the Buckeyes in tackles. Ohio State had the ball on the Michigan 44, and the Old Man went to old reliable: Archie, Archie, Archie, Archie, four times for 27 yards. At that point, the Wolverines could only hope to hold Ohio State to a field goal, and they did just that. Another shaky snap, another great hold by Baschnagel, another accurate kick by Klaban. Michigan led, 10–6.

Schembechler sent Lantry in to try a field goal on Michigan's next drive, but it was, literally and figuratively, a long shot: a 51-yarder from the left hash, into the wind. The kick fell short.

Ohio State took over on its own 20. Around a minute remained in the half. Woody Hayes seemed like a sure bet to stay conservative and go into the locker room trailing 10–6. But then Griffin picked up a first down, and Greene carried twice more, and without really try-ing to score, Ohio State found itself on its own 49-yard line with 21 seconds left.

Now even Hayes was willing to take a shot downfield. Greene had plenty of time to throw, and he hit Dave Hazel for 25 yards. On the next play, Griffin was supposed to run to his left to center the ball for a field goal, but he made a rare mental mistake and ran right instead. Nonetheless, Klaban converted his third field goal of the game, a 43-yarder.

At halftime, Michigan led 10–9. ABC's Lampley ventured into the stands for a quick interview with a Buckeye fan who had been of-fered $3,000 for three tickets. (And as Lampley pointed out, "The seats aren't even that good!")

Ohio State had the first scoring chance of the second half: yet an-other field goal attempt for Tom Klaban. ABC briefly cut to the side-lines so Lampley could do twenty-four seconds on the meaning of the Buckeye leaves on the Ohio State helmets. Ohio State's coaches handed a leaf decal to any player for a particularly impressive action on the field—a touchdown catch, a big block, a sack—and Tom Kla-ban was about to earn another. He kicked his fourth field goal of the afternoon, this one a 45-yarder with the wind at his back. It was the first third-quarter score of any kind against Michigan in 1974. Ohio State led 12–10.

On the ensuing drive, the Wolverines lined up with two wide receivers for the first time all day.

"Maybe they're going to start throwing that football," Paterno said from the broadcast booth. Michigan did try to throw on that drive—once—but the pocket collapsed and Franklin had to swallow the ball.

The Wolverines could not sustain a drive. They had not run a single play inside the Buckeyes' 20-yard line. They forced an Ohio State fumble, took over on their own 45, and still couldn't get into field goal range.

Michigan's next chance came early in the fourth quarter, but it ended when Franklin threw an interception at midfield. The Wolverines stopped Ohio State on the next drive, then fielded a punt on their own 11-yard line and returned it two yards. There was 11:06 left in the game—plenty of time, in theory. But with points at such a premium, and Ohio State leading by two . . . well, with 7:40 left, ABC's Keith Jackson set the scene for the millions in the viewing audience.

"I want to say it one more time: the wind is at the backs of Michigan," Jackson said. "That is very important, because if they get that ball down within reasonable field goal range, Mike Lantry will get a helping hand from Mother Nature. Remember, it was Lantry last year who missed a 44-yard try that might have won the game for Michigan in that famous 10–10 tie."

The Wolverines mixed runs and short passes to advance to the Ohio State 42. They were still not in "reasonable field goal range," not really, but they were in the neighborhood. On third and 12, Franklin threw a pass behind running back Rob Lytle. It fell incomplete.

"It is fourth down for Michigan at the Ohio State 42-yard line," Jackson said. "Now what do you do?"

"I'd punt," Paterno said.

"It would be a 59-yard effort at a field goal," Jackson said, "which we used to say was absurd . . ."

Paterno: "I'm pretty sure they'll punt."

Schembechler did not want to punt. He sent Mike Lantry in to try the 59-yarder. Only a few kickers in history had converted on such a long field goal. The rules of the day stated that if Lantry missed, Ohio State would get the ball on its own 20. In later years, the rules would change to give Ohio State the ball on the line of scrimmage (the Michigan 42)—under those rules, Schembechler probably would not have tried the field goal. But now a missed field goal would effectively be like a 22-yard punt.

Lantry's kick was straight, but it was several yards short.

"If they had punted it might have been the same sort of a thing," Jackson said.

"They know the range of that kicker, how good he is," Paterno said. "He gave it a good shot."

"Last year, Lantry just barely missed one from 58," Jackson said.

ABC then cut to Lampley, who reminded viewers that Michigan had the best record in the country over the last three years but had not been to a bowl game. Ohio State got the ball on its own 20 and immediately threw a pass—clearly, Hayes's assistant coaches were not going to let him repeat the 1973 disaster. Greene threw complete to Dave Hazel.

Griffin then ran for three yards. He was over 100 for the twenty-second straight game—and when the play ended, there was Michigan's Larry Banks, lying on his stomach. Over his dead body, indeed.

Soon, though, the Buckeyes had to punt. Michigan had the ball with barely three minutes left on its own 30. Dennis Franklin needed one drive to finally beat his home-state team, to cap his career with a moment that would trump his "only the good ones" comment in 1972 and broken collarbone in 1973.

Franklin dropped back to pass. Incomplete. And again: incomplete. On third down, he was sacked.

Michigan had to punt, hope its defense could stop Ohio State, then try to coax some magic out of an offense that had been lifeless since the first quarter.

Ohio State ran for one yard. Michigan called timeout to stop the clock with 1:51 left. The camera flashed to Franklin.

"Dennis Franklin, frustrated on the sidelines," Keith Jackson said. "The Michigan quarterback watching, hoping that lightning will strike in favor of the Wolverines . . ."

Another short Ohio State run; another Michigan timeout.

"Actually, if they can stop them now and make them kick, and get any kind of return, they're still in pretty good position," Paterno said.

On third down, Greene rolled right, one of those plays where he could throw if anybody was open or keep it if everybody was covered. Everybody was covered. Ohio State had to punt. Michigan's Calvin O'Neal just missed blocking the punt.

The Wolverines had the ball on their own 47, trailing 12–10. There were 57 seconds left.

In the east stands, twenty-four-year-old Vietnam veteran Mike Oliver turned to Linda Lantry and said, "It's going to come down to a last-second kick again." She looked at him and pleaded: "No . . . *That can't happen again.*"

Franklin dropped back and looked for Jim Smith on a curl pattern. Complete! Twenty yards. Michigan had a first down on the Ohio State 32. Fifty-two seconds left. Franklin rushed his team to the line of scrimmage and threw a quick pass out of bounds to stop the clock.

Forty-six seconds left.

"They're in pretty good position here," Paterno said.

Schembechler certainly thought so—he called for a running play. Rob Lytle picked up 10 yards, down to the Buckeyes' 22.

ABC cut to No. 36 in the maize and blue, senior placekicker Mike Lantry, walking on the sideline. Was he pacing? Or just trying to stay loose?

Lantry looked down and made the sign of the cross on his chest.

"Thirty-nine ticks remaining on the clock," Jackson said. "What a ballgame."

Lytle ran up the middle, to the Ohio State 16. Schembechler used his last timeout. ABC cut to Jim Lampley on the sideline.

"Once again the pressure is apparently coming down on the shoulders of Mike Lantry, the Michigan field goal kicker," Lampley said. "Remember that twice in the last five minutes a year ago, Lantry missed field goals that would have won the ballgame for Michigan and sent them to the Rose Bowl . . ?"

The camera flashed to the clock, which showed 18 seconds left, and then over to Schembechler, who grabbed Lantry by the arm and sent him in.

"... remember that he hasn't had a great year this year. Before last week he was four for 13 on the year, and the Michigan coaches were worried about his kicking. Remember that he missed his last two attempts today—both of them were long ones."

Lampley's twenty-four seconds were up.

"Now back up to Keith Jackson," he said.

"It will be a 33-yard try," Jackson said, "as Mike Lantry has come on, out of the hold of Tom Drake. He is a remarkable story. He is from Oxford, Michigan. He was a walk-on. He just showed up one day and said, 'Coach, I want to play football for you.' He right now might very well write his name indelibly into Michigan football history—one of the richest collegiate history books of them all. He is a left-footed kicker. He is a senior. He hit a 37-yarder. This one is from 33 yards, the wind is at his back. Only 18 seconds to play in the ballgame."

Lantry lined up on the right hash mark. The ball was snapped. Lantry stepped forward.

"The kick," Jackson said, "it is up . . ."

It was up. *Way* up. Linda Lantry expected that—she knew, better than anybody, that Mike kicked the ball so high, which made his kicks especially hard to follow. Now everybody in Ohio Stadium, much of the state of Ohio, a big chunk of the state of Michigan, and of course the national television audience was watching what could have been the final kick of Mike Lantry's Michigan career.

The ball sailed over the left upright. Because it was going from right to left, it was virtually impossible for any fans to tell if the ball was just inside the upright or just outside of it. Linda immediately thought, "It's good!" If she was correct, that would almost certainly mean a 13–12 victory for Michigan, a Rose Bowl bid, maybe a national title, and permanent hero status in the state of Michigan for Oxford's own Mike Lantry. Then, instinctively, Linda looked down at the officials under the upright, who made their signal . . .

". . . it is no good!" Jackson said.

Mike Lantry went numb. His holder, Tom Drake, briefly argued with the officials. ABC showed Lantry touching his helmet, stunned, as the Buckeyes celebrated in the foreground. Ohio State fans charged the field—once again, they had beaten That School Up North.

"The people have broken out of the stands," Jackson said, "and come swarming onto the field with 16 seconds to play in the football game. As Lantry missed from 33 yards out . . . Let's have another look at it, as the goalposts are being ripped down . . ."

The Ohio Stadium fans were watching the bedlam on the field and celebrating with each other; the Michigan fans were stunned. Only a few people in the stadium kept their eyes on Mike Lantry. Linda Lantry was one. An ABC cameraman was another. The camera stayed on Lantry as offensive lineman Dave Metz walked past him. Lantry had his hands on his hips.

Jackson, narrating the action on the screen, said "Mike Lantry walks disconsolately to the sidelines."

"I thought he had it from this angle," Paterno said.

"All right, let's have another look," Jackson said. "Slow-motion replay. Here's the snap. It is good. Drake's hold is just fine. Lantry's kick is in the air . . .

"Well," Jackson continued, "it's impossible to tell from this angle. He missed to the left side, so apparently the ball had not crossed . . . it veered just to the outside of the uprights. It was waved off by the officials as no good. Now the field has been cleared. We have 16 seconds to play on the game."

The television audience watched Lantry take his helmet off and run his hand through his brown hair as he looked down. None of his teammates came near him.

ABC showed one more replay.

"There is absolutely no way to tell from here as to where the ball was over the crossbar," Jackson said. "It looked good as far as the uprights are concerned, but at this point you cannot tell where the ball was. I am perfectly content myself to agree with the men in the striped shirts on the field."

Ohio State ran out the final 16 seconds and the celebration started up again. The Buckeyes were going back to the Rose Bowl. Steve Luke found his childhood friend Dennis Franklin and gave him a hug. Franklin's career was over—he had gone 0-2-1 against Ohio State and 30–0 against everybody else. His three Michigan teams would finish with rankings of six, six, and three in the final Associated Press poll, yet Franklin's career would forever be defined by his bowl record: 0–0.

That night, Jim Lampley would go out on High Street, the main drag on Ohio State's campus, and see fistfights between Buckeye and Wolverine fans. He would go to a fraternity party and feel a fervor that seemed, to him, to be almost religious. But before he did any of that, he had work to do.

Lampley stopped Mike Lantry on the field and asked him for a quick interview. Lantry declined.

In the Michigan locker room, Schembechler told his team not to put it on Mike Lantry's shoulders. But it was too late. By that time, the telecast was off the air.

It was a long ride back to Ann Arbor for Mike Oliver and Linda Lantry. Not much was said; not much could be said.

By the time Mike Lantry arrived at his apartment in northeast Ann Arbor, the first few telegrams from Western Union had already arrived. To his surprise, several were from Ohio State fans sitting in the south end zone, who told him they were happy they won the game but thought his field goal had actually been good.

Then came the letters: a dozen, then a few dozen, then more than a hundred. Some letters were sent to Lantry's apartment. Most were sent to the athletic department. Some were simply addressed:

Mike Lantry
University of Michigan
Ann Arbor, Michigan

No other identification was needed. The nation knew Mike Lantry now: he was the guy who missed the kick to beat Ohio State. But it was more than that: he was the guy who walked off the field alone, without so much as a hug from a teammate.

A woman in Lima, Ohio, wrote, "I wanted SOMEONE to put an arm around you as you walked back to the bench to show some appreciation for your great effort under unmeasurable pressure. To me and I'm sure millions of T.V. viewers you are a CHAMP!"

A Columbus woman wrote, "Just finished watching the game and my heart goes out to you. Please don't despair—there is a big, beautiful world outside the football field."

A woman in Jackson, Michigan, wrote, "It was easy for my husband and me to turn off the television set on Saturday and say that's it for another year. However, I couldn't erase from my mind the thought that perhaps you may have felt that you *alone* were solely responsible . . ."

A fifteen-year-old girl in Wyandotte, Michigan, wrote, "I believe teammates are there to work with you and encourage you . . . as I watched you walking alone, I could not believe no one came up to you to give you a pat on the back or comfort you, probably when you needed them the most."

When Lantry had made the sign of the cross on his chest, he didn't even know the ABC camera was on him. But that brought a wave of letters about faith in Jesus Christ.

One Ann Arbor woman sent a list of Bible verses with a note: "I felt bad you looked so lonely after the kick and no one comforted you." She put a "GOD LOVES YOU" sticker on the envelope. A man in Louisville, Kentucky, enclosed a pamphlet from the Reverend Billy Graham. An Alabama fan in Birmingham wrote, "It really broke my heart when the TV camera showed you walking off the field so dejected, sitting down on the bench and no one saying anything to you. This just about killed me." She enclosed a pamphlet entitled "GOD'S PLAN AND YOU." A pastor at Free Methodist Church in Jackson, Michigan, wrote, "I cried with you Saturday because I know you were the loneliest fellow in Columbus. Jesus Christ was also very lonely—more lonely than you when he realized the whole world was against him."

The letters kept coming. Before long, there were hundreds. Then more than a thousand. Athletic department employees were kidding Lantry: *Mike, enough already—we're swimming in your mail.* But it wouldn't stop. The football coach at Foothill High School in Bakersfield, California, sent a three-page handwritten note. Another three-page handwritten letter from Grand Rapids reminded Lantry that "all things are in God's providence" and that the Lord had a plan for him. A Florida man wrote that "thousands of people are holding your hand." An eighteen-year-old in South Bend, Indiana, wrote that "there should be more people in this world just like you."

If ABC wanted to know if its experiment with "college-age reporters" had an effect on the audience, the proof was right here, in Mike Lantry's mailbox. Jim Lampley had done his job well. People felt like they knew Lantry. A Columbus man addressed his letter, "Dear Son," and wrote, "I take the privilege to call you that because I am the father of eight children . . . after watching yesterday's game I can't get you off my mind." A grandmother in Virginia wrote, "My heart aches for you."

Lawyers compared Lantry's miss to their own trials: sometimes, even when they did everything right, they lost a case. An Ohio State fan in Fairborn, Ohio, wrote about losing his right index finger in a car wreck. University of Montana placekicker Bruce Carlson wrote Lantry about his own miss, with 11 seconds left against Idaho. A high school football player in South Bend, Indiana, recovering from surgery to his right (and writing) hand, wrote a letter with his left hand instead. Lantry even got a sympathetic letter from a quadriplegic.

NBC baseball announcer Joe Garagiola sent a letter. So did University of Detroit basketball coach Dick Vitale, who wrote, "You have not a damn thing to be ashamed of!"

Lantry was stunned, not just by the outpouring of support, but by the tone: most people were appalled that his fellow Wolverines abandoned him after he missed the kick. Lantry didn't feel that way at all. He thought his teammates were stunned, just as he was, and if anything, they wanted to give him space. Millions of viewers could not shake the image of Mike Lantry all alone. Lantry and his teammates would never even discuss it.

After a while, Lantry stopped reading the letters. There were simply too many, and they were too similar. Besides, Lantry couldn't shake the thought he shared with Bobby D. Crim, Speaker-elect of the Michigan House of Representatives, who ended his letter with this: "P.S. I was sitting behind the Michigan bench at the game. That kick was good."

A week after Ohio State beat Michigan, Woody Hayes flew out to Los Angeles to provide color commentary for the Notre Dame–Southern California telecast. It was one of the most memorable games in college football history. Just before halftime, Notre Dame led, 24–0. But USC scored 55 points in the final 30 minutes and 10 seconds to win, 55–24.

After the game, Hayes drove his rental car down the coast to San Clemente, California, to visit an old friend.

When Hayes arrived, Richard Nixon was wearing a scarlet jacket and gray slacks. Nixon and his wife, Pat, had dinner waiting. Nixon gave Hayes two neckties—one for Hayes, one for his son Steve.

President Ford had pardoned Nixon in September, ending the disgraced president's legal troubles. But Nixon was still essentially in hiding. He had not spoken publicly since his resignation, and the pardon had damaged Ford's reputation more than it had helped Nixon's; there was immediate speculation that Nixon had offered to resign only if Ford would pardon him. In Nixon's statement after the pardon, he acknowledged that "I was wrong in not acting more decisively and more forthrightly in dealing with Watergate," but he stopped short of a true apology.

Now, on a late November night in Nixon's San Clemente home, there was no need to discuss Watergate. For one of the rare times in the twenty years that he had known Richard Nixon, Woody Hayes was content to talk mostly about football. Hayes understood, better than anybody, why Nixon would not say he was sorry—the Old Man never said it himself. He didn't believe in it.

"If you would serve your brother," Emerson wrote, "because it is fit for you to serve him, do not take back your words when you find that prudent people do not commend you . . . a simple, manly character need never make an apology."

Befitting a team that still had a chance at the national championship, Ohio State was a big winner at the postseason awards. Archie Griffin won the Heisman Trophy. Defensive lineman Pete Cusick was a finalist for the Lombardi Award as the nation's top lineman.

The Lombardi banquet was in Houston, and Cusick had to fly through Atlanta to get back to Columbus. On that flight to Atlanta, he sat in first class next to *Monday Night Football* announcer Howard Cosell, who asked him the same question everybody asked: what was it like to play for Woody Hayes?

Cusick said Hayes was a great person and a character, largely responsible for Cusick's success, and who wouldn't want to play for a man who won a bunch of games and was famous around the country?

Cusick had seen Hayes's concern for people up close—the hospital visits, the emphasis on academics. A few months earlier, when Champ Henson's mother, Liz, was admitted to a hospital, Anne Hayes showed up to the Henson farm in Ashville, thirty-five miles from Columbus, at 6 a.m. "You can't run a farm without a woman," Anne told Champ's father, Raymond. "What do you want for breakfast?" She stayed for three days.

"Let me tell you something," Howard Cosell told Pete Cusick. "I think Woody Hayes is a Neanderthal boor."

Cusick asked Cosell if he had ever met the coach.

"No," Cosell responded. "I haven't had the displeasure."

Cosell then rattled off a list of Hayes's transgressions: the time he tore up the sideline markers, the way he screamed at officials, the way he talked to the press. Cosell, like so many members of the national media, thought Hayes was a relic—a 1940s coach in 1970s America—and he needed to disappear.

But getting rid of the Old Man would not be easy. That same month, Ohio State assistant coach Mickey Jackson was driving home from a recruiting trip to Youngstown when state troopers sounded their sirens behind him. There had been reports of somebody who looked like Jackson driving with a dead man riding shotgun. The cops pulled Jackson's car over and shined their flashlight inside at the fully reclined front seat, when the supposed "corpse" woke up from his nap. That wasn't a dead man. It was Woody Hayes, alive and well.

Woody Hayes had given Tom Klaban a "battlefield promotion" after beating Michigan—Klaban, a walk-on, was now on scholarship. When they arrived in Pasadena, Klaban and his teammates had a chance at a bigger prize: the national title.

Undefeated Oklahoma was a sure bet to finish No. 1 in the Associated Press poll; The Sooners were on NCAA probation and therefore ineligible for a bowl. But Oklahoma was not eligible for the coaches' poll because of the sanctions, so that vote was up in the air. If Ohio State beat Southern California and Notre Dame upset Alabama in the Orange Bowl, the Buckeyes would likely regain a piece of the national title they thought they had lost in East Lansing.

It would not be the unbeaten, unquestioned national championship that Hayes desired. But would he retire if they won it?

"I haven't made my mind up on that yet," he told reporters. He said former Bowling Green coach Doyt Perry, former Oklahoma coach Bud Wilkinson, and former Marine general Lewis Walt all advised him not to quit.

From early in the Rose Bowl, there was a sense that the victor would not win as much as survive. On the opening kickoff, Ohio State's Doug Plank sprinted downfield and put his helmet in the chest of the biggest USC player he could find. Plank got up and his head felt funny. His helmet had cracked on the play; the Ohio State equipment managers put tape through the earhole and out the facemask just to hold it together the rest of the day.

Archie Griffin suffered a rib injury and was limited to 75 yards. (His streak of 100-yard games technically remained intact because the NCAA did not count bowl games in its records.) The Heisman runner-up, running back Anthony Davis of USC, also suffered a rib injury and missed the entire second half.

Ohio State took leads of 7–3 into halftime and 17–10 in the fourth quarter. But with two minutes left, USC quarterback Pat Haden hit Johnny McKay (the son of Trojans coach John McKay) for a 38-yard touchdown pass.

The coaching McKay decided to go for two points and (potentially) a share of the national title. He called for Haden to roll out and either run or look for Johnny McKay in the end zone. When Haden rolled out, neither option was there. He threw to receiver Shelton Diggs, who dove and caught it.

USC led, 18–17. The Buckeyes had one last chance, but a 62-yard field goal by Tom Skladany fell short.

A few hours later, Notre Dame shocked Alabama in the Orange Bowl. USC would finish first in the coaches' poll. Woody Hayes's Buckeyes had come within a single point of sharing the national title.

8

Roses

Five years had passed since the University of Michigan promised to increase its black enrollment to 10 percent of the student population. The school still hadn't met the threshold. In mid-February 1975, a group of black students tried to make the university pay for it.

Three hundred minority students occupied the Administration Building and vowed not to leave unless the university complied with their demands. Five hundred employees of the Graduate Employees' Organization rallied outside to support them.

It looked like 1970 all over again. But it was not 1970. By the second day of the occupation, there were only 150 students in the Administration Building. The next day, they ended the sit-in after President Robben Fleming promised to negotiate the following Monday. But then Monday came and none of the demands were met.

Vietnam was over and Richard Nixon was an ex-president. The culture that had embraced the 1970 protests had disintegrated. Now it was hard to get the masses to protest anything.

Sometimes at parties, Don Canham would idly remark that he could have become president of Chrysler or General Motors if he had chosen that particular career path. Fewer and fewer people doubted him. In the July 28, 1975, issue of *Sports Illustrated*, celebrated sportswriter Frank Deford cemented Canham's status as the king of athletic directors.

The article was headlined "No Death for a Salesman," and it took up nine pages in the magazine. There was a large photo of Canham in

Michigan Stadium, wearing a plaid jacket, dark pants, and white loafers, and surrounded by Michigan mugs, plates, a helmet lamp, bumper stickers, and other merchandise he was peddling.

Deford began by breaking down the state of intercollegiate athletics. "Something like 90 percent of all U.S. college athletic departments are losing money," he wrote. "And every indication is that it will get worse before it gets lots worse. The panic is on."

Public funding for colleges was shrinking, leading to a rise in scholarship costs *and* a reduction in funding for athletics. Title IX looked like it might radically change the face of college sports. (That summer, Bo Schembechler would write a letter to his friend and president, Gerald Ford, begging him to help "prevent the great injury to intercollegiate athletics which imposition of these unreasonable rules will bring about.") Pro football and basketball were siphoning interest from college games.

"Which brings us to Don Canham," Deford wrote.

Deford noted some of Canham's successes: alumni gifts to the athletic department had gone from $46,000 annually to $300,000; Michigan was now making $100,000 a year off *parking*, of all things; and football attendance had jumped from an average of 67,000 per game to 90,000. The piece also noted that twenty-eight universities, from state schools to Yale, had either paid for Canham to visit their campus or sent a representative to Ann Arbor to try to replicate his magic touch.

Canham appreciated the article. He understood that it increased his power in college athletics and added to the perception that Michigan athletics were in demand. But he was a bit miffed that Deford used approximately sixty-five hundred words in his piece and somehow neglected to include an important one:

"Schembechler."

Bo Schembechler was 58-7-1 at Michigan, including 50-4-1 in his last five seasons. He was no longer known as an up-and-comer, the guy who beat his mentor Woody Hayes's Team of the Century in his first season. He was considered an elite coach, the guy who beat everybody *except* Woody Hayes. Since that 1969 upset (and not counting the ensuing Rose Bowl, which Schembechler had missed because of his heart attack), he was 1-3-1 against Hayes and 49-1 against the rest of the planet.

Now, entering the 1975 season, at least Schembechler knew that Ohio State could not keep Michigan out of a bowl game. The Big Ten had finally eliminated its Rose Bowl–only rule, allowing other conference teams to play in other bowl games. Schembechler would forever tell people that the 1973 tie had forced the Big Ten's hand, but the truth was that Big Ten commissioner Wayne Duke had wanted the change from the moment he arrived in 1971. It just took some time to convince the Rose Bowl representatives to sign away their monopoly on Big Ten teams.

And Duke wasn't trying to help Michigan. He was trying to help everybody else.

Duke believed that sending multiple teams to bowls would create parity in the conference—no longer could Woody Hayes and Bo Schembechler tell recruits that the only roads to a bowl game went through Ann Arbor and Columbus. (Duke was not the only one with that ambition. A new NCAA rule limited schools to ninety-five football scholarships, to spread the talent more evenly. The Big Ten already had the limit in place, but some national powers, such as Nebraska, were known to hand out 150 scholarships or more.)

Yet even with the new rule, the Rose Bowl was clearly the nation's premier bowl game. Sixty-seven million people were expected to watch the January 1, 1976, game on television. The Rose Bowl payout (which was split evenly among Big Ten teams) was bigger than the Orange, Sugar, and Cotton Bowl payouts combined.

Schembechler was desperate to get back to the Rose Bowl. But in order to do it, he had to first find a quarterback to replace Dennis Franklin. The leading candidate was senior Mark Elzinga, but Schembechler had high hopes for a left-handed recruit from Southwestern High School in Flint named Rick Leach.

Leach had been a passing quarterback in high school, but the

Michigan coaches were not interested in veering from their run-heavy offensive attack. Leach would have to fit them, not the other way around. The coaches felt he had the right blend of athleticism and poise to do it. Leach had been an all-state football, basketball, and baseball player and was one of the highest-regarded high school athletes ever in the state of Michigan. His father and uncle had both played baseball at Michigan. Yet he was no lock to end up in Ann Arbor—he was such a gifted batter that the Philadelphia Phillies offered him $100,000 to skip college and play in their minor-league system.

Schembechler was determined to bring Leach to Michigan. But he was going to do it on his terms. He signed five high school quarterbacks in Leach's class (though some were destined for other positions, and one, Rick Sofield, would skip school altogether to play for the Minnesota Twins). There would be a dozen or so quarterbacks in Michigan's fall camp. Leach was promised a chance to compete. Nothing more.

Leach asked Schembechler if he could play both baseball and football at Michigan. Schembechler had played both sports at Miami, but as a coach he did not like the idea of *anybody* playing two sports, let alone his quarterback.

Schembechler had already allowed defensive back Don Dufek to play hockey after the football season ended. Dufek would captain the 1975 team and earn All-American honors. So Schembechler offered Leach a compromise: he would skip baseball as a freshman, then play as a sophomore.

Like many schools, Michigan found summer employment for its players, who were not allowed to hold jobs during the school year. Schembechler got Leach a job working in an auto shop, painting car parts from 6 a.m. to 2 p.m., five days a week. There were certainly cushier jobs (and better hours), but Schembechler wanted to test Leach's resolve.

Leach would get up before sunrise, work at the shop for eight hours, then drive down to Ann Arbor to watch film or work out with the Wolverines. He would then drive home and play baseball in the evenings and do it all again the next day.

Schembechler tabbed Leach as his starter for the season opener at Wisconsin. Schembechler did not love the idea of playing a freshman, but Leach was an exceptionally quick learner who had adapted to Michigan's system and outplayed the other quarterbacks on the team. Schembechler knew he had not handed the job to Leach. Leach had earned it.

The night before the Wisconsin game, two of Schembechler's best defensive players, Calvin O'Neal and Tim Davis, arrived a few minutes late to the team dinner. When they walked in the room, O'Neal felt like everything stopped—dishes stopped clanging, players stopped eating. Lateness was simply not tolerated on Bo Schembechler teams, even if it was only for dinner.

O'Neal and Davis would tell Schembechler there was an obese lady in the elevator who had fallen and broken her leg and they had helped her to the ambulance. That's why they were late. It was not just a lie; it was a really *bad* lie. Yet Schembechler, whose temper was now common knowledge around the country, did not say a word.

Rick Leach threw more interceptions (three) than completions (two) against Wisconsin, but Michigan still managed to win, 23–6.

The next morning Schembechler went to Detroit for a live broadcast of his new weekly television show, *Michigan Replay*. The show was Don Canham's idea. Canham wanted to "get Bo off the rubber-chicken circuit," referring to Schembechler's banquet speeches for money, and the new show would pay him more than his old one had. Schembechler did not know the producers well, and though he took direction easily, he tended to treat them like reporters instead of folks who worked with him. But he started to show the poise and skill with the language that his players had seen for years. The film for the first *Michigan Replay* highlight was loaded backwards; Schembechler wryly noted that the video showed Leach as a righty, instead of a lefty, and continued his narration.

That afternoon, at the Wolverines' regular Sunday afternoon meeting, Schembechler asked Calvin O'Neal and Tim Davis to stand up and tell the team why they had been late to the Friday night meal.

The players started to talk about the fat lady and the elevator, and the whole team burst out laughing. Schembechler had managed to call O'Neal and Davis on their lie without even saying a word about it.

Michigan was a three-touchdown favorite at home against Stanford the next week, but Leach struggled and Stanford kicked a field goal with nine seconds left to force a 19–19 tie. The next week, the Wolverines were again three-touchdown favorites, this time against Baylor. Schembechler benched Leach for Elzinga, but when Elzinga struggled, Leach played the second half. This one ended in a 14–14 tie.

Michigan was 1-0-2. The season was in peril.

The Wolverines bounced back, beating fifth-ranked Missouri, 31–7, and No. 15 Michigan State, 16–6. That should have eased Schembechler's concerns. But the night before the sixth game of the season, against lowly Northwestern, Schembechler sat in his hotel room, watching films and worrying.

"Goddamn, Northwestern is good and we aren't ready," he told his assistants. "I am sitting on an upset."

He then started screaming at anybody in the hotel who had the misfortune of being associated with Michigan football.

The next day, the Wolverines beat Northwestern 69–0.

From there, the season took on a typical Schembechler quality: whip Indiana, beat Minnesota, shut out Purdue, beat Illinois. Michigan still had not lost to a team from outside of Columbus in four years.

If this was it for the Old Man, the last season in his legendary career, it would begin with a team he could not stand: Michigan State. The Spartans were considered the third best team in the Big Ten, and they had handed Woody Hayes his last two conference losses, in 1972 and 1974. Michigan State quarterback Charlie Baggett had said the Buckeyes would be "scared" to come back to East Lansing and promised "we'll whip their ass," and that chapped Hayes even more.

Hayes did not like how Michigan State operated its program. He thought the Spartans had been giving illegal recruiting inducements to players for years. The NCAA had recently boosted its investigative staff from three people to eight, but that was still woefully inefficient to monitor cheating, which was growing rampant. The Spartans were probably not going to get caught cheating unless somebody turned them in to the NCAA, and the next year, somebody would.

Woody Hayes would proudly claim responsibility.

In the meantime, Hayes spent much of the summer preparing for Michigan State, instead of his usual habit of focusing on Michigan. Late in the week leading up to the game, he asked his four captains—Archie Griffin, Tim Fox, Brian Baschnagel, and Ken Kuhn—to address the team. Before they spoke, Hayes pulled Baschnagel aside.

"Brian," Hayes said, "I want you to swear."

As the coach knew, Baschnagel rarely swore. The request made him uncomfortable.

"Coach, I'm not an actor," Baschnagel said.

Hayes, of course, cussed like the Navy sailor he had once been. But he was not proud of it. He considered it a weakness. Before one practice, he gathered the Buckeyes and told them there would be no profanity that day; when practice started, the players kept count of how many times Hayes violated his rule: *twenty-three, twenty-four, twenty-five* . . .

Why would Hayes suddenly ask one of his best-behaved players to swear at the whole team? Did he think that was the only way to connect with the others? Perhaps Hayes saw what others saw, that some of his players were starting to view the Old Man as just that: an old man.

Some Buckeyes were openly making fun of Hayes. The coach had a funny voice—he spoke with a lisp, had a higher-pitched voice than one expected from a man his size, and had an Ohio country accent that surfaced sometimes. Like in practice, he would often tell a player to "set up right here," but the way he said it sounded like "right he-yur." Or he would say, "We're not going to let anybody sneak up behind us and hit us over the head with a sack of shit," and it sounded like "sack of sheet." This was the kind of thing players had joked about for years—in their dorm rooms. But now guys were making tackles in practice, pointing to the turf, and saying, "I got him right he-yur."

Baschnagel remembered one incident at the Rose Bowl, when Hayes had gathered the entire team in the lobby of the Huntington Hilton to go for a walk. As the Buckeyes walked behind their coach, one of them started whistling the theme to *Patton*. He seemed to be mocking the Old Man for acting like a general. But Woody perked up and picked up his pace, and then the rest of the team started whistling, and pretty soon they really *were* marching behind Hayes, and maybe it wasn't mocking after all. Maybe it was inspiring. At least that's how Hayes seemed to view it.

Now Hayes was asking Brian Baschnagel, Rhodes Scholarship candidate, to cuss at the whole team. Baschnagel declined. When the captains were finished speaking, Hayes tried to fire up his guys by hurling a pitcher of water against a wall. That, like his request for cussing, was part of a plan. Earlier that week, he had told somebody on his staff to make sure the water was in plastic pitchers instead of glass so they did not shatter when he threw them.

The night before the opener, an East Lansing disk jockey blasted rock music outside the Buckeyes' motel rooms until midnight. The Ohio State coaches were so worried about attacks from a hostile crowd after the controversial ending in 1974 that they brought baseball batting helmets to the game. But neither the fans nor the Spartans did any damage. Ohio State beat Michigan State, 21–0. The Buckeyes' defense intercepted three of Charlie Baggett's nine passes and limited him to minus nine yards rushing.

"They played a heck of a game," a humbled Baggett said afterward.

The next week, Ohio State faced No. 7 Penn State, the dominant power in the East. On the field before the game, Penn State coach Joe Paterno asked how Hayes was doing and told him not to overwork—normal pregame chitchat to Paterno, especially in light of

Hayes's heart attack the year before. But Hayes didn't see it that way. By the time he made it back to the locker room for his pregame talk, he was fuming.

"You know what they tried to do to us this week?" he asked his team. "They've been the nicest shit asses in the world. Joe comes out: 'Coach, how's your health? Do you want to take it easy?' Why, I had notion to *slap* the son of a bitch. *Take it easy?* Goddamn, I'll take it easy when they put me UP THERE!"

He pointed toward heaven.

"Or down there!"

And he pointed toward hell.

"But I know where I'll go!"

Was he serious? Was he really offended? Nobody knew for sure. But Hayes was on a roll now, and pretty soon he was shouting:

"Anything less than a man's best effort demeans him! Spoils him! Ruins him! Cheapens him!"

("Men suffer all their life long under the foolish superstition that they can be cheated," Emerson wrote. "But it is as impossible for a man to be cheated by anyone but himself, as for a thing to be and not be at the same time.")

The Buckeyes beat Penn State, 17–9. The next week, they whipped North Carolina. Then came the game that showcased Ohio State's dominance: the Buckeyes flew to Los Angeles and crushed No. 13 UCLA, 41–20. Hayes said afterward that his team played "pretty doggone good football until we got ahead 38–7 and let up." Cornelius Greene played like a man nicknamed "Flam" *should* play in Hollywood: he ran for 120 yards and passed for 98 yards.

"Cornelius did a super job today," Hayes said afterward, "but there was one better back on the field and that was our tailback." Archie Griffin had run for 160 yards. Hayes then added his standard line on Griffin: "He's a better young man than he is a football player, and he's the best ball player I've ever seen."

In late October, Griffin set the NCAA career rushing mark against Purdue. "I wish we could have had a shutout," Hayes said afterward, but he had to settle for a 35–6 victory. Griffin felt awkward about all the attention, and he asked Hayes not to talk about him so much. Hayes proudly told reporters that Griffin had asked him to clam up, creating another wave of stories about selfless Archie.

When it came time to vote for the team's most valuable player, Hayes told his players that if Griffin won, he could make history: the Big Ten MVP was chosen from the ten team MVPs, and nobody had ever won the league MVP for three straight years. But Cornelius Greene beat Griffin in the team voting. Hayes asked Archie how he had cast his vote. Griffin said he had voted for Greene. Hayes then told the press that was the kind of man Archie Griffin was—he gave up a chance at history for Cornelius Greene! Hayes was not so quick to mention that Greene had voted for Griffin.

Greene would be named the Big Ten's MVP. But Griffin would become the first two-time winner of the Heisman Trophy.

The 1975 team seemed to capture the entire Hayes era at Ohio State. Before Griffin came along, Hayes's favorite player was probably Howard "Hopalong" Cassady, the 1955 Heisman Trophy winner. Now Hopalong's son Craig was a defensive back for the Buckeyes; he led the Big Ten in interceptions. Griffin's brother Ray had moved from running back to defensive back and was now a rising star.

Hayes had also found a new, trusted aide-de-camp. In order to keep the coaches focused on football, every Ohio State coach had a student manager essentially acting as a personal assistant. Being the head coach, Woody Hayes naturally had a manager assigned to him, but this was not a coveted job—as a general rule, the closer you got to Woody, the tougher he was to deal with, and student managers inevitably spent many hours with him.

For the 1975 season, a sophomore named Mark George volunteered. George had been assistant coach Dick Walker's manager the year before and had done a good job, but when he offered to be Woody's manager he had long hair and a three-day-old beard.

"I'd like to make you my manager," Hayes said, "but you look like a goddamn communist bomb-thrower."

George got a haircut and a shave and came back the next day. Soon after, without asking if it was okay, he decided to tidy up Hayes's

office. For all he knew, that could end his time as Hayes's manager—
Hayes might come back, see that George had cleaned his office without his permission, and start yelling. But Hayes thanked him and
admired his initiative, and a friendship was born. Despite the forty-plus
years of age difference, George and Hayes would become extremely
close.

As the season unfolded, George got a strong sense that Hayes was
planning on retiring after the 1975 season—assuming that Ohio State
won the national championship.

People close to Hayes had long believed he cared even more than
most coaches about retiring on top. Put another way: there were
doubts about whether Hayes could leave if he *wasn't* on top. George
Patton said success was how high you bounce when you hit bottom,
and Hayes had always told his players they would be measured by how
well they came back from failure. How could he leave after, say, a loss
to That School Up North?

Jeff Kaplan, the "brain coach," sensed that this was a once-in-
a-lifetime kind of year. He bought a Radio Shack cassette recorder,
stuck it under his coat in the locker room, and surreptitiously recorded
the coach. Even Paul Hornung, whose *Dispatch* dispatches seemed to
come directly from Hayes's typewriter, could not avoid the retirement
rumors. He acknowledged, in print, that Columbus was buzzing with
the possibility.

Hornung also wrote that Hayes was recruiting high school prospects awfully hard for a man who did not plan to coach them. But
Hornung, of all people, should have known better. If anything, Hayes
would work *harder* than usual on the eve of his retirement, just so
nobody could say he had coasted to the finish line. He didn't want
anybody to say he had cheated Ohio State University out of anything.
He even apologized to staffers for going through too many of the
department's red felt-tip pens.

Spurred by its blowout win over UCLA, Ohio State beat its next
six opponents by an average of 34 points. The Buckeyes would enter
the game against Michigan as the undefeated, untied, and undisputed
No. 1 team in the country. Griffin had run for at least 100 yards in

his last thirty-one regular-season games, the longest streak in college football history—an astounding fourteen games more than the second longest streak.

This could be the ultimate ride off into the sunset: a national championship, a second straight Heisman Trophy for Griffin, and a senior class that had won four straight Big Ten championships and never lost to Michigan. Nobody could say Woody Hayes had been forced to quit, like they said about President Nixon. Hayes would not say whether he planned to retire. But when reporters asked him about it, he never said he was coming back, and there was no denying that the possibility was tantalizing. Woody Hayes had a chance at the perfect ending to his career. He was two wins away.

All Andy Sacks wanted was a picture of Bo Schembechler talking to Rick Leach. That was it. Sacks, a Michigan grad and freelance photographer, called Michigan sports information director Will Perry with his request. The photo would go out on the United Press International wire and likely run in newspapers around the country.

Perry told Sacks the coach was way too busy to accommodate him. Many photographers would have given up. But when Sacks was a Michigan student, he had lived at 1307 South State Street, across from the Michigan athletic campus, and he knew there were a few new apartment buildings there that had balconies overlooking the football practice field, which was surrounded by a brick wall. One afternoon, while the Wolverines were practicing, Sacks went to one of the buildings, walked up to the second floor, and knocked on a few doors until somebody let him in.

Sacks walked to the balcony, took out his 500-millimeter telephoto lens, and started shooting. Two Michigan graduate assistants walked toward him and hollered that Bo wanted to see him. And Sacks thought, "Oh—*now* he's got time to pose."

No, the assistants said. Sacks was not allowed to take photos of practice. Schembechler had spotters all around his field, looking for journalists and other spies.

Sacks was no wallflower. He had been arrested on the job once before, for taking pictures of kids who were removing billboards to cleanse the environment. (The charge was "aiding and abetting the illicit destruction of property." He was not convicted.) Sacks said he would stay on the balcony.

A few minutes later, he saw Bo Schembechler and most of his football team walking across the street. Sacks was worried about getting his ass kicked. He told the guys who lived in the apartment to call the police. Schembechler and his troops walked into the building, up to the second floor, into the apartment, and demanded that Sacks turn over his film.

"You have no scruples!" Schembechler barked.

Sacks told Schembechler to call the UPI editor. And as Schembechler was on the phone, giving the editor an earful, the police showed up. The cops told Sacks they would take his film, cameras, and tripod and walk out with them. Sacks did not have a choice. There was no way he could get past the football team on his own. The cops told him he could have everything back as soon as the game started on Saturday.

The incident made national news. It was more evidence of how big this game had become—and, some said, how paranoid the coaches were. Schembechler did not care about the reaction. He was keeping the media out of his practices all week, just like Hayes was doing in Columbus. The No. 1 team in the country was coming to Michigan Stadium, where the Wolverines had not lost in forty-one games, and there was a Rose Bowl bid on the line. Schembechler was not going to let some son-of-a-bitch photographer screw it up.

"This game, I want more than any game I've ever played!" Woody Hayes shouted to his Buckeyes. "You and I will remember this game more than the other ten, a hundred times over."

They were in the locker room now, huddled beneath the biggest football crowd in the country. Safety Tim Fox started telling his teammates that they could beat Michigan because they did it the year before, and Hayes cut him off: "Fuck last year! This is us! This is *this* year!" When somebody mentioned the national championship, Hayes interrupted again: "The national championship, hell, it will fall in our laps! That's nothing!"

Hayes talked briefly of the battles at Lexington and Concord, when Paul Revere had alerted Samuel Adams and John Hancock that the British were coming.

"I want this one more than anything I've lived for!" Hayes said.

In seven years under Bo Schembechler, Michigan was 27-0-1 in Big Ten home games. Yet the fourth-ranked Wolverines were underdogs in this one, for good reason. Ohio State had been the best team in the country, and Michigan, though rapidly improving, was still young, especially at the most important position on the field.

Rick Leach stood on the field before the game and was almost overwhelmed by the moment. He had followed the Michigan–Ohio State rivalry closely for years, and now, just a few months after graduating from Southwestern High School in Flint, he was one of the game's marquee players. As he warmed up, Michigan equipment manager Jon Falk walked up to him. The two had become close over the course of the season.

"How's your helmet?" Falk asked.

His *helmet*? It was fine. On his head. Right where it was supposed to be.

Then Falk started talking about Leach's chinstrap.

"Make it tighter," Falk said, "because you're going to get hit harder than in any other game. This game is different."

Leach tightened his chinstrap and got ready for the opening kickoff.

To nobody's surprise, Ohio State's senior-laden, talent-laden offense drove all the way to the end zone on its first possession of the game. Fullback Pete Johnson finished the drive with a touchdown run. To everybody's surprise, the Buckeyes did almost nothing for the rest of the half. Cornelius Greene, the senior star, was making freshman mistakes: he threw two interceptions in Michigan territory. Rick Leach, the freshman, was not exactly playing like a senior (he too threw an interception, and he also fumbled), but at least he was making some positive plays as well.

Late in the second quarter, Leach and running backs Rob Lytle and Gordon Bell led the Wolverines from their own 20 down to the Ohio State 11. Leach pitched the ball to Bell on an apparent sweep. The Ohio State defense, which had seen a thousand sweeps, swarmed. But it was a trick play. Bell stopped and threw a pass to Jim Smith in the end zone. Touchdown.

And now Andy Sacks figured he knew why Bo Schembechler had been so mad. He did not want anybody finding out about his secret halfback pass.

Ohio State was way out of its element: its senior quarterback was playing poorly and the other team was asking its halfback to throw touchdown passes. There were 24 seconds left in the second quarter. The Buckeyes just wanted to get out of the half without further damage, and they almost didn't do that. On the ensuing kickoff, Archie Griffin fumbled. Michigan recovered and had a chance for a 36-yard field goal. It missed. The halftime score was 7–7.

Despite the missed field goal, Michigan was just thirty minutes away from earning its first Rose Bowl bid in four years—and killing Ohio State's national title hopes. Yet ABC sideline announcer Jim Lampley noticed that the Michigan Stadium crowd was not nearly as loud as the one at Ohio Stadium the year before.

This was partly because of the wide-open configuration of the stadium, which did not contain noise well. In earlier years, one could have argued that the fans in Ann Arbor were more interested in politics than in football. That was no longer the case. The Human Rights Party, a socialist political party that had used student support to build power in Ann Arbor city government, was down to a single member on the city council. Earlier in 1975, Human Rights Party candidates had been defeated in the city's student-dominated first and second wards. Conservatives had won all three open seats on the Ann Arbor school board that summer.

Now the students were knee deep in football. They just weren't as loud about it, and when Lampley stepped into a Michigan Stadium restroom, he discovered why. He got a contact high from all the marijuana smoke. The students in Columbus had been fueled largely by alcohol. They were loud and out for blood. Many Michigan students were there to have a good time. Beating Ohio State was only part of the fun.

The second half started but the Ohio State offense did not. This was unbelievable. Despite all these senior starters, the Buckeyes couldn't go anywhere. They got nine yards on their first drive, then punted. Forget about touchdowns; the Buckeyes could not even get a *first* down.

Before the game, there had been a sense that Ohio State would outplay Michigan, but the Wolverines would have a chance to win if they could just hang around long enough. Now the opposite was happening. The Wolverines were clearly outplaying the Buckeyes, yet the score remained tied at seven.

Midway through the fourth quarter, Michigan forced the Buckeyes to punt from their own four-yard line, then took over at the Ohio State 43. Chances like this were scarce, and the Wolverines desperately needed to take advantage. They did. They quickly moved down to the Ohio State one-yard line, where Leach kept the ball on an option play and ran into the end zone. Michigan led, 14–7.

An announcement came over the Michigan Stadium public address system: No. 7 Oklahoma was leading No. 2 Nebraska, 7–3. The crowd roared. If the Wolverines held on to beat the top-ranked Buckeyes and Oklahoma beat Nebraska, Michigan would be in prime position to capture Bo Schembechler's first national championship.

Barely seven minutes remained. One of the finest senior classes in Ohio State history needed to go 80 yards for a game-tying score. The Buckeyes had not even picked up a first down since early in the second quarter.

On first down, Greene threw deep. Incomplete. Second down. Greene dropped back to pass again. Michigan middle guard Tim Davis burst through the line and looked, for all the world, like he would chase Cornelius Greene right out of Michigan Stadium. Greene ran back to his left, then changed directions and ran the other way, and finally found himself in his own end zone, 20 yards behind the line of scrimmage. He chucked the ball into coverage—a desperate, ill-advised pass. Three Wolverines had a chance to make the interception. None of them did. The ball fell to the ground.

Third down, 10 yards to go.

Greene asked his teammates to hold hands so he could say a prayer. Brian Baschnagel was stunned, almost *offended*. Was Flam really asking God for a victory? No. He was not. Greene didn't pray for a win. He prayed for the strength to deal with whatever happened—for the Buckeyes to keep their composure and keep it in perspective.

Greene dropped back to pass and threw to Baschnagel along the right sideline. Baschnagel caught it for a 17-yard gain. First down.

Greene passed again, this time to Lenny Willis. Another first down.

Greene passed to Willis again. And again, they picked up a first down.

Griffin ran for 11 yards, and then Greene ran down to the Michigan eight. All this passing had been well and good, but now the Woody Hayes's boys were honing in on Bo Schembechler's end zone, and he was going with his beloved "robust" offense. He would load up the backfield and run the fullback.

Pete Johnson ran for six yards, down to the Michigan two. Johnson ran again, almost to the end zone—Greene held his hands up, thinking Johnson had scored—but not quite in. On third down, Johnson ran again. He was stopped short.

Fourth down. Ohio State needed less than a yard for the touchdown. Hayes called on Johnson again, and this time he scored. Ohio State now trailed 14–13, leaving Hayes with a choice: kick the extra point to tie the game, or go for a two-point conversion and the win. The Buckeyes could not afford for the game to end in a tie—they would get the

Rose Bowl bid but likely lose their chance at a national championship, just like in 1973. But Hayes knew Michigan *really* couldn't afford a tie. The Wolverines needed to win to go to the Rose Bowl. So there was no way Schembechler would try to run out the clock.

Hayes decided to kick the extra point instead of going for a two-point conversion. The score was tied, 14–14. Michigan took possession on its own 20 with 3:18 left in the game. Schembechler pulled Rick Leach aside and told him they were going for the score, the win, and the Big Ten championship.

Michigan's freshman quarterback would pass with the game on the line.

Woody Hayes liked his chances.

On first down, Leach was sacked. On second down he threw incomplete. It was third and 18. Leach dropped back and threw to Jimmy Smith, but he put too much on it. The pass went over Smith's head and into the hands of Ray Griffin, Archie's brother, who intercepted it and ran it all the way down to the Michigan three-yard line.

On the next play, Pete Johnson scored his third touchdown of the day.

Ohio State 21, Michigan 14.

Pretty soon, Leach threw another interception, and then it was over.

The still-unbeaten Buckeyes carried the Old Man off the field. Somebody handed him a bouquet of roses. Ohio State was going back to Pasadena. Michigan would settle for the Orange Bowl.

In the jubilance of the postgame locker room, after one of his best teams recorded its greatest victory, against the team and town and state he had been battling for most of his professional lifetime, Woody Hayes noted the date.

"November 22," he said. "That was a Friday twelve years ago. We'd just started to have our quarterback meetings at one o'clock in Ypsilanti at an old hotel. Our team manager came in and said, 'The president has been shot.'

"I've had the feeling in the last twelve years that that's the worst thing that ever happened to this country, because we've sort of had a downhill run ever since. They said it was a great big plot. I don't think it was. I think it was a goddamn kook and there's never been the slightest shred of evidence otherwise. But I think we oughta pray that people stay together like we stay together . . . without it, we couldn't have won today."

Griffin had been stopped short of 100 yards, but nobody in scarlet and gray seemed to care, least of all Griffin. In his postgame press conference, Hayes was asked if this was his sweetest win.

"I'd say it's the sweetest one, maybe because it's the last one," he said.

The reporters' ears perked up. The last one? Did he mean "last" as in most recent? Or last because he was going to retire?

"I wouldn't give you that information if I knew it," Hayes said, "and I don't know it."

A thousand fans greeted Ohio State's charter flight when it landed at Port Columbus International Airport. Somebody handed Hayes more roses. He had a little time before filming *The Woody Hayes Show*, so he directed his driver to Riverside Hospital.

Hayes brought the roses with him to Riverside. He walked through the halls with a nurse, stopping in each room, handing a rose to each patient, whispering in their ears, kissing them on the forehead, then walking to the next room. He kept going until he was out of roses.

Ohio State was a 15-point favorite in the Rose Bowl, and not even the Buckeyes' opponent could argue with the spread. After all, UCLA had played Ohio State just three months earlier, and the Buckeyes had won 41–20. UCLA seemed overmatched in every way. Ohio State was 11–0 and No. 1 in the nation; UCLA was 8-2-1 and not even in the top ten. Ohio State was one of the premier programs in the country; UCLA was not even the top program in its own city.

The Bruins' thirty-nine-year-old coach, Dick Vermeil, was in awe of Hayes. He was mesmerized when Hayes gave a thirty-minute speech at a Tournament of Roses brunch. Vermeil told reporters that after listening to Hayes speak, *he* was ready to go out and win for Ohio State. "This is the type of man I was raised by, my dad," he said. Hayes appreciated Vermeil's admiration. As he told the writers, "I've been a hero worshipper from back in the 1920s."

As expected, Ohio State dominated the first half. The Buckeyes piled up 174 yards to UCLA's 49 and gained eleven first downs to the Bruins' two. Yet Ohio State only led 3–0.

At halftime, Vermeil decided his running game wasn't working and he needed to mix in short- to medium-range passes. UCLA kicked a field goal on the opening possession of the second half. A game that Ohio State had dominated was now tied, 3–3.

On the Bruins' next drive, they used a variety of plays—a play-action pass, a flanker reverse, an option pitch, and another pass—to put together a touchdown drive. The Bruins missed the extra point, but they suddenly led Ohio State for the first time in seven quarters of trying.

Later in the third quarter, UCLA scored again, on a pass from quarterback John Sciarra to Wally Henry. Ohio State, which had opened a 38–7 lead in the first meeting between the teams, now trailed 16–3.

The national championship was slipping away.

The Buckeyes scored to cut it to 16–10, but late in the fourth quarter, UCLA tailback Wendell Tyler ran 55 yards through a worn-out Ohio State defense for a touchdown. Tyler ran right through the end zone and started dancing against the upright.

The Bruins now led 23–10. Nobody would score again. With eight seconds left and the clock stopped, a pair of UCLA players put Vermeil on their shoulders, ready to carry the rising coaching star off the field. But Vermeil looked out on the Pasadena field and realized his players had to put him down . . . because there, slowly walking alone across the Rose Bowl field, his hands at his hips, was Woody Hayes.

Hayes walked all the way over to the UCLA sideline and gave Vermeil a hug. He knew he wouldn't have a chance to do it in the pandemonium after the clock expired, so he did it with eight seconds left.

Then Hayes took the long walk back to the Ohio State sideline, the officials ticked those final eight seconds off, and the Buckeyes' national championship hopes had officially disappeared into the Southern California air. Hayes kept the Ohio State locker room closed for forty-five minutes after the game, then ducked out a side door without talking to reporters.

Spurred (they said later) by UCLA's upset of Ohio State, the Oklahoma Sooners came into the Orange Bowl that night and beat Michigan, 14–6. Some of the Wolverines felt like they had peaked a week before the game—Bo Schembechler, so fired up about finally coaching in a bowl game, overdid the practices once again. It had felt like fall conditioning instead of game preparation. But the Wolverines also admitted that Oklahoma simply had a better team, and some said that, in the wake of UCLA's stunning upset of Ohio State, the Sooners deserved the national title. Oklahoma would finish No. 1 in both polls.

With the two bowl losses, Michigan and Ohio State were now a combined 1–7 in bowl games since the start of the Schembechler era. Almost every result, on its own, made some sense. Twice they had lost by a point in the final moments (Stanford's 13–12 win over Michigan in the 1972 Rose Bowl and USC's 18–17 win in the '75 Rose Bowl). Another time the Michigan players had opened the game without knowing if Schembechler was alive. Three of the teams that beat Michigan or Ohio State won at least a share of the national title.

Yet 1–7 was still 1–7, and people across the Midwest searched for answers. Some argued that Big Ten football simply wasn't that strong, but that was an oversimplification. Ohio State had dominated that same UCLA team in the regular season. Only one of the seven losses was a blowout—and that came to the 1972 USC team, one of the best ever.

Many Buckeyes and Wolverines felt they put so much into their "season-ending" game against each other that they could not reach that emotional high again for a bowl game. Woody Hayes's proclamation to his team before the Michigan game summed up the feeling: *The national championship, hell, it will fall in our laps! That's nothing!*

But there was something else, too. Michigan and Ohio State dominated Big Ten teams that were similar to them—just not as good. The
bowl season was different. In Pasadena, the Big Ten champion played
on grass, instead of the artificial surfaces favored in the weather-
beaten Big Ten, before a crowd that favored the opponent, against a
team that inevitably passed more than anybody in the Big Ten.

In the Rose Bowl, UCLA quarterback John Sciarra had passed for
212 yards, compared to 90 for Cornelius Greene. And it was *how* Sciarra gained those yards that stood out. Many came on short passes
to the sidelines or underneath the coverage, instead of the more traditional deep passes. When Ohio State had the ball, UCLA stacked
eight men on the line of scrimmage to stop the run. On those occasions when Greene dropped back to throw, he was often swamped by
Bruin defenders before his receivers could complete their patterns,
which almost always took them downfield.

Even when UCLA was leading in the fourth quarter, Vermeil was
not afraid to throw. Sciarra, in fact, had thrown an interception with
UCLA up 16–10.

Hayes and Schembechler had built their programs on fundamentals, repetition, and error-free football. They had used the pass as a
change-up pitch—every once in a while, they would throw downfield.
Now passing attacks were more varied, and coaches were willing to
risk a few mistakes in exchange for larger rewards.

The game was changing. It would be up to Hayes and Schembechler to change with it.

In the wake of Ohio State's Rose Bowl defeat, Woody Hayes would
return to coach the Buckeyes in 1976. But Ohio State athletic director
Ed Weaver still had to hire a coach—for basketball. Longtime basketball coach Fred Taylor resigned in the spring of 1976 after a 6–20
season, and the school needed somebody to revive the program. The
brightest young coach in America at that time was a thirty-five-year-
old Ohio State graduate named Bob Knight.

Knight had built a juggernaut at Indiana: he had nearly won the national championship in 1975 and would win it in 1976 with an undefeated team. He had done it with the same authoritarian, ultra-intense, fundamentals-first approach that had worked so well for Woody Hayes. This was not a coincidence. Knight had idolized Hayes since he was a kid growing up in Orrville, Ohio.

Pursuing Knight was a no-brainer. But Ohio State did not go after him, not at first. The Buckeyes simply went to him for advice. Associate athletic director Hugh Hindman (one of Hayes's former assistants) and chemistry professor Harold Schechter, the athletic department's acting faculty representative, met with Knight at a hotel in Louisville, Kentucky, for almost seven hours, discussing all aspects of the job and what it would entail. By the end, Hindman and Schechter got the sense that Knight was interested in being more than just a consultant.

Schechter asked if he would consider coaching at Ohio State. Knight replied that he had the best team in the country at Indiana and an excellent recruiting class coming in. But he could never turn down Ohio State.

Schechter and Hindman flew back to Columbus and told Weaver, the athletic director, that Knight wanted the job. Schechter figured an offer was forthcoming. But a few days passed and Knight was left dangling.

Knight was angry. He wondered why Weaver hadn't gone to Louisville to meet with him, and he suspected that Ohio State's administration wasn't committed to hiring him. His suspicions were accurate. Knight was known as a volatile coach, and Ohio State president Harold Enarson told people that he didn't think he could handle both Woody Hayes and Bob Knight at his university.

Hayes eventually stepped in to woo Knight, but it was too late. Knight withdrew from the search and Ohio State hired Western Michigan coach Eldon Miller.

In September of that year, Knight sent a letter to Hayes to let him know that the process had not changed his opinion of the football coach.

"The relationship I have had with you is one of the most enjoyable that I have had in athletics," Knight wrote, "and there is no one I respect more than you. I am sorry that things did not work out last spring and wish they would have involved you in the situation earlier. I greatly appreciate your thoughtfulness and consideration at the time. Here's hoping that your season is the best ever."

9

Independence

Woody Hayes hung up the phone, looked over at brain coach Dutch Baughman, and started walking out the door. Baughman knew he was about to drive Hayes someplace. He just didn't know where. They could be heading out for a pecan roll or a recruiting visit or both. As it turned out, they were going to a hospital. That was no surprise—in the offseason, Hayes visited hospitals whenever somebody asked, and somebody always asked. This trip was unusual only because of the hospital (St. Joseph Mercy in Ann Arbor) and the name of the patient: Glenn Edward Schembechler.

Typically, Don Canham had seen this coming, and just as typically, he was blunt about it.

"Bo will probably have to have an arterial bypass someday," Canham had told an alumni gathering in East Lansing, Michigan, two weeks before the surgery. "The question is when."

Schembechler thought he had an answer to the question of when: "Later." The coach had missed spring practice because of chest pains and a gall bladder problem, and he had been told he needed the bypass, but he refused to believe it. He spent much of the spring scouring the country for a doctor, *any* doctor, to tell him he didn't need surgery. Finally, Schembechler gave in. On May 20, 1976, he underwent six hours of surgery to remove blockage in his heart.

Hayes and Baughman did not reach Ann Arbor until late that night. And such was the legend of Woody and Bo that the security guard outside the hospital looked at Hayes and said, "Coach, we've been expecting you."

Hayes went up to Schembechler's room, sat down, put his hand on

Schembechler's shoulder, and leaned over. Baughman stayed on the other side of the room, and for the longest time, he couldn't tell if Hayes was talking or praying.

Genetics and cheeseburgers had caught up with Schembechler again. After his heart attack at the 1970 Rose Bowl, he had improved his diet and exercised regularly, but within a few years he ate what he wanted and spent most of his days holed up in his office, watching film. Now he had to recover from another heart surgery and work himself back into shape. He stayed in the hospital for almost two weeks before being released.

Schembechler would start exercising and eating more sensibly. But he had no interest in reducing his daily intake of football film. A few weeks after the surgery, he joined a group of Michigan alumni on a tour of Scandinavia. On the charter flight to Copenhagen, Michigan alumni director Bob Forman discreetly walked up and down the aisle and asked the alums to give the recovering coach a break by not asking about football.

Two days later, Forman asked Schembechler how the trip was going.

"I can't understand this damn group of people," Schembechler grumbled. "I haven't had a question about football from any of them. Apparently they're not interested."

At a cocktail reception that night, Forman announced that the embargo was off.

Bo Schembechler was not the only Ann Arborite who was eager to return to football. That summer, hundreds of Michigan students packed up their books, playing cards, and bedrolls and formed a tent community outside Michigan's ticket offices. Tickets would not go on sale for another three weeks.

The demand for tickets was so high that Don Canham was sometimes asked if he would build a second deck on Michigan Stadium. Eight years after Canham joked about planting shrubs in the seats, the nation's biggest college-owned stadium suddenly wasn't big enough.

Canham looked into it. He concluded that building a second deck would cost as much as $100 million—way too high.

But he did have another idea for increasing his ticket revenue.

"What we're doing is considering putting in a private box, like the press box, on the other side," he said. "We could add more than 5,000 seats and pay it off in one year."

If Canham could get the school's regents to sign off on his plan, he would have the first private luxury box in a collegiate stadium. He could charge big money for the luxury seating without soaking the blue-collar season-ticket holder. He was sure he could make a profit quickly, but he wasn't sure if the regents would go for it.

In the meantime, Canham had the plans drawn up. He would spread them across his desk or his kitchen table at home and ask people what they thought. Mostly, though, it was the other way around: people wanted to know what Canham thought.

James Michener's *Sports in America* had been published, and though Michener wrote only a small portion of the book about Canham, he described the Michigan athletic director as one of its heroes. Canham appeared before President Ford's Commission on Olympic Sports and proposed that Olympic athletes should be paid to put them on equal footing with Russians and Eastern Europeans. (His recommendations were not heeded.) Canham was the man other athletic directors turned to for advice. He was the most influential member of the NCAA's television committee, which was negotiating to sign a four-year, $118 million TV package.

In 1976, Canham finally landed a contract to broadcast Michigan games on Detroit's WJR, the most powerful and influential radio station in the state. For years, WJR had been affiliated with Michigan State. The new radio deal came with a bonus: Canham's old friend and Michigan track teammate, Bob Ufer, would now be broadcasting to a mass audience. Ufer had been loyal to WPAG, a small Ann Arbor station. Ufer didn't care about the exposure, or the money. As he often told his audience, "Football is a religion and Saturday is the holy day of obligation."

Ufer spent his days selling insurance and Michigan football, and not always in that order. He once said that besides his family, two things were important in his life: "Michigan and Michigan football."

Ufer was the perfect frontman for Canham's perpetual marketing campaign. While other broadcasters at least feigned impartiality, Ufer seemed to live and die with every possession. He would shout that running back Harlan Huckleby ran "like a penguin with a hot herring in his cummerbund." And that fullback Rob Lytle charged "like a big bull with a bee in his ear." To Ufer, Rick Leach was not just a quarterback—he was "the guts and glue of the Maize and Blue."

And like many Michigan fans, Ufer relished the class struggle against Ohio State. He would break down the Ohio Stadium crowd of 88,000 as "4,000 Michigan fans, 10,000 alumni, and 74,000 truck drivers." He playfully called Woody Hayes "Dr. StrangeHayes." But Bob Ufer's sharpest dig at Woody Hayes was unintentional: he often referred to Michigan's coach as "Bo 'George Patton' Schembechler." Ufer was using Woody Hayes's hero against him! He often compared the Wolverines' ground assault to Patton's marches through Europe.

"Wasn't that Michigan drive just great?" Ufer once asked on the air. "That was like riding into Berlin!"

Never mind that Hayes, not Schembechler, was the one who idolized Patton, or that Hayes had been comparing his team's offense to Patton's army for decades. That was not Bob Ufer's problem. He was a Michigan man, spreading the gospel to anybody who would listen.

Michigan began the 1976 season ranked No. 2 in the country, then beat Wisconsin in the opener and moved up to No. 1. For some teams, earning a No. 1 ranking would have been the highlight of the season. For Michigan, it was not even the highlight of the week. Four days after beating Wisconsin, the Wolverines were practicing in Michigan Stadium when the president of the United States showed up.

President Gerald R. Ford spent twenty minutes watching his Wolverines practice. At one point, one of Ford's Secret Service agents was in the path of a planned running play. Schembechler asked the man to move, and when the agent refused, Schembechler told Rick Leach to run the play anyway. Leach obliged, and the agent jumped out of the way just as he was about to get leveled.

The players would laugh about that one for years. Bo would not even let the president interfere with practice.

That evening, Ford joined the Wolverines for their training-table dinner at the Michigan Union and gave a short speech. Then he left for the real purpose of his visit: his general-election kickoff rally at Crisler Arena.

Just three years earlier, it was inconceivable that a Republican president would visit Ann Arbor at all, let alone kick off a campaign there. Had the city changed that much? Bo Schembechler wasn't convinced; he skipped the rally because he feared protesters would cause him to lose his temper.

There *were* a few sporadic boos from hecklers, and one scary moment during Ford's speech when people thought a gunshot had been fired. (It was actually a firecracker.) The next day, the *Michigan Daily* would print an editorial about "Ford's Hot Air." And university president Robben Fleming acknowledged that some alumni were upset about the public university hosting a partisan political rally.

But Ford, the proud Michigan alum, was largely greeted as a hometown hero. Afterward, the chief complaint of Michigan students was that they couldn't get in to Crisler Arena to see the president. Four thousand tickets admitted the ticketholder "and family," making it impossible to determine how many people entered the arena on a single ticket. The students wanted to see Ford, who had just defeated California governor Ronald Reagan for the Republican nomination and was gearing up to face the Democratic nominee, Georgia governor Jimmy Carter.

Ford's speech felt like a Michigan pep rally before a really big game. Bob Ufer gave Ford a rousing introduction. Then Ford took the stage in the same arena where John Lennon had sung in support of John Sinclair less than five years earlier.

"It's great to be back at the University of Michigan—home of the No. 1 Wolverines," Ford said. "After what you did to Wisconsin, I'll tell you one thing—I'd rather run against Jimmy Carter than Harlan Huckleby any day of the week."

The crowd roared.

Harlan Huckleby and the Wolverines lived up to the president's hype. They beat Stanford 51–0. They beat Navy by the absurd score of 70–14. They whipped Wake Forest by 31 and Michigan State by 32. That set up a trip to Northwestern, the worst program in the Big Ten by almost any measure. Everybody figured Michigan would win big, so Don Canham made a pitch to Northwestern officials: why get whipped in front of a few thousand people at home when you can get whipped in front of 100,000 people in Ann Arbor?

Canham promised to split the gate fifty-fifty if the game was moved to Michigan Stadium. It would have given Michigan five Big Ten home games instead of the customary four, infuriating the rest of the conference, but the financial benefits were undeniable: Canham guaranteed at least $250,000 for each school. Northwestern declined the offer. The game remained in Evanston, where it drew 31,045. Michigan won, 38–7.

The Wolverines then beat Indiana and Minnesota by the combined score of 80–0. They took an 8–0 record to West Lafayette, Indiana, in early November, to play lowly Purdue. Schembechler openly wondered if anybody would even test his team before the season-ender in Columbus. He was about to get an answer.

On paper, there was no reason to worry about Purdue. The Boilermakers had just lost to Michigan State by 32 points. They were 3–5. Their coach, Alex Agase, was on the verge of being fired. The Wolverines were confident and relaxed at their Friday practice and subsequent evening meal—so confident and relaxed that co-captains Rob Lytle and Calvin O'Neal were worried. Their teammates seemed to think they could not lose. O'Neal and Lytle talked about calling a team meeting to set everybody straight. They decided against it.

By halftime the next day, Lytle and O'Neal knew they had made a mistake. Purdue led, 13–7. Michigan took the lead in the third quarter with a Schembechler rarity: a 64-yard touchdown pass from Leach to receiver Jimmy Smith. But with less than five minutes left, Purdue's Rock Supan kicked a field goal to give Purdue a 16–14 lead.

The Wolverines had one more chance to show they had both the nation's No. 1 team and its No. 1 offense. Leach led a march into Boilermaker territory. On first down from the Purdue 23, Schembechler called a running play. Then he called another. And another. The three plays picked up a total of four yards. Now it was fourth and six with 14 seconds left.

Schembechler was clearly setting up the potential game-winning field goal. Michigan placekicker Bob Wood, a reliable second-year starter, lined up for a 37-yarder to preserve his team's perfect record. Lytle thought, *Okay, we escaped.* Wood had converted six of eight for the year.

Wood kicked it wide left.

"When you depend on winning on a forward pass or a field goal," Schembechler said afterward, "you're in trouble."

Michigan fell to No. 4 in the Associated Press poll and came home to play Illinois in its final home game. The game against Illinois was uneventful—the Wolverines, shaken out of their doldrums, won 38–7. The most interesting statistic was the attendance: 104,107, meaning that Michigan had drawn at least 101,000 fans to every game of the 1976 season. No other college-owned stadium could even seat 100,000, and here Don Canham had drawn that many for every game.

To Canham, sellout crowds were the heart of his job. He had once taken his family to see comedian Pat Paulsen at the Cherry County Playhouse in the Michigan resort town of Traverse City, and before Paulsen took the stage, he looked around the theater and started mumbling under his breath. He was counting seats and multiplying by the ticket price. Another time, he and his right-hand man, Will Perry, were photographed in an empty Michigan Stadium. Perry was smiling. Canham scrawled in a corner of the picture: "Will—what the hell you smiling for? The seats are empty."

And of course, how could anybody attend a Michigan game without wearing maize and blue? Eight years after Canham drew up a few simple designs on his kitchen table, Michigan paraphernalia was all over the world. It was better than free advertising—people were paying Canham to advertise for him. What few people realized, and fewer questioned, was that with the exception of the university's official seal, royalties from every product went directly to the athletic department, not the university's general fund. Financially and philosophically, that big block "M" (or gray "O") did not represent the school itself; it represented the school's athletic teams.

The Canham influence was usually measured geographically: *I saw a Michigan shirt in Japan!* The more telling measurement was not how *far* big-time sports had spread, but where: they had seeped into corners of the culture that had rejected them just a decade earlier.

Every year, on that late November Saturday when Michigan and Ohio State battled, a man who used to be in the headlines would find his way to a bar to watch the Michigan–Ohio State game. The man did not own a TV. He was living a fugitive life, bouncing from town to town, hoping nobody would recognize him. But he would not miss this game.

Federal agents were searching for the man and his fellow would-be revolutionaries, a group that used to call itself the Weathermen. The man told people his name was Joe Brown. But his real name was Bill Ayers.

Rob Lytle had spent part of the summer of 1976 working out with an old high school teammate, Bob Brudzinski. They would run a few 800-yard or mile races at their old high school, Fremont Ross in northern Ohio, then go next door to lift weights at the local YMCA. For Lytle, this was all the motivation he needed: Brudzinski was now a defensive end at Ohio State, the one school Lytle had never beaten.

The offseason workouts were important, because college football had become a year-round game. Bo Schembechler's first Michigan team barely lifted any weights—the legendary offseason workouts were all running and hitting. By the mid-1970s, players were expected to build muscle mass throughout the year. And it was at offseason workouts, in the summer of 1976, where Duncan Griffin first noticed the cracks in Woody Hayes's machine.

Duncan was the youngest of the three Griffin brothers to play at Ohio State. When Duncan was still in high school, Archie would take him over to the Ohio State campus in the summer to work out with the Buckeyes. Now, entering his sophomore season, Duncan saw that the voluntary workouts did not have as many volunteers. Players seemed to work out on their own—or not at all.

Hadn't they listened to Hayes all these years? *I might not be the smartest but nobody can outwork me.* Didn't they know that every day, they were competing against the guys working out in Ann Arbor? *You're either getting better or you're getting worse.*

The pollsters couldn't see this, of course. They figured Hayes would simply plug new talent into the holes left by the illustrious 1975 senior class—Rod Gerald would replace Cornelius Greene at quarterback, Jeff Logan would replace Archie Griffin at tailback, and the Buckeyes would keep rolling. And for two games, it looked like the pollsters were right: Ohio State beat Michigan State and seventh-ranked Penn State to move to No. 2 in the country, right behind No. 1 Michigan.

But in their third game, the Buckeyes blew a 21–7 lead at home against Missouri and lost 22–21. The next week, they had a chance to exact revenge against UCLA, which had yanked the national championship away from them just a few months earlier. But the Buckeyes could manage only a 10–10 tie.

Ohio State was now 2-1-1, which wasn't terrible, but it was shocking for a program that had not lost in September or October in five years. The Buckeyes won their next two, but the seventh game, against Purdue, brought another blow: their quarterback, Rod Gerald, fractured three vertebrae, sidelining him for the rest of the regular season.

Gerald was an electrifying talent in the mold of Cornelius Greene, who had mentored him in 1975. But while Gerald had Flam's moves, he did not have Flam's moxie. Gerald was a raw athlete trying to establish himself as Ohio State's quarterback, and his back injury rattled him. He doubted whether he could come back at full speed, and he bristled when backup Jim Pacenta, an Akron native, stepped in and led Ohio State to three straight victories. Gerald felt like Ohio State fans had wanted the switch all along.

Pacenta was a better passer than Gerald but not nearly as athletic. Quarterbacks coach George Chaump pushed Hayes to pass more. Chaump had been fighting this battle, to various degrees, for years, and he was starting to wonder if he had stuck with Hayes too long. He was tired of banging his head against a wall while the Old Man kept yelling "Robust!" and handing the ball to his fullback.

During some home games, Ohio State's assistant coaches would ask Mark George, Woody's student manager, to keep the sideline phone away from the Old Man, so they could call plays that made sense. *Do you want to win this game, Mark? Then get the hell as far away from him as you can!*

Sometimes, it seemed like everybody and everything were getting as far away from Woody Hayes as they could. While the rest of the country seemed like it wanted to forget Vietnam, Hayes had sponsored a family of Vietnamese refugees, taking them into his home for a while at the conclusion of the war. His idea of a nice treat was giving his student managers five dollars to take their girlfriends for ice cream. Many Buckeyes, like the rest of their classmates, had other ideas. They would go to a campus joint named Papa Joe's and buy buckets of beer—not a bucket full of beer bottles, but a bucket filled up with beer. They went in and dipped their silver buckets into a bigger bucket and drank away.

In December, Hayes would give Mark George a blank check and tell him to go to the Ohio State golf course and buy slacks for the players who couldn't afford them. Hayes wanted his boys to have a decent pair of pants to wear on Christmas. But some Buckeyes had figured out other ways to improve their financial status: they would give football tickets to a car dealer and get a break on a car.

Hayes's passion for Ohio State—both the university and its football program—was as strong as ever. That spring, while dining at the Faculty Club, Hayes was introduced to a young doctoral candidate named Tom Engler. "You're coming to Ohio State, aren't you?" Hayes asked an awestruck Engler, then proceeded to sell the school. Engler picked Ohio State. But Hayes was finding it easier to recruit doctoral candidates than football players.

At least everybody expected doctoral candidates to go to class. With football players, who could tell anymore? The NCAA had approved the concept of "redshirting"—giving a player an extra year of eligibility as long as he spent one year on the bench. Hayes was incredulous. The NCAA was telling kids *before they arrived on campus* that they were not expected to graduate in four years. For a while, Hayes refused to redshirt anybody. But that hurt the Buckeyes, because other teams were taking advantage of the redshirt rules and getting the performance of players who were five years out of high school instead of one. Hayes had to relent.

While some other coaches worried mostly about keeping their players eligible, Hayes's commitment to academics took on a new intensity. In the spring of 1976, he had called Brian Baschnagel into his office and asked what he planned to do after graduation. Baschnagel pointed out the obvious: the Chicago Bears had picked him in the third round of the NFL draft. Hayes slammed a book to the ground and screamed, *"If you do that, you will never get your law degree!"*

After his rookie season with the Bears, Baschnagel would come back to see Hayes, and the Old Man wouldn't even turn from his desk and look at him. *Don't come back here until you're enrolled in law school.*

All those people who had fought him all those years, who claimed that too much emphasis was placed on football . . . where were they now? Academically, financially, didn't they realize they were losing? Hayes always said that the Ohio State coach should never earn more than the governor. His salary in 1973 had been $29,400; the Ohio State administration was raising it incrementally, without giving him a chance to turn down the raises, but he still hadn't hit $30,000. Up north, even Bo Schembechler was clearing $80,000, an even split—$40,000 for coaching and another $40,000 for his television show, a tacit acknowledgment that being a coach was half about being a TV personality.

Ah, Bo. Hayes had beaten the poor bastard in three of the last four years—and the other time they tied and Hayes got the Rose Bowl bid, which sent Schembechler into a rage for weeks. This year's game would be in Columbus, where Bo had never won. This is what Hayes still loved most: plotting against his closest colleague and fiercest rival, a man who coached old-time, slug-it-out, win-it-in-the-trenches football, just as he did.

It was like George C. Scott's monologue in *Patton*, as he looks across the desert and daydreams:

"Rommel's out there somewhere, waiting for me. You know, if I had my way, I'd send that genius son of a bitch an engraved invitation in iambic pentameter—a challenge in two stanzas to meet me out there in the desert. Rommel in his tank and me in mine. We'd stop at about twenty paces. We'd get out and shake hands. And we'd button up and we'd do battle, just the two of us. And that battle would decide the outcome of the war . . .

"The world grew up.

"It's a hell of a shame . . .

"God, how I hate the twentieth century."

On Monday, November 1—the day before election day—President Ford campaigned in Ohio, a crucial swing state. Ford spoke on the steps of the Statehouse in Columbus. He was joined there by the most prominent Republicans in Ohio: Governor James Rhodes, Congressman Robert Taft, former senators Frank Lausche and John Bricker, and head coach Woody Hayes.

"He believes in winning," Ford said of Hayes, "and that's what we're going to do."

The next day, Ford lost the election to Jimmy Carter. The margin was 297 electoral votes to 240, but the election was really closer than that. If Ford had won Ohio and Hawaii, he would have won the election, 270–268. The vote difference in Hawaii was barely 7,000 votes, and the difference in Ohio was tiny—Carter received 48.92 percent of the vote, to 48.65 for Ford. The margin in Ohio was just 11,000 votes, or barely an eighth of the crowd on a fall Saturday in Ohio Stadium.

Woody Hayes later said that if he could do it all over again, he would have left his team for a few weeks in the fall of 1976 to campaign for Gerald Ford in Ohio. Maybe he meant it and maybe he didn't. But he was sure he could have secured those 11,000 votes and returned Gerald Ford to the White House.

In Ohio State's final game before facing Michigan, the Buckeyes beat Minnesota, 9–3, in Minneapolis. Once again, Woody Hayes made bigger news than his team, but this time it wasn't Hayes's doing. ABC television announcers told a national audience that there was a rumor Hayes would announce his impending retirement the following Friday—the day before facing That School Up North. It would have been the ultimate motivation tactic, but Hayes angrily denied the rumor.

"I'll tell you one other thing," Hayes said. "If I ever do [retire], before ABC knows it, Paul Hornung will know it."

With the win over Minnesota, the Buckeyes had clinched at least a share of the Big Ten title. But if they lost to Michigan, the Wolverines would go to the Rose Bowl and Ohio State would go to the Orange Bowl.

Now Hayes was in his Biggs Facility bunker, plotting to beat Michigan. He skipped a television showing of *Patton* for a staff meeting, and he told his staff to "get the pictures." When Ohio State was about to play Illinois, Hayes would ask for "the Illinois pictures," and when the Buckeyes were facing Indiana, he said "get the Indiana pictures." When he wanted to watch film of That School Up North, all Hayes said was "get the pictures." Everybody knew what he meant.

Hayes saw that Purdue had used a passing play featuring a curl route to beat Michigan. He decided to install the same play. Quarterback Jim Pacenta and assistant George Chaump were baffled. The same play? Didn't Hayes know that since losing to Purdue, Michigan had surely spent hours defending that play in practice? Did he really think the Wolverines would fall for it again? Hayes seemed to know he needed *something* new for his passing game, but was apparently incapable of figuring out what. Sometimes he would install new plays to use against Michigan and throw them out by the end of the week. The players would roll their eyes. "Woody is getting a tight ass again," they'd say.

The night before the game, Hayes took his team to see a John Wayne movie, *The Shootist*. It was about an aging, terminally ill gunfighter trying to die with his dignity intact.

Meanwhile, Bo Schembechler made the rounds at Michigan's hotel, trying to assure his players that this was finally their year. Nobody on Schembechler's roster had ever beaten Ohio State. The last five Ohio State–Michigan games had been so breathtakingly close that four of them were *still* in dispute: Ohio State fans were convinced they got robbed on that missed pass interference call in 1971, and Michigan fans thought officials had screwed them out of a winning touchdown run in 1972 and a winning field goal in 1974. And in 1973, the dispute was about what happened after the 10–10 tie, when Ohio State won the Rose Bowl vote.

Only the 1975 game had a clear-cut winner. But even in that one, Michigan had led 14–7 midway through the fourth quarter before Ohio State came back.

"Gentlemen, here we are again," Schembechler told defensive tackle Greg Morton and linebacker Calvin O'Neal in their Columbus hotel room. "You know how close we've come in the past, but something has always happened to stop us. Some people are even saying we choked. Now, we know that's not true. We've just made some mistakes we shouldn't have made. But tomorrow we're not going to make those mistakes because tomorrow we're going to win."

O'Neal did not need any convincing. When assistant coach Jerry Hanlon came by the room, O'Neal told him not to worry.

"Coach, we're going to blow them out tomorrow," O'Neal said. "We're going to blow them out. We're going to *shut* them out."

Hanlon looked at O'Neal like he was insane.

* * *

Ohio State had gone 122 consecutive games without being shut out. That was the second longest streak in college football history—just one shy of Oklahoma's record.

Yet for most of the first half, the Buckeyes looked like they would indeed get shut out . . . and go to the Rose Bowl anyway, thanks to a 0–0 tie. In the first quarter, the teams combined for just 66 yards, all of them on the ground. Michigan finally put a drive together late in the first half, but on fourth down Rob Lytle was stopped by his summer workout partner, Bob Brudzinski.

Late in the first half, Ohio State drove all the way down to the Michigan 10, where Woody Hayes called a play he had installed that week. The Buckeyes lined up in their "robust" formation, with three running backs, as though they were planning to run their famous "26" or "27" play. Then they sent two tight ends into a crossing pattern.

It was a fine play but the wrong time to call it. Ohio State faced second down and eight, an obvious passing situation. The Wolverines were not going to stack the line to stop the fullback. Pacenta dropped back. A blitzing linebacker drilled him. The pass was intercepted, and the Wolverines and Buckeyes soon went to their locker rooms tied at zero.

Bo Schembechler had thirty minutes to avoid an upset, and his offense had done squat. Schembechler did not panic. He believed he had the better team, and his defense had stopped Ohio State cold. Michigan just had to get its offense moving.

On the first play of the second half, Rick Leach ran for eight yards. On the third play, Leach turned a broken play into a 45-yard run. Michigan, which could barely move the ball in the first half, soon found itself with a third-and-one on the Ohio State seven. Leach tried to draw Ohio State offside with a "hard count"—changing the volume of his voice over center in the hope that the Buckeyes would think the ball had been snapped. It worked. Ohio State jumped offside, and on the next play, Russell Davis ran three yards for a touchdown.

Up in the press box, Bob Ufer squeezed his new favorite prop: a horn from George Patton's jeep. One of Patton's nephews had heard Ufer refer to "Bo 'George Patton' Schembechler" and offered the horn, which Ufer gleefully accepted. Ufer would honk it three times for every Michigan touchdown, twice for every field goal, and once for every extra point. Now Ufer honked three times for Davis's score, and then once more when Bob Wood kicked the extra point. Michigan led, 7–0.

The Wolverines stuffed Ohio State on the next possession, then got the ball on their own 48. They moved down the field with relative ease and scored on another Davis run, bringing three more honks from George Patton's horn.

The Wolverines still had not completed a pass. It did not matter. They led 13–0, and on the point-after, Schembechler tried some trickery—he had Jerry Zuver take the snap, then run with it. Zuver ran into the end zone for a two-point conversion. Michigan led 15–0.

The rout was on. By the middle of the next Michigan drive, the Wolverines had outgained Ohio State 231–141. Every one of those 231 yards had come on the ground. Leach threw an interception at the Ohio State 11, but even that only delayed the misery for the Buckeyes, because Michigan's Zuver quickly got the ball back by intercepting Pacenta. Lytle scored Michigan's third touchdown of the game. It was 22–0, less than halfway through the fourth quarter.

The Buckeyes, who had not been shut out in twelve years, had eight minutes to salvage some pride. They could not even do that. The Wolverines won 22–0—their most lopsided win over Ohio State since 1946.

As time expired, the Wolverines carried Schembechler off the field, but what they would remember—more than the touchdowns or their coach's joy or even the final score—was the quiet in Ohio Stadium in that fourth quarter. Four years of frustration had melted away. They had silenced Ohio at last.

Bo Schembechler's wife, Millie, had been so worried about the game that she had stayed home. Now she was overjoyed. Just a few months earlier, Bo had gone in for bypass surgery and they didn't know if he would ever coach again. He had just beaten the Old Man for the first time in five years, and he was heading to the Rose Bowl.

The game had been televised nationally, from the coast of Southern California all the way to the Oval Office, where 1934 Michigan football MVP Gerald Ford, now a lame-duck president of the United States, watched it. Ford tried calling Schembechler from a helicopter late that afternoon but did not reach him. He tried again that evening and congratulated Schembechler. The two spoke for two minutes while Bo's seven-year-old son Shemy listened in on an extension.

At the Rose Bowl luncheon in late December, Bob Ufer gave a seven-minute speech that was so inspiring, NBC announcers Curt Gowdy and Don Meredith refused to take the podium afterward. They did not want to follow his act.

Ufer and Michigan were extremely confident about the matchup against No. 2 Southern California. The Wolverines, ranked third, led the nation in scoring offense (38.7 points per game) and scoring defense (7.2). They still felt they had the best team in the nation. They were convinced that if they had just shown up to play at Purdue, they would have won the national title. But that Purdue game was instructive—not only because Michigan lost, but because of Bo Schembechler's comments afterward:

When you depend on winning on a forward pass or a field goal, you're in trouble.

Michigan had attempted just 99 passes all season—and rushed 660 times. The Wolverines blocked and ran so masterfully, with such discipline, that lesser Big Ten teams were powerless to stop them. Even against Ohio State, the Wolverines had not completed a single pass.

Schembechler hoped to beat USC the same way he had dominated the Big Ten. For a while, it worked: Michigan scored first, on a Rob Lytle run in the second quarter. (The extra-point attempt was blocked.) But USC was loaded—three of the first five picks in the 1977 NFL draft would be Trojans. Unlike most Big Ten teams, USC could stack the line of scrimmage and reasonably contain Michigan's running game.

The Wolverines caught an early break when Southern California star Ricky Bell suffered a head injury in the first quarter and left the game. He was replaced by a little-known freshman named Charles White. But USC mixed its runs with passes, and White was much better than the Wolverines realized. He ended up rushing for 114 yards, more than Michigan's top two rushers combined. USC took a 7–6 lead into the fourth quarter. With three minutes left, White scored on a seven-yard run to give USC a 14–6 lead. The Wolverines had one last chance, and they made it all the way to the Trojans' 17, but they turned the ball over on downs.

For the game, Leach completed only four of 12 passes for 76 yards. But just as importantly, the Wolverines struggled to *stop* the pass. A season of playing ground-oriented Big Ten teams had not prepared Michigan for USC's passing attack. Trojans quarterback Vince Evans had completed 14 of 20 passes for 181 yards.

Bo Schembechler was now 0–4 in bowl games. All four games had been decided by eight points or less, two had come down to the final seconds, and Schembechler was laid up in a hospital bed for one of them. But as far as fans were concerned, so what?

Rod Gerald wished he were back home in Texas. Or maybe in Columbus. Anywhere but Miami, Florida. Ohio State had literally left him behind after he injured his back—because of NCAA limits on the number of players who could travel to regular-season road games, he had stayed in Columbus when the Buckeyes went on the road.

Gerald felt neglected. So when the season ended with that loss to Michigan, and Woody Hayes told him he was expected to go to Miami for the Orange Bowl, Gerald balked. He was sure Jim Pacenta would start against Colorado. Gerald told the coaches he was skipping the trip. Running back Ron Springs and Hayes convinced him to change his mind.

So Gerald went down to Miami, competed against Pacenta in

practice, and what happened? The Old Man chose Pacenta to start anyway. Pacenta had practiced well—so well, in fact, that when Miami Dolphins coach Don Shula watched him at Buckeyes practice one day, he asked Hayes about Pacenta's NFL prospects. (Hayes, never a fan of playing football for money, told Shula not to bother: Pacenta was going to medical school.)

Now it was January 1, 1977. Pacenta was getting ready to face Colorado. Gerald was depressed and swimming in self-pity. The whole trip had been a waste, he thought. And so when a former Buckeye teammate came to him that day and offered him cocaine, Gerald thought, *Why not?*

Like many of his teammates, Gerald had smoked pot before. But he had never tried cocaine.

Now it was right in front of him.

What did he have to lose?

He tried it.

Just a little bump.

That evening, Ohio State quickly fell behind Colorado, 10–0. Eight minutes into the game, Woody Hayes sent Rod Gerald in to replace Jim Pacenta. Gerald ran for 17 yards on his first carry. Soon after, he led the Buckeyes on a 99-yard touchdown drive. Ohio State went on to beat Colorado, 27–10.

A few hours after using cocaine for the first time in his life, Rod Gerald was named the Orange Bowl MVP.

10

The Ultra Secret

On January 20, 1977, Jimmy Carter was sworn in as the thirty-ninth president of the United States. In his inauguration speech, Carter promised "a new spirit" to a nation looking to move past both Watergate and Vietnam.

"We will maintain strength so sufficient that it need not be proven in combat," Carter promised, "a quiet strength based not merely on the size of an arsenal, but on the nobility of ideas."

This was easier in rhetoric than in practice, of course. It raised as many questions as it answered. "DEFENSE," *Time* magazine blared on one cover early in the Carter administration, "How Much Is Enough?" Another *Time* cover announced that "Uncle Jimmy Wants You," before asking the follow-up question: "But Will America Enlist?"

Woody Hayes was paying close attention. He scanned newspapers and magazines and marked the articles he wanted to read, then gave the publications to secretary Woonsin Spalding. The secretary would cut out the stories and paste them in a spiral notebook, separated into categories such as "Russia/China," "Nuclear Energy," "Sports," "Behavior," and "Education and Books."

And while many Americans wanted to hear that the United States could build a foreign policy with ideas instead of combat, Hayes never tired of war stories. His office was still stocked with books about war, and he kept adding to his collection. One of his latest favorites was called *The Ultra Secret*, by former British secret service official Frederick William Winterbotham.

The Ultra Secret was about how the Allies broke a crucial German

247

code in World War II. Not surprisingly, Hayes immediately related the book to football. What if he could come up with a code that opponents simply couldn't crack? His team could run a no-huddle offense—every play would have more than one name, to confuse the opposition. Having multiple names for a single play could be the Ohio State equivalent of multiple plays; Woody's boys could confuse the opposition but still maintain a relatively limited playbook. Hayes wrote down ten consecutive plays and made his coaches memorize them in order. One day he burned the list, lest somebody rifle through his trash and find his plays.

The Ultra Secret was just the kind of book that could spur Hayes into one of his long lectures about the similarity between war and football. Now he was deep into his own version of it.

Woody Hayes was writing a book about the relationship between military strategy and football.

He had toyed with the idea for years. He had often told people he would write this book someday. Now he was in the thick of it.

He would write about how Napoleon had tried a power run into Russia, and how Hitler had tried the same thing. The Old Man said Napoleon and Hitler "weren't option people." But Ohio's own General William Tecumseh Sherman, now *he* was an option guy— Sherman ran the triple option all through the South, hitting towns off to the side, so nobody knew where he would strike next. That element of surprise was important—like when General Douglas MacArthur surprised the North Koreans in the Inchon landing in 1950. Hayes said a football team could learn from the Inchon landing.

Hayes would call one chapter "Goal Line Stand." It would describe how British air marshal Hugh Dowding put together an almost perfect defense in the Battle of Britain.

This was the book Woody Hayes had been preparing to write for three decades. And unlike his previous three books, which were self-published, he wanted to find a major publisher this time. A major publisher meant a national audience. Woody Hayes wanted to be heard. He wanted to be read.

Befitting a man who always said exactly what he was thinking,

Hayes always gave his books straightforward titles that told readers precisely what was on the author's mind at the time. In 1957, when Hayes was forty-four, he was mostly concerned with football at Ohio State, and that was the title of his debut book: *Football at Ohio State*. In 1969, fresh off a national championship and invigorated by winning, the fifty-six-year-old Hayes published *Hot Line to Victory*. In 1973, the sixty-year-old Hayes was terribly disturbed by the longhairs and radicals who didn't seem to give a damn about anything, and to emphasize the importance of individual character, he wrote *You Win with People!*

Now, in 1977, the sixty-four-year old Hayes was angry at all the snooty professors and liberal media types who kept tearing down the two American institutions that he most revered: the military and football. Sometimes, while addressing his team, he would go off on a tangent about the media or politics or World War II—not just an aside, but a long rant. The players would wonder when he would ever get back to talking about football.

All around him, Hayes saw people who forgot that the United States was built on military might and strong-willed, tough men—the kind produced by the great game of football. As a Navy veteran and career football coach—as well as a sixty-four-year-old who had suffered a heart attack and battled diabetes—he surely thought about his own legacy. And so, for his planned fourth book, the Old Man came up with another straightforward title:

Football, History and Woody Hayes.

In April 1977, Ed Weaver retired as Ohio State's athletic director. Hayes had been livid, years earlier, when he was not consulted on Weaver's appointment. But the two men had forged a good relationship.

"We started out as good friends," Hayes told Weaver, "and now we are great friends."

A reporter from the *Lantern* called Hayes's house to see if he wanted the job. Woody wasn't home. Anne told the reporter that she and Woody never talked about that kind of thing.

"Either we're talking about love or we're making love," she cracked.

Right as she said it, Woody walked into the house.

"What if he prints that?" he asked.

Anne replied, "If you're lucky, you'll come out like a sex maniac. It'll help your image."

To answer the *Lantern* reporter's question: no, Woody was not interested in being athletic director. Even if he *had* been interested, it is doubtful that Ohio State would have put him in charge of all its men's and women's teams, anyway. Ohio State president Harold Enarson likely wouldn't go for that.

The school did not look far for Weaver's replacement. Ohio State chose Weaver's deputy (and Woody's old assistant coach), Hugh Hindman.

Fritz Seyferth had heard the rumors: *Bo's mellowed. The heart problems slowed him down.* Seyferth had played fullback and special teams for Bo Schembechler's first three Michigan teams. Now he was living in New York, working for the accounting firm Arthur Young and Co. In the spring of 1977, Seyferth returned to his alma mater to recruit MBA students. He decided to stop by the Wolverines' spring practice and see if his coach had really changed.

It didn't take long to find out. An offensive lineman made a mistake, and Schembechler, who always expected the most out of his offensive linemen, grabbed the son of a bitch and started shaking him madly. Then he took his "M" cap and threw it to the ground and screamed. Finally, he walked over to pick up his cap, looked up and saw Fritz Seyferth . . . and *winked* at him.

Holy shit, Seyferth thought. *He knows exactly what he's doing.*

So much had changed in college sports. Schembechler knew he couldn't be as physical with his players as he once was. They just wouldn't go for it anymore. He was down to ninety-five scholarships, limiting his depth. He had to play freshmen, whether he wanted to or not. But Seyferth was right: Bo Schembechler knew exactly what he was doing.

Sure, the coach fought Rick Leach every time Leach wanted to go play baseball instead of practice with the football team, but ultimately Schembechler got Leach for most of his practices, and he did it without alienating the quarterback. When Schembechler thought Atlantic Coast Conference officials were robbing his team in an early-season game against Duke, he accused Big Ten officials of standing around "like goons" instead of keeping the ACC zebras in line. Big Ten commissioner Wayne Duke reprimanded him, but the Wolverines liked that their coach stood up for them.

They rewarded him on the field. Texas A&M came to Ann Arbor ranked No. 5 in the nation and left as a 41–3 loser. Would the Wolverines finally win a national title for Bo Schembechler?

"I'd just as soon not be No. 1," Schembechler told reporters after the A&M game. "It's a pain in the neck. No. 1, No. 1, No. 1, No. 1. It's only been four games. Who cares?"

A week later, Michigan moved up to No. 1.

And two weeks after that, Minnesota beat Michigan, 16–0. There was no good reason for it. ("We played poorly and they played well," Schembechler said. "I've never seen our offense so bad.") The Wolverines dropped to No. 6 in the country when they returned home.

The national championship would probably have to wait another year. But the loss did nothing to dampen the passion of Ann Arborites for Bo Schembechler's team. Don Canham was selling everything imaginable in maize and blue; in Ann Arbor, you could even buy toilet paper with Woody Hayes's image on every sheet.

Just nine years earlier, Michigan State had been the dominant team in the state. Now Michigan dominated the local radio airwaves, the Detroit television market, and the state's newspapers like never before. When the Wolverines beat the Spartans in early October, the *Detroit Free Press* headline was telling: "U-M Struggles, 24–14."

Adding to the insult for the folks in East Lansing was that Michigan–Michigan State was not even the most discussed rivalry in the state anymore. The official 1977 road map of the state of Michigan featured two towns just over the border in Ohio that nobody had ever heard of—because they did not exist. Their names were in small type. One was called "Goblu." The other was "Beatosu."

*   *   *

Columbus had been asking the question, in earnest, for two solid years: when will Woody retire? A lot of people wondered if 1977 would be the last year for the Old Man. Once again, he had the talent to win the national championship.

People inside and outside the program speculated about his successor. Everybody knew that Hayes's choice was George Hill, his longtime defensive coordinator. Ralph Staub, the offensive coordinator, had left in January to be the head coach at Cincinnati, but if Hayes retired, maybe Ohio State would bring him back. Another of Hayes's old assistants, Lou Holtz, had just been named head coach at Arkansas. Hayes complained that the glib Holtz was already politicking for the Ohio State job. Quarterbacks coach George Chaump seemed to be angling for it. Chaump had been a strong candidate for an assistant coaching job with the Oakland Raiders two years earlier; John Robinson ended up taking the job, and Robinson had parlayed it into the head coaching job at Southern California. Chaump wished he had left Ohio State when he had the chance. The only way to make up for it would be to land the head coaching gig.

The tension started to seep into the program. But even if Hayes sensed it, what could he do about it? He had never fired an assistant coach, and he wasn't going to start now. No. He would *teach* them.

At morning meetings, Hayes would ramble about politics or the military and offer a silver dollar to any coach who could answer one of his history questions. The coaches would kick each other under the table: *Here he goes again!* Just a few years earlier, Hayes knew the names of his players' wives and girlfriends. Now he was referring to starting receiver Jimmy Harrell as "Jimmy Herbstreit" and calling graduate assistant coach Kevin Rogers "Roger." At a banquet, Hayes introduced assistant coach Gary Tranquill as "Gary Transoo."

Hayes would sometimes tell his assistant coaches, "When we play That School Up North, we have to pass eighteen to twenty times."

The coaches were skeptical. They felt that Woody Hayes either did not understand, or would not accept, that football was a different kind of game now.

Hayes never seemed comfortable with the passing game. Hell, quarterbacks had to drop back to gain yardage. Did Patton move backward to acquire territory?

Hayes was trying to believe. In early May, he brought Stanford's new head coach, a passing-game whiz, to Columbus. The coach, whose name was Bill Walsh, had yet to make his collegiate head coaching debut, but Hayes brought him in to teach at the Ohio High School Football Clinic anyway. Walsh's presentation was called "Developing the Young QB," and while he was in Columbus, he tried to do just that. He spent several days tutoring Ohio State quarterback Rod Gerald on the fundamentals of passing.

Gerald struggled to learn the lessons. In the 1977 opener against unranked Miami of Florida, Ohio State scored just 10 points and gained just 347 yards. The Buckeyes still won, 10–0. But Hayes was not happy.

"You will not win many conference games with 10 points," Hayes told reporters afterward. "And we've got to get more juice in our attack. Let me tell you that 347 yards is not nearly enough against a team like Miami."

Rod Gerald knew that as well as anybody. He wondered: was he faster before injuring his back the year before? Gerald weighed just 175 pounds. If he *had* lost a little speed, he would take a pounding in the Big Ten. He might injure his back again or lose his starting spot.

Gerald was looking for an edge, any edge. He thought back to his last game of the previous season, when he snorted cocaine during the day and won the Orange Bowl MVP award at night.

Was it a coincidence?

At the time, Gerald thought so. Now he wasn't so sure. Woody Hayes wanted more juice in his attack. Rod Gerald thought he had the solution: cocaine on game day.

The next week, Gerald did one or two lines of cocaine before Ohio State kicked off against Minnesota. And look what happened: the Buckeyes rolled, 38–7. Gerald was convinced the cocaine made the difference. It wasn't just the final score. It was how he *felt*: faster, more elusive, like he had never injured his back. The coke gave Gerald a mental boost, too. He didn't worry about the Old Man on the sidelines. He just tried to make plays.

That's why Gerald was concerned the next week, when third-ranked Oklahoma came to Columbus and he couldn't score any coke beforehand. The rest of the Buckeyes had another reason to worry. Star running back Jeff Logan had sprained his ankle, so Hayes moved his best defensive back, All-American candidate Ray Griffin, to running back. Griffin had played running back behind his brother Archie as a freshman in 1974 before moving to safety.

Four minutes into the game, Oklahoma led 14–0. Pretty soon the score was 20–0. Gerald suffered a concussion. Ray Griffin was barely playing—for the day, he would carry the ball just seven times—and he wondered why Hayes had moved him from safety. Ray felt like Hayes had a personal objection to him, simply because he wasn't Archie. He wondered: was Woody trying to keep him from becoming an All-American?

Somehow, the Buckeyes came back. They scored two touchdowns in the second quarter and two more in the third to take a 28–20 lead. With less than two minutes left, the Sooners scored on a two-yard run. Ohio State led, 28–26.

Oklahoma had to go for two. The national title hopes of two states were on the line.

The Sooners ran an option to the right, the Buckeyes stopped them, and Ohio Stadium erupted. After trailing 20–0, the Buckeyes were going to win! All they had to do was recover the inevitable onside kick.

The ball hopped toward Ohio State's Mike Strahine, and as far as the Buckeyes were concerned, it could not have bounced into a better pair of hands. Strahine was an infielder on the Ohio State baseball team. But this time, he couldn't field the ground ball. Players from both teams jumped on it. Oklahoma ended up with possession.

Four plays later, the Sooners kicked a field goal to win, 29–28.

Woody Hayes's hopes for that final, elusive national title had taken a big hit. But there was still a season to play. The week after losing to Oklahoma, the Buckeyes hosted Southern Methodist, and Rod Gerald was not taking any chances. He snorted at least a gram of cocaine when he got up that morning, then went to the pregame quarterbacks meeting. It was there, with Hayes in the room, that Gerald noticed his nose was bleeding. He thought he'd been caught.

That's it, he thought. *I'm gone.*

The team physician, Dr. Bob Murphy, gave Gerald a towel to stop the nosebleed. Woody Hayes watched Murphy do it. Neither man had a clue as to *why* Gerald's nose was bleeding; they figured it was an aftereffect of his concussion. That afternoon, Ohio State beat SMU, 35–7. Rod Gerald and his team were flying high again.

Ohio State's quarterback and one of Ann Arbor's most famous radicals had at least one thing in common: a growing addiction to cocaine.

By 1977, Pun Plamondon had become a cokehead. Plamondon was working as a personal bodyguard and roadie for Ann Arbor native Bob Seger, who had become a full-fledged rock star. Seger, who had written the first antiwar rock song of the Vietnam era and had performed at the Concert for John Sinclair, had his biggest hit in 1977. *Rolling Stone* would name it the best single of the year. It was called "Night Moves," and it was a tribute to the days when Seger was a teenager growing up in Ann Arbor, back when it was a quiet midwestern college town, before the war in Vietnam had changed America.

In the fall of 1977, 23 percent of Ohio State's incoming freshmen students scored so low on the English portion of their entrance exam that they had to take remedial courses. Twenty-seven percent had to take remedial math.

Woody Hayes was not going to just stand there and let his university's standards fall apart. He had been saying for years that football players were better people than other students—they had to work harder and be more disciplined. Now his passion for academics became manic.

The previous semester, he had walked into brain coach Larry Romanoff's office to look at the grades for the hundred-plus players on his team. Romanoff was proud: just one guy with a grade point average below 2.0. He thought that was pretty impressive. But when Hayes looked at the list and got to that one player, he threw the sheet down, stomped on it, tried to rip it apart, and told Romanoff he was fired. Of course Romanoff wasn't *actually* fired; the Old Man just wanted to keep Romanoff on edge. But Hayes was getting frustrated with any academic slippage. When a few Buckeyes struggled with their Russian culture class, Hayes got the textbook and started quizzing them at study table. Every six weeks he would call his old center, Steve Myers, and urge him to come back and finish his degree.

As far as Hayes was concerned, they *had* to get their degrees. Otherwise, how would they help right the world? Didn't they realize what was at stake? Didn't they read newspaper and magazine stories? Like this one, from *U.S. News and World Report*: "Marxist Ideas Spread on U.S. Campuses." Hayes had the article cut out and put in his files, which were expanding rapidly. Anything about the United States' reliance on foreign oil went into the file, too—Hayes had started driving to work again, but he still worried about the consequences.

Hayes read a column in the *Columbus Citizen-Journal* about the emerging something-for-nothing culture, and he underlined a few sentences:

"We are against so many things that we can't remember what we are for. We want more money for less work. People with money want more tax shelters."

Woody Hayes had always asked for less money and more work. He despised luxury. On the road, he preferred cheap, bare hotels or motels, and he would keep going back to the same one as long as Ohio State won there. In early November 1977, the Buckeyes traveled to Champaign, Illinois, and stayed at a place called the Lincoln Lodge. The Lincoln Lodge was outdated for Ohio State's needs. The team had to pile three coaches into two-person rooms, with the third coach sleeping on a cot, and there were no conference rooms for Friday evening meetings. But Ohio State kept beating Illinois, so Hayes kept booking the Lincoln Lodge.

The night before the game, the team went to see the movie *Slap Shot.* Assistant coach Mickey Jackson was in charge of picking the movies, and he and trainer Billy Hill decided *Slap Shot* seemed like a safe bet. It was a sports movie starring Paul Newman. What could go wrong?

A few minutes into the movie, Jackson realized he had made a mistake. *Slap Shot* was littered with profanity and sexual references. Then, a half hour into the movie, Newman's character, Reggie Dunlop, finds himself in bed with a woman named Suzanne, who had recently split with her husband. Suzanne sits topless in bed and . . .

Suzanne: "You're the first man I've slept with since I left Hanrahan."

Reggie: "Aw, Suzanne—beautiful woman like you?"

Suzanne: "I've been sleeping with women . . . Are you shocked?"

Woody Hayes was sure as hell shocked. He stood up in the middle of the theater and shouted, "This is *TRASH!* This is *TRASH!*" Mickey Jackson slunk as low into his seat as he could so Hayes would not see him. The Buckeyes did not have the theater to themselves— there were other paying customers there—but the Old Man was too pissed off to care. He walked out to the candy counter and asked for the manager, and when the manager came out, Hayes barked, "You're fired!" He then went outside and left a note on the team bus to let everybody know he was walking back to the Lincoln Lodge. And he did.

Ohio State recovered from Suzanne's revelation to beat Illinois, 35–0, and Indiana, 35–7. The Buckeyes were ranked No. 4 and favored to beat Michigan. They were relatively healthy (Jeff Logan, whose Heisman candidacy had ended because of the ankle injury, was healthy) while Schembechler's top two tailbacks were hurt. If Ohio State beat

That School Up North, won the Rose Bowl, and got a little luck, Hayes might get that national title yet.

"I can't give you a story this week," Hayes told reporters. "Nope. Not on this game. I can't see any point in it at all. Not at all."

To fans, Hayes's team appeared as strong as ever. The Buckeyes were 9–1, and their one defeat had been that crazy 29–28 loss to Oklahoma. Who could tell that the Buckeyes were not quite as disciplined or together as previous Ohio State squads? Only an expert film-watcher, sitting alone in a dark room, would notice that kind of thing.

Two weeks before the game, Bo Schembechler was talking to Don Canham when the conversation turned to the last game of the season.

Don't worry, Schembechler told his boss. *If we beat Purdue, we'll beat Ohio State.*

Michigan beat Purdue, 40–7, to set up another showdown for the Big Ten championship.

As the little black baseball hat with the block "O" emerged from the tunnel under Michigan Stadium, the crowd broke into a chorus of boos. The man beneath the hat, Woody Hayes, clenched his fists by his sides.

"That's respect, boys," he said. "That's respect. Now let's go out and make them sit on their hands."

They took an indirect route—straight to the "GO BLUE" banner at midfield, just like in 1973. This time, the "M Club" supporters were determined to protect their banner, and a melee broke out at midfield: thirty seconds of pushing and shoving, including one Michigan fan apparently taking a swing at the Old Man.

For years, everybody had understood that players and coaches belonged on the field and fans and reporters did not. Now Michigan fans pelted the Ohio State marching band with eggs, fruit, and toilet paper. The area between the 30-yard lines was supposed to be reserved for players and coaches, but before the game, ABC cameraman Mike Freedman was on the 50. When Ohio State officials asked him to move, Freedman simply replied, "I'm with ABC."

Two minutes into the game, Freedman was on the field again, trying to capture the emotion of the moment. An Ann Arbor sheriff ordered Freedman to move, and he did. But moments later he was back again. The strangest thing about his determination to get as close as possible to the action was that it was going to waste.

The game wasn't being televised. Anywhere.

Oh, ABC had *planned* to show the game to the whole country. But then Egyptian president Anwar Sadat chose the day of the game to visit Israel for the first time in his tenure. This was a landmark moment in the modern history of the Middle East; Egypt and Israel had been enemies for twenty-nine years, and Sadat broke an Arab policy of not dealing publicly with Israel by meeting with Israeli prime minister Menachem Begin.

Sadat's plane was due to land after sundown on the Jewish Sabbath. That meant early afternoon in Ann Arbor. And that left ABC with a problem.

For a while, the network cut from Ben Gurion Airport outside Tel Aviv to Michigan Stadium and back again. ("We will make sure we don't miss anything in Ann Arbor," reporter Harry Reasoner assured viewers.) But when Sadat's arrival coincided with the opening kickoff, the network stayed with its cameras in Israel. ABC's live coverage of this historic moment prompted thousands of calls to network headquarters, all with one basic response: *PUT THE GAME ON!*

Six minutes into the first quarter, with CBS and NBC continuing their coverage of Sadat's arrival, ABC switched to the Michigan–Ohio State game for good.

A few minutes into ABC's broadcast, Ohio State kicked a field goal to take a 3–0 lead. That was all Don Canham could handle. Despite Bo Schembechler's assurance that Michigan would win, Canham bolted Michigan Stadium for the sanctuary of his office.

For the first quarter, the Buckeyes outgained the Wolverines 106–

5, thanks mostly to quarterback Rod Gerald, who was slicing through the Michigan defense. Gerald had brought cocaine to Ann Arbor on Friday, snorted some Saturday morning, then stuck some inside his wristband to keep him high throughout the game. He would snort it on the sidelines or even in the huddle. He felt unstoppable.

Over the course of the season, Gerald's cocaine use had increased. It was no longer just a game-day thing; he was using during the week, too. But Saturdays were when he needed it most.

Could anybody tell what he was doing? Gerald wasn't sure. Before the game, when ABC had filmed the starters in the empty stadium, Gerald had looked down instead of into the camera.

But now he glided to his left for six yards. He passed to Ron Springs for eight more. He dropped back to pass, felt the pressure of Michigan's pass rush . . . and what did Woody Hayes's quarterback do? He *improvised.* Gerald scrambled away from the defense and dumped the ball off to Springs. His oversized jersey looked like it would fall off at any moment—the numeral 8 swung back and forth as he ran.

Gerald wasn't worried about the Old Man. He wasn't worried, period. And that was probably why, in the midst of an otherwise brilliant performance, he caused two fumbles in the first half. On both plays, Gerald was running the option when the Michigan defense collapsed on him, and instead of just accepting a loss of yardage, he tossed the ball to a teammate. Partly because of miscues like those, Ohio State trailed 7–3 at halftime.

Before the game, the Buckeyes thought they were the more talented team. Now they had thirty minutes of evidence to back it up. They had outplayed Michigan. They just needed to play the same way in the second half—without the mistakes. Just play fundamentally sound football, like the Old Man always preached.

It should have been so simple. But on the Buckeyes' first possession of the second half, they moved nine whole yards before fumbling. Michigan recovered and scored four plays later. In a game the Buckeyes had dominated, the Wolverines somehow led, 14–3.

Rod Gerald wasn't done yet. He pitched to Ron Springs on the option. He threw a bomb on target to Jimmy Harrell. Ohio State drove deep into Michigan territory before the drive bogged down. On third and 13 from the Michigan 14-yard line, Gerald was pressured, and he should have just taken the sack, but how boring was that? He threw the ball as he was being tackled. Officials ruled that he was already down.

The Buckeyes settled for a field goal. They trailed 14–6.

On the next possession, Michigan fumbled on its own 26. Ohio State ran three times and missed a field goal. It was still 14–6.

Early in the fourth quarter, the Buckeyes moved down to the Michigan 10, where they faced fourth and one. Hayes decided to go for it. Paul Campbell ran for . . . well . . . slightly less than one yard. Michigan took possession. Still 14–6.

Maybe the Buckeyes just needed to give the ball to their quarterback. They got the ball on their own 10 and Gerald took over. He passed to Jimmy Harrell for five yards. He passed to Harrell again for 21 more. He threw a swing pass to Springs for nine yards. He escaped pressure and sprinted up the field for 16 more. On third and inches from the Michigan 25, Gerald lateraled to Springs, who ran all the way down to the Michigan eight, where he was pushed out of bounds.

First and goal.

The ball sat on the right hash mark, waiting to be snapped.

Woody Hayes called for an option run to the right side of the field.

Up in the press box, quarterbacks coach George Chaump was furious. Didn't the Old Man see that the ball was on the right hash mark? The option depended on making defenders miss. Why was Hayes running it to the short side of the field, where all the players would be bunched into a relatively small space? Ohio State didn't even have any receivers lined up on the right side of the field, which left Michigan with defenders just waiting to pounce. Didn't Hayes see what he was doing? He was forcing Rod Gerald into the sideline—into the alps!

"Don't call that play!" Chaump screamed. "Don't call that play!"

On the Michigan sideline, high school senior Art Schlichter of Bloomingburg, Ohio, watched with interest. Schlichter was the most sought-after high school quarterback in the country. Everybody figured he would either go to Michigan or Ohio State. Now, on his official visit to Michigan, he looked through his binoculars and saw Chaump, the man recruiting him for Ohio State, literally hanging out of the press box, screaming:

"Don't call that play! Don't call that play!"

The Old Man had already called that play, and he wasn't going to let Chaump change his mind. Ohio State snapped the ball. Gerald faked a handoff to Jeff Logan, then darted right. Michigan linebacker John Anderson came right after Gerald. There was no chance for a play there. A clean and sober quarterback would have seen that. But Rod Gerald tried to lateral the ball, just as Anderson wrapped him up.

The ball fell to the turf. Michigan's Derek Howard recovered it.

On the Ohio State sideline, Hayes had a brief phone conversation with his angry assistants in the press box. He ended the conversation by slamming the phone down. *Goddammit.* Two straight losses to Bo. Hayes looked to his right and saw ABC cameraman Mike Freedman, capturing his tantrum for all those viewers who wanted to watch Woody Hayes meeting Bo Schembechler instead of Anwar Sadat meeting Menachem Begin.

Hayes walked over, lunged toward Freedman, and gave him a quick punch. The whole country saw it, and in case anybody missed it, ABC replayed it several times.

For the game, Ohio State would outgain Michigan 352 to 196. But the Wolverines had won, 14–6.

Schembechler found Hayes in the tunnel and tried to speak to his old coach, but in the pandemonium, Hayes didn't hear him. When the two men crossed paths again later, Schembechler attempted to explain himself.

"I tried to say hello to you," Schembechler said, "and you didn't know it was me."

Hayes looked at Schembechler.

"No, no," Hayes corrected. " 'You didn't know it was *I*.' "

*   *   *

Hayes did his best to be gracious afterward. "Gentlemen," he told the assembled media, "that was the best game we ever played and lost." He admitted that Michigan "outguessed us." For a man who had twice ended Michigan Stadium press conferences in less than a minute, Hayes was behaving remarkably well. Yet there was an air of inevitability to the proceedings—at some point, somebody was going to ask about punching that cameraman. Finally, somebody did.

"I'm darned disgusted with having cameras pushed at me," Hayes said. "Your team makes a mistake, you're mad, and you turn around and there's that thing pointing at you."

Hayes immediately ended the press conference.

Bo Schembechler was effusive in his praise for Rod Gerald ("he has the quickest feet I've ever seen") and acknowledged that Ohio State had outplayed his team. But he was not about to apologize for the win.

"I've been down there when we got all the stats and they got the points," he said.

That evening, a gleeful Schembechler climbed in a car with Don Canham and Canham's right-hand man, Will Perry, to go record his television show in the Detroit suburb of Southfield. Was it just twelve months earlier that people were saying he couldn't beat the Old Man? Look at him now: two straight wins over Woody, two straight Rose Bowl bids, a 4-4-1 record against Ohio State.

"Hiya, men!" Schembechler said with a smile as he walked into the studio. He was drinking tea out of one of those maize mugs Canham was selling. The two men had the happiest athletic director–coach marriage in the nation. Canham said he had never seen Schembechler so relaxed.

"I think we're in the last year of a five-year contract," Canham told a *Detroit News* reporter that night. "I don't know. I'd have to look it up. But as far as I'm concerned, we've got an unlimited contract."

The writer asked Bo about Woody shoving the ABC cameraman, but Schembechler wouldn't bite. "I'm not the judge of his actions,"

Schembechler said. "He may have been provoked. We've got to get some restrictions on the cameras on the sidelines." There *were* restrictions, but they didn't seem to matter anymore, and when Canham was asked why cameras were allowed on the sidelines at all, he had a simple answer: "Oh, $600,000, that's why."

Woody Hayes would soon make peace with Mike Freedman. The cameraman would work the Sugar Bowl, and the two men would joke around at an Ohio State practice in New Orleans.

But by then, the whole country had seen the replay. Big Ten commissioner Wayne Duke had publicly reprimanded Hayes. Duke said Hayes had acted in violation of the conference's rules regarding unsportsmanlike conduct. If Hayes had a similar infraction at any time in the next twelve months, Duke warned, he would be suspended for two games.

The media reaction was just as harsh. *Sports Illustrated* led its coverage of the game by asking, "Well, why wouldn't poor old Woody Hayes feel like hitting somebody?" The story was more about Hayes's outburst and the frustration that caused it than about Bo Schembechler's triumph. Even the Columbus media was growing tired of Hayes's outbursts. The *Citizen-Journal* printed an editorial headlined, "Coach Hayes, you are wrong."

"Commit a crime," Emerson wrote, "and the earth is made of glass."

Fourth-ranked Michigan was headed to Pasadena to play No. 13 Washington. If the Wolverines won, they had a chance at the national title . . . as long as No. 9 Ohio State beat No. 3 Alabama in the Sugar Bowl, and No. 5 Notre Dame beat No. 1 Texas in the Cotton Bowl, and No. 6 Arkansas beat No. 2 Oklahoma in the Orange Bowl.

This was how college football had operated for years—there was no system for producing a clear national champion. But the clamor for a playoff was increasing. The *Football News* told fans that if they wanted a playoff, they should write to the three most powerful men in college football: Walter Byers, the executive director of the NCAA; Roone Arledge, the president of ABC sports; and Don Canham.

Canham was not interested in a playoff. He didn't want to extend the season, and he thought the automatic Rose Bowl bid gave the Big Ten a huge advantage over other conferences. But the *Football News* was right: if Canham *had* wanted a playoff, he was one of the few men who could help create one.

Canham had that kind of power, and part of the reason he had it was that he only used it when he thought he could succeed. That's why, after much deliberation, he shelved his plan to build luxury boxes. Canham wanted the boxes, and he was sure they would be profitable. But the Michigan economy was in a slump, and the political environment was not right for an expensive stadium renovation.

Even as he gave up that fight, Canham kept a firm grip on his department. He ran it the way he saw fit. In early December 1977, Crisler Arena hosted a basketball doubleheader: the women's team would play first, followed by a televised men's game. With less than nine minutes left in the women's game, Canham realized they were running late.

The score was close. It did not matter. The referees were told to speed the game up. A few minutes later, they went to a running clock—it did not stop for substitutions, timeouts, or anything else. In Don Canham's athletic universe, time stopped for no woman. Women's basketball was fun, but men's basketball was business.

With the exception of the loss in Minnesota, Michigan had swept through the regular season, forcing most of its opponents to play catch-up. Yet those opponents had still averaged more than twice as many rushing attempts (44) as passing attempts (20). That's how football was played in the Big Ten. It was *not* how football was played in the Pacific-8.

So the Wolverines were not surprised Washington quarterback Warren Moon threw fourteen passes in the first half of the Rose Bowl.

The surprise was that Washington led 17–0 at halftime. Early in the third quarter, Moon hit receiver Spider Gaines for a 28-yard touchdown to give the underdog Huskies a 24–0 lead. The regular season had not prepared the Wolverines for the Huskies' aerial attack—and while Moon was pitching the ball around the field, Bo Schembechler had stubbornly stuck with his running game. Now Schembechler had to scrap the game plan that had worked the entire season and ask Rick Leach to pass his team to victory.

Well, what do you know? On the next drive, Leach threw a 76-yard touchdown pass to Curt Stephenson. After a Washington field goal, Leach completed four straight passes to lead to another Michigan touchdown. Soon after that, Leach threw a 32-yard touchdown pass to freshman Stan Edwards.

The Wolverines had cut the margin to 27–20. They just needed a touchdown and a two-point conversion to beat Washington. There was no doubt that Bo Schembechler would go for the win instead of the tie. He still had an outside chance at a national title, and he did not come to Pasadena to get his first Rose Bowl *tie*.

Late in the fourth quarter, Leach led the Wolverines down to the Washington eight-yard line. It was first and goal. The comeback was nearly complete. There was a minute and a half on the clock—plenty of time for Schembechler to go back to his kind of football, stuff the ball down the throat of the reeling Huskies, and set up a two-point conversion. But the frenzy of the second-half comeback must have inspired Schembechler. He called for a swing pass to Stan Edwards.

Edwards was open, but Leach threw the ball slightly off-target, and Edwards turned upfield before he had secured the reception. The ball bounced up in the air. It landed in the hands of Washington linebacker Michael Jackson.

Game over.

Bo Schembechler was now 0–5 in bowl games. From 1972 to 1975, the book on him was that he could beat everybody except Woody Hayes. Now he was beating Hayes, but he couldn't win the bowl game. Schembechler's teams were 0-8-1 in their last game of the season.

For Schembechler, the Rose Bowl defeat was another bitter disappointment.

But it was pure ecstasy compared to what was happening to the Old Man in New Orleans.

Ohio State assistant coach Gary Tranquill was the team's entertainment chairman for the Sugar Bowl, the man who would make sure the Buckeyes spent their non-practice time wisely. When the team arrived in the Big Easy, somebody handed Tranquill a bunch of tickets good for a free "hurricane" at Pat O'Brien's, a legendary bar in the French Quarter. Tranquill barely looked at the tickets before passing them along to all the players and coaches. He didn't realize that a hurricane was a rum drink. Pretty soon, a whole bunch of Ohio State Buckeyes were drinking them.

Woody Hayes walked into Pat O'Brien's and asked one of the players what was in the drink. He was told it was some sort of fruit punch.

The Old Man took a sip.

"Jesus Christ!" he screamed. "This thing has *alcohol* in it!" Hayes threw the glass down against the floor, where it shattered. Players started ducking under tables to avoid his wrath. The tone for the trip was established right there. Some players drank heavily. Others found New Orleans to be a foreign land. The Buckeyes didn't want to be there. They wanted to be in Pasadena, playing for the national title.

Rod Gerald had another reason to panic: by the time the game finally rolled around, he didn't have any cocaine and didn't know where to get it.

The game had been touted as the first-ever matchup between Hayes and Alabama's Bear Bryant, the two winningest coaches in the country. Both men downplayed that storyline, yet within the Ohio State camp, it was clear how much this meant to Hayes.

On the morning of the game, some Buckeyes were laughing in their team meeting.

That night, Alabama whipped Ohio State, 35–6.

"They beat us," Hayes said, "with a team that had half the talent we had. Our team had about a quarter of the coaching their team got."

The Old Man's frustration had been building throughout the night. At one point he got so mad he ignored his assistant coaches and went to his old "robust" offense, even though Ohio State needed to pass to have any chance at a comeback. Late in the first half, when the Buckeyes had been stopped short of the goal line, Hayes had thrown his hat onto the field.

Pictures of him throwing the hat would run in the *Columbus Citizen-Journal* the next day, along with a story in which a writer documented the grumbling in Columbus bars. Several fans said they thought it was time for Woody to retire—an inexact survey, to be sure, but one that never would have appeared in a Columbus paper just two years earlier.

Most fans and players did not see what happened *after* Hayes threw his hat. As he ran off the field at halftime to head to the locker room, he stopped at a goalpost and punched it several times. These were not casual punches. They were an assault on the goalpost.

That Woody Hayes would have such an explosion in a game called the Sugar Bowl was appropriate, for some of his close friends suspected that sugar played a major role in his temper tantrums. Hayes's diabetes had been a problem for years, and it got worse as each season progressed; Woody might follow his diet in the offseason, but once football practice began, he would invariably stray. People who wanted to get some time with him learned to bring donuts to his office.

As September became November, the long workdays would take their toll, and Hayes would eat more sweets at odd hours. His blood sugar got more and more out of whack and his ability to control himself diminished. He was capable of blowing up in practice at any time of year—and many times, the eruptions were staged for dramatic effect—but some friends noticed that almost all his public meltdowns occurred at the end of seasons, when he had let himself go: tearing up the sideline marker in Ann Arbor in November 1971 . . . shoving Art Rogers's camera back in his face in January 1974 . . . assaulting Wayne

Duke in the locker room after the Michigan State loss in November 1974 . . . and now, in 1977, two incidents: punching Mike Freedman at the Michigan game and pounding on the goalpost in New Orleans.

Some of the Old Man's friends thought he should retire before his body broke down completely. But "retiring" sounded like "quitting" to Woody Hayes, especially after a disappointing season. He did not even want to discuss his health. His physicians told Buckeyes team doctor Melvin Olix that the coach wasn't taking care of himself, but when Olix broached the topic, Hayes told him to mind his own business.

"That's enough of my personal life," Hayes said.

Olix told him that for a man who had suffered a heart attack, he was behaving irresponsibly.

"I didn't have a heart attack," Hayes said.

Olix asked him how he could say that.

"I didn't have a heart attack," Hayes repeated.

It was the equivalent of telling an assistant coach he was fired. End of conversation.

11

The Final Days

In late January of 1978, the worst blizzard on record swept through the United States. Experts later said they saw a storm coming but had no idea it would be so lethal. The storm grew so intense and fast-moving that its warm and cold fronts became reversed. It twisted like a corkscrew, a winter tornado, threatening everything in its path.

The blizzard killed more than a hundred people in eighteen states but focused its fury on the Midwest. At least thirty-five Ohioans perished. Winds over Lake Erie reached 103 miles per hour. Gusts up to 70 and 80 miles per hour were common throughout Ohio. The temperature, with the wind chill factor, was 60 degrees below zero. More than 150,000 Ohioans lost power, but utility companies were having trouble accessing the downed lines, which were often buried under snowbanks as high as fifteen feet.

Ohio's state highway patrol rescued 5,700 motorists on the first day of the storm, and another 2,100 cars were abandoned. Most people accepted that they couldn't go anywhere for a few days, which meant Bo Schembechler was stuck in Cincinnati, where he had been recruiting. Thankfully for Schembechler, his best friend Joe Hayden lived there. Schembechler stayed at Hayden's house for so long that Hayden and his family started calling him Monty Woolley, after the actor from *The Man Who Came to Dinner*, a movie about a man who is confined to another family's house after slipping on ice and breaking his leg. Schembechler really wanted to get out and recruit. Instead, he stayed in and ran up a huge phone bill from Hayden's house. ("It's for a good cause, Joe," Schembechler said.)

On the first morning of the storm, Woody Hayes trudged into his office a little later than usual. Only one of his assistant coaches was there—graduate assistant coach Larry Kindbom, who lived maybe a hundred yards away. Kindbom kidded the Old Man about sleeping in. Hayes told Kindbom he had a reason for being late: he had walked the three miles from his house. The whole city was shut down.

Hayes made a few calls. Nobody else was coming to work. They were all snowed in. Hayes made another call or two, then turned to Kindbom and said, "You and I are going for a ride."

As they walked outside, Kindbom started to grasp the magnitude of the storm. There was snow and ice everywhere, and . . . what's that, pulling into the parking lot? A snowplow? Hayes and Kindbom climbed in a car. Hayes told Kindbom to follow the snowplow. Kindbom did just that—onto Interstate 670 (where the only cars in sight were abandoned on the side of the road) and all the way down to Gahanna, thirteen miles away, where Hayes was scheduled to visit high school stars Tim O'Cain and Ted Hall.

Kindbom parked across the street from O'Cain's house. Hayes got out, walked down the O'Cains' six-hundred-foot driveway, and stepped inside the house. He spent several hours with the O'Cain family and never mentioned the weather or football.

Before Hayes left, Tim O'Cain promised to attend Ohio State. So in that sense, the day was a success. But all things considered, Woody Hayes probably would have preferred to be in Bloomingburg, Ohio, recruiting the best high school passer in America.

Art Schlichter could throw the ball fifty yards in the air while sitting on his ass. In pregame warm-ups in high school, he would intimidate his opponents by throwing sixty- and seventy-yard passes. Then the game would start, and Schlichter would run his team's sophisticated offense to perfection. The Panthers usually scored at least four or five touchdowns before halftime. Schlichter passed for more than 6,000 yards in his high school career. He never lost a game at Miami Trace High School. He had never lost an organized football game of *any* kind, going back to fifth grade.

Virtually every school in the country wanted Schlichter, but he quickly narrowed his choices to two schools: Michigan and Ohio State. Schlichter was the kind of recruit that Bo Schembechler and Woody Hayes loved. He was a country kid raised on sports. He would practice by throwing passes into a net hung between two telephone poles in his backyard—ten passes from one knee, ten from the other, until he had thrown five hundred passes. He would come back the next day and do it again. He rarely drank. He didn't smoke. In the spring of his senior year, a classmate hosted a graduation party at a farmhouse, with a hayride and kegs of beer. Schlichter and his friends grabbed some potato chips and soda pop and played tennis.

Woody Hayes decided he had to have Art Schlichter. He went after him with more gusto than he had shown for any recruit in twenty-eight years. It was customary for assistant coaches to try to recruit several players each year, because of the sheer size of a typical recruiting class (twenty-five players or more) and the reality that some heavily recruited players would end up elsewhere. But for the 1978 recruiting class, Ohio State offensive coordinator George Chaump recruited only one player: Schlichter.

Art's father, Max, made it clear that he expected his son to start at quarterback as soon as he arrived on campus. Not only that, Max said, but Art wasn't going to be like the other quarterbacks who had played at Michigan and Ohio State—running the option, handing off to the fullback, throwing only on third and long. Max Schlichter told recruiters that he expected Art to throw at least twenty times per game as a freshman. He also said he expected Art to play basketball as a freshman, as soon as the football team finished its regular season.

When Bo Schembechler was presented with these demands, he slammed his fist on the Schlichters' coffee table and told Max he was crazy. Schembechler had senior Rick Leach returning at quarterback. Did Max really think Schembechler would send Leach to the bench so Art could play as a freshman—without even holding a competition? And as for basketball . . . well, Leach had waited a year to play baseball. Why couldn't Art do the same?

Woody Hayes also had a senior star, Rod Gerald, returning at quarterback. But Hayes shook Max Schlichter's hand and said they had a deal: Art would start, Ohio State would throw twenty passes per game, and when Art wasn't playing football, he could play basketball.

What on earth was going on here? Was this the same man who said three things could happen when you passed, and two of them were bad? Who said a team could expect one loss for every *sophomore* in the starting lineup? Who had told his players for almost three decades that the only way to get anything in life was to work for it?

Hayes had always prided himself on honesty; even the Old Man's critics acknowledged that. Was he so desperate now that he was *lying* just to land Art Schlichter?

No.

Hayes meant every word.

Woody Hayes's closest friend from his Navy days was probably a man named Eloy Cueto, whom Hayes referred to simply as "Bud." (Hayes said "Eloy" was too effeminate. "Your name is Bud," he said.) Hayes and Cueto stayed in touch for years after leaving the USS *Rinehart*. They became friendly with each other's wives. When Ohio State played at Illinois, near Cueto's home, Hayes would leave tickets for Cueto.

But Hayes and Cueto were not close when they were actually in the Navy; Hayes was Cueto's captain and was determined to maintain some distance. Their most intimate contact was their most violent: Hayes liked to box, and sometimes he asked Cueto to be his sparring partner. Cueto did not imagine the man he was fighting would be a lifelong friend.

The 1968 Ohio State Buckeyes understood how Eloy Cueto felt. They were the last team to win a national title for Hayes, yet so many of them hated the Old Man when they played for him. Everywhere they went, there he was, demanding more work and less fun. One of the stars from the '68 team, Jim Stillwagon, remembered his sophomore year, when he and a few buddies were laughing in the locker room the day before they played Minnesota, and Woody walked in and said, "Goddammit, don't you know too much levity will beat you every time?" When Hayes walked away, Stillwagon had to ask what "levity" meant. But he knew enough to shut up and listen when Hayes spoke. They all did.

Ten years had passed since those Buckeyes won the national championship. The players had come to appreciate Hayes—how he demanded a level of discipline they didn't know they could reach, how he forced them to go to class, how he helped them find jobs or medical assistance long after they stopped playing football.

Now it was the spring of 1978. Several of those 1968 Buckeyes were back in Columbus for a ten-year mini-reunion. They went to practice, just to see Woody in action again. Wouldn't this be fun? Remember how Woody used to scare the shit out of them? Remember how they all stayed quiet on bus rides, because that's what he wanted? Shoot, guys were so uptight, they couldn't even eat their pregame meals.

In the Ohio State locker room, Hayes introduced the 1968 players to his 1978 team:

I've got some of the boys back . . .

These are the men who won the national championship . . .

The 1968 Buckeyes looked around. Some of the current players were holding private conversations. They weren't even whispering. Others were slamming lockers or walking around. It was like the Old Man wasn't speaking at all. And worst of all, he just kept going, like this was how it was supposed to be.

The 1968 Buckeyes were stunned. As Stillwagon and his teammate Dirk Worden walked to their car, they talked about how embarrassing it was—not for them, but for Woody. Ron Maciejowski, the backup to Rex Kern in '68, thought Hayes had lost control of the team. Bill Urbanik, who had stayed in football and become an assistant coach at Wake Forest, blamed Hayes's staff. He thought the assistants had let the kids get away with too much. But Urbanik knew that ultimately, it wouldn't matter who was at fault. As he told a friend afterward, "This ain't gonna last real long."

*   *   *

Michigan's spring football game fell on the same day the university's baseball team was hosting Minnesota, which meant Rick Leach had a problem. Obviously, the baseball game counted and the football game did not. But Bo Schembechler did not want to lose his senior quarterback for the spring game. He reached a compromise: Leach would play the first half of the spring game, then head to the baseball stadium.

That afternoon, Leach showed the spring-game crowd why he was a leading contender for the 1978 Heisman Trophy.

Then he left, joined the baseball team, and drove in the winning run.

In August, with the 1978 season just weeks away, Woody Hayes called defensive coordinator George Hill into his office. Hayes probably had a better relationship with Hill than with any of his other assistants, because he gave Hill the most latitude. Hayes, an offensive coach, rarely spent extended time with the defense. He had come to look at Hill as more than an assistant coach—Hill was like the head coach of the defense. And unlike some of the other assistants, who felt stifled by Woody's stubbornness, Hill was always deferential to the Old Man.

"Sit down," Hayes said. "I want to talk to you about something."

Hill figured Hayes would mention a story in that day's *Dispatch*, or maybe one of President Carter's foreign policy initiatives.

"Do you think I should resign?" Hayes asked.

Hill tried to deflect the question. He said Hayes had to make the decision himself. He said he didn't want any input into the decision. Without either man saying it, both understood that the timing of the question—in August, just before the start of the season—was almost as important as the question itself. Schools around the country were gearing up for the season. There was no chance of hiring another school's head coach in August. If Hayes resigned then, Ohio State would have to choose his successor from the current staff. That probably meant Hill would get the job. Hayes would have effectively named his successor.

Hill told Hayes he should keep coaching—because he could still coach.

Hayes said he wasn't sure.

Was he fatigued? There was a time when Hayes thought he knew everything about his team. That time had passed. There were even rumors that his starting quarterback of the last two years, Rod Gerald, was using drugs; the coaching staff felt powerless to do anything about the rumors.

Did he sense that he was losing support, even at home? Hayes had long been a polarizing figure among sports fans around the country, but now he was even losing support in Columbus. He was a Nixonian in a time of Carter and a military historian when many Americans wanted to forget their last war, and his temper tantrums were becoming harder to defend. Plus, he had lost two straight to That School Up North.

That summer, a Columbus television station asked Columbus residents the same question Hayes asked George Hill: should Woody Hayes retire?

Fifty-six percent of respondents said yes.

Columbus sportscaster Marty Reid asked Hayes about the poll at one of the coach's weekly media lunches at the Jai Lai. Hayes was defiant as ever.

"Well, I don't care," he barked. "There's nobody around in this league or any other league that has won as many games as I have. I'm not going to let their opinion decide a thing . . . and if you're one of the 56 percent, I don't give a damn about you, either!"

But privately, he wondered.

Was it time to retire?

How many people believed in Woody Hayes anymore?

"I admit without shame that he is my favorite American," wrote renowned *Chicago Tribune* columnist Bob Greene, a native of Columbus, just before the start of the 1978 season. "I have yet to find one other person who agrees with me."

The weeks before the 1978 Michigan season were filled with anticipation—not just because Bo Schembechler had another national title contender, but because of the schedule. In Week 2, the Wolverines would travel to South Bend to play Notre Dame for the first time since 1943.

The schools had avoided each other mainly because of a feud between coaches Fritz Crisler of Michigan and Frank Leahy of Notre Dame. Don Canham didn't care about the feud. He thought that bringing the Fighting Irish to Michigan Stadium every two years would be a huge boost to season-ticket sales and guarantee a huge television audience.

But Canham was not content to simply schedule Notre Dame. He asked Notre Dame athletic director Ed "Moose" Krause to let the home team keep 100 percent of the gate receipts. Krause balked. He pointed out that Michigan had almost twice as many seats, and the standard throughout college football was a fifty-fifty split. Why would Notre Dame let Canham keep all that revenue?

Canham told Krause the deal would serve as a blueprint for all their other contracts. Krause could bring Duke or Tulane into Notre Dame Stadium for a reduced price and say that if it was good enough for Michigan, it should be good enough for them. Krause agreed. Within a few years, guarantees would become the norm throughout college football.

Now Canham had a home-and-home contract with the most storied team in his sport, virtual assurance that he would sell more season tickets than anybody else in the country, a chance to keep 100 percent of the revenue off a guaranteed sellout every two years, and a contract that would give Michigan a bigger chunk of the pie in future seasons. All in all, a pretty good deal.

Of course, there *was* the matter of the game. Notre Dame, the defending national champion, took a 14–7 halftime lead, but Rick Leach outplayed Fighting Irish quarterback Joe Montana in the second half to lead Michigan to a 28–14 win.

By the end of the season, Leach would set an NCAA record for touchdowns accounted for (running or passing) and earn acclaim as the best player of Bo Schembechler's tenure. Schembechler's plan had worked: Leach had survived the grueling summer before his freshman year, when he painted car parts in the morning and worked out with the team in the afternoon. He had earned the starting spot and withstood the early struggles and subsequent criticism. Now he was one of the biggest college football stars in the country.

Oh, the quarterback and the coach had their battles. Leach pushed to pass more. Schembechler wanted to stick with his option running attack. For the season, Michigan would average only fifteen passes per game—more than the ten per game in 1975, Leach's freshman year, but still not a lot. But even Leach had to acknowledge that, in the wake of the Rose Bowl debacle against Washington, Schembechler was coming around. (Bo had bigger plans in mind, too. He was recruiting a high school kid from Florida named Anthony Carter, a make-you-miss sprinter, to be his game-breaking receiver.)

Schembechler had good reason to stick with his running game: it worked every day of the year except the first of January. He had one of the best sets of running backs in the Big Ten and another overpowering offensive line. The linemen got bigger every year— offensive tackle William Paris, just a freshman, was listed at 284 pounds and might have weighed more. Paris was so big that nobody called him William. He was "Bubba."

Dan Dierdorf came back to Ann Arbor for a clinic, took one look at Bubba Paris, and asked Schembechler what the hell had happened. Back in 1970, Dierdorf had damn near killed himself to get down to Schembechler's prescribed weight of 245 pounds. Now a *freshman* was pushing 290 and Schembechler was giving him playing time? Schembechler laughed. Times, he said, had changed.

In virtually every interview he gave in 1978, Bo Schembechler said that Rick Leach was the finest player he had ever coached. Of course, there weren't that many interviews. Schembechler, always wary of "the media people," was growing more insulated by the year. He had begun shutting the media out of all his practices. It didn't matter if the reporters were local or national, print or TV. Why should Schembechler trust them? What could he gain? Don Canham was selling every ticket he printed whether Schembechler helped the media or not.

In his first few years at Michigan, Schembechler had simply been a reluctant interviewee. Now he was determined to stop the flow of information, and his gift with the language served him as well with the press as it did with his players. He would growl, or pause for dramatic effect, or drop a self-deprecating line to lighten the mood. With closed practices, limited access to players, and increasing fan interest, reporters had no choice but to write more about Schembechler. Naturally—because he kept them at bay, and charmed them while doing it—they depicted him as a charismatic control freak. The coach didn't care much about that. He was more worried about what reporters *didn't* write.

Schembechler knew Michigan fans would support him as long as he won—which he continued to do. Heading into the Ohio State game, Michigan had lost only once, to Michigan State—the first time since 1969 that Schembechler had lost to his in-state rival. After the season, Michigan State coach Darryl Rogers would tell a reporter that the win was special, not just because of the rivalry, but because the Spartans beat those "arrogant asses in Ann Arbor." Michigan State's victory wasn't a fluke, either. The Spartans were as good as anybody in the Big Ten in 1978. But they couldn't go to the Rose Bowl. They were ineligible because Woody Hayes had turned them in for cheating.

The Ohio Stadium crowd roared as the Buckeyes took the field for their first possession of the 1978 season, against Penn State. Who saw this coming? Art Schlichter was starting! The Old Man went with the freshman!

Woody Hayes had kept his starting quarterback a secret until that moment—like General MacArthur at the Inchon landing, he wanted the element of surprise. He closed his preseason practices to the media for the first time ever. ("What was it Churchill said?" Hayes asked reporters. "Truth is so valuable that it must be protected by a bodyguard of lies.'') Hayes didn't even tell the television crew that morning; when they filmed quick shots of the starters, Rod Gerald was the quarterback.

But while the crowd was thrilled, many Buckeyes were not. They held out hope until the day of the game that Gerald would get to keep his job. Some of them thought there was an unseemly undercurrent to the crowd's reaction: black out-of-staters had started at quarterback for five straight years, and now it was time for the all-American white kid from down the road to take over. Others simply wondered if Gerald really ever had a chance to keep his starting job. The whole thing seemed rigged from the beginning: Schlichter had even visited Ohio State spring practice a few months earlier, which was unheard of for a high school senior. When the players reported to camp, Gerald split his time between quarterback, under the guise of a competition, and wide receiver.

Woody Hayes was suddenly determined to win through the air. Heaven knew Art Schlichter could make all the throws. But wait— wasn't there an element of risk? What about all those Penn State blitzes? Wouldn't Penn State sack Schlichter, force him to move *backward*? Hayes decided to keep seven guys back to block and send three on long pass routes.

Offensive coordinator George Chaump was furious. With only three receivers running pass patterns, he worried that Schlichter would be forced to throw downfield into double and triple coverage.

On Ohio State's first possession, Chaump's fear was realized. Schlichter threw deep into triple coverage and was intercepted.

On their next possession, the Buckeyes came out in the wishbone. If they were running the wishbone, why not start Rod Gerald? They picked up one first down and punted.

On Ohio State's third possession, Schlichter threw deep to Gerald, who caught it. But Gerald lost both a shoe and the ball on the play. Penn State recovered the ball.

On Ohio State's fourth possession, Schlichter nearly threw another interception.

Ohio State's fifth possession started on its own eight-yard line.

Hayes was not going to let a freshman pass from there. He put Gerald in at quarterback to run the option. Now Gerald's teammates were *really* mad. Was this how it was going to work? How come Schlichter got to play quarterback when the Buckeyes had good field position, but Gerald only played when they were backed up against their own end zone?

On Ohio State's sixth possession, Schlichter threw his second interception.

It just got worse from there. In the second half, Schlichter threw three more interceptions. After one of those interceptions, linebacker Tom Cousineau got in the freshman's face: *Throw it to the guys in our color, you asshole.* Penn State won, 19–0.

Just a year earlier, Ohio State had won its opener, 10–0, and Hayes told reporters the team needed "more juice" in its attack. Now, when asked about the five interceptions and 19–0 embarrassment, Hayes told reporters, "When you get into the passing game, you can expect that sort of thing to happen, particularly in a first game."

What did he think of Schlichter, who had completed twelve passes to his own team and five to his opponent?

"A lot of the mistakes weren't his fault," Hayes said. "I think our new quarterback is probably as fine a passer as there is in college football."

If anybody had a reason to feel slighted by the quick elevation of Art Schlichter, it was Rod Gerald. After all, he was the one who had to give up the position he'd held for two years. Yet Gerald did not harbor any resentment. He knew his only chance at an NFL career was at receiver, and in fall practice he thought that Schlichter was the greatest pure passer he'd ever seen.

Plus, Gerald genuinely liked the kid. The two were roommates for road games, and Gerald realized that Schlichter was truly a high school all-American, and not just in the football sense. Schlichter practiced hard and stayed away from the party scene. He really only had one vice, and it seemed like a small one: in high school he would join his best friend and favorite wide receiver, Bill Hanners, at Scioto Downs, a racetrack in Columbus. Hanners's family was in the horse business, and he and Schlichter would place two-dollar bets on horses.

So Gerald was content with Schlichter starting. Many other Buckeyes were not. They started to play like a team that had no chemistry or belief in itself. In their fourth game, the Buckeyes tied Southern Methodist. The next week, Schlichter completed 20 of 34 passes for 289 yards against Purdue, his best passing day so far. But Gerald broke a bone in his elbow, the Buckeyes fumbled six times, and Purdue won, 27–16. Ohio State fell to 2-2-1 and dropped out of the Associated Press rankings for the first time since the injury-ravaged 1971 season.

Hayes insisted after the Purdue game that "as [Art] gets better, we'll pass even more." But pass protection was a constant problem. Ohio State linemen had always been taught to overpower the men in front of them and pave the way for running backs, but pass blocking required a different technique. Linemen had to stay behind the line of scrimmage and keep pass rushers in front of them. Hayes could not get used to it.

Hayes essentially relieved George Chaump of his responsibilities as offensive coordinator and gave more power to Alex Gibbs, the offensive line coach. In the ten games leading up to the Michigan game, Schlichter passed just 155 times—and 60 of those passes came in the losses to Purdue and Penn State. In the other nine games, Schlichter was mostly an option quarterback.

Art's father, Max, grew angry. Hadn't Hayes promised Art would throw twenty times per game? Rumors circulated that the freshman would transfer. One wire service quoted Max as criticizing the Ohio State coaches. Art later said it was actually his grandfather, who thought a friend was playing a practical joke, and the wire service issued an apology. But the story rang true. Max was complaining to the Ohio State coaches all the time.

The Buckeyes won their next five games, but almost every one featured the same storylines: How many passes did Art throw? Was

Woody still committed to a passing offense? And if there was a controversial call, what did Hayes think of it?

Hayes had a standard response to that last question: "Remember, I'm on probation." He knew that one transgression could bring a suspension from Big Ten commissioner Wayne Duke.

Of course, the probation did not apply to practice, where Hayes's outbursts became more frequent and more pronounced. He would often smack himself in frustration, or slug a player to make a point. If the 1978 Buckeyes had anything in common with their predecessors, it was that they knew to stand on Hayes's left, so he had to hit them with his right hand.

Mostly Hayes was exhausted, and he was running out of time in every way. He had stopped teaching an English class to the players; instead, he would grab three freshmen before practice and try to improve their vocabulary and grammar in the car. Some of the freshmen would hide rather than get picked for the short ride with the Old Man.

Hayes had promised himself he would finish his book about the parallels between war and football before the start of the 1978 season. With every other book, he had set a due date and met it; in 1973, he had even ignored signs of an impending heart attack to finish *You Win with People!* But now he was late for the first time, and his publisher, Random House, wanted the manuscript. There was just so much to write, so many parallels to draw. (Adolf Hitler, he said, had taken France by using the "40 trap," one of Ohio State's running plays.)

Sometimes Hayes would dictate a passage into a tape recorder and ask secretary Woonsin Spalding to type it up. On one such dictation, Hayes told his version of hitting photographer Art Rogers of the *Los Angeles Times* at the 1973 Rose Bowl. It was as though he was getting ready for a trial and wanted to present his case to the jury.

Hayes was sixty-five years old. How much longer could he coach? His friends sensed that the end was near. Harold Schechter, the liaison between the athletic department and the faculty, nominated him for a teaching award. Hayes was one of the last coaches in the country to be an active member of the faculty. Schechter knew how much that meant to Woody, and he wanted somebody to acknowledge it.

Hell, they had to do *something* for the Old Man, because he sure wasn't going to get the retirement gift he really wanted: one more national championship. The Buckeyes looked like they were headed to some second-tier bowl game like the Peach or the Gator, and some folks in Columbus thought those games were beneath them. In mid-October, at athletic director Hugh Hindman's recommendation, the Ohio State Athletic Council voted to restrict the Buckeyes from attending any bowl game besides the Rose, Orange, Sugar, or Cotton.

Art Schlichter was one of the few Ohio State starters who was genuinely excited about a trip to a lesser postseason game. He had never been to a bowl game, and he thought it would be nice to go somewhere warm in winter. But Schlichter couldn't share these feelings with his teammates, because he felt removed from them. His fellow freshmen dressed in another locker room, away from the starters. And the starters, of course, would barely acknowledge him.

Schlichter had arrived in Columbus as a ready-made quarterback. He had broken high school records. He had played in a sophisticated offense. He was prepared to succeed immediately. What he was *not* prepared to do was fail. The downside of having always won was that he had never lost, and he didn't know how to handle it. He was a farm kid who wasn't prepared for the magnitude of Ohio State football. Schlichter was recognized everywhere he went. It made him uncomfortable, and he began to search for his own identity. He didn't drink or smoke, so he couldn't go party on High Street with the rest of the guys. He started taking solace at Scioto Downs, the racetrack outside Columbus. He went there first as a social release, but after a while, he discovered that he loved to gamble. Pretty soon, he couldn't live without it.

Rod Gerald had no idea Schlichter was developing a gambling problem. Gerald was more concerned with hiding his own addiction. He no longer felt the need to get high on game day—the pressure was on Art now—but he spent most days using cocaine, speed, barbiturates, and "black mollies" and other amphetamines.

There they sat in the Ohio State team hotel on Friday nights before road games: the freshman who was disdained by the rest of the starters and the senior who couldn't go two days without getting high. Meanwhile, Hayes was still telling his players he had only two rules: "No drugs and no haters."

Ten days before the Buckeyes would face Michigan, the Ohio State Athletic Council changed its mind about second-tier bowls. Woody Hayes had asked them to reconsider. He said a trip to a bowl—any bowl—would be good for his team, especially his young quarterback. Some of his assistant coaches and friends felt Hayes didn't really want to go to a lesser bowl, either. He was asking because he thought he should ask.

The only bowl Hayes wanted was the Rose Bowl—which was still a possibility. Thanks partly to Michigan State's ineligibility, the winner of the Michigan–Ohio State game would head to Pasadena. Big Ten commissioner Wayne Duke announced that the loser would go to the Gator Bowl in Jacksonville, Florida.

Hayes would not let the media watch practice during the week leading up to the Michigan game. When he was asked about the secrecy, Hayes talked about the Battle of Khalkin Gol in 1939, when the Japanese invaded Siberia, with disastrous results. The battle convinced the Japanese they did not want to fight the Russians again. They would fight the United States instead. A reporter asked Hayes what that had to do with the Michigan game; Hayes just said it was "a matter of security."

Even without any access to practice, the Columbus newspapers still had to provide plenty of stories for the insatiable Ohio State fan base. The *Citizen-Journal* noted that Ohio State had lost its last four televised games, and in another story, the *Citizen-Journal* sports editor pointed out that Hayes was a television attraction, whether he wanted to be or not. The story was headlined, "Move over, TV stars! Introducing: Woody."

And speaking of introducing Woody . . .

"Let me tell you about Woody," Bo Schembechler told the media four days before the game.

Schembechler started smiling.

"Nah, I'd better not."

A Columbus reporter played along: "Go ahead. We won't tell Woody."

"You say that," Schembechler said, "but when you guys get back to Columbus, you're going to have to line up one at a time." Schembechler was playing to his audience now. He gave a long detailed description of how the Columbus writers would deal with the wrath of Woody as soon as they crossed the Ohio-Michigan border.

"He's going to be waiting for you," Schembechler said. "And they're going to take you to this interrogation room. It's going to be dark and cold. And they're going to make you talk."

As always, the inflection on every word was perfect. The reporters laughed. Finally, somebody asked him about his control over the press in Michigan. Schembechler pretended to be angry.

"I . . . DON'T . . . CONTROL . . . THE . . . PRESS!" he said in mock anger. "That's for damn sure."

Then he cracked, "You're damned right I'd like to."

One reporter, eager to blow the game up as much as he could, asked Schembechler what could possibly be bigger than beating Ohio State.

"A lot," Schembechler said, laughing. "A lot."

Woody Hayes acknowledged to the ABC announcers before the game that "we have not been that good this year." Yet Michigan was only a six-point favorite, partly because the game was in Columbus, and partly because these Bo-Woody matchups had been so close and low-scoring.

For ABC, the best storyline was Rick Leach, the senior Heisman Trophy candidate, versus Art Schlichter, the freshman gunslinger. But underneath that storyline was the true theme of each team's season. Leach, supposedly the running quarterback, had more touchdowns passing (14) than running (12). Bo Schembechler had slowly incorporated the pass without losing his team's identity. But Schlichter, the kid with the golden arm, had run for 11 and passed for only four. Schlichter had also thrown 19 interceptions. Woody Hayes had taken one of the most gifted passers in the country and shoehorned him into a run-first system.

Midway through the first quarter, after a long punt return, Ohio State found itself with a first down on the Wolverines' 19-yard line. Would this be it—the moment when Art Schlichter started building his legend at Ohio State? No. Schlichter kept the ball on the option for six yards. He kept it again and slipped. On third and four, Ron Springs ran for two yards. Ohio State settled for a field goal.

Michigan responded in most unusual fashion: Leach threw three straight passes. He had plenty of time to throw each one; Schembechler's team had worked vigorously on pass blocking. Each pass was complete. The third one went for a touchdown, to Rodney Feaster. Michigan led, 7–3.

The Wolverines should have scored again, late in the second quarter, when Leach completed a pass to Gene Johnson inside the Ohio State one-yard line. But Johnson fumbled and the Buckeyes recovered.

Michigan was clearly outplaying Ohio State, but the Wolverines' bad fortune was piling up inside that huge horseshoe. The bad luck had started before the game: star tailback Harlan Huckleby was out with a knee injury and fullback Russell Davis had the flu and had barely practiced. There had even been a water-main break at Michigan's team hotel, which limited the Wolverines' water access that morning. Now Gene Johnson had fumbled less than three feet from the end zone.

Now, in the locker room at halftime, Schembechler faced his biggest problem of the week: Rick Leach had pulled a hamstring in the second quarter.

Schembechler suddenly had a running quarterback who couldn't run. Fortunately for Schembechler, Ohio State had a passing quarterback who was not allowed to pass.

*   *   *

Ohio State's first possession of the second half featured three short runs and a punt. Next possession, same thing: run, run, run, punt. Michigan responded with a mix of runs and passes to move down to the Ohio State 11-yard line. From there, Rick Leach showed his coach, his opponent, and the nation just how far he had come.

It was third down. Leach took a snap and rolled left, looking for a receiver. Nobody was open. Leach patiently rolled a few more steps to his left, then dumped a pass to Roosevelt Smith, who barreled into the end zone. Touchdown.

Michigan led, 14–3.

Down 11 points, Hayes tried to pass on the next possession, but the result was the same: three and out. Then the Buckeyes got the ball back on their own one-yard line, and Hayes inserted Rod Gerald at quarterback. Once again, the coach wanted to stick to a ground game rather than pass out of his own end zone. And once again, some Buckeyes thought Hayes was asking Gerald to climb out of a hole that Art Schlichter had dug.

Schlichter was on the sidelines in a red Ohio State windbreaker. After three running plays gained just seven yards, Gerald joined him there.

Boos rained down from the Ohio Stadium stands. Were they booing Gerald? The team? The Old Man? All of the above? It didn't matter. Ohio State was finished. Schlichter went back in the game in the final minutes and completed a pass to Gerald—the Buckeyes' only first down of the second half. Two plays later, Schlichter threw an interception. Ohio State had lost its third straight game to That School Up North—14–3 this time, and really not that close.

"He's the best football player in the United States of America," Bo Schembechler said of Rick Leach afterward. "If he doesn't get the Heisman Trophy, I'll be surprised. He's the greatest football player I've ever been associated with."

Leach had completed 11 of 21 passes for 166 yards. He had arrived as a highly touted freshman, earned a starting spot that year, withstood fan criticism, balanced two sports, and finished with three straight wins against Ohio State. In doing so, he had given his coach an edge, however temporary, against Woody Hayes: Schembechler was now 5-4-1 against his mentor.

Reporters waited fifty minutes for Woody Hayes to come out of the locker room.

"He's talking to prospects," said an Ohio State aide.

"He *needs* to talk to prospects!" one writer cracked.

Hayes finally sat down for his press conference more than an hour after the game ended. "We weren't quite good enough to win," he said quietly. Ohio writers tossed him a few softballs: *It's a shame your players slipped on the field, isn't it, Coach? Are you going to get a new artificial surface next year? What did you think of Michigan?*

And then: How are you feeling right now?

"Happy as a lark," Hayes snapped, his voice rising.

The last Ohio State Buckeye to score a touchdown against the Wolverines was Pete Johnson in 1975. *Chicago Tribune* columnist David Israel asked Hayes if he was aware that his team had gone three years and twelve quarters without scoring a touchdown against Michigan.

"What's that?" Hayes asked, though he had clearly heard the question.

Are you aware . . .

"I'm aware of that and you're the guy to mention it!" Hayes snapped at Israel as he stood up. "You're the guy who cut [Notre Dame coach] Dan Devine up so badly three years ago. You almost cost him his job. People like you, I have no use for, and I want you to know that.

"You're not the kind of guy I ever want to spend any time with. And I won't!"

Hayes said good night and left the press conference.

Two days later Art Schlichter started practicing with the Ohio State basketball team. He was exhausted. He wasn't in basketball shape: he had added muscle for the football season and wasn't ready to run up and down the gym floor. Since the football season started, Schlichter had suffered bursitis in his elbow, jammed his right hand, injured ligaments in his thumb, and hurt his shoulder. But his father had made Woody Hayes promise that Art could play basketball as a freshman, and so he did.

Four weeks later, the Ohio State football team landed in Jacksonville, Florida. Their Gator Bowl matchup against Clemson was just three days away. Woody Hayes's teams had always arrived for their January 1 bowl games by December 20, so Hayes could run training camp–style practices. But in 1977, his players had complained about being in New Orleans for too long, so he decided to scale back on the pre-bowl practices this time. Rather than cut down to eight or even six days, he decided to hold a few practices in Columbus and let his players spend Christmas at home, then head to Jacksonville only three days before the December 29 game.

Hayes had even given his players the option of flying to Florida on the team plane or getting there on their own. But he seemed stunned when many players traveled on their own. A few days before leaving Columbus, he was asked about the long-held assumption that he wanted to win one last national title before retiring. He looked up, smiled a little, and said, "I don't think I'll get it this year."

The day before the Gator Bowl, Woody Hayes took the Buckeyes to the naval base in nearby Mayport, where they toured the USS *Forrestal*. Hayes's old ship, the USS *Rinehart*, had been sold for scrap in the late 1960s. The *Forrestal* was as close as he could get to being on the *Rinehart* again.

Many Buckeyes figured this was just another one of Hayes's side trips—no more special than the Wisconsin state capitol in Madison or Herbert Hoover's gravesite. But those who knew Hayes well, like George Hill and student manager Mark George, sensed the Old Man's melancholy. Hayes grew quiet and introspective.

Thirty-three years had passed since Hayes commanded the *Rinehart*. On the ship he had a punching bag outside his quarters and would spar every afternoon, when the sea was calm. When the *Rinehart* stopped somewhere for "R&R"—when the troops "got liberty"—Hayes would warn them about venereal disease. But even that was only a temporary concern. Soon they were back at sea and Hayes was captain again.

The *Rinehart* was where Hayes learned of the birth of his son Steve. Woody celebrated by buying cigars for all the smokers on board and candy bars for all the nonsmokers. He would not meet his son until he arrived home.

Was Hayes thinking about all that now, as he walked around the *Forrestal*? Was he thinking of how much his country had changed since he was a young captain of a Navy ship, where everybody was always in uniform and everybody had the same haircut? Or did he just feel like it all happened so very long ago?

At a luncheon the day before the Gator Bowl, ABC announcer Keith Jackson presented Woody Hayes with a pair of boxing gloves. Former Clemson coach Frank Howard added that Hayes might have to retire for health reasons, just like he did: "The alumni got sick of me."

When Hayes addressed the crowd, he talked about how age had changed his perspective.

"I sometimes get the feeling that football is not important [to others]," he said. "I feel it means darn near everything."

The Gator Bowl would kick off at 9 p.m. on December 29, a Friday night. ABC wanted the late start, to maximize ratings for the lackluster game. With television rights fees soaring, bowl organizers had to acquiesce to the network's wishes.

Because of the second-rate nature of the game, ABC made another unusual decision. The network decided to save a few thousand bucks by not purchasing a "net return" feed of the broadcast, which meant the network could not show instant replays. ABC could only show separate slow-motion replays shot by a different camera.

* * *

The fog was thick as Ohio State and Clemson took the field for the Gator Bowl. It was so thick that "Misty" was played over the stadium loudspeakers. It was so thick, in fact, that from his seat on the 50-yard line, on the opposite side of the field from the Buckeyes' sideline, Ohio State president Harold Enarson could barely see what was happening on the field.

Enarson had much in common with Woody Hayes. Both men vacationed at a rustic cabin. (Enarson's was in Colorado, Hayes's in Ohio.) They both served in World War II. (Enarson joined the Air Force; Hayes, of course, was in the Navy.) Enarson frequently ate lunch at the Faculty Club, often struck up impromptu conversations with Ohio State students, and kept an office that was relatively unimpressive for a man of his station.

Yet on the one issue that mattered most in their relationship—Ohio State football—Enarson and Hayes fundamentally disagreed. Enarson was not a fan of the game, either personally or professionally. He was an academic who sometimes resented that so many people saw his university as a football program with some classes attached. He had even talked about embracing the California model of public higher education—with many colleges on many campuses, each with its own specialties. If the state of Ohio had gone that route, it would have decreased the importance of the Ohio State University—and, by extension, the powerful pull of Ohio State football.

So Enarson probably did not mind that the fog impeded his view of Hayes's team. He was just there as part of his official duties.

Of the 72,000 fans in the Gator Bowl, approximately 60,000 were cheering for Clemson. To Woody Hayes, it was just like the Sugar Bowl the year before: Ohio State had gone down South, into enemy territory.

Ohio State's first two plays from scrimmage were passes—one incomplete, one complete for a first down. ABC color man Ara Parseghian told partner Keith Jackson he was surprised Hayes went to the pass so early. The surprise did not last long. The Buckeyes ran ten straight times before being stopped on fourth down from the Clemson two-yard line.

On the Buckeyes' next first down, Schlichter threw an ill-advised pass to Rod Gerald. It was nearly picked off. Schlichter was now one for three on the day. It looked like the 1978 season would end just as it started, with Schlichter having a disastrous game. But it would not. Schlichter completed a throw to tight end Ron Barwig, then lofted a gorgeous pass into the arms of Doug Donley along the sideline. Donley was well covered. It didn't matter. The pass was perfect, and Donley caught it for a 34-yard gain.

Ohio State kicked a field goal, and after a Clemson touchdown, the Buckeyes drove down the field again. Schlichter threw an 11-yard pass to Paul Campbell, his fourth straight completion. He rifled a throw to Gerald. Five straight. Between plays, Schlichter looked like a calm veteran; he was not jumping around every time he completed a pass, like he had earlier in the season. He tossed one over the top of the Clemson defense, to Barwig again, for 34 yards. Six straight completions. Schlichter finished the drive with a four-yard touchdown run.

The extra point was blocked.

Ohio State led, 9–7.

In the final minute of the half, Clemson quarterback Steve Fuller orchestrated a mad, pass-fueled drive to set up a 47-yard field goal. Clemson led 10–9 as the bands took the field at halftime.

What did the Old Man think of his freshman, the kid he had recruited harder than any other, completing six straight passes? Not much, apparently: on the first drive of the second half, Ohio State ran twice, completed a screen pass short of the first down, and punted. Art Schlichter completed another short pass (his eighth straight) to Ron Springs on the next possession, but on third and 13 from their own 42, the Buckeyes ran a draw play. They punted again.

Clemson drove down for a touchdown. And unlike the Buckeyes, the Tigers successfully kicked their extra point.

Ohio State had the ball, trailing 17–9. Schlichter completed his ninth straight pass—an improvisational flip under pressure—but the Buckeyes lost five yards on the play. Schlichter rolled left and threw to Chuck Hunter along the sidelines; Hunter caught it, but he couldn't get a foot in bounds, so it was incomplete. Ohio State soon punted again. But Art Schlichter wasn't finished.

When Schlichter got his hands on the ball again, he threw one of those passes that had sent college recruiters racing to Miami Trace High School—a run-left-and-throw-it-back-across-the-field 34-yarder to Hunter.

Art Schlichter was fulfilling all of his considerable promise. He completed an eight-yarder to Cal Murray. Even when he was off, he was on—a Clemson player tipped his next pass into the air, but the ball went right into the hands of Rod Gerald, who was not even the intended receiver on the play.

Six plays later, Schlichter ran for another touchdown to make the score 17–15. He had completed 13 of his last 14 passes. If not for the blocked extra-point attempt in the first quarter, Ohio State could have just kicked an extra point to tie it at 17. But now the Buckeyes had to go for two.

Woody Hayes called timeout to discuss the two-point conversion attempt. Ohio State asked for the ball to be placed just inside the left hash mark, then ran an option play to that side of the field. It was similar to the crucial play against Michigan the year before, when Rod Gerald fumbled away the Buckeyes' chance at a victory. This time, Schlichter was stopped. Clemson still led 17–15.

On the ensuing kickoff, a Clemson player hit Duncan Griffin of Ohio State with a forearm to the temple. Griffin responded with a forearm of his own, and as often happens in those kinds of plays, the retaliator was the one who got caught. Griffin was flagged for unsportsmanlike conduct and ejected from the game. It was the last play for any of the Griffin brothers at Ohio State.

Clemson tried to put together a game-sealing touchdown drive, but Ohio State recovered a fumble. There were less than five minutes on the clock. The Buckeyes had one more chance.

Art Schlichter immediately started taking advantage. He threw to

Rod Gerald for 14 yards. He threw to Chuck Hunter for 12. He rolled right and ran for seven yards. Ohio State faced third and five from the Clemson 24, needing at least a field goal to take the lead. Barely two minutes remained. The Buckeyes really didn't need to pass at that point—a short run would have set up a reasonable field goal. But the kid was playing so well that the Buckeyes decided to throw.

Max Schlichter must have been pleased as Art Schlichter dropped back for his twentieth pass of the night.

Pass protection had been a weakness for Ohio State all year, but it would not be a problem on this play. The Buckeye linemen expertly executed their assignments. Poor Clemson noseguard Charlie Bauman tried to make a move to his right and got nowhere. Bauman went left and Tim Vogler blocked him. Bauman could have pass-rushed for another fifteen seconds and he never would have touched Art Schlichter.

Schlichter was in the pocket, going through his progressions. He looked for receiver Doug Donley, but Donley was covered. Next he looked for Ron Springs, who was open.

Schlichter threw to Springs. He didn't see Charlie Bauman—had no reason to even *look* for Charlie Bauman—because Bauman was near the line of scrimmage after failing to get to Schlichter.

Bauman stepped to his left and intercepted the pass and took off. *Goddamn.* Now this was the sort of thing you expected when you got into the passing game. The Buckeyes had done everything right—Schlichter had gone through his progressions and thrown to the right man, the linemen had blocked perfectly—and they still threw an interception. This just didn't happen when you ran the ball—you handed it to Archie or Otis or Hopalong, the linemen executed their perfect blocks, and you conquered some territory.

Goddamn, Goddamn . . .

Bauman kept running. It was late now—in the game, in the season, in the Old Man's career, and in the night. Too late. Bauman was finally pushed out of bounds on the Ohio State sideline, right next to the Buckeyes' sixty-five-year-old head coach.

Goddamn . . .

Bauman got up, looked up at all those southerners in the crowd, and raised his hands in celebration.

Why, that son of a bitch.

Woody Hayes grabbed the back of Charlie Bauman's jersey, wound up, and punched him in the chest, just below the neck. Bauman looked over at the Old Man like he might have looked at a poodle nipping at his pants. Bauman was in full pads and a helmet; Hayes was in a windbreaker and a black cap, flailing at him. Bauman didn't strike back. He didn't even push Hayes away. He just retreated toward his teammates on the field as Hayes kept grabbing at him. Clemson players ran over to the sideline; Ohio State players scuffled with them. *Somebody* had to remove Hayes from Charlie Bauman.

One of Woody's captains, Byron Cato, pulled him off.

Word spread quickly at the Palladium in Hollywood, California, where the Big Ten Club of Southern California was holding its annual Dinner of Champions. *Did you hear about Woody? He hit a kid from Clemson.* Up on the dais, Bo Schembechler was stunned.

From his seat behind the Clemson sideline, Ohio State president Harold Enarson could not see what happened. It was too foggy, too confusing.

Ohio State athletic director Hugh Hindman had a better view. He saw the Buckeyes pull their coach off Charlie Bauman, and he thought he had seen what happened before. Hindman was sitting in the stands next to his right-hand man, Jim Jones, who had been Hayes's old brain coach.

"If he hit that kid, Jim," Hindman said, "he's done."

ABC's cameraman didn't even have to move; he was already focused on Bauman when Woody Hayes entered the picture. But up in the press box, Keith Jackson had not seen the punch. All he saw was the melee.

"And we've got a big fight going on," Jackson said on the air. "The officials buried in the middle. Oh, come on now. Quiet down, folks . . . I don't know what it was that triggered the fight."

ABC producers kept talking into Jackson's earpiece, telling him Hayes had punched Bauman. But Jackson had not seen it, and because ABC had decided not to pay for a "net return" feed, there was no replay available. Jackson did not want to comment on what he had not seen. He and Ara Parseghian would not mention the punch for the rest of the broadcast, and they would not see it until they were off the air.

Across the country, former Ohio State players and coaches were watching the Old Man's career disintegrate in their living rooms. America would not let him get away with this one—not in 1978, not on national television. One punch had ended it—and not much of a punch, either.

Heck, Woody obviously did not mean to hurt the kid. After all, he punched Bauman with his right hand.

Woody Hayes's postgame address to his team was mostly about the Civil War. Hayes's great-grandfather had been killed in the autumn of 1862 at the battle of Antietam, the bloodiest single-day battle in American history. Woody's great-grandmother had already died before that, so his great-grandfather's death left his grandfather, Isaac Hayes, an orphan.

The locker room cleared out fairly quickly. Star linebacker Tom Cousineau didn't even shower. Defensive coordinator George Hill addressed the media in Hayes's place. Hill hadn't even seen the punch— as soon as Charlie Bauman intercepted Art Schlichter's pass, Hill had turned to get his defensive players back in the game.

"Whatever I say would be wrong," Hill told reporters.

In the locker room, athletic director Hugh Hindman told Hayes to "be prepared for the worst." Hindman and most of the coaches were out of the locker room when Hayes sent word that he wanted to see Mark George—his student manager, his aide-de-camp.

When George arrived, the Old Man was sitting on a folding chair in the middle of the locker room, his glasses in his hand, his head down.

"Mark," Hayes said, "I'm going to need your help for the next few days."

Hayes did not want to go back to the hotel with the Buckeyes. He had embarrassed them enough for one night. He asked George to go get Paul Hornung of the *Dispatch*. When Hornung arrived, he and Hayes sat and talked for twenty minutes. Hornung took some notes, but Mark George, off on the other side of the locker room, could tell this was not a case of a reporter interviewing a coach. It was, like so many other conversations between Paul Hornung and Woody Hayes over the years, a friend talking to a friend. Hayes told Hornung he intended to resign.

The next morning, Hayes called Hornung and gave him the news, on the record, as he had always promised he would when the time came: "I am resigning as of now." The banner headline blared across that afternoon's *Dispatch*:

WOODY HAYES RESIGNS

But he had not resigned. He had talked about resigning; at the Sheraton, Hayes had told both George Hill and Mark George he would resign. And he had told Hornung he would resign. But he had not told Ohio State's athletic director or president that he would resign.

He had spent several hours in his room at the Jacksonville Sheraton, trying to piece together what had happened, before falling asleep in the sport coat and tie he had worn to the game. Perhaps, given a day to cool down, he would have gone through with it. But he did not have a day or two. Ohio State wanted Hayes out as quickly as possible. President Harold Enarson was worried that the school's image would be tarnished over an incident in a *football game*, of all things. Besides, Hayes had come back so many times, from so many incidents, that the administrators did not want to give him a chance to do it again, as unlikely as that might have been.

At 2 a.m., Enarson and Hugh Hindman had met at the president's hotel room in nearby Ponte Verde and agreed Hayes had to go immediately. At 8 a.m., Hugh Hindman went to Hayes's room and gave him the opportunity to resign. Hayes knew his career was finished. He just couldn't bring himself to quit.

"That would make it too easy for you," Hayes told Hindman. "You better go ahead and fire me."

At 10 a.m., Hindman held a press conference at the Sheraton. He announced that "Coach Hayes has been relieved of his duties as football coach at Ohio State. I prefer not to go beyond that."

Enarson's plane was diverted to Pittsburgh because of visibility concerns, and he didn't even wait until he got to Columbus to address reporters. He held a press conference at the Pittsburgh airport.

"There was no difficulty in reaching the decision," Enarson said. "There is not a university or an athletic conference in the country which would permit a coach to physically assault a college athlete."

Hayes had finished his twenty-eight-year career at Ohio State without ever firing an assistant. The only coach who was fired in Woody Hayes's coaching tenure was Woody Hayes.

The Ohio State team plane was already in the air when Hugh Hindman was holding his press conference at the Sheraton. The Buckeyes did not know their coach was caught in a dispute over whether he had quit or been fired. All they knew was that he had punched the guy who picked off Art Schlichter's pass.

Hayes made an announcement over the plane's loudspeaker. He said he had three things to tell his players. The first was that it was New Year's Eve weekend, and he wanted them to be careful on the roads, because there were a lot of crazy people and drunks out there. The second thing was that they had to talk to the brain coach, Larry

Romanoff, because classes were about to begin again and he wanted them to get off to a good start. The last thing, Hayes said, was that "I regret to say that next year, I will not be your coach."

The loudspeaker was so weak that some players couldn't even hear him.

Hayes went home for a couple hours, then met Mark George at his office. Their relationship was back to where it first flowered, with George cleaning Hayes's office. But back then, George had cleaned the office on his own. Now Woody was asking him to do it, and he had a specific request: *Throw it all away.*

Everything? *Everything.* The pictures with generals and presidents? The coach-of-the-year-plaques, the trophies, the notebooks from seasons past? The letters from President Nixon? The get-well cards? *Everything.* They could say what they wanted about Woody Hayes, but nobody was going to say he took a goddamn thing he didn't earn. He wouldn't even take a T-shirt or one of those block "O" caps he was famous for wearing. *Throw it all away.*

George couldn't believe it. He did something he had rarely done before: he defied the Old Man. How could he throw this stuff out? George put all the items in his car and hauled them over to his mother's house. They would remain there for the rest of Woody Hayes's life.

Perhaps the most unusual mementos were the ones Hayes never wanted in the first place. They were in his desk drawers, tossed aside like bottle caps: dozens of uncashed checks, worth thousands of dollars, from charity dinners where Woody Hayes was the featured speaker.

"I don't have a lot to say other than that I'm saddened by it," Bo Schembechler told reporters in Pasadena. "I hate to see something like this happen . . . I was shocked. Not shocked, but disappointed. I hope you all look back over his career and all the good he's done . . . and not dwell so heavily on his indiscretions."

Schembechler instinctively tried to steer the conversation back to his upcoming Rose Bowl matchup with USC. He started talking about turnovers. But he couldn't get his mind off the Old Man.

"There's the pressure of coming to the end of a career," Schembechler said. "Things are slipping away from you and you're not winning enough. I just wish his career would have ended differently."

Schembechler also doused any speculation before it could catch fire: no, he said, he would not be the next coach at Ohio State.

Charlie Bauman's first comment to reporters, on the field after the Gator Bowl, was, "I don't want to talk about it now. He hit me in the facemask." Clemson's thirty-year-old coach, Danny Ford, quickly got to Bauman, and Bauman clammed up completely.

The newspaper photos of the incident seemed to show Hayes grabbing the facemask of one of his own players, Ken Fritz. Nobody really had a picture of him hitting Bauman. Ohio State's president had not seen the punch. The school's athletic director thought he saw it, but he wasn't sure. The only undeniable proof was in the television broadcast.

Network affiliates had recorded the game for their newscasts, so they were able to show the punch. They showed it again and again. It was irresistible television: an old coach getting so mad after an interception that he actually slugged the guy who did it.

But ABC had shown it only once. The lack of an instant replay had people buzzing throughout the country. Fans had come to expect replays and the story of the game, beyond just the play-by-play. ABC had failed to deliver both. Network executives knew why: they had foolishly skimped on the "return feed" that would have allowed them to show instant replays. But fans were suspicious about a cover-up. A headline in the *Detroit Free Press* summed it up:

"No TV replay—football Watergate?"

The next day, a Sunday, Archie Griffin and Daryl Sanders showed up at the white house at 1711 Cardiff, unannounced. Sanders had played for Ohio State from 1959 to 1962. Griffin did not start playing until ten years after Sanders left. Their only link was Woody Hayes. Now they felt like their old coach needed them.

Hayes let them in. Sanders and Griffin sat in the living room for hours, talking to the Old Man. Hayes never offered them a glass of water. He never even turned the lights on. They just sat in the dark and talked. Sanders and Griffin were mentally exhausted when they left, and they wouldn't even remember what they discussed. But they knew they did not talk about the Gator Bowl.

Sanders would remember a moment, maybe an hour or two after they arrived, when he heard a cough from behind a wall, and he thought, *Oh—Anne is here.* He never saw her.

Bo Schembechler thought he had seen every possible way to lose a bowl game. He had lost on a last-second field goal and from his hospital room, after taking a lead and after making a comeback, to national champions and heavy underdogs. But this, *this* was something else.

In the second quarter, Southern California running back Charles White had fumbled on the Michigan three-yard line. The Wolverines' Jerry Meter recovered. So what happened? Official Gil Marchman, standing twenty yards away, ruled that White reached the end zone before he fumbled. White wasn't *close* to the end zone—that was obvious from the television replay. Yet the touchdown stood, and it was the margin of victory: USC won, 17–10, despite gaining just 157 yards all day. Southern California went on to win a share of the national championship.

Schembechler was reserved in the postgame press conference. He wanted to see the replay before he complained. But once he saw it, he lashed out.

"We've got to get some protection from the officials," he said. "I don't give a damn about them. When are they accountable for anything? Maybe they'll all quit and we'll play without them. It might be a better game."

*   *   *

Woody Hayes kept his position as a tenured member of the Ohio State faculty. But he never received the teaching award his friend Harold Schechter had wanted for him; after the Gator Bowl incident, there was simply no way to give it to him.

Bo Schembechler called Hayes and said he wanted to come down to Columbus to talk to him. Hayes said they should meet halfway, at former Bowling Green coach Doyt Perry's house. When they got there, Schembechler told Hayes he should apologize.

Hayes said he would not. He did not believe in apologies.

Two weeks later, Hayes fulfilled a previous commitment to speak at the Columbus Area Chamber of Commerce's annual meeting. He talked about his conversation with Schembechler.

"It was my attitude not to apologize," Hayes said, "'cause I don't apologize for anything. When I make a mistake, I take the blame for it and go on from there. I've seen too many people who quickly apologize and sort of cop out. I just don't think there are easy ways out of anything like that.

"And yet, the thing that makes me apologize is this: I feel very, very sorry for it, because of the wonderful people it's affected—my coaches, five of whom are without jobs, and several graduate students."

As for Bo, Hayes could finally reveal his true feelings, after ten years of battle.

"Confidentially," Hayes told the audience, "I like the man."

Hayes also expressed serious concern about the future of his sport. He feared the influx of TV money, the increase in under-the-table payments to recruits, and the lowering of academic standards. The following spring, Ohio State would reduce the number of credit hours required for a freshman to be eligible from forty-five to thirty-six, bringing the school in line with the rest of the Big Ten. Hayes would have the story cut out of the *Dispatch* and placed in one of his notebooks.

"Maybe I've read Emerson too much," Hayes said at the Chamber of Commerce meeting. "But I know this: there's a great, great price . . . as I told a newsman day before yesterday, there's a great price on everything. Nothing worthwhile comes cheap. You give a man something and it amounts to nothing. It destroys him. I know that. Of that I'm certain."

Ohio State replaced Woody Hayes with one of his former assistants, Iowa State coach Earle Bruce. There was sound logic behind the decision: Bruce was highly regarded and had strong Ohio State ties (in addition to his coaching tenure, he played there in Hayes's early years) but had established himself independent of Hayes.

Bruce also understood the magnitude of Ohio State football in Columbus. Perhaps he understood it too well. When others said that Hayes was fired for punching Charlie Bauman, Bruce cut them off.

"If he had beaten Michigan three years in a row and hit that kid, would he have been fired?" Bruce would ask.

In case there was any doubt, Bruce gave his own answer: No.

"We are not scrupulous," Emerson wrote. "What we ask is victory, without regard to the cause."

Slowly, Woody Hayes resurfaced in the town he had owned. Ohio State made him an associate professor of military history and gave him an office in the Military Science building. Hayes would go there and work on his book, about the parallels between football and the military—he had the chapter titles on a large blackboard. He had written more than five hundred pages but was still not satisfied with it.

After three or four months, Hayes started going back to the Faculty Club. He would often ask several friends to eat with him, and sometimes he would bring a guest speaker—often somebody from the government or the military.

In the spring of 1979, Hayes invited several friends to meet former Marine general Lewis Walt in a private room on the second floor of the Faculty Club. A decade had passed since they were at the height of their powers, with Walt commanding the Marines in Vietnam and

Hayes guiding the best college football team in America. In 1968 Walt had addressed Hayes's Buckeyes at halftime of the Purdue game, spurring them to victory and the national championship.

Now Walt told the gathering at the Faculty Club there were two messages he wanted to express about the United States' involvement in Vietnam—two reasons, essentially, why the mission had failed.

The first reason was that the media had worked to undermine the U.S. military and divide the country, severely hampering the American effort. The second reason was that the rules of engagement had changed. The United States had self-imposed limits on whom it could attack and when, instead of going all out to win the war.

Woody Hayes voiced his wholehearted agreement.

12

Football, History, and Bo Schembechler

Let us bid even our dearest friends farewell, and defy them, saying, "Who are you? Unhand me: I will be dependent no more." Ah! seest thou not, O brother, that thus we part only to meet again on a higher platform, and only be more each other's because we are more our own?

—**Ralph Waldo Emerson**, *"Friendship"*

With the firing of Woody Hayes, forty-nine-year-old Bo Schembechler became the longest-tenured coach in the Big Ten.

Schembechler coached eleven more years at Michigan after Hayes retired, and the Michigan–Ohio State rivalry kept humming along. But Schembechler never felt the same anticipation that he had felt before meeting his mentor at midfield in late November.

After going 96-15-2 in his first ten seasons, Schembechler slipped to 98-33-2 in his final eleven—still an excellent record, but not quite as remarkable as his first decade. After the 1980 season, he finally won a Rose Bowl; his electrifying new receiver, Anthony Carter, helped pull him into the passing age. But the Wolverines had lost their first two games that year, so they had no shot at the national title. Schembechler never won a national title. Yet in his final eleven years, his profile rose higher than ever.

In January 1982, Texas A&M offered Schembechler an unprecedented ten-year contract for $250,000 per year. It would have made him the highest-paid coach in the country by a wide margin. Schembechler was tempted. Michigan was simply not going to pay that kind of money to a football coach. Don Canham counteroffered $125,000: an $80,000 salary and another $45,000 from television and radio deals. Michigan media outlets and fans were nervous as Schembechler weighed his options.

Schembechler finally decided to stay in Ann Arbor. When he announced his decision at a press conference, broadcasters and writers scrapped professional decorum and broke into a round of applause. It wasn't just that a winning coach was staying put. Schembechler had chosen loyalty to his players over money. He had chosen the Michigan program—*his* program, run *his* way—over a school in the rogue Southwest Conference, where there was a waiting list to get on NCAA probation.

Why, Schembechler was asked, did he even think about going to Texas A&M?

"Did you ever wonder what it would be like, being a millionaire?" he responded.

(As an incentive to stay, Michigan booster Tom Monaghan gave Schembechler a franchise in his thriving Domino's Pizza chain. There was only one catch: the franchise was in Columbus.)

By turning down A&M, Schembechler solidified his reputation as both a one-school icon and model of integrity in an era that was woefully short on both. College football in the 1980s seemed to be a cesspool, unbecoming of the nation's most prominent universities. At many institutions, academic standards were comically low and cheating was rampant, and in the wake of Watergate, journalists were less inclined to give anybody in power a free pass. Yet most sportswriters were fans before they were journalists, and they still wanted to believe in *somebody*.

Many of them believed in Bo Schembechler. He was not just a coach. He was the people's idea of what a coach should be. Sure, Bo was gruff. That became part of his charm. He could say "most writers aren't worth a damn," as he told *Sports Illustrated*'s Douglas S. Looney in 1981, and get away with it.

"He talks straight ahead; no matter what the circumstances," Looney wrote. "He says exactly what's on his mind; he makes judgments on everything; he is secure in every way; he dominates everywhere and everybody. All of which makes him, remarkable as it sounds, a good guy up close. A really good guy."

In 1973, a Michigan freshman named David Turnley tried to walk on to the football team as a wide receiver. After two or three weeks, Turnley realized he would probably never play a down at Michigan—there were too many talented players. He quit.

Turnley later became one of the world's most respected photojournalists, won the Pulitzer Prize in 1990, covered every virtually major war of the 1980s and 1990s, and worked in more than seventy countries. He spent extensive time with the Dalai Lama, Nelson Mandela, Muhammad Ali, Bill Clinton, and Norman Schwarzkopf, among others.

"I've been around a lot of generals," Turnley would say. "I've never been around anybody in any army that had [Schembechler's] kind of presence, that inspired his kind of authority."

As he grew older, Schembechler became comfortable wielding that authority outside his football program. He and his wife, Millie, campaigned to increase Ann Arbor's famous five-dollar fine for marijuana possession. He railed against under-the-table payments to recruits and the increasing use of anabolic steroids to gain strength. He had the credibility to complain: in his time at Michigan, Schembechler never got in trouble with the NCAA. Indiana basketball coach Bob Knight said Schembechler was "the best coach coaching anything in American sports."

People occasionally wondered if he would have a career-ending temper tantrum like Woody Hayes. Schembechler had some flare-ups—on one occasion, he pushed a writer from the *Michigan Daily*, and his abuse of game officials was legendary. But he insisted privately that he was acting—dramatizing to make a point. He never did anything to warrant dismissal.

In 1989, Schembechler published a book called simply *Bo*, with immensely popular *Detroit Free Press* columnist Mitch Albom. Thanks to Schembechler's old-school, no-nonsense reputation and Albom's writing, it became a national best-seller.

Schembechler was something of an accidental author—Albom did dozens of interviews to complement Schembechler's memories—but he grew to embrace his tough-guy persona. This was particularly evident on his weekly television show, *Michigan Replay*. Schembechler learned to use his gifts with the language on television, often playing off his cohost to great effect. In later years, that cohost was Jim Brandstatter, the lineman Schembechler nearly killed for missing a block in practice. Many of the same people who spit on Brandstatter for wearing a ROTC uniform in 1969 came to embrace him on television every week.

By the time he retired, in 1990, Schembechler was most associated not with a specific game or a play, but a quote: "A Michigan man will coach Michigan." The Wolverines' basketball coach, Bill Frieder, accepted a job at Arizona State before the 1989 NCAA tournament but said he would coach Michigan through the tournament. Schembechler told Frieder to leave immediately. *A Michigan man will coach Michigan.* The Wolverines went on to win the national championship.

Frieder had no choice but to follow Schembechler's orders. By that time, Bo Schembechler was not just Michigan's football coach. He was the athletic director, too.

On December 3, 1979, the *Chronicle of Higher Education* quoted Don Canham as saying, "Cable television has more potential than anyone has had a chance to think about." The nation's first all-sports cable channel, something called the Entertainment and Sports Programming Network, was less than three months old. "Only a few people in college athletics, however, share Mr. Canham's enthusiasm for the money-making possibilities of cable T.V.," the *Chronicle* reported.

Canham was right about ESPN, and about most things. In the 1980s the Michigan brand grew exponentially. Everything Canham touched turn to cash. His athletic department's budget went from $2.6 million in 1968 to $9 million in 1980 to $16 million in 1986.

For years, as something of an inside joke, the PA announcer at

Michigan Stadium had dropped the score of Slippery Rock games in with the big-time matchups of the day. Slippery Rock was a small school in western Pennsylvania. In September 1979, almost on a lark, Canham brought Slippery Rock and Shippensburg into Michigan Stadium and charged five dollars a head. The game drew more than 61,000 people. The same day, Michigan played before 57,000 in Berkeley, California.

In 1985, the *Arizona Republic* polled athletic directors, television executives, writers, and conference commissioners, asking them to name the best athletic director in the country. Canham received more votes than the next three vote-getters combined. In 1986, when University of Maryland basketball star Len Bias died of a drug overdose and the NCAA investigated the Terrapins, the school called Canham for advice.

Canham retired in 1988. He was so successful that he ultimately proved himself wrong about one thing: his 1971 comment that "Ohio State without Hayes would mean 30,000 less people in the stands" now seemed silly. Ever since the middle of the 1975 season, Michigan had drawn at least 100,000 fans to every home football game—a streak that was entering its fourth decade when Don Canham died in May 2005, at age eighty-seven.

From a few drawings on Don Canham's kitchen table, an industry had been born. By the 1990s, college athletic departments were putting their logos on every imaginable item—license plates, light-switch plates, even shot glasses and beer mugs. Years after Bill Ayers got past his Weathermen-related legal troubles, he would open a beer bottle for his father with an opener that played the Michigan fight song.

Ayers had finally turned himself in to authorities in 1981, but charges were dropped due to government misconduct. Ayers, like many of his fellow would-be revolutionaries, took a respected position in society; he went on to become a Distinguished Professor of Education and Senior University Scholar at the University of Illinois at Chicago.

Despite the efforts of Black Action Movement leaders, the University of Michigan never did reach its goal of 10 percent black enrollment. But when that became a national story in the late 1990s and beyond, it was the school's administration, not its student body, that pushed for more black students. The administrators defended their affirmative-action admission policies all the way to the U.S. Supreme Court in a landmark case, *Grutter v. Bollinger*. (The court upheld the principle of affirmative action.)

And as the shadow of Vietnam receded, so too did the protest movement.

"I don't want to have anything to do with [benefit concerts]," John Lennon told *Playboy* in 1980. "I have been benefit-ed to death. . . . There's always this terrible atmosphere, equipment problems, double time for the unions—the guy who is putting on the lights, carrying the bags, promoting it—everybody else is getting paid except for the musicians. It's an absolute ripoff, but it makes the artist look good: 'Isn't he a good boy?'

"It's all a goddamn ripoff. So forget about it. All of you who are reading this, don't bother sending me all that garbage about, 'Just come save the Indians, come and save the blacks, come and save the war veterans.' Anybody I want to help will be saved through our tithing, which is 10 percent or whatever of what we earn."

A few days after the *Playboy* interview hit newsstands, Lennon was assassinated just outside his New York City apartment building. Much of the country heard the news from Howard Cosell on *Monday Night Football*.

Bo Schembechler asked Dr. Bob Murphy, the Ohio State team physician, about what happened that fateful night at the Gator Bowl. Murphy said that Hayes had let his blood sugar get so out of whack, he might not have known what the hell he was doing when he punched Charlie Bauman.

Shortly after Hayes was fired, a group of his former players gave him a new car to replace his old Ranchero pickup truck. They also re-furbished and modernized his Noble County cabin. The cabin would have been the perfect place for Hayes to work on his book about football and the military. But he never finished it.

In the early 1980s, screenwriter Budd Schulberg spent several months researching a movie about Hayes's life. Schulberg, who won an Academy Award for his screenplay for *On the Waterfront*, spent sev-eral days with Hayes in Columbus. Schulberg expected to hate the coach. He found that he liked him a great deal, and his screenplay might have created the same empathy for the Old Man that *Patton* had created empathy for General George Patton. But the movie never got made.

Hayes *did* succeed in getting another movie made: *The Ten Year War*, a retrospective on his ten-year battle with Bo Schembechler. When Hayes called Schembechler with the idea, the Michigan coach was surprised. He didn't think Woody would want to do that kind of thing. But Schembechler could not say no to Hayes; they sat to-gether and discussed each game, on camera. The video was quite popular, but it did little to change the perception of Hayes outside Ohio.

For the most part, Woody Hayes's players were not bitter about the fact that he was fired; rather, they were bitter about the *way* he was fired. The school seemed eager to dismiss him instead of giving him a chance to leave with some dignity.

Ohio State president Harold Enarson thought Hayes might be bitter. In 1981, Hayes underwent gall bladder surgery at Ohio State's hospital, but the surgeon left a sponge inside him, causing an ab-scess. Hayes needed another surgery to remove the sponge and his recovery was arduous. Enarson sent him a letter, basically thanking him for not suing the university. Hayes had never even considered it. He had joked to the surgeon that he didn't know how such a mistake could happen, because he had never made one in all his years of coaching.

Hayes kept his office in the Military Science building and rarely showed any resentment about how his firing was handled. Only an astute Woody observer would notice that he sometimes referred to Hugh Hindman simply as The Athletic Director, in the same way he referred to That School Up North.

Hayes's players and friends had always feared he could never live without football. They were surprised that his post-coaching years were some of the happiest of his life. His former tackle Daryl Sanders sensed that the reason Hayes never finished his book is because he realized he didn't need it.

In April 1982, on the hundredth anniversary of Ralph Waldo Emerson's death, Hayes delivered an address commemorating Emerson at Harvard University. Elliot Richardson, who had been defense secretary and attorney general under Richard Nixon, also spoke. So did Watergate special prosecutor Archibald Cox. (Richardson famously resigned as attorney general rather than follow Nixon's orders to fire Cox—it's unclear whether Hayes told Richardson what he thought of that defiance of authority.)

"I'm sure you're wondering what a football coach is doing here tonight," Hayes said. "It's simple. I've come to pay back something I owe . . . Emerson was an inspiration to me all my life—he was a big factor. Not the only factor, of course, but an important one."

Hayes told the crowd he had read Emerson's essay "Compensation" at least fifty times.

"My father gave it to me when I was a college student at Denison, in Ohio. He told me that Emerson said that the more you give, the more you get in return. I was charmed by the fancy of this endless compensation. And doggone if it isn't true. It became the cornerstone of my coaching philosophy."

What did the folks at Harvard think of the Old Man? Were they impressed? Amused? Did they roll their eyes? Surely some of them found it bizarre that Woody Hayes was sharing the Harvard stage for a salute to Emerson. Maybe they thought, like Howard Cosell had said years earlier, that Hayes was a "Neanderthal boor." And maybe some saw him as a lonely, sad figure, disgraced by punching that guy in that bowl game, living outside the only realms of the culture where he belonged: football and the military.

Maybe they saw a man whose self-esteem was inextricably tied to coaching a famous football team, and who was lost and alone when his team was taken away from him.

Maybe that's what they saw. But then, they hadn't read Emerson like Woody Hayes had read Emerson. They hadn't read "Compensation" fifty times, with each reading as vigorous and passionate as a preacher reading a Bible passage. They hadn't read, time and again, the passage in "Compensation" in which Emerson wrote:

"Has he a defect of temper that unfits him to live in society? Thereby he is driven to entertain himself alone and acquire habits of self-help; and thus, like the wounded oyster, he mends his shell with pearl."

On March 21, 1986, Woody Hayes gave the commencement speech at Ohio State. He was awarded an Honorary Doctor of Humanities. For Hayes, it was an acknowledgment that the school saw him as an educator, not just a fired coach, and that he was remembered for more than just the Gator Bowl.

"Today," Hayes told the graduates, "is the greatest day of my life."

He told them to never feel sorry for themselves. He told them Emerson had taught him that you can never pay back, but you can pay forward. He told them to stay away from drugs and alcohol, and to work hard and to get married only once—preferably early in adulthood, and preferably to a fellow Buckeye.

"All right," he said, "there's one more thing I want to get into and then I will let you get graduated."

He went on to discuss: the Battle of Salamis ("the Greeks outfoxed the Persians, then founded a new type of government: 'Demo-cra-tos'"); an interview he had done with the mayor of Stuttgart, Germany, who was the son of legendary German field marshal Erwin Rommel; the Battle of Britain ("they were four-to-one underdogs against Hitler's hordes"); all the great men in history who were fired (he named General Douglas MacArthur, Richard Nixon, and British air marshal Hugh Dowding); Admiral Chester Nimitz and the miracle of Midway against Japan; why Harry S. Truman had to use the atom bomb; the Soviet threat ("communism came right out of the First World War, directly. The German general staff put Lenin in Russia to start that revolution . . ."); the problem with helping Communists; and a daughter of one of his former Ohio State captains—a pianist who wanted to learn Russian and go to Russia ("I think she'll be as fine an ambassador as we can have there," Hayes said, "because she is a lovely, lovely lady").

In the stands at St. John Arena, Hayes's niece Mary Hoyt was stunned. A few weeks earlier, she had brought her son John over to see her uncle Woody. Hoyt was surprised to see Woody dressed in a suit and tie. He sat John down and talked about all sorts of topics, from Emerson to drugs to the great men in history who had been fired. Hoyt now realized Woody had been practicing his commencement speech. He could no longer see well enough to read it, so he memorized it.

One night in the mid-1980s, while Jeff Kaplan was visiting Woody Hayes, Kaplan asked to use Hayes's cassette player. Hayes said yes. Kaplan, the former brain coach, popped in one of his tapes from the 1975 season, when he had surreptitiously recorded the Old Man.

At first, Hayes was livid. *You goddamn son of a . . .*

But then Hayes started to reminisce. Less than a decade had passed, but he seemed so far removed from his days as the toughest coach Ohio State ever had. He suffered a stroke on an airplane in 1985. That was followed by a mild heart attack, nagging ulcers, and phlebitis.

Hayes's former players had trouble accepting this weakened version of their coach. Was this the same man who told *Chicago Tribune* columnist Bob Greene that when he had his 1974 heart attack, in the middle of the night, he waited until the morning to call his doctor? ("Well, I knew I'd had one," Hayes said. "I didn't want to bother him.")

The players tried to help. Former fullback Champ Henson would bring Hayes out to the Henson family farm and load up his car with sweet corn and other fresh vegetables. One time Hayes struggled to get his leg over a low threshold.

"Well, Coach," Henson said, "you'd have a hard time kicking me in the ass now, wouldn't you?"

"Oh, I'd just have an assistant do it," Hayes replied.

He remained close with many former players. In many ways, he was still their coach. He was still trying to help the ones who needed it. He called Rod Gerald, addled by drug addiction, and begged him to come back to Columbus to finish his degree. It took some time, but Gerald eventually went into drug rehab and graduated. (The golden boy who took Gerald's job, Art Schlichter, had put together a stellar career at Ohio State, but his gambling addiction destroyed his NFL career. Schlichter spent the 1980s and 1990s in and out of various prisons for theft, forgery, writing bad checks, and other gambling-related crimes.)

Hundreds of Woody's boys lived in Columbus. Many of them worked together. Archie Griffin would eventually become president and CEO of the Ohio State University Alumni Association. Hayes tried to stay in contact with them. But there were some he did not see as often as he would have liked.

One in particular.

In all those years of plotting to beat one another, Bo Schembechler and Woody Hayes had barely spoken to each other. But after Hayes retired, they were able to resume their friendship. In the early 1980s, Schembechler invited Hayes to speak to his Wolverines. Hayes gladly accepted the invitation, and he was proud when Bo introduced him as "our nemesis." The two talked on the phone regularly.

On March 5, 1987, Schembechler attended a dinner for Woody Hayes in Columbus. Five days later, Hayes returned the favor, introducing Schembechler at a banquet in Dayton. After Hayes gave his speech, he realized he and Schembechler were seated on opposite ends of the table.

"You sit next to me," Woody told Bo. "I don't care where those name tags are. You sit next to me. The other night you were at the other side of the table and I didn't get a chance to talk to you."

Two days later, Anne Hayes awoke and her husband Woody did not. He had died of a heart attack in his sleep. He was seventy-four.

After a private funeral, approximately fourteen hundred people attended a memorial service at First Community Church in the Columbus suburbs. One of the reverends at First Community was Jeb Magruder, who had been President Nixon's deputy communications director. Magruder had joined the church staff in 1981, after serving seven months in prison for obstruction of justice and perjury during the Watergate scandal.

Magruder had not seen Richard Nixon in thirteen years. But on this day, he led the former president to his seat.

Then Nixon delivered a eulogy.

"I got to know the real Woody Hayes, the man behind the media myth," Nixon said. "I found . . . that he was a Renaissance man, a man with a sense of history, with a profound understanding of the forces that move the world."

To accommodate the Ohio State faithful, another memorial service was held, at Ohio Stadium. Fifteen thousand people showed up. It was there that Schembechler called Hayes "the greatest football coach the [Big Ten] Conference ever had.

"He set the tone," Schembechler said, "and that is why you see so little of the cheating and violations [of national recruiting rules] that are current within our country in the conference. For twenty-eight years, if you violated the rules, you had to face the Old Man."

Former student manager Mark George still had everything he had cleared out of Woody Hayes's office on December 30, 1978. He gave most of it to Anne Hayes. She died in 1998; the items eventually ended up in the Ohio State University Archives.

Sorting out the Old Man's legacy was not as easy. Earle Bruce could never live up to it. Bruce was fired after the 1987 season, despite winning 75.5 percent of his games at Ohio State (just a shade off of Hayes's 76.1 percent). There was speculation that Bruce fell out of favor because he liked gambling (he switched Ohio State's spring game from the first Saturday in May so he could attend the Kentucky Derby, and rumors circulated that he had been seen at Columbus racetracks with Art Schlichter); because he wanted more money for his television show and switched stations to get it; and because the station he left, WBNS, was owned by major Ohio State contributor (and *Columbus Dispatch* owner) John Walton Wolfe.

Bruce was replaced by John Cooper, who committed the unpardonable sin of going 2-10-1 against Michigan. When Cooper was fired, in 2001, Ohio State found Jim Tressel, who would become the most beloved Ohio State coach since Hayes. In 2002, Tressel's Buckeyes won the national title.

The school used Hayes's "pay forward" mantra in its fundraising campaigns, and Hayes's family, friends, and fans raised enough money to establish a Woody Hayes Chair of National Security Studies at Ohio State. In 1987, the school named its new state-of-the-art football building the Woody Hayes Facility. That tribute was genuine but ironic; when Hayes saw the plans for the new football facility, he replied, "Do we need all this goddamn stuff?"

Ohio State put a big sign in the atrium of the facility that reads, "You Win With People." And the school placed a huge picture there of Hayes on the sideline—looking north, of course.

Bo Schembechler's heart forced him out of coaching after the 1989 football season, when he was sixty. He'd had another heart attack in 1987, and doctors said if he kept coaching it would probably kill him. Schembechler left both his coach and athletic director jobs to become president of the Detroit Tigers. Tom Monaghan, the Domino's Pizza magnate, owned the Tigers and convinced Schembechler to go back to his baseball roots.

Schembechler's tenure with the Tigers was short and painful. It would be remembered mostly for the firing of beloved announcer

Ernie Harwell—which, even Harwell said later, was not Schembechler's decision, though Bo possibly could have stopped it. In August 1992, just before selling the team to fellow pizza magnate Mike Ilitch, Monaghan fired Schembechler.

Schembechler would sue Monaghan, claiming Monaghan had broken a contract written on a napkin. (Don Canham thought their years of handshake agreements had given Schembechler a false sense of security.) Schembechler and Monaghan settled out of court.

Thirteen days after Schembechler was fired by the Tigers, his wife, Millie, died of adrenal cancer.

In a span of five years, Bo Schembechler had lost two jobs, his wife, and his mentor. Yet his players and friends always figured that as long as his heart was ticking, he would be okay. They were correct. Schembechler remarried and traveled the world with his new wife, Cathy. He never tired of football—he would watch all day Saturday and all day Sunday—and grew to accept and appreciate that it had become primarily a passing game. He also continued to do television and radio shows in metro Detroit, and he often told stories about the best days of his coaching life, going against the Old Man for ten years. He referred to that era simply by the name of the video he had done with Hayes: the "Ten Year War."

The "Ten Year War" had at least one warlike aftereffect: its participants felt a bond with each other that was unlike anything else in their lives. They even felt a connection to their opponents. Steve Luke and Dennis Franklin remained fast friends, even though Luke lived in Columbus and Franklin lived in Southern California. And several Ohio State players, upon meeting former Michigan placekicker Mike Lantry, would say, "Mike Lantry, how *are* you?" as though they weren't sure he had summoned the will to live beyond 1974. To answer the question: Lantry was just fine. He was a successful businessman in Michigan who routinely attended the Wolverines' games.

In retirement, Schembechler became more interested in politics. His friendship with Gerald Ford reached the point where the former president asked him to be a pallbearer at his funeral. Schembechler was not shy about expressing his political opinions.

"I like to think most people would agree that I know football," Schembechler wrote in an October 2004 op-ed piece in the *Detroit Free Press*. "I also know a little something about character, commitment and leadership. The past three years, President George W. Bush has dealt with situations no president has ever faced, and he has emerged as one of the most principled leaders our country has ever seen. . . . He is dedicated to defending our nation at home and abroad. And he defends through smart offense—bringing the war to the terrorists so we don't have to fight them again here at home. . . . It goes to show that the best defense is a good offense."

Long after Schembechler retired, the Ohio State–Michigan rivalry flourished. At the end of the century, ESPN.com named it the greatest rivalry in sports. And for those with a rooting interest, The Game was still epitomized by Woody and Bo. When *Sports Illustrated* asked Ohioans to name an "Enemy of the State," Schembechler finished second, behind only Art Modell, who had moved the Browns out of Cleveland. At the time of the poll, Schembechler had not coached in almost fifteen years.

Just as Schembechler and Hayes never left the public consciousness, Hayes was never far from Schembechler's thoughts. As filmmaker David Crouse interviewed Schembechler for a documentary called *Beyond the Gridiron: The Life and Times of Woody Hayes*, he was struck by the reverential tone in Schembechler's voice. Crouse asked him if Hayes reminded him of his father.

"He did, he did," Schembechler said, and tears filled his eyes, and he had to compose himself before continuing the interview.

The program Schembechler built lasted long after he was gone. Schembechler tapped longtime assistant Gary Moeller to replace himself for the 1990 season. In the spring of 1995, Moeller was arrested after a drunken tirade at a Detroit-area restaurant. Schembechler thought it was a one-time mistake and desperately tried to save Moeller's job, but after a while he got the uncomfortable sensation that he was the only one trying to do so. Moeller was fired and replaced by another Schembechler hire, Lloyd Carr. In 1997, Carr won the national championship that had eluded Schembechler.

The sign Schembechler hung in the winter of 1969—THOSE WHO STAY WILL BE CHAMPIONS—had come to epitomize his program. From 1969 on, only one class of Michigan football players stayed four years without winning a big title. The Wolverines had not missed a bowl since 1974, the last year the Big Ten only sent one team. It was the longest streak in college football history, and it might have been Schembechler's crowning achievement.

Almost four decades after getting lost on his way to Ann Arbor, Bo Schembechler was the person most closely associated with the University of Michigan. He still kept an office in Michigan's football facility, which was called Schembechler Hall. (Schembechler spent most of his office hours talking on the phone with former players such as Rick Leach, who had enjoyed a ten-year Major League Baseball career.) The school's regents had even approved a plan to add the luxury suites Don Canham had wanted in 1976.

The unrest of the late 1960s and early 1970s were a distant memory. The Black Action Movement, White Panthers, Weathermen, and Human Rights Party were long gone; Schembechler had outlasted them all. Far more people wanted to hear stories about Bo and Woody than about the unrest of the Vietnam era. Schembechler was always happy to talk about the Old Man.

"He is the best teacher," Schembechler said of Woody Hayes, almost two decades after Hayes had died. "When he goes to the board in a classroom, he is magnificent."

Bo Schembechler continually told friends he could not believe he was still alive. Almost thirty-seven years had passed since his first heart attack. He had been diagnosed with diabetes. But as long as Schembechler was alive, he was going to *live*. Thirty-three years after he told Joe Falls he couldn't understand why anybody would want to read a book about him, Schembechler was writing his third. It was called *Bo's Lasting Lessons* and was a guide to leadership intended for business-people, and of course, football fans.

The coauthor of *Bo's Lasting Lessons*, John U. Bacon, had asked Schembechler what he would ask for if he had one more week as Michigan's coach. Schembechler said he would want one week of preparation for a game against Woody Hayes and Ohio State. He didn't even want to coach the game. He just wanted to prepare for it.

In late November 2006, Michigan and Ohio State were headed for the most hyped clash in the history of the rivalry—No. 1 Ohio State against No. 2 Michigan, both undefeated, with a likely national title on the line. Though he obviously wasn't coaching, Schembechler was hot with anticipation, and naturally the media wanted to hear from the godfather of Michigan football. The Michigan media relations staff brought the seventy-seven-year-old Schembechler into the team's weekly press conference.

As Schembechler limped to the podium, a school official offered him a stool.

"I don't need this," Schembechler said. "I think I can stand for a while."

Schembechler stood for twenty-nine minutes, mesmerizing the reporters in attendance with Woody stories and thoughts on the rivalry. The room was quiet as a church as he spoke.

Three days later, Schembechler was having trouble breathing.

"I can't live like this," he told Michigan coach Lloyd Carr.

The next morning, Schembechler collapsed in the studios of WXYZ-TV outside Detroit, where he was getting ready to tape his weekly television show, *Big Ten Ticket*. His heart had given out for the last time. A little more than two hours later, Bo Schembechler was pronounced dead.

Ann Arbor residents flowed into St. Andrew's Church for the visitation. Schembechler's closed casket rested with an American flag on one side and a Michigan flag on the other, along with a blanket of yellow and blue flowers. Thousands would gather in Michigan Stadium for a memorial service.

The media coverage of Schembechler's death was wall-to-wall. ESPN devoted several hours to Schembechler and his legacy, and most major newspapers played his obituary prominently. This was partly because of the timing; sports fans around the country were already talking about Michigan and Ohio State that week. (Ohio State would win the game, 42–39, and, in an oddly appropriate salute to the Woody and Bo era, both teams would lose their postseason bowl games.) But it was also because, for an entire generation, Schembechler was a lovable, larger-than-life throwback.

"It was not just a man who died last Friday in Michigan, but another piece of a college football institution whose time is nearly gone," read the *Sports Illustrated* obituary. "The modern coach is part strategist, part salesman, part mercenary. Soon there will be no more giants."

John Sinclair was back in Ann Arbor.

Sinclair had moved to Detroit in the mid-1970s, then to New Orleans in the '90s, and then, in the winter of 2003, to Amsterdam. Now it was December of 2006. The Michigan Theater on Liberty Street in Ann Arbor was screening *The U.S. vs. John Lennon*, a documentary about Lennon's deportation fight.

Over time, Sinclair had come to believe that America would never change in the ways he wanted it to. He had launched his total assault on the culture, and the culture had won. Of all the new developments that scared Ann Arborites in the late '60s and early '70s, only one remained: Briarwood Mall, on the edge of town. The locals had feared Briarwood would siphon customers away from downtown business, and some of those businesses had indeed closed. But so many strip malls had sprouted up around Briarwood that it no longer seemed like the edge of town.

Now, at the Michigan Theater, Sinclair commiserated with old friends. Fellow White Panther Pun Plamondon was there, selling his self-published memoir, *Lost from the Ottawa*. So were Sinclair's lawyer and his concert promoter. Sinclair, who played a fairly significant role in *The U.S. vs. John Lennon*, spoke to the audience after the screening. One current Michigan student asked for advice in organizing students. Others in the audience wanted to know what had happened to the movement.

Why were so many people apathetic today?

"Television," Sinclair said.

Well, what was the best way to fight apathy?

"I don't know," Sinclair said. "I've never suffered from apathy."

When the Q&A session ended, Sinclair left the theater. It was 10:15 p.m. on a clear night in mid-December. Students and townies milled about.

John Sinclair walked outside, stopped on the sidewalk of Liberty Street, and lit a joint.

Acknowledgments

Throughout this project, I was asked the same question dozens of times: "How did you come up with the idea?" I never had a good answer, and I finally realized why: I never "came up" with the idea. The narrative took shape over time, thanks to the generosity and help of hundreds of people, who gave me a sense of the time, places, and (most important) the two men at the heart of the book.

Before I really knew what I was writing, I tried to explain the concept to Bo Schembechler. After listening for a few minutes, Bo told me he thought the real untold story of his rivalry with Woody Hayes was the era in which he coached and added that I might be on to something. Those words meant so much to me. Schembechler graciously sat down for interviews—in my last conversation with him, four days before he died, we talked about setting up another. I am sure he could have made this project difficult for me if he had so desired; I am thankful he chose to make it easier.

I was fortunate to have an editor, Rick Wolff, who was perfect for this project. Rick played baseball at Harvard in the 1970s and understood the book instinctively. A great editor improves material without leaving fingerprints; that was Rick. The rest of the team at Grand Central was a tremendous help; specifically, thank you to Bob Castillo, Tracy Martin, and Flamur Tonuzi.

Thanks, too, to Greg Dinkin and Frank Scatoni of Venture Literary for negotiating the deal. And to Mitch Albom, Christine Brennan, and Mark Kriegel for their kind words, which appear on the cover.

I lucked into two outstanding researchers. Kevin Bruffy in Columbus was eager and bright and showed a nose for finding great material. He never tired of this project, even when I sent him back to libraries for a fourth or fifth time because I had yet another request. Nixon researcher Matthew Hogan searched for everything I wanted and found almost all of it. He also went beyond that, sending material that he discovered and thought would be of interest to me (and all for a flat fee!).

I owe a special thanks to my various bosses at the *Free Press*— Gene Myers, Dave Robinson, Paul Anger, Caesar Andrews, and Jeff Taylor—for supporting me on this project, even at times when it took me away from my day job. My bosses at Foxsports.com were understanding as well. I would also like to thank the entire *Free Press* staff, except for Mick McCabe.

My friend Jeff Eldridge read each chapter when I finished it and provided thoughtful and detailed feedback; Jeff reads more than any three people I know, and his criticism and encouragement were invaluable. Several friends read the finished manuscript and provided important feedback and editing. Thanks so much to Rachel Bachman, Bill McGraw, Jim Schaefer, and Matt Rennie. Any mistakes that remain are Rennie's fault. No, I'm kidding: They are of course my fault.

If you are a fan of Michigan or Ohio State, you have probably heard this story: *After his team took a 48–14 lead on Michigan in 1968, Woody Hayes decided to go for two. When he was asked why, Hayes said, "Because they wouldn't let me go for three!"*

That is a great story. Unfortunately, it is at least half false: As I wrote in the first chapter, based on interviews with both Jim Otis (who scored the two-point conversion) and George Chaump (who was on the sideline with Hayes), Hayes never wanted to go for two. It is certainly possible that when a reporter questioned Woody about it, he got annoyed and snapped, "Because they wouldn't let me go for three!" But I found no evidence of that, either in the coverage of the 1968 game or the buildup in 1969, which is why it does not appear in the text.

As I researched this project, I heard many stories that I later found out were either not true or were exaggerated—not because anybody was lying to me, but because memories get foggy. This is the risk of writing historical narrative nonfiction based at least partly on interviews. Thankfully, so many people shared their time and memories with me that I was able to double-check and reconfirm stories and write an accurate book.

I hesitate to mention any interviewees ahead of the rest, because so many were helpful. But a few went far out of their way to assist me, and it would be rude not to acknowledge them.

Shemy and Megan Schembechler were accommodating and open in discussing Bo. Mary Hoyt, Woody's niece, was a great resource for family history, especially since Woody's son, Steve, rarely gives interviews (and chose not to talk to me, which was certainly his prerogative). Mark George, George Hill, and Daryl Sanders spent hours giving me insight into the Old Man. Jerry Hanlon did the same with Bo.

Clare Canham-Eaton and Don Eaton not only shared Don Canham stories with me, but they gave me access to Canham's personal scrapbooks.

I would not have faulted Mike Lantry if he did not want to discuss either his Vietnam experience or his games against Ohio State. I am fortunate that he was so honest, matter of fact, and patient in discussing both. He also put me in touch with his exwife, Linda Lantry; his sister Michelle Beardsley; and his childhood friend Mike Oliver. Each of them helped fill in the edges on Mike's story.

Rod Gerald, Steve Strinko, and Art Schlichter were open in discussing some of the most difficult days of their lives. Jeff Kaplan was kind enough to meet me in Toledo and play audiotapes of Woody that he had surreptitiously recorded in 1975. Champ Henson and John Hicks spent an afternoon talking about Woody and helped put me in touch with several teammates.

Pun Plamondon, John Sinclair, and Bill Ayers all shared their experiences as radicals in the 1970s. They were especially patient in answering followup questions and e-mails.

Several people helped me contact former Michigan and Ohio State players; without them, this book might have taken another two years. At Michigan, Jamie Morris, Bruce Madej, Dave Ablauf, Jim

Schneider, Mary Passink, and Michelle Guidry-Pan all helped immensely (but don't tell Bruce I said that). Mary Basinger and Taryn Jones of the Ohio State alumni association greeted my requests with an enthusiasm I probably didn't deserve. Shelly Todd at Ohio State must have gotten tired of my requests, but she never showed it. Thank you to her and to Steve Snapp.

Quite a few current coaches and former coaches provided great insight into the personalities and coaching styles of Hayes and Schembechler. Thank you to Dave Adolph, Dutch Baughman, Earle Bruce, Tirrel Burton, Larry Catuzzi, George Chaump, Carm Cozza, Ed Ferkany, Dino Folino, Bill Gunlock, Rudy Hubbard, Mickey Jackson, Larry Kindbom, Frank Kush, Bill Mallory, Frank Maloney, George Mans, Gary Moeller, Bill Myles, John Pont, Kevin Rogers, Larry Romanoff, Ralph Staub, Gary Tranquill, and Jim Young.

Wayne Duke talked to me extensively about his time running the Big Ten. Robben Fleming sat with me and discussed the challenges he faced as president of the University of Michigan. Thank you to both.

Several friends of Bo and/or Woody provided anecdotes and insight. Thanks to Art Adams, Eloy Cueto, Gene D'Angelo, Bob Greene, Jon Falk, Bob Forman, Joe Hayden, Bob Lipson, Melvin Olix, Jim Otis Sr., Tom Pequignot, Will Perry, and Harold Schechter.

Thanks to the Griffin family—Archie, Duncan, Ray, and Margaret—and to the Griffins' high-school coach, Bob Stuart.

On the rare occasions when a former Buckeye or former Wolverine was hesitant to speak to me, I told them my impressions of the coaches would be formed largely on what the former players said. That usually convinced them the portraits would be fair, and dozens of former players happily cooperated. Many spent a significant amount of time talking to me. In addition to those mentioned above, thank you to:

Brian Baschnagel, Gordon Bell, Jim Betts, Mike Boren, Jim Brandstatter, John Brockington, Dick Caldarazzo, Tom Cousineau, Garvie Craw, Pete Cusick, Scott Dannelly, Thom Darden, Tom DeLeone, Dan Dierdorf, Glenn Doughty, Don Dufek, Stan Edwards, Bruce

Elia, Bruce Elliott, Tom Engler, Dennis Franklin, Dennis Franks, Richard Galbos, David Gallagher, Cornelius Greene, Frank Gusich, Jim Hackett, Greg Hare, Pete Johnson, Mike Kenn, Jim Kregel, Ken Kuhn, Greg Lashutka, Rick Leach, Jeff Logan, Steve Luke, Jim Lyall, Rob Lytle, Ron Maciejowski, Dick Mack, Jim Mandich, Jack Marsh, Reggie McKenzie, Lenny Mills, Jimmy Moore, Don Moorhead, Steve Myers, Pete Newell, Tim O'Cain, Calvin O'Neal, Jim Otis Jr., Jim Pacenta, Ted Provost, John Prusiecki, Bruce Ruhl, Kurt Schumacher, Mike Sensibaugh, Fritz Seyferth, Phil Seymour, Paul Staroba, Jim Stillwagon, Greg Strinko, Billy Taylor, Frank Titas, Doug Troszak, Bill Urbanik, Dick Wakefield, Jan White, Dave Whitfield, and Dirk Worden.

Other interviewees who helped paint this picture: David Crouse, Bill Cusumano, John Haldi, Bill Hanners, Mike Harden, Alan Haber, Ernie Harwell, James Jones, Kaye Kessler, Wayne Kramer, Dale Laackman, Jim Lampley, Bob Maruschak, Daniel Okrent, Art Rogers, Andy Sacks, Budd Schulberg, Leonard Shapiro, Jay Smith, Ronald Thompson, David Turnley, Bob Ufer Jr., Tom Ufer, Robert Vare, Pete Waldmeir, and Mary Carran Webster.

Allan Millett shared his excellent piece, "Woody at War," months before it was published in *Timeline,* the Ohio Historical Society's quarterly magazine. World War II veterans Norm Kouba, Gregory McFarland, William Moore, and Maurice Northcutt also helped.

Incredibly, I wrote an entire book about Woody Hayes and Bo Schembechler and only talked to one referee. Thanks to Jerry Markbreit.

And of course: Thank you, Ralph Waldo Emerson, for inspiring Woody Hayes—and, in turn, inspiring me.

This book taught me the value of a great librarian, and I was fortunate to work with several. Bertha Ihnat and Michelle Drobik patiently helped me navigate the Ohio State University Archives. Greg Kinney and the staff of the Bentley Historical Library did the same in Ann Arbor. Bill McNitt and the staff at the Gerald R. Ford Presidential

Library were helpful as well, as was archivist Sahr Conway-Lanz of the Nixon Presidential Materials Project at the National Archives.

A slew of books provided source material as well as context. On the Woody front, they included: Paul Hornung's *Woody Hayes: A Reflection*; Robert Vare's *Buckeye: A Study of Woody Hayes and the Ohio State Football Machine*; Woody Hayes's three books, *You Win with People!*, *Football at Ohio State*, and *Hot Line to Victory!*; Paul Underwood's *The Enarson Years*; Alan Natali's *Woody's Boys*; Jack Park's *The Official Ohio State Football Encyclopedia*; *Ohio State '68: All the Way to the Top*, by Steve Greenberg and Larry Zelina; Jerry Brondfield's *Woody Hayes and the 100-Yard War*; John Lombardo's *A Fire to Win: The Life and Times of Woody Hayes*; Monte Carpenter's *Quotable Woody*; Norman Lewis's *Word Power Made Easy*; and *Woody Hayes: The Man and His Dynasty*, an anthology edited by Mike Bynum.

On the Bo/Michigan front: Mitch Albom and Bo Schembechler's *Bo*; Don Canham's *From the Inside: A Half Century of Michigan Athletics*, written with Larry Paladino; Joe Falls's *Bo Schembechler: Man in Motion*; Robben Fleming's *Tempests into Rainbows: Managing Turbulence*; Howard H. Peckham's *The Making of the University of Michigan*; Jonathan Marwil's *A History of Ann Arbor*; Will Perry's *The Wolverines: A Story of Michigan Football*; Jim Brandstatter's *Tales from…Michigan Stadium*; Bo Schembechler and John U. Bacon's *Bo's Lasting Lessons*; *A Dynasty in Blue: 25 Years of Michigan Football Glory*, edited by Francis Fitzgerald; and *What It Means to Be a Wolverine*, by Kevin Allen, Nate Brown, and Art Regner.

On the Woody/Bo front: Joel Pennington's *The Ten Year War: Ten Classic Games Between Bo and Woody*; Greg Emmanuel's *The 100-Yard War*; and Bill Cromartie's *The Big One: Michigan vs. Ohio State*.

Pun Plamondon's memoir, *Lost from the Ottawa: The Story of the Journey Back*, and Bill Ayers's memoir, *Fugitive Days*, provided great insight into the minds of revolutionaries in the Vietnam era. (Because of the nature of both books—some facts and names were changed by the authors—I did not use any facts from either unless I could independently confirm them.)

General George S. Patton Jr.'s memoir, *War as I Knew It*, provided some insight into Hayes's hero.

Woody's second cousin Christine Hayes was kind enough to send me information about her family (including pictures of Woody's cabin in Noble County) and to send me a copy of her father's book, *The Ben Hayes Scrapbook*, edited by Mike Harden and Tom Thomson.

Other books that helped: Keith Dunnavant's *The 50-Year Seduction*; William M. Kunstler's *My Life as a Radical Lawyer* (with Sheila Isenberg); F. W. Winterbotham's *The Ultra Secret*; James A. Michener's *Sports in America*; Michael and Judy Ann Newton's *The FBI Most Wanted: An Encyclopedia*; David Sheff and G. Barry Golson's *The Playboy Interviews with John Lennon and Yoko Ono*; H. R. Haldeman's *The Haldeman Diaries*; Jon Wiener's *Gimme Some Truth: The John Lennon FBI Files*; and Todd Jackson's *Road to the Rose Bowl: 50 Years of Lawry's Beef Bowl*.

Two lengthy magazine stories became essential resources: "The Times They've Been a-Changin'," Sandra Gurvis's May 1990 look back at the 1970 Ohio State riots, which appeared in the *Ohio State Alumni Magazine*; and Betty Garrett's October 1978 *Ohio Magazine* story about Hayes, "Lion in Autumn."

Thanks to the wonders of the Internet, I was able to buy copies of nine of the ten games between Bo and Woody. (The one I missed was the 1971 game, which was not televised; for that one, I relied primarily on newspaper accounts and interviews.) I also found copies of several other pivotal games, including bowl games. I'm sure my video library would have been incomplete without the help of Art Vuolo. Art describes himself as "radio's best friend"; he is a good friend to book researchers as well.

Other videos that helped: All Green Video's *10.4.2: John Sinclair Freedom Rally*, the "Buckeye Classics" series of game highlights, the terrific documentary *The Weather Underground*, and especially the Duncan Group and Crouse Entertainment Group's excellent *Beyond the Gridiron: The Life and Times of Woody Hayes*.

Tom Ufer provided several CDs of his father Bob's broadcasts. (If you've never heard Bob Ufer, I recommend going to ufer.org and giving him a listen.)

A slew of fellow journalists helped in ways big and small. Eric Adelson, Christine Brennan, Chuck Culpepper, Rick Morrissey, Mike Vaccaro, Dan Wetzel, Gene Wojciechowski, Adrian Wojnarowski, Mark Snyder, Bruce Hooley, Jim Carty, Angelique Chengelis, Marsha Low, and Ken Gordon were the most prominent.

Thank you to the journalists who covered Woody Hayes and Bo Schembechler during their rivalry, some of whom are still doing an excellent job today: most notably, Joe Falls and Curt Sylvester of the *Detroit Free Press*; Wayne DeNeff of the *Ann Arbor News*; Pete Waldmeir, Jerry Green, and Bill Halls of the *Detroit News*; Tom Keys and Kaye Kessler of the *Columbus Citizen-Journal*; and Tim May and Paul Hornung of the *Columbus Dispatch*. Thanks to the dozens of student reporters at the *Michigan Daily* and Ohio State *Lantern* from that era as well.

Thanks also to Howard Bragman, Keith Dunnavant, Julie Peterson, and Robert Falls.

I'm one of those lucky people who knows his family would be proud of him no matter what he did for a living, and I'll always be thankful for that. Thank you to my mom and dad and my brother, David, for continued support. Thanks, too, my extended family, and to all the friends who were excited when I told them I was writing a book—and also to those who faked excitement.

I don't know if it's true that all writers are obsessive pains in the ass, but I hope it is, because I'd hate to think I'm the only one. Two ladies inspired me and kept me (relatively) sane throughout the process.

One is my daughter, Audrey, who had no idea Daddy was writing a book and therefore didn't care if it ended up being a big pile of poop.

The other is my wife, Erin. She encouraged my dream of writing a book, even when we were young and I showed no ability to actually, you know, *write a book*. She supported me throughout this endeavor. She never complained about the fact I had basically taken on a second full-time job. She never made me feel guilty when my work took me away from my family. She listened to every worry and every complaint. She somehow swallowed the staggering news that the book would be delayed by a year. She believed me when I told her I would only need a few more months instead of the whole extra year, and did not complain when, to my great embarrassment, I took every day of that year. She also provided the first edit of every chapter.

For a million reasons, I never could have written this book without her. I can't possibly thank Erin as much as she deserves to be thanked, so I guess she will just have to settle for seeing the four words she dreamed about for almost three years:

The book is finished.

Michael Rosenberg
April 2008

Notes

NOTES ON THE NOTES: In researching this book, I combined my own interviews with accounts from newspapers, periodicals, and books. (The interviewees can be found in the acknowledgments.) In the notes, I tried to be thorough without being excessive. I provided attribution for most material that came from another publication, except in instances where the material was clearly nonexclusive (i.e., from a press conference). As a general rule, I tried to attribute anything between quote marks in these notes, unless there is attribution in the text, or the quote was so widely circulated and repeated that attribution was unnecessary. In some cases, quotes were taken from my individual interviews; those quotes are also identified in the notes. Facts and anecdotes that are not attributed in the notes were either widely circulated or provided to me in interviews.

CHAPTER 1: What Kind of Game?

3: *national convention*: "SDS mulls new attack on U-M research," *Detroit News*, December 29, 1968.

4: *Haber had left Ann Arbor*: Interview with Alan Haber.

4: *fuel shortage*: Don Canham and Larry Paladino, *Don Canham's From the Inside: A Half Century of Michigan Athletics* (Ann Arbor, MI: Olympia Sports Press), pp. 96–97.

4: *a salary of $21,000*: Canham and Paladino, *From the Inside*, p. 96.

5: *staying up until 6 a.m.*: *Ohio State University Monthly*, September 1969.

5: *his "best" trip*: "Hayes Visits Vietnam," *Ohio State University Monthly*, February 1969.

5: *had watched the Rose Bowl with a special guest*: Tom Brownfield, "Tributes to Hayes," *Sports Illustrated*, April 13, 1987, p. 6.

6: *met Colonel George Patton III*: "Hayes Visits Vietnam," *Ohio State University Monthly*, February 1969.

8: *students had taken over*: Madison Foster papers, Bentley Historical Library, Ann Arbor, Michigan.

8: *"How are you coming?"*: Interview with Robben Fleming.

8: *the Jesse James Gang*: Howard H. Peckham, *The Making of the University of Michigan* (Ann Arbor: University of Michigan Press, 1994), p. 293.

9: *Even the new Briarwood Mall*: Jonathan Marwil, *A History of Ann Arbor* (Ann Arbor: University of Michigan Press, 1987), p. 157.

9: *"What kind of game?"*: Interview with Pete Newell.

10: *"We will not forget this"*: Interview with Jim Mandich.

12: *"I'm quitting"*: Interview with John Prusiecki.

13: *"You precipitated the fracas!"*: Interview with Dick Caldarazzo.

13: *In 1952 and 1956*: Marwil, *History of Ann Arbor*, p. 146.

14: *In a 1960 campus straw poll*: Ibid.

14: *McNamara had lived*: Paul Hendrickson, *The Living and the Dead* (New York: Alfred A. Knopf, 1996), pp. 22–24, 34–35.

14: *"God made you and put you on earth"*: Interview with Daryl Sanders.

17: *three dozen insurance companies*: Robert Vare, *Buckeye: A Study of Woody Hayes and the Ohio State Football Machine* (New York: Harper's, 1974), p. 54.

20: *In the spring of 1949*: Joe Falls, *Bo Schembechler: Man in Motion* (Ann Arbor, MI: School-Tech Press, 1973), p. 69.

20: *During a game of handball*: Ibid., p. 71.

20: *told Schembechler to take summer classes*: Ibid., pp. 72–73.

21: *"Oh yeah?"*: Interview with Bo Schembechler.

22: *"George, goddammit"*: Interview with George Chaump.

23: *"Congratulations"*: Interview with Bill Ayers.

24: *said most of the rioters were not students*: "The University President . . . ," *Ann Arbor News*, June 18, 1969.

24: *There were forty-seven arrests*: "Police, Youths, Clash Near U-M," *Ann Arbor News*, June 18, 1969.

24: *took his family to the Leelanau Peninsula*: Falls, *Man in Motion*, p. 5.

24: *Win Schuler held a picnic*: Canham and Paladino, *From the Inside*, p. 100.

24: *his recommended daily allowance*: Falls, *Man in Motion*, pp. 1–3.

25: *was valued at $5 million*: "Here's the Man Behind the U. of M's New Sporty Look," *Detroit News Sunday Magazine*, July 20, 1968.

25: *"whaddaya say"*: "Marketing the Wolverines," *Chicago Tribune*, November 8, 1981.

25: *with 25,000 tickets still unsold*: Canham and Paladino, *Man in Motion*, pp. 107–9.

25: *a track team road trip to UCLA*: Ibid., pp. 105–6.

25: *he bought used sweatsocks*: "Marketing the Wolverines," *Chicago Tribune*, November 8, 1981.

CHAPTER 2: The Fall of '69

29: *"you're all wrong"*: Interview with Rudy Hubbard.

31: *"They are the finest college team"*: "62–0," *Sports Illustrated*, October 6, 1969.

31: *"I'm not one to hide"*: "Finest Team Ever," *Columbus Dispatch*, September 28, 1969.

31: *"In that towering gray edifice"*: "62–0," *Sports Illustrated*, October 6, 1969.

32: *"I never go to a movie"*: Interview with Earle Bruce.

33: *"Michigan Football Offers New Excitement in '69"*: *Michigan Daily*, August 27, 1969.

33: *"Until we start planting shrubs"*: *Detroit News Sunday Magazine*, July 20, 1968.

34: *He let a friend at ABC know*: Don Canham and Larry Paladino, *Don Canham's From the Inside: A Half Century of Michigan Athletics* (Ann Arbor, MI: Olympia Sports Press), p. 111.

34: *"I'll make you a promise"*: Interview with Jerry Markbreit.

35: *The day before the opener*: "Vietnam teach-in draws over 5,000," *Michigan Daily*, September 20, 1969.

35: *"We have also the rather naïve notion"*: Robben W. Fleming, *Tempests into Rainbows: Managing Turbulence* (Ann Arbor: University of Michigan Press, 1996), p. 195.

35: *12,000 spectators marched*: "12,000 join peace march," *Michigan Daily*, September 21, 1969.

35: *"Politics and Tartan Turf"*: "Wolverines smash defenseless Vanderbilt, 42–14," *Michigan Daily*, September 21, 1969.

35: *"I don't know if it's any indication"*: Interview with Garvie Craw.

36: *"We will never get a punt blocked"*: Interview with Jim Brandstatter.

36: *"Oh, shit," Brandstatter thought*: Ibid.

36: *sixty demonstrators had seized the ROTC building*: "60 demonstrators seize ROTC Building; Sheriff Mobilizes Force of 200 Deputies," *Michigan Daily*, September 23, 1969.

36: *"Don't go"*: Ibid.

37: *"You guys have accepted me"*: Interview with Pete Newell.

37: *"I'll tell you what I'm gonna do"*: Interview with Dick Caldarazzo.

37: *the rally drew 20,000 people*: "Wide 'U' participation in moratorium," *Michigan Daily*, October 10, 1969.

38: *Cars were overturned*: "Cops, Troops Guard City," *Chicago Tribune*, October 10, 1969.

38: *"Hit-and-run guerrilla tactics"*: "City High Schools Targets of S.D.S. in Strategy for Havoc," *Chicago Tribune*, October 6, 1969.

39: *removed the backseat of a late-model Buick*: Pun Plamondon, *Lost from the Ottawa: The Story of the Journey Back* (Cloverdale, MI: Plamondon, Inc., 2004), p. 146.

40: *"I don't believe they should go"*: "Valek Suggest Bucks For Southern Bowl," *Columbus Dispatch*, October 26, 1969.

40: *"Not much you can do about it"*: "Coatta Thinks Bucks Must Be Supermen," *Columbus Dispatch*, November 9, 1969.

42: *"No, I don't think so"*: Interview with Jim Jones.

42: *"mentally depressing and morally discouraging"*: "Irate Black Athletes Stir Campus Tension," *New York Times*, November 16, 1969.

43: *When he first heard the song*: *Democracy Now!*: Interview with Pete Seeger, December 8, 2005.

43: *He stayed inside and watched Ohio State*: "Washington Comes of Age; The Vietnam Protests: When Worlds Collided," *Washington Post*, September 27, 1999.

43: *standing behind a fifty-seven-bus barricade*: Ibid.

44: *"I knew they were good"*: *Columbus Dispatch*, Nov. 16, 1969.

44: *"It would be some crash, boy"*: "Ohio State: Alone at the Top," *Sports Illustrated*, November 24, 1969.

44: *"He's our defensive player of the week"*: Interview with Pete Newell.

45: *"Our defense was the best"*: *Columbus Dispatch*, November 16, 1969.

46: *"I hate to be defended in a newspaper"*: Ralph Waldo Emerson, "Compensation."

46: *President Nixon cut off a budget meeting*: H. R. Haldeman, *The Haldeman Diaries: Inside the Nixon White House* (New York: G. Putnam's Sons, 1994), p. 110.

48: *Hayes gave the cameraman a shove*: "'Outplayed, Outcoached,'" *Detroit Free Press*, November 23, 1969.

49: *"Jim, if you would have run the ball"*: Interview with Jim Otis.

50: *"There's only one tough son of a bitch"*: Interview with Jim Young.

52: Dear Bo: Joe Falls, *Bo Schembechler: Man in Motion* (Ann Arbor, MI: School-Tech Press, 1973), p. 13.

CHAPTER 3: Using the Enemy's Tactics

55: *had been running a preschool in Ann Arbor*: "Diana Oughton, 1942–1970: Portrait of a radical," *Michigan Daily*, March 21, 1970.

56: *eighty faculty members formed a group*: "New faculty group threatens class strike," *Michigan Daily*, February 17, 1970.

56: *Recruiters from DuPont*: "Recruiter locked in at W. Engin," *Michigan Daily*, February 19, 1970; "Five more arraigned on charges of contention for GE lock-in," *Michigan Daily*, February 21, 1970.

56: *Fleming said he would give the names of students*: "Sit-in names denied to HEW," *Michigan Daily*, Febuary 7, 1970.

57: *an instant three-mile protest*: "Convict 5 of Chicago 7 on Riot Charges; 2,000 Marchers Routed at City Hall; Police Arrest 12 at Recruiter Protest," *Michigan Daily*, February 19, 1970.

57: *More than a hundred black students*: "100 blacks resume library disruption after meeting with Regents," *Michigan Daily*, February 21, 1970.

57: *at least four "stink bombs"*: "Stink bombs hit S. Quad, UGLI, Union," *Michigan Daily*, February 22, 1970.

57: *not to give in to "coercion"*: "Regent warns of 'coercion,'" *Michigan Daily*, March 18, 1970.

57: *On March 9*: "150 march to back BAM," *Michigan Daily*, March 10, 1970.

58: *Later they would wonder*: Interview with Ronald Thompson.

58: *class attendance dropped to 50 percent*: "Estimate effect at up to 50%," *Michigan Daily*, March 24, 1970.

58: *"refusing to support niggers"*: "40% attend classes in Lit School," *Michigan Daily*, March 26, 1970.

59: *"goddamn Italians"*: Interview with Dick Caldarazzo.

60: *"He treats us all the same"*: Interview with Jim Betts.

60: *Fleming promised that black enrollment would increase*: "BAM Ends Class Strike," *Michigan Daily*, April 2, 1970.

60: *Spiro Agnew*: "Fleming blasts Agnew on 'U', BAM settlement," *Michigan Daily*, April 8, 1970.

61: *Schembechler started jogging*: Joe Falls, *Bo Schembechler: Man in Motion* (Ann Arbor, MI: School-Tech Press, 1973), p. 17.

61: *"Billy Taylor hasn't shown us anything"*: "Offense disappoints Bo," *Michigan Daily*, April 5, 1970.

61: *a list of black demands*: "The Times They've Been A-Changin'," *Ohio State Alumni Magazine*, May 1990.

62: *The crowd on the Oval*: "Student Rioters Battle Police," *Lantern*, April 30, 1970.

63: *school president Novice Fawcett left for a trip*: "Officials React to Strikers," *Lantern*, April 30, 1970.

63: *Some students predictably saw the strike*: "Violence, Gas, Fire Bombs," *Lantern*, May 1, 1970.

63: *more than four hundred arrests*: Ibid.

64: *Three hundred protestors roared their approval*: "A Student Strike Roundup: Our Tense, Explosive Spring," *Lantern*, May 19, 1970.

64: *a burgundy sport coat*: "Woody Attends Rally as Silent Observer," *Lantern*, May 20, 1970.

64: *Hayes told* Lantern *reporter Jay Smith*: Ibid.

65: *they could "win together"*: "PEP TALK," *Lantern*, May 22, 1970.

65: *"Sometimes you can't get a touchdown"*: Interview with Harold Schechter.

65: *"First and ten—do it again!"*: Interview with Mike Harden.

65: *In the wake of the riots*: "The Times They've Been A-Changin'," *Ohio State Alumni Magazine*, May 1990.

66: *"I was putting black kids through college"*: Interview with Art Adams.

66: *stopped a Volkswagen van*: "'60s radical takes long trip back to his roots," *Detroit Free Press*, October 27, 2004.

66: *Plamondon sat with a .38 caliber Derringer*: Pun Plamondon, *Lost from the Ottawa: The Story of the Journey Back* (Cloverdale, MI: Plamondon, Inc., 2004), pp. 240–41.

68: *"You're the best player"*: Interview with Dan Dierdorf.

69: *"Look at 'em down there!"*: Ibid.

69: *"I'm proud of [the soldiers]"*: "Surprise visit stuns students," *Lantern*, October 20, 1970.

73: *"Well, Coach, you sent in a play"*: Interview with Ron Maciejowski.

74: *the red color tube in the projector went out*: "Bucks look faded," *Columbus Dispatch*, October 19, 1969.

74: *"We haven't formulated our plans yet"*: "Nixon Phones Bucks, Hayes Lauds Defense," *Columbus Dispatch*, November 15, 1970.

75: *"The president will just have to wait this time"*: "Bucks' Locker Room Just Big Open House," *Columbus Dispatch*, November 22, 1970.

75: *"I read your book"*: Interview with Champ Henson.

76: *"Can't you hear anything?"*: "Wolves' Spirit High, But Performance Off," *Columbus Dispatch*, November 22, 1970.

76: *"the most publicized and televised single game"*: "Hayes Salutes Victory as OSU's 'Greatest,'" *Columbus Dispatch*, November 22, 1970.

76: *"was greatly impressed with our ballclub"*: Ibid.

76: *"It's a funny thing"*: Ibid.

CHAPTER 4: Napoleon; or, The Man of the World

83: *"I'd kick you in the ass"*: Interview with Jim Brandstatter.

84: *"You're getting* placid*"*: Interview with George Mans.

88: *"I'm a football coach up at the university"*: Interview with Bob Greene.

88: *his mother baked pies*: "Woody at Denison," *Columbus Dispatch*, November 26, 1947; reprinted in *The Ben Hayes Scrapbook* (Columbus, OH: Ravine Books, 1991), p. 96.

89: *"The stars awaken a certain reverence"*: Ralph Waldo Emerson, "Nature."

90: *"I'm your new roommate"*: Interview with Mike Lantry.

91: *"Don't you think"*: Ibid.

92: *He guaranteed Lions general manager Russ Thomas*: Don Canham and Larry Paladino, *Don Canham's From the Inside: A Half Century of Michigan Athletics* (Ann Arbor, MI: Olympia Sports Press), pp. 117–18.

92: *"I think he's up there"*: Ibid.

93: *"Of course we're not* for *the war"*: Interview with Frank Gusich.

93: *"Bring All the Troops Home Now"*: *Ann Arbor News*, October 31, 1971.

93: *"In the words of the student body"*: "U-M Football Fans Hail Anti-War Half-time Show," *Detroit Free Press*, October 31, 1971.

94: *"We got the fucking shit kicked out of us"*: "'It was a nightmare,'" *Michigan Daily*, November 7, 1971.

95: *"We are the best"*: "We Are the Best—Bo," *Ann Arbor News*, November 14, 1971.

96: *"A lot of people bought tickets"*: "You'll Admit It Was a Doozy of a Finish," *Columbus Citizen-Journal*, November 22, 1971.

96: *"We know what kind of battle we're against"*: "Silent Bucks Cut 'Rah-Rah,'" *Columbus Dispatch*, November 16, 1971.

97: *"We're going to tackle toward the north"*: "19 Buckeyes Take Senior Tackle," *Columbus Dispatch*, November 19, 1971.

99: *"It was a little confusing out there"*: Ibid.

100: *"When you see officials decide the ball game"*: Ibid.

100: *"The only right"*: Ralph Waldo Emerson, "Self-Reliance."

101: *The latest Ann Arbor asininity*: *Lantern*, December 8, 1971.

101: *"My big concern"*: Don Canham papers, Bentley Historical Library, University of Michigan, Ann Arbor, Michigan.

101: *"We can have electronic machines"*: "Woody Advocates 'Instant Replay,'" *Columbus Dispatch*, November 25, 1971.

102: *As Lennon sang*: Jon Wiener, *Gimme Some Truth: The John Lennon FBI Files* (Berkeley and Los Angeles: University of California Press, 1999), pp. 113–15.

103: *"We have played our schedule"*: "It's U-M's Power vs. Stanford's Dazzle," *Detroit Free Press*, January 1, 1972.

103: *"Is anyone as nervous as I am?"*: "Don Bunce Ruined Season for U-M," *Detroit Free Press*, January 2, 1972.

CHAPTER 5: Only the Good Ones

107: *"tell her the names of the priests"*: Interview with Jim Young.

108: *"Only the good ones"*: "Ohio State fans re-live, re-love fantastic victory," *Columbus Citizen-Journal*, November 27, 1972.

109: *"A prophet is without honor"*: Interview with Ed Ferkany.

110: *"If the king is in the palace"*: Ralph Waldo Emerson, "Nature."

110: *"Well, you're here for the interview"*: Interview with Ed Ferkany.

111: *legal experts said*: "Court pot ruling brings confusion," *Michigan Daily*, March 14, 1972.

111: *"Proceed with caution"*: Ibid.

112: *"I don't see anything"*: "Cops stand by as kids get high," *Michigan Daily*, April 2, 1972.

113: *"the danger posed by the new barbarians"*: William H. Rehnquist speech to Kiwanis Club of Newark, 1969.

113: *The issue before us*: United States v. United States District court 407 U.S. 297 (1972).

114: *Kunstler believed that Rehnquist*: William M. Kunstler with Sheila Isenberg, *My Life As a Radical Lawyer* (New York: Citadel Press, 1994), pp. 205–8.

114: *"Archie Griffin made me change my mind"*: "Hayes Sees Griffin As Gate Attraction," *Columbus Dispatch*, October 1, 1972.

115: *"You could sell more seats"*: Ibid.

115: *"I've been meaning to talk to you"*: Interview with Brian Baschnagel.

117: *"Well, no—not really"*: Interview with Bo Schembechler.

118: *"I didn't want to do it"*: Ibid.

120: *"To say it was dull football"*: "Dull Football? You've Got To Be Kidding," *Ann Arbor News*, October 16, 1972.

120: *"Hey, Mr. President"*: Interview with Bo Schembechler.

121: *"a bunch of donkeys"*: Robert Vare, *Buckeye: A Study of Woody Hayes and the Ohio State Football Machine* (New York: Harper's, 1974), p. 227.

122: *"We don't like ties"*: "Hayes, Foe, Quiet, Ready," *Columbus Dispatch*, November 22, 1972.

123: *"This is not a game"*: Interview with Archie Griffin.

126: *he pulled a calf muscle*: "'Great Experience,' Hayes Says; Deplores Fans' Conduct," *Columbus Dispatch*, November 26, 1972.

126: *"Each year it gets a little worse"*: Ibid.

127: *"A game like this brings kids together"*: Ibid.

127: *"I just wish there was some way"*: "We should have won—Schembechler," *Ann Arbor News*, November 26, 1972.

127: *"We deserve to be underdogs"*: "Rose Bowl Odds Biggest Ever Against Buckeyes," *Columbus Dispatch*, January 1, 1973.

127: *Between 60 and 70 million people were expected to watch*: Ibid.

127: *injured Rogers's right eye*: "Bucks Are Inert But Hayes Explodes," *Columbus Dispatch*, Jan. 2, 1973.

128: *"If that's all you have to ask me"*: Ibid.

CHAPTER 6: Books

131: *"And now this Watergate thing comes up"*: Robert Vare, *Buckeye: A Study of Woody Hayes and the Ohio State Football Machine* (New York: Harper's, 1974), p. 32.

131: *Hayes had called the White House*: Nixon Library, National Archives and Records Administration (NARA), College Park, Maryland, White House Central Files (WHCF), Subject Files, (JL) Judicial—Legal Matters, Box 15, File: "EX JL 3 Criminal Matters, [36 of 89] June 4–5,1973," Memorandum from Stephen Bull to Richard Nixon, dated May 8, 1973.

132: Dear Woody: Nixon Library, National Archives and Records Administration (NARA), College Park, Maryland, White House Central Files (WHCF), Subject Files, H to Kai-shek/Chiang, Box 9, File: "Hayes, W. Woodrow [McKay, John]," Letter from Richard Nixon to Woody Hayes, dated January 2, 1973.

132: *"I know just how Nixon feels"*: Vare, *Buckeye*, pp. 30–31.

132: *a court ruled*: Paul Underwood, *The Enarson Years* (Columbus: Ohio State University Press, 1985), pp. 38–39.

132: *the American Association of Universty Professors*: Ibid., p. 41.

132: *a U.S. district court*: Ibid., p. 48.

132: *spring commencement*: Ibid., p. 43.

132: *"So you see"*: Vare, *Buckeye*, p. 32.

134: *"We have worked closely together"*: Woody Hayes, *You Win with People!* (Columbus, OH: Typographic Printing Company, 1973), p. iii.

134: *"I have a deep and abiding respect"*: Ibid., p. 11.

135: *why his coaches did not get divorced*: Ibid., pp. 135–36.

136: *"But if you apply to law school"*: Interview with Jeff Kaplan.

137: *"The town council at one Big Ten university"*: Hayes, *You Win with People!*, p. 177.

137: *"How do you tell them about pot"*: Joe Falls, *Bo Schembechler: Man in Motion* (Ann Arbor, MI: School-Tech Press, 1973), p. 119.

139: *"I can give you something every day"*: Ibid., p. 176.

139: *"I don't know how much a football coach can do"*: Ibid., p. 126.

139: *"No man can write anything"*: Ralph Waldo Emerson, "Nature."

140: *"I'm not sure our guys got a lot out of it"*: "Michigan Blows 'Em Out Quickly," *Ann Arbor News*, November 4, 1973.

140: *"Where did you learn"*: Interview with Dan Dierdorf.

141: *"The players know"*: Joe Falls, *Bo Schembechler: Man in Motion* (Ann Arbor, MI: School-Tech Press, 1973), p. 139.

144: *"the flamboyant flim-flam man"*: Interview with Leonard Shapiro.

144: *"Does anybody know"*: Interview with Steve Luke.

145: *"Coach, you gotta be kidding me"*: Interview with Kurt Schumacher.

145: *"student interests have shifted"*: Paul Underwood, *The Enarson Years* (Columbus: Ohio State University Press, 1985), p. 15.

145: *the Ohio State Marching Band*: Ibid., p. 31.

145: *the Ohio Staters*: Ibid., p. 31.

146: *"But goddamn can they play football"*: Interviews with Champ Henson and John Hicks.

147: *"It is almost as if"*: "Michigan, Bucks, Look Alike," *Ann Arbor News*, November 4, 1973.

148: *"I'm so excited"*: James A. Michener, *Sports in America* (Greenwich, CT: Fawcett Publications, 1976), p. 238.

149: *"Is television that important?"*: Ibid., pp. 238–39.

151: *"Bullshit"*: Interview with Ed Ferkany.

151: *"We are reformers in spring and summer"*: Ralph Waldo Emerson, "The Conservative."

156: *"Our passing is not good"*: "For the Buckeyes, It's Just like A Loss," *Ann Arbor News*, November 25, 1973.

157: *Ohio State trainer Alan Hart*: "Bucks Feast Before 3rd season," *Columbus Dispatch*, November 26, 1973.

157: *picked up Schembecheler in his station wagon*: Will Perry, *The Wolverines: A Story of Michigan Football* (Huntsville, AL: Strode Publishers, 1974), pp. 375–76.

158: *"Have you heard the vote?"*: Ibid.

158: *"petty jealousies"*: "Everything's coming up weeds!," *Michigan Daily*, November 27, 1973.

159: *"it's only natural"*: "Bo 'Very Bitter' As Athletic Chiefs Vote for Woody, Buckeyes," *Detroit Free Press*, November 26, 1973.

159: *"A great wrong has been done"*: Ibid.

159: *Letters of support*: "Bo's Mailbag Overflows," *Ann Arbor News*.

159: *"sister institution"*: "Why Big 10 voted against Michigan," *Detroit News*, November 26, 1973.

160: *Gerald Faye filed a lawsuit*: "Suit Filed As Bowl Controversy Boils On," *Ann Arbor News*, November 28, 1973.

160: *"I'll be a thorn in their side"*: "Totally Disillusioned With College Football," *Ann Arbor News*, November 29, 1973.

160: *"typical of today"*: Associated Press, November 28, 1973.

160: *They got together and voted*: Vare, *Buckeye*, p. 236.

161: *"Now, who doesn't want to go?"*: Ibid., p. 237.

161: *He would loosen his curfew restriction*: Ibid., pp. 236–37.

161: *The Old Man loosened up, too*: "'New' Hayes Continues Light Touch," *Columbus Dispatch*, December 30, 1973.

161: *"We're still going to pass"*: Interview with Cornelius Greene.

162: *"I would rather talk about World War II"*: "'My Topper,' Hayes Says," *Columbus Dispatch*, January 2, 1974.

CHAPTER 7: Television

163: *"If you want to quit law school"*: Interview with Jeff Kaplan.

164: *his salary was only $29,400*: Robert Vare, *Buckeye: A Study of Woody Hayes and the Ohio State Football Machine* (New York: Harper's, 1974), p. 20.

165: *"Coach, don't say anything"*: Interview with Jim Otis.

166: *"He'll be fine"*: Interview with Ed Ferkany.

167: *"sometimes known as the land of the free"*: "Ford Stresses Jobs with Sense for Grads," *Columbus Evening Dispatch*, August 30, 1974.

168: *"Besides being 'the research center of the Midwest'"*: "Images of an activist past: Ann Arbor's SDS veterans," *Michigan Daily*, November 24, 1974.

171: *"You'll be referring to this book"*: Interview with Dutch Baughman.

172: *"The dorms are so fucking filthy now"*: Vare, *Buckeye*, p. 45.

172: *"I can tell in a minute"*: Ibid., p. 45.

172: *"These fellas they have today"*: Ibid.

172: *"They've gotten so goddamned liberal"*: Ibid., p. 38.

174: *"I ain't hip"*: Interview with Pete Johnson.

174: *"rising costs"*: Interview transcript provided by Mark George.

177: *"I am the winning coach!"*: "MSU Stuns Buckeyes, 16–13," *Michigan Daily*, November 11, 1974.

177: *"They snapped the ball"*: "Angry Hayes Awaits Films," *Columbus Dispatch*, November 10, 1974.

177: "What are you going to do about it?": Interview with Champ Henson.

178: *"Let me drive!"*: Interview with Champ Henson.

178: *"dirty football"*: *Associated Press*, November 12, 1974.

179: *"Certainly losing the game"*: "All Those for Ohio State Can Stand Up and Blush," *Washington Post*, November 16, 1974.

180: *D'Angelo simply bumped Hayes up*: Interview with Gene D'Angelo.

180: *"The heroic soul does not sell its justice"*: Ralph Waldo Emerson, "Heroism."

181: *"Bullshit!"*: Interview with Pete Cusick.

181: *"There may be some doubt"*: "Michigan's Athletic Big Sell," *New York Times*, November 20, 1974.

182: *"You know, I couldn't win a popularity contest"*: "Candid Canham converses in exclusive Daily interview," *Michigan Daily*, September 14, 1974.

182: *"There is no distinction made"*: "Women's Athletics: A Conflict Over Regulations," *New York Times*, December 29, 1974.

186: *"Good luck, Mike"*: Interview with Mike Lantry.

192: *"It's going to come down to a last-second kick"*: Interviews with Mike Oliver and Linda Lantry.

195: *Then came the letters*: All letters reprinted courtesy of Mike Lantry.

199: *"If you would serve your brother"*: Ralph Waldo Emerson, "Heroism."

199: *"You can't run a farm without a woman"*: Interview with Champ Henson.

199: *"Let me tell you something"*: Interview with Pete Cusick.

200: *"I haven't made my mind up"*: "Klaban Uses Sister as Toe Coach," *Columbus Dispatch*, December 31, 1974.

CHAPTER 8: Roses

203: *Three hundred minority students*: "Minorities occupy Ad. Bldg.; vow to remain until demands are met," *Michigan Daily*, February 19, 1975.

203: *there were only 150 students in the Administration Building*: Ibid.

207: *"get Bo off the rubber-chicken circuit"*: Interview with Bob Lipson.

208: *"Goddamn, Northwestern is good"*: "Bo," *Sports Illustrated*, September 14, 1981.

208: *had said the Buckeyes would be "scared"*: "Calm Settles Over Buck-MSU Tilt," *Columbus Dispatch*, September 12, 1975.

209: *"I want you to swear"*: Interview with Brian Baschnagel.

210: *"They played a heck of a game"*: "Subdued Baggett Lauds Buckeyes," *Columbus Dispatch*, September 14, 1975.

211: *"You know what they tried to do to us"*: Tape provided by Jeff Kaplan.

211: *"Men suffer all their life long"*: Ralph Waldo Emerson, "Compensation."

211: *"pretty doggone good football"*: "Greene Sparks 41–20 Victory," *Columbus Dispatch*, October 5, 1975.

211: *"Cornelius did a super job today"*: Ibid.

212: *"I'd like to make you my manager"*: Interview with Mark George.

215: *"You have no scruples!"*: Interview with Andy Sacks.

215: *"This game, I want more than any game"*: Tape provided by Jeff Kaplan.

216: *"How's your helmet?"*: Interview with John Falk.

220: *"November 22"*: Tape provided by Jeff Kaplan.

222: *"This is the type of man"*: "Hayes Not Concerned On 'Timing,'" *Columbus Dispatch*, December 31, 1975.

225: *Knight replied that he had the best team in the country*: Interview with Harold Schechter.

225: *"The relationship I have had with you"*: The Ohio State University Archives, Wayne W. Hayes Papers (RG 40/111-B/2/14), "Correspondence 1976."

CHAPTER 9: Independence

227: *"Bo will probably have"*: "Nothing happens under table, Canham tells alums," *Lansing State Journal*, May 6, 1976.

227: *had missed spring practice*: "Bo's Surgery Scheduled for This Week," *Ann Arbor News*, May 19, 1976.

227: *"Coach, we've been expecting you"*: Interview with Dutch Baughman.

228: *"I can't understand this damn group"*: Interview with Bob Forman.

229: *"What we're doing"*: "Canham won't expand stadium," *Detroit News*, September 22, 1976.

229: *the first private luxury box*: "Stadium May Have Private VIP Boxes," *Ann Arbor News*, October 1, 1976.

229: *Ford's Commission on Olympic Sports*: "Byers, Canham have similar views," *Chicago Tribune*, April 9, 1976.

229: *four-year, $118 million TV package*: "Huckster Label Doesn't Bother Canham," *Ann Arbor News*, September 8, 1977.

231: *he skipped the rally*: "Ford Outlines Goals for America," *Michigan Daily*, September 16, 1976.

231: *people thought a gunshot had been fired*: Ibid.

231: *university president Robben Fleming acknowledged*: Ibid.

231: *the chief complaint of Michigan students*: "Crisler Crisis," *Michigan Daily*, September 16, 1976.

231: *"It's great to be back"*: "Ford Outlines Goals for America," *Michigan Daily*, September 16, 1976.

233: *"Will—what the hell you smiling for?"*: "Marketing the Wolverines," *Chicago Tribune*, November 8, 1981.

235: *fractured three vertebrae*: "Gerald Injured in 24–3 Win," *Columbus Dispatch*, October 24, 1976.

236: *Hayes had sponsored a family of Vietnamese refugees*: "Explosive Woody Hayes," *Reader's Digest*, September 1977.

237: *"You're coming to Ohio State, aren't you?"*: Interview with Tom Engler.

237: *Schembechler was clearing $80,000*: "102,415 U-M Crowd Monument to Canham," *Detroit Free Press*, November 9, 1975.

238: *"He believes in winning"*: "Columbus Welcomes President," *Columbus Dispatch*, November 1, 1976.

239: *Woody Hayes later said*: Paul Hornung, *Woody Hayes: A Reflection* (Champaign, IL: Sagamore Publishing, 1991), p. 228.

239: *"I'll tell you one other thing"*: "Hayes Denies Rumor," *Columbus Dispatch*, November 14, 1976.

239: *He skipped a television showing*: "Favorite wish for Mich," *Sports Illustrated*, November 29, 1976.

240: The Shootist: Ibid.

240: *"Gentlemen, here we are again"*: Ibid.

240: *"Coach, we're going to blow them out tomorrow"*: Interview with Calvin O'Neal.

242: *had been so worried about the game*: "Finally, Bo Enjoys a Good Night's Sleep," *Detroit Free Press*, November 26, 1976.

243: *Ford tried calling Schembechler*: Gerald R. Ford Library, President Gerald R. Ford's Daily Diary, 11/20/76, folder 11/19–30/74 (Staff Secretary's copy), Box 71.

243: *Shemy listened in*: Ibid.

244: *Rod Gerald wished he were back home*: Interview with Rod Gerald.

CHAPTER 10: The Ultra Secret

248: *Hayes would call one chapter*: Letter from Woody Hayes to Rick Pearson, The Ohio State University Archives, Wayne W. Hayes Papers (RG 40/111-B/l).

249: Football, History and Woody Hayes: "Lion in Autumn," *Ohio Magazine*, October 1978.

250: *"Either we're talking about love"*: "Woody's Woman's Wit and Wisdom," *Sporting News*, November 20, 1978.

251: *standing around "like goons"*: "In the Second Half It Was Pure Aggie-ny," *Sports Illustrated*, October 10, 1977.

251: *"I'd just as soon not be No. 1"*: Ibid.

251: *"We played poorly"*: "It's Goodbye No. 1, Perfect Season and Brown Jug! U-M Flops, 16–0," *Detroit Free Press*, October 23, 1977.

253: *"You will not win many conference games"*: "Hayes Happy With Defense After Victory," *Columbus Dispatch*, September 11, 1977.

255: *23 percent of Ohio State's incoming freshmen*: Paul Underwood, *The Enarson Years* (Columbus: Ohio State University Press, 1985), p. 89.

256: *"We are against so many things"*: *Columbus Citizen-Journal*, August 31, 1979.

257: *"This is* TRASH*!"*: Interview with Mark George.

257: *"You're fired!"*: Interview with Mark George.

258: *"I can't give you a story this week"*: "Buckeyes' Chief Speaks of Big Game in Silence," *Columbus Dispatch*, November 14, 1977.

258: *Two weeks before the game*: "Mature, happy, Bo never stops on longest day," *Detroit News*, November 21, 1977.

258: *"That's respect, boys"*: Interview with Bill Myles.

258: *one Michigan fan apparently taking a swing*: "ABC exec berates Bucks' Hayes," *Columbus Citizen-Journal*, November 21, 1977.

258: *eggs, fruit, and toilet paper*: Ibid.

259: *"I'm with ABC"*: "Woody isn't only sinner," *Columbus Citizen-Journal*, November 22, 1977.

259: *An Ann Arbor sheriff*: Ibid.

259: *Canham bolted*: "Mature, happy, Bo never stops on longest day," *Detroit News*, November 21, 1977.

262: "Don't call that play!": Interviews with Art Schlichter and Mark George.

262: *"I tried to say hello to you"*: "Bucks, Bear in Sugar," *Columbus Citizen-Journal*, November 21, 1977.

263: *Schembechler climbed in a car*: "Mature, happy, Bo never stops on longest day," *Detroit News*, November 21, 1977.

263: *"Hiya, men!"*: Ibid.

263: *"I think we're in the last year"*: Ibid.

263: *"I'm not the judge of his actions"*: Ibid.

264: *Wayne Duke had publicly reprimanded Hayes*: "Hayes Violated Conference Rule," *Columbus Dispatch*, December 2, 1977.

264: *media reaction was just as harsh*: "So It's Two In A Row For Bo," *Sports Illustrated*, November 28, 1977; "Coach Hayes, you are wrong," *Columbus Citizen-Journal*, November 22, 1977.

264: *"Commit a crime"*: Ralph Waldo Emerson, "Compensation."

265: *In early December 1977*: "Fair Play," *Michigan Daily*, October 27, 2005.

267: *"Jesus Christ!"*: Interview with Mark George.

267: *some Buckeyes were laughing*: "'Great' Again Eludes Let-Down Buckeyes," *Columbus Dispatch*, January 3, 1978.

268: *"They beat us"*: "Who is No. 1?...Certainly Not Ohio State," *Columbus Dispatch*, January 3, 1978.

268: *a writer documented the grumbling*: "The disappointed agree in opinion of Woody," *Columbus Citizen-Journal*, January 3, 1978.

269: *"That's enough of my personal life"*: Interview with Mel Olix.

CHAPTER 11: The Final Days

271: *its warm and cold fronts became reversed*: "As we guessed, Blizzard worst in U.S. history," *Columbus Citizen-Journal*, January 28, 1978.

271: *At least thirty-five Ohioans perished*: "Ohio slowly gains upper hand in fight with snow," *Columbus Citizen-Journal*, January 30, 1978.

271: *Winds over Lake Erie*: "As we guessed, Blizzard worst in U.S. history," *Columbus Citizen-Journal*, January 28, 1978.

271: *More than 150,000 Ohioans lost power*: "Blizzard lashes through Ohio; Life locked in by raging cold," *Columbus Citizen-Journal*, January 27, 1978.

271: *"It's for a good cause, Joe"*: Interview with Joe Hayden.

272: *"You and I are going for a ride"*: Interview with Larry Kindbom.

274: *"Your name is Bud"*: Interview with Eloy Cueto.

275: *"Goddammit, don't you know"*: Interview with Jim Stillwagon.

275: *"This ain't gonna last real long"*: Interview with Bill Urbanik.

276: *"Sit down"*: Interview with George Hill.

277: *Marty Reid*: "Woody and Hero Suffer Same Fate; Hayes' Tantrums Worry His Friends," *Washington Post*, December 31, 1978.

278: *let the home team keep 100 percent*: Don Canham and Larry Paladino, *Don Canham's From the Inside: A Half Century of Michigan Athletics* (Ann Arbor, MI: Olympia Sports Press), pp. 123–30.

280: *"What was it Churchill said?"*: "Hayes plans to surprise Penn State," *Columbus Citizen-Journal*, September 15, 1978.

282: Throw it to the guys in our color: Interview with Tom Cousineau.

282: *"A lot of the mistakes weren't his fault"*: "There will be other days for Bucks and Schlichter," *Columbus Citizen-Journal*, September 18, 1978.

283: *"as [Art] gets better"*: "Hayes Rates Victory Above Exciting Loss," *Columbus Dispatch*, October 15, 1978.

284: *his publisher*: "Lion in Autumn," *Ohio Magazine*, October 1978.

284: *the "40 trap"*: "Split personality," *Detroit Free Press*, November 24, 1978.

286: *Hayes had asked them to reconsider*: *Lantern*, November 16, 1978.

286: *the Battle of Khalkin Gol*: "Will Woody cure his case of TV-itis?" *Columbus Citizen-Journal*, November 25, 1978.

287: *"Let me tell you about Woody"*: "A 'mellow' Bo has fun with Woody," *Detroit Free Press*, November 22, 1978.

289: *"He's the best football player"*: "Leach's 2 TD passes, iron defense send Michigan to Rose Bowl, 14–3," *Detroit Free Press*, November 26, 1978.

290: *"He's talking to prospects"*: "Woody explodes at writer: 'I have no respect for you,'" *Detroit Free Press*, November 26, 1978.

290: *Art Schlichter started practicing*: "Only Wins Count With Schlichter," *Columbus Dispatch*, December 17, 1978.

291: *"I don't think I'll get it this year"*: Associated Press, December 24, 1978.

291: *the naval base in nearby Mayport*: "Woody promises 'a few surprises,'" *Columbus Citizen-Journal*, December 27, 1978.

292: *Woody celebrated by buying cigars*: "Woody at War," *Timeline*, April/June 2007.

292: *"The alumni got sick of me"*: *Columbus Citizen-Journal*, December 29, 1978.

292: *"I sometimes get the feeling"*: "Hayes has respect, no fear of Clemson's 10–1 Tigers," *Columbus Citizen-Journal*, December 29, 1978.

292: *The network decided to save a few thousand bucks*: Keith Dunnavant, *The 50-Year Seduction* (New York: Thomas Dunne Books, 2004), pp. 102–3.

293: *Enarson could barely see what was happening*: Interview with Harold Schechter.

297: *Word spread quickly at the Palladium*: Interview with Bo Schembechler.

297: *"If he hit that kid, Jim"*: Interview with Jim Jones.

298: *Hayes's great-grandfather*: "Lion in Autumn," *Ohio Magazine*, October 1978.

298: *"Whatever I say would be wrong"*: "Hayes's Spirits Tumbled Before Decision to Quit," *Columbus Dispatch*, December 30, 1978.

299: *"I'm going to need your help"*: Interview with Mark George.

299: *he had told Hornung he would resign*: "Hayes Ponders Uncertain Future," *Columbus Dispatch*, December 31, 1978.

300: *At 2 a.m., Enarson and Hugh Hindman had met*: "The end: Officials move quickly following game," *Columbus Citizen-Journal*, January 1, 1979.

300: *"That would make it too easy for you"*: *Associated Press*, December 31,1978.

300: *At 10 a.m., Hindman held a press conference*: Ibid.

300: *he had three things to tell his players*: Interviews with Larry Romanoff, George Hill, and Mark George.

301: *"I regret to say"*: "Decision Sends Out Shock Waves," *Columbus Dispatch*, December 31, 1978.

301: Throw it all away: Interview with Mark George.

301: *dozens of uncashed checks*: Interview with Jimmy Moore.

301: *"I don't have a lot to say"*: " 'Saddened' Bo points to pressures," *Detroit Free Press*, December 31, 1978.

302: *"I don't want to talk about it now"*: "Clemson claws OSU in Gator Bowl, 17–15," *Columbus Citizen-Journal*, December 30, 1978.

303: *"We've got to get some protection"*: "Bo rips official: 'I can't believe' call," *Detroit Free Press*, January 3, 1979.

304: *Ohio State would reduce the number of credit hours*: "OSU Council discusses many issues," *Columbus Dispatch*, May 9, 1979; The Ohio State University Archives, Wayne W. Hayes Papers (40/111-G-3/3).

305: *"If he had beaten Michigan"*: Interview with Earle Bruce.

305: *"We are not scrupulous"*: Ralph Waldo Emerson, "Success."

305: *He had written more than five hundred pages*: "The way we were just wasn't his way," *Columbus Citizen-Journal*, January 1, 1979.

305: *In the spring of 1979*: Walt anecdote courtesy of Daryl Sanders, who was in attendance; quotes are similar to other public statements by Walt.

CHAPTER 12: Football, History, and Bo Schembechler

307: *$250,000 per year*: "Bo received $25,000 pay hike as part of Canham deal," *Ann Arbor News*, January 19, 1982.

308: *Don Canham counteroffered $125,000*: Ibid.

308: *"most writers aren't worth a damn"*: "Bo," *Sports Illustrated*, September 14, 1981.

309: *"I've been around a lot of generals"*: Interview with David Turnley.

309: *"best coach coaching"*: Bo Schembechler and Mitch Albom, *Bo: Life, Laughs, and Lessons of a College Football Legend* (New York: Warner Books, 1989).

310: *His athletic department's budget*: "Variety his life's spice," *Ann Arbor News*, June 29, 1980; "Michigan is clean, but wins; the key: A powerful coach," *USA Today*, October 14, 1985.

313: *spent several days with Hayes in Columbus*: Interview with Budd Schulberg.

313: *Hayes underwent gall bladder surgery*: Hornung, pp. 225–26.

314: *In April 1982*: "Football Success Formula: Recruit a Philosopher," *New York Times*, April 27, 1982.

314: *"I'm sure you're wondering"*: Ibid.

316: *"Well, I knew I'd had one"*: Transcript provided by Bob Greene.

317: *"Well, Coach"*: Interview with Champ Henson.

318: *"You sit next to me"*: "Bo remembers Woody," *Detroit Free Press*, April 13, 1987.

318: *he led the former president to his seat*: "Watergate conspirator Magruder leads Columbus drive for honesty," *St. Petersburg Times*, March 12, 1989.

319: *because he wanted more money*: "No Tuxedo for Earle Bruce," *New York Times*, November 28, 1987.

319: *"Do we need all this goddamn stuff?"*: Interview with Jim Jones.

320: *Harwell said later*: Interview with Ernie Harwell.

321: *"He did, he did"*: Transcript provided by David Crouse.

322: *he got the uncomfortable sensation*: Interview with Bo Schembechler.

322: *"He is the best teacher"*: Ibid.

323: *As Schembechler limped to the podium*: "Bo has the stories no one else can tell," *Ann Arbor News*, November 14, 2006.

Index